Artificial Intelligence

Handbook of Perception and Cognition
2nd Edition

Series Editors
Edward Carterette
and Morton Friedman

Artificial Intelligence

Edited by
Margaret A. Boden

School of Cognitive and Computing Sciences
University of Sussex
Brighton, England

Academic Press

San Diego   New York   Boston
London   Sydney   Tokyo   Toronto

Copyright © 1996 by ACADEMIC PRESS, INC.

Academic Press, Inc.
A Division of Harcourt Brace & Company
525 B Street, Suite 1900, San Diego, California 92101-4495

United Kingdom Edition published by
Academic Press Limited
24-28 Oval Road, London NW1 7DX

Library of Congress Cataloging-in-Publication Data

Artificial intelligence / edited by Margaret A. Boden.
          p.   cm. -- (Handbook of perception and cognition, 2nd ed.
    series)
    Includes bibliographical references and index.
    ISBN 0-12-161964-8 (case : alk paper)
    1. Artificial intelligence. I. Boden, Margaret A. I. Series:
Handbook of perception and cognition (2nd ed).
Q335.A7857   1996
006.3--dc20   95-44625
                                                       CIP

PRINTED IN THE UNITED STATES OF AMERICA
96   97   98   99   00   01   BC   9   8   7   6   5   4   3   2   1

Contents

3   *Representation of Knowledge*
Derek Partridge

4   *Machine Learning*
Stuart Russell

5   *Connectionism and Neural Networks*

Harry Barrow

6   *Expert Systems and Theories of Knowledge*

John Fox

10 Human–Computer Interaction

Mike Sharples

11 Artificial Life and the Animat Approach to Artificial Intelligence

Jean-Arcady Meyer

Contributors

Numbers in parentheses indicate the pages on which the authors' contributions begin.

Harry Barrow[1] (135)
School of Cognitive and Computing
  Sciences
University of Sussex
Brighton BN1 9QH, England

Margaret A. Boden (267)
School of Cognitive and Computing
  Sciences
University of Sussex
Brighton BN1 9QH, England

Andy Clark[2] (1)
School of Cognitive and Computing
  Sciences
University of Sussex
Brighton BN1 9QH, England

John Fox (157)
Advanced Computation Laboratory
Imperial Cancer Research Fund
Lincoln's Inn Fields,
London WC2A 3PX, England

David C. Hogg (183)
School of Computer Studies
University of Leeds
Leeds LS2 9JT, England

Robert Inder (23)
Human Communication Research
  Centre
University of Edinburgh
Edinburgh EH8 9LW, Scotland

[1]Present Address: Schlumberger Research Lab, Cambridge CB3 0EL, England.
[2]Present Address: Philosophy/Neuroscience/Psychology Program, Washington University,
St. Louis, Missouri 63130

Jean-Arcady Meyer (325)
Groupe de Bioinformatique
Ecole Normale Supérieure
75230 Paris, France

Derek Partridge (55)
Department of Computer Science
University of Exeter
Exeter EX4 4PT, England

Stuart Russell (89)
Computer Science Division
University of California, Berkeley
Berkeley, California 94720

Mike Sharples (293)
School of Cognitive and Computing
   Sciences
University of Sussex
Brighton BN1 9QH, England

Mark Steedman (229)
Department of Computer and
   Information Sciences
University of Pennsylvania
Philadelphia, Pennsylvania 19143

Foreword

The problem of perception and cognition is understanding how the organism transforms, organizes, stores, and uses information arising from the world in sense data or memory. With this definition of perception and cognition in mind, this handbook is designed to bring together the essential aspects of this very large, diverse, and scattered literature and to give a precis of the state of knowledge in every area of perception and cognition. The work is aimed at the psychologist, the cognitive scientist in particular, and at the natural scientist in general. Topics are covered in comprehensive surveys in which fundamental facts and concepts are presented, and important leads to journals and monographs of the specialized literature are provided. Perception and cognition are considered in the widest sense. Therefore, the work will treat a wide range of experimental and theoretical work.

The *Handbook of Perception and Cognition* should serve as a basic source and reference work for those in the arts or sciences, indeed for all who are interested in human perception, action, and cognition.

Edward C. Carterette and Morton P. Friedman

Preface

Computational psychologists use computational concepts in formulating their theories. They typically employ computer models to improve the theories' clarity and internal coherence and to test their generative power (and limitations). These concepts and methods are drawn from artificial intelligence (AI).

AI is the study of how to build or program computers to enable them to do what minds can do (for introductory texts, see Boden, 1987; Broadbent, 1993; Rich & Knight, 1991). AI is a broad church, whose members differ about general methodology as well as detail. Accordingly, computational psychology is diverse, too. This volume outlines the major theoretical approaches and some promising recent developments.

Some of the work herein discussed was done by psychologists. But most was done by AI professionals. However, the distinction is not always clear. Many AI workers are not primarily interested in technological "fixes," ingenious ways of getting computers to do things irrespective of how real minds do them. Rather, they hope to illuminate the structural and processing principles underlying minds in general and human minds in particular.

Even technological AI has a psychological tinge, since its ideas are often suggested by the human (or animal) case. For instance, a team designing an early lunar robot, capable of switching between its goals without waiting for radio signals from Earth, modeled the role of the mammalian reticular formation in scheduling different instinctive behaviors (Kilmer, Mc-

Culloch, & Blum, 1969). Technological AI has benefited enormously from the psychologically motivated work of Allen Newell and Herbert Simon (Newell, 1990; Newell, Shaw, & Simon, 1957; Newell & Simon, 1961, 1972).

Newell and Simon's 40-year research program on human thinking pioneered several lasting AI techniques: list processing, hierarchical planning, heuristic search, production systems, and "blackboard" memories. This example illustrates the potential for links between advances in AI and in computational psychology. Significantly, if sadly, a recent overview of AI written by and for AI professionals (Bobrow, 1993) includes 200 pages reviewing Newell's last book, *Unified Theories of Cognition,* plus an obituary by his intellectual alter ego (Simon).

Early AI (from the mid-1950s), like current "symbolic" AI, ignored neurophysiology. This attitude sprang from a reasoned philosophical position, the "physical symbol-system hypothesis" (see Chapter 1). Some philosophical critiques, and work on parallel-processing "connectionist" systems, have suggested that computational psychologists ignore the brain at their peril. These issues are featured in Chapters 1 and 5, and relevant neuroscientific work is cited there, but there is not a chapter devoted to computational neuroscience (for a review of this area, see Churchland & Sejnowski, 1992).

Nor does any chapter concentrate on motivation and emotion. Little computational work has been done on these matters. Purposive behavior has been a concern of AI from the early days (Boden, 1972), although most AI models still have only one or two goals (plus subgoals). Truly multiple-goal systems will show aspects of emotional behavior. Any intelligent system capable of scheduling multiple conflicting goals, and of reacting to emergencies and opportunities, would need the sorts of goal-scheduling mechanisms characteristic of emotions (Frijda, 1986; Ortony, Clore, & Collins, 1991; Sloman, 1990).

Whether the conscious aspects of emotion—or anything else—could be explained in AI terms is more controversial (see Chapter 1). Most computational psychologists simply ignore this question. The same is true of most other psychologists: consciousness is typically taken for granted, no scientific or philosophical explanation being sought. These comments would have been even more apt 10 years ago. Recently, however, several extended discussions of consciousness have appeared, both within (Dennett, 1991; Jackendoff, 1987) and outside (Bock & Marsh, 1993; Marcel & Bisiach, 1988) the computational paradigm.

Fundamental philosophical questions such as this are discussed in Chapter 1. Other topics explored there include the differences between symbolic and connectionist AI, and the nature of computation and representation. Chapter 1 also comments on the philosophical significance of artificial life

(ALife), a recently revivified research field described in the final chapter. ALife uses computer modeling to study self-organizing systems, and refers more often to insects than to human beings. It merits inclusion in this volume partly because of its ethological interest, and partly because AI can be seen as a subarea of ALife: ALife studies self-organization in general, while AI focuses on intelligent systems (Boden, 1996).

The intervening chapters tackle specific topics within computational psychology and AI. These are planning and problem solving, knowledge representation, learning, connectionism, expert systems, vision, natural language, robotics, creativity, and human–computer interaction. Most of these topics are studied by noncomputational methods too, so for a rounded view the reader should also consult other volumes of the *Handbook of Perception and Cognition* series.

The diversity and excitement of computational psychology life not only in its "in-house" theoretical disagreements, but also in its interdisciplinarity. This characterized the field from the start. The lunar-robot team which imported neurophysiology into space technology included the polymath Warren McCulloch. McCulloch was a psychiatrist, a physiologist, a cybernetician, a philosopher, a poet . . . and his most influential work was published with a mathematician, Walter Pitts. Their papers of 1943 ("A Logical Calculus of the Ideas Immanent in Nervous Activity") and 1947 ("How We Know Universals: The Perception of Auditory and Visual Forms") were crucial in founding both computational psychology and AI, of both the symbolic and connectionist varieties. McCulloch (and Pitts) also co-authored, in 1959, the neurophysiologically influential paper on "What the Frog's Eye Tells the Frog's Brain" (McCulloch, 1965.)

We cannot all hope to be a McCulloch. But AI and computational psychology are inescapably interdisciplinary. They need insights from the sciences (biology, ethology, psychology, neuroscience, physics, and computer science), and from the humanities too (philosophy, linguistics, and the history of art and science). If this wide-ranging enterprise appears difficult, even daunting, so be it. We should expect no less, in aiming to understand the mind.

References

Bobrow, D. G. (Ed.). (1993). Artificial intelligence in perspective [Special issue]. *Artificial Intelligence, 59*, 1–462.

Bock, G. R., & Marsh, J. (Eds.). (1993). *Experimental and theoretical studies of consciousness.* Chichester: Wiley.

Boden, M. A. (1972). *Purposive explanation in psychology.* Cambridge, MA: Harvard University Press.

Boden, M. A. (1987). *Artificial intelligence and natural man* (2nd ed.). New York: Basic Books.

Boden, M. A. (Ed.). (1996). *The philosophy of artificial life.* Oxford: Oxford University Press.

Broadbent, D. (Ed.). (1993). *The simulation of human intelligence.* Oxford: Blackwell.

Churchland, P. S., & Sejnowski, T. J. (1992). *The computational brain.* Cambridge, MA: MIT Press.

Dennett, D. C. (1991). *Consciousness explained.* Boston: Little, Brown.

Frijda, N. (1986). *The emotions.* Cambridge, UK: Cambridge University Press.

Jackendoff, R. (1987). *Consciousness and the computational mind.* Cambridge, MA: MIT Press.

Kilmer, W. L., McCulloch, W. S., & Blum, J. (1969). A model of the vertebrate central command system. *International Journal of Man-Machine Studies, 1,* 279–309.

Marcel, A. J., & Bisiach, E. (Eds.). *Consciousness in contemporary science.* Oxford: Oxford University Press.

McCulloch, W. S. (1965). *Embodiments of mind,* Cambridge, MA: MIT Press.

Newell, A. (1990). *Unified theories of cognition.* Cambridge, MA: Harvard University Press.

Newell, A., Shaw, J. C., & Simon, H. A. (1957). Empirical explorations with the Logic Theory Machine. *Proceedings—Western Joint Computer Conference, 15,* 218–239.

Newell, A., & Simon, H. A. (1961). GPS—A program that simulates human thought. In H. Billing (Ed.), *Lernende automaten* (pp. 109–124). Munich: Oldenbourg.

Newell, A., & Simon, H. A. (1972). *Human problem solving.* Englewood Cliffs, NJ: Prentice-Hall.

Ortony, A., Clore, G. L., & Collins, A. (1991). *The cognitive structure of emotions.* Cambridge, UK: Cambridge University Press.

Rich, E., & Knight, K. (1991). *Artificial intelligence* (2nd ed.). New York: McGraw-Hill.

Sloman, A. (1990). Motives, mechanisms, and emotions. In M. A. Boden (Ed.), *The philosophy of artificial intelligence* (pp. 231–247). Oxford: Oxford University Press.

CHAPTER 1

Philosophical Foundations

Andy Clark

I. AN EVOLVING ENGAGEMENT

In the beginning, the nature of philosophy's engagement with artificial intelligence and cognitive science was clear enough. The new sciences of the mind were to provide the long-awaited vindication of the most potent dreams of naturalism and materialism. Mind would at last be located firmly within the natural order. We would see in detail how the most perplexing features of the mental realm could be supported by the operations of solely physical laws upon solely physical stuff. Mental causation (the power of, e.g., a belief to cause an action) would emerge as just another species of physical causation. Reasoning would be understood as a kind of automated theorem proving. And the key to both was to be the depiction of the brain as the implementation of multiple higher level programs whose task was to manipulate and transform symbols or representations: inner items with one foot in the physical (they were realized as brain states) and one in the mental (they were bearers of contents, and their physical gymnastics were cleverly designed to respect semantic relationships such as truth preservation).

A compelling virtue of this image lay in its unique combination of physical dependence and multiple realizability. Everything bottomed out in a solid physical implementation with impeccable causal credentials. But one

Artificial Intelligence

higher level program could have any number of distinct physical implementations. This was (rightly) perceived to be an advance over the previous best shot at vindicating naturalism and materialism; namely, the so-called mind–brain identity theory developed in the middle to late 1950s by U. T. Place, J. J. C. Smart, D. Armstrong, and others (see, e.g., readings in Borst, 1970; Lycan, 1990). The mind–brain identity theory, in its strongest form, claimed that types of mental state were identical with types of brain state. Thus, to feel pain (or even to believe that such and such) was to be identified with being in some specific neural state. But, as H. Putnam (1960) famously pointed out, this leads rapidly to an uncomfortable kind of species chauvinism. For on the face of it, there is no reason to suppose that a being lacking neurons, but equipped with, say, a silicon brain, could not feel pain or believe that such and such. The identification of mind with program avoids this pitfall because it can be silent about the details of any implementation.

A simple and satisfying view thus has it that artificial intelligence vindicates the basic claims of the materialist–naturalist. It does so by revealing the brain as one physical implementation of a class of sophisticated, representation-manipulating programs, the operation of which gives rise to the rich panoply of semantically governed behaviors we associate with the presence of minds.

An endearing feature of the continuing relationship between philosophy and artificial intelligence, however, is that the story does not end there. On the contrary, this basic image has given rise to a mountain of new questions whose resolution demands a much more intimate interweaving of philosophical enquiry and empirical research. These questions concern, for example, the proper understanding of the key concepts of representation and symbol, the nature of the (putative) implementation–program dichotomy, and the precise relationship between gross mentalistic discourse (about beliefs with specific contents, etc.) and the (putative) inner representation-manipulating events.

The subterranean force that has pushed these fascinating questions to the surface is an increased awareness of more complex, less intuitive ways in which physical devices might be arranged to exhibit various kinds of semantically constrained behavior. Connectionist models (see later) have raised questions concerning the form of internal representation and the nature of the processing underlying cognition. Artificial life (see later) questions even the need to invoke representations and symbols as the meat in the perception–action sandwich in the first place. One implication of these new visions is that, although the mind surely does have its place in nature, the final scientific story may not literally recapitulate the contentful states posited by daily mentalistic talk. Instead, it may postulate a quite different kind of inner economy; one which nonetheless leads, in some perfectly physically respectable way, to the characteristic behaviors of which we then make sense by using familiar content ascriptions.

Artificial intelligence and cognitive science are, therefore, no longer mere tools whose philosophical role is simply to vindicate a naturalistic view of the mind. Instead, philosophy and the other cognitive sciences have emerged as genuine companions in the quest to discern and articulate the full and unexpected range of ways in which the mind might be located in the natural order. In this common quest, key concepts like representation, symbol, and even program and implementation can no longer be taken for granted. Nor can we afford to assume that the relation between mental talk and inner states is a simple or transparent one.

Given this state of conceptual flux, it is impossible to legislate on the philosophical foundations for a mature science of the mind. Those foundations do not yet exist, and their ultimate construction will be a fully interdisciplinary task. What follows is therefore better seen as a kind of historical prolegomenon to the search for such a foundational understanding. The goal is to sketch what I see as the three main artificial intelligence (AI) based visions of the mind, and to highlight the specific philosophical and cognitive scientific questions to which they give rise. The three visions are

1. Symbol-system AI
2. Connectionist AI
3. Artificial life

These will be discussed in turn, then.

II. SYMBOL-SYSTEM AI

Consider the following question: how is it possible to learn the meaning of a public language concept? One obvious answer is "by definition." Someone tells you the meaning, using words that you already understand. But such a model obviously cannot be invoked to explain our initial acquisition of concepts in the context of first language learning. How, then, is this to be explained?

Fodor (1975) argues that we acquire such knowledge by a process of hypothesis generation and test conducted using the resources of an innate representational base. The idea is that the child is genetically programmed to develop an initial repertoire of internally represented predicates. The process of learning the meaning of a natural language term is then cast as a process of formulating hypotheses about possible meanings, using the innate expressive resources of the inner code (the infamous "language of thought") and then testing those hypotheses against observed public usage. The most that concept learning can therefore do is to promote the development of inner abbreviations, which can ultimately replace the complex defining expressions in the language of thought (see Fodor, 1975, p. 152). What concept learning cannot do is to expand the expressive power of any innate representational system. The innate system provides both a base for learning and (hence) a limit on what can be learned.

Fodor's vision is thus symbol assuming in a very strong sense. But it is not just symbol assuming. It is also symbol-system assuming, and this feature has lately (see, e.g., Fodor, 1987; Fodor & Pylyshyn, 1988) come to dominate discussions concerning the differences between so-called classical artificial intelligence and its rivals (see later). In essence, a symbol system comprises both a set of atomic symbols and a special kind of processing environment in which they are embedded. The relevant kind of processing environment is modeled on our understanding of formal logical systems and artificial grammars (for a nice critical discussion, see Oaksford & Chater, 1991). What is important about such an environment is its provision of a fixed combinatorial framework for the embedded symbols. Such a framework is often described (a little opaquely, I feel) as quasi-linguistic. But, all this means is that

1. Atomic symbols can combine in a predetermined variety of ways.
2. The contents of the symbol strings resulting from such recombinations are systematically determined by the contents of the participating atomic symbols and the mode of combination.

Given these properties, some nice features follow. Strings of inner symbols will then exhibit structure that can be exploited by computational operations. For example, it will be possible to define an operation to apply to all and only strings involving some particular atomic symbol or sequence of symbols or to apply to all and only those strings exhibiting a given combinatorial form (e.g., conjunction) and so on. As a result, it is easy to see how to implement rational (e.g., truth theoretic) processes of reasoning by allowing only certain kinds of symbol string to be created in response to other kinds (think here of the premises and conclusions in logical arguments). The key property of what have become known as classical cognitive models (see, e.g., Clark, 1989, Chap. 1) is that, courtesy of their reliance on symbol systems, it is possible within them to define semantically well-constrained mental operations in very neat ways. As Fodor and Pylyshyn put it:

> In classical models, the principles by which mental states are transformed, or by which an input selects the corresponding output, are defined over structural properties of mental representations. Because classical mental representations have combinatorial structure, it is possible for classical mental operations to apply to them by reference to their form. (1988, pp. 12–13)

The symbol-system idea was itself originally formulated by Newell and Simon in their idea of a physical symbol system; namely, any member of a general class of physically realizable systems meeting the following conditions:

1. It contains a set of atomic symbols, physical patterns that can be strung together to yield a structure or expression;
2. It contains many such structures and a set of manipulative processes capable of creating, modifying, reproducing, and destroying expressions according to instructions that may themselves be coded as symbol structures.
3. Its states relate consistently to a wider world of real objects.

Thus a physical symbol system (see Newell & Simon, 1976, pp. 40–42) is any system in which highly manipulable tokens can be assigned meanings and operations on such tokens defined to preserve desired semantic relations. The ubiquitous talk of classical AI as a "symbol-manipulating paradigm" is best understood as gesturing at this quite specific proposal.

The focus of computational psychology is, at least in part, on natural biological cognition. A question therefore arises concerning the extent to which the symbol system idea will serve as a useful model of natural information processing. In particular, it is fair to ask: does human thought and cognition arise out of the operation of an internal symbol system of the Fodor–Newell–Simon stripe? The proponents of the symbol system view suggest two (related) reasons to think so.

The first is that we are indeed remarkably semantically well-behaved (this terminology is drawn from Clark, 1993). We do, quite often, enjoy trains of thought (Fodor, 1987, Chap. 1) that make rational sense. The simplest explanation of all this is (we are told) that we reason using a symbol system and a set of semantically sensible transformation rules (for a neat summary of this line of reasoning, see Haugeland, 1981).

The second reason concerns the productivity and systematicity of thought. Human thought looks to be productive in the sense that there is no obvious limit to the number of distinct thoughts we can have. One explanation of this putative fact is that we command a finite set of resources and a set of iterable mental operations. Such a combination yields an, in principle, infinity of thoughts out of a finite base of materials. But even if you deny that human thought is thus fully productive, you must at least concede, so Fodor and Pylyshyn (1988) argue, that it is systematic. The observation here is simply that the cognitive abilities of human cognizers are in a certain respect interanimated: if you are capable of having, say, the thought that John loves Mary, then you will be capable also of formulating the thought that Mary loves John. Likewise, if you can have two thoughts, such as (1) the cup is on the floor and (2) the book is on the table, then you will also be able to have thoughts such as (3) the cup is on the table and (4) the book is on the floor.

The best explanation for this kind of systematicity (of potential thoughts) is, so Fodor and Pylyshyn (1988) claim, to posit the operation within us of a symbol system complete with reusable elements and combinatorial operations. The explanation of systematicity is thus to posit structured internal representations whose parts are effectively interchangeable. The internal representations of "John loves Mary" and of "Mary loves John" will be "made of the same parts" (Fodor & Pylyshyn, 1988, p. 39).

A final, more outrightly philosophical benefit of the symbol system approach lies in the ease with which it accommodates the idea of mental causation. The causal powers of our mental states, according to such a view, need be nothing other than the causal powers of the physical tokens in the inner symbol system. Therefore, a belief that P (for example) is able to act as a cause of some action A, since there is tokened inside the agent a symbol or symbol string which means such P and which (qua physical token) can act upon the bodily parameters that drive whatever motions (if any) constitute action. The symbol-tokening vision is thus sold as

> a vindication of intuitive belief/desire psychology [insofar as it] shows how intentional states could have causal powers; precisely the aspect of common-sense intentional realism that seemed most perplexing from a metaphysical point of view. (Fodor 1987, p. 26)

The attractions of the symbol system assuming approach are clear and powerful. But there is a threefold cost.

First, a great deal is left unexplained. In particular, the symbol system hypothesis does not cope very well with the explanation of skillful behaviors (catching a ball, controlling locomotion, recognizing a scene). And it is not immediately obvious how well it allows us to integrate our image of human reasoning with cognition in other animals (see P. M. Churchland, 1989, chap. 10).

Second, the bridge between the symbol system view and what is actually known about the computational style of the brain is unclear. The brain (see, e.g., P. S. Churchland & Sejnowski, 1992) relies heavily on the use of parallel processing and appears to favor distributed or semi-distributed styles of representation. As a result, the image of thought as a process involving the serial manipulation of discrete symbols looks profoundly un-biological. At the very least, the symbol-system theorist needs to address, in some detail, the issue of how real brains realize the kinds of computational description she favors.

Third, the assumption of symbols and symbol systems merely serves to shift an explanatory task. It is now the job of evolutionary theory to explain the origin of the rich innate symbolic base and the highly articulated manipulative system. It would be better, many believe (see, e.g., P. S. Churchland, 1978) not to shift the total burden thus to evolution. Instead, we should investigate ways in which processes of genuine learning might contribute to the development of whatever computational structures underlie mature adult cognition. To even contemplate addressing this question of origins, however, is to begin to countenance alternatives to the full-blooded (innate symbols and symbol-system) classical vision.

Since it is not my primary purpose to attempt to adjudicate between the rival approaches, I shall not pursue these three criticisms here (see, e.g., P. M. Churchland, 1989; Clark, 1989, 1993, for more detail). Instead, I turn now to the details of the major alternative approach: connectionism.

III. CONNECTIONISM

The trouble with symbol-system style artificial intelligence, according to many of its critics, is that it illegitimately back-projects the structures of language and conscious, reflective problem solving on to the basic mechanisms of human cognition. Such structures are, however, evolutionarily recent and likely to represent at best the tip of a cognitive iceberg, whose underlying bulk involves a quite different style of representation and computation. This alternative style of representation and computation will be adapted to serve the more basic needs we share with other animals. These will include rapid pattern recognition and the control of bodily movement. Connectionism constitutes a proposal concerning broad representational and computational style that is consonant with just such a picture.

The distributed connectionist approach (see later) presents itself as a genuine alternative to classical "rule and symbol" systems. It relies on (1) an alternative form of knowledge representation, (2) an alternative type of basic processing operation, and (3) a set of powerful learning algorithms.

Regarding knowledge representation, the distributed connectionist eschews representations that consist of symbolic atoms concatenatively combined to form symbolic expressions (for a good discussion, see Van Gelder, 1990). Instead, connectionism exploits activation patterns among large numbers of idealized "neurons" (small processing units) to encode specific contents. The resulting scheme turns out to resemble prototype based encoding insofar as similar contents tend to be represented by similar patterns of activation [hence the inner "symbols" are in a sense nonarbitrary: if content A is represented as pattern of activation P, it will be semantically significant if a content B is assigned a closely related pattern (see Clark, 1993, Chap. 2 for a full discussion)].

In such systems, the basic processing operations are defined over such numerical vectors. Information retrieval consists of a process of vector completion, given a partial vector as a cue. Generalization is achieved by the superpositional storage of activation patterns in a single set of long-term weights. The weights consist of numerical values assigned to local links between idealized neurons. These weights allow the system, given a partial vector (pattern of activation across a set of input units) as a cue, to complete the vector (by activating, courtesy of the connection weights, a specific pattern of units). If several contents are stored superpositionally in a single network of units and weights, an input cue appropriate to several such patterns will induce an activation pattern that in a sense averages the patterns of the individual contents that fit the cue. Hence so-called free generalization (see P. M. Churchland, 1989, Chap. 9).

All the semantically significant items in such an encoding can thus have significant internal structure. In a very real sense, there are no symbolic atoms here; that is, no items that are both clearly representational and lack semantically significant inner structure. Moreover, complex contents are not represented by concatenations of more basic representations but by new activation patterns (ones that need not actually embed the "components") created by processes involving mathematical operations on the numerical vectors that constitute the "activation patterns". Once again, the departure from the classical paradigm is quite marked (see Fodor & McLaughlin, 1991; Smolensky, 1988, 1991).

Such networks are also heir to some powerful learning algorithms. Starting with random weights on the connections, a network can automatically alter these random weights in a way that should lead it to encode a desired input–output mapping. This kind of learning is usually driven by exposing the net to a set of inputs alongside a set of desired outputs. The net uses the (initially random) weights to yield an (initially hopeless) output. If the output is incorrect, an automatic procedure slightly amends those weights most heavily implicated (along the path of activation between input and output) in the mistake, in whatever direction (increase or decrease of specific weights) will yield a reduction in the numerical error measure. Such a process (of "gradient descent learning"; see, e.g., P. S. Churchland & Sejnowski, 1992, pp. 106–107) gently leads the network in the direction of an assignment of weights that will support the target input–output mapping and (usually) will generalize to deal with new cases of the same type (e.g., a net trained to map coding for written text to coding for phonemes will then perform the mapping for text on which it was not specifically trained; see Sejnowski & Rosenberg, 1987).

Two features of this summary sketch bear immediate expansion. They involve, first, the idea of a subsymbol system and, second, the potential for strong representational change.

Connectionist approaches that exploit distributed representations (see later) are able to learn not just isolated representations but rather whole systems of representation, complete with an inbuilt similarity metric. This feature, I believe, constitutes their greatest advance over the kind of classical symbol system described earlier. To see how this works, we need first to clarify the notion of distributed representation itself.

A connectionist representation is sometimes said to be local if it has as its computational vehicle a single unit. This immediately suggests that any representation whose vehicle comprises several units should count as distributed. But this is misleading. As Van Gelder (1991) points out, distributedness conceived as the mere extendedness of a representational vehicle is not in itself a very interesting property. Instead, what matters is that these extended representations display significant internal structure. An example will help.

Consider a net whose task is to represent the letters of the alphabet. A pure localist coding would use a single unit for each individual letter. Now consider a second scheme in which the letters are represented as patterns of activity across 78 units. And let the encoding scheme be as follows. The joint activity of units 1, 2, and 3 represents *A*, that of units 4, 5, and 6 represents *B*, that of units 7, 8, and 9 represents *C*, and so on. Such a scheme involves extended representational vehicles, but it has no especially interesting properties. It is still effectively localist, since the representations, although indeed spread out, do not exploit their extendedness in any semantically significant way.

Now consider the following alternative scheme. Let individual units stand for the features that make up the letters (in a given font). For example, let one unit stand for the vertical upstroke found in, say, a capital *E*. And let another stand for the topmost horizontal arm found in, say, a capital *F*, and so on. The system's distributed representation of the letter *F* can then be the joint activity of those units that encode the various features (microfeatures, if you will) that characterize it. Here at last we are dealing with distributed representation in an interesting sense. Note that such a scheme captures facts concerning the gross similarity of letter forms. That *E* shares more gross features with *F* than with *C* will be reflected in the system's use of resources to encode the letters. The *E* activation pattern will overlap more with the *F* one than with the *C* one. In this sense, such systems embody a similarity metric. The semantic (broadly speaking) similarities between contents can be reflected in a similarity between their computational vehicles. More precisely, if each relevant unit is treated as a dimension in a hyperspace, then similar contents get assigned to neighboring locations in that space (see, e.g., P. M. Churchland, 1989, Chaps. 9 and 10). The use of the kind of learning algorithms briefly described earlier allows connectionist systems to discover such similarity metrics for themselves. That is to say, they are able to generate sets of representations which together constitute systems embodying such similarity metrics.

One point worth drawing out here is that there therefore *is* a kind of systematicity to connectionist knowledge encoding. It is just that it displays itself below the level of propositional specifications of content. The connectionist can thus give a neat computational account of, for example, the internal relations between concepts by depicting semantically related concepts as occupying neighboring regions of a high dimensional space (see, e.g., P. M. Churchland, 1989, Chaps. 9 and 11; for a critical attack, see Fodor & Lepore, 1992, Chap. 7). The problems facing such an account of concepts are also pursued in Clark (1993). The price of this neat account of the systematic internal structure of concepts is doing without a neat account of the larger structures (propositions) in which they figure.

The second feature to be highlighted concerned what I earlier dubbed *strong representational change*. For connectionist learning is a powerful existence proof of the possibility of types of learning that are both rational and yet do not require an antecedent and limiting representational base. The rationality issue is a little elusive. Fodor (1975, 1981) claims that the notion of hypothesis generation and test constitutes our only model of rational concept acquisition (nonrational routes include being hit on the head, having your cortex surgically rewired, and so on; see Fodor, 1981, p. 275). Although the contrast is intuitive, the distinction is never fully pinned down. Nonetheless it seems clear that a connectionist network that begins life with random weights and then learns some given mapping is

1. Not learning by formulating hypotheses using the representational elements of a predetermined code, and
2. Not acquiring the knowledge by accident or by any means which involves external interventions like surgical rewiring.

In addition, note that, even if a network were to begin life with some knowledge (some body of representations) already in place, such knowledge would not itself determine a limit to what could be learned. Thus, even if connectionists are (as they may well be) driven to postulate some initial representational base, that base will not be such as to limit future learning to whatever can be expressed by means of those specific representational resources (see Rumelhart & McClelland, 1986a, p. 141).

Distributed connectionist approaches thus constitute a genuinely different paradigm for understanding cognition. They depart fundamentally from the combinatorial, logicist vision embodied in the physical symbol system hypothesis and exploit new and powerful styles of representation and learning. The value of such models to computational psychology, however, will depend crucially on the extent to which they can be constrained by psychological and neurological data. The basic connectionist techniques of representation and processing allow us to approximate just about any function we can coherently imagine. But merely mimicking some input–output pattern is clearly not sufficient. What other factors can be invoked to ensure the relevance of the models to human psychology? One such factor whose role is increasingly prominent concerns actual neurophysiological data. As brain theory becomes more advanced (and new nonintrusive techniques for recording widespread neural activity are developed) it will become increasingly possible to use what is known about the structure of the brain to help shape various parameters of connectionist models.

It is important, however, that such a constraint should not be too rigidly understood. Models of cognitive phenomena are always to be assessed relative to a specific kind or level of interest. Thus, if a connectionist network is meant to model the structure of the brain at some quite high level (e.g., the level of modules and not of circuits or neurons), it will be inappropriate to "constrain" it to model the details of within-module organization. One of the clearest and most important lessons of recent years has been that the classic tripartite distinction between computational, algorithmic, and implementation detail is just too blunt an instrument with which to taxonomize the spectrum of explanatory interests and endeavors characteristic of cognitive science. What is (mere) implementation detail relative to a computational model of modular organization may be (profound) algorithmic detail relative to a model of intramodular processing (see P. S. Churchland & Sejnowski, 1992). This is obvious enough in principle, but in practice, it is often hard to be sure what level of physiological detail a model is supposed to be capturing. Working connectionists are too often content just to specify a problem and offer a model. But without specifying the proposed grain of interest of the model, it is impossible to assess and criticize it from a psychological–neurophysiological point of view.

Other constraints on good models can flow from a developmental dimension. Since a central focus of the connectionist paradigm is on learning, it is often fair to ask whether the principles that determine the nature and course of knowledge acquisition in a given network are (at some grain of description) the same as those that govern human knowledge acquisition. One of the most famous disputes in the history of connectionist psychological modeling centers on just this issue. Rumelhart and McClelland (1986b) presented a connectionist model of the acquisition of the English past tense, but Pinker and Prince (1988) objected that, although the model did mimic some of the distinctive developmental data, it did so for reasons that involved manipulations of the training data that could not apply to the human case. This whole debate has recently been reopened (K. Plunkett & Marchman, 1991). But the moral is still important. It is that good developmental connectionist models must be sensitive to the actual nature and temporal distribution of ecologically realistic training inputs.

The complexity of the methodological issue is such, however, that it is necessary to beware *also* of rejecting a putative model too quickly. Even if it is demonstrated that the training data to which the child is exposed lack, say, a certain distributional property that the data used by a given simulation exhibit, the case is not closed. It is possible that the incoming data (or "gross input") to the child undergo various stages of preprocessing before they are used as training data by a downstream network. Such preprocessing may filter the data or systematically distort it (expanding and contracting the similarity space) and hence yield a body of downstream (or "effective") training data whose statistical properties are quite radically different (for more on this, see Clark, 1993). Once again, what matters is just to be as clear as possible about the target of the model. Is it supposed to model what happens to the gross input data or is some preprocessing assumed? If the latter, is the assumption plausible?

Further levels of interest, with attendant constraints, are specified by attention to the pattern of failures produced by physical damage to a network or a brain. And still further ones are suggested by attention to the detailed time course of processing and problem solving. What constraints are appropriate always depends on the specific explanatory target of a model. Clarity is all.

To close the present section, it is worth noting a variety of ways in which the connectionist approach remains (it seems to me) unsatisfactory. Most of these are accidental (i.e., remediable) features of actual practice rather than deep features of the paradigm. They represent a kind of vestigial classicism, which continues to depict the brain as a kind of disembodied symbol cruncher, despite countenancing some new styles of representation and processing.

First, there is a problem (noted by, e.g., Dennett, 1991a) concerning the nature of the inputs and outputs. These continue to be specified, often as not, in what are essentially symbolic terms. Yet the real task of the brain is not (generally) to take symbols as input and give symbols as output. Instead, it is to take environmental stimuli as input and yield actions as output. But it is at least possible that once the stress is thus put on the sensing–action cycle, the kind of inner representational states needed as intermediaries may be significantly altered. It is even possible (see later) that the very idea of representations (in any familiar sense) as intermediaries may be challenged.

Second, existing connectionist models suffer from both "single-mindedness" and excessive functional localization. By this, I mean that they tend to focus on just one, single problem (e.g., mapping text to phonemes or producing past tenses) and assume that it is reasonable to charge a single, isolated network with the task of solving it. Yet real neural nets (in the brain) seem to be implicated in the solutions to multiple tasks. And in addition, for a great many tasks, it seems that several different networks make contributions to the solution. The brain, we may say, distributes gross tasks across multiple inner resources. If connectionist models are to be constrained by what is known about functional neuroanatomy, we shall need to study the use of single nets to perform multiple tasks (see, e.g., Karmiloff-Smith, 1992; Plunkett, 1993). And we shall need simultaneously to address the issue of cooperative problem solving, using the partial knowledge embodied in several networks. In this vein, Arbib (1993) depicts the brain as exploiting multiple interacting partial representations (distributed across several subsystems) in its problem-solving activities. The trick is to see how these partial representations can come to interact appropriately without, for example, central or explicit executive controls (see Dennett, 1991b). A philosophically important consequence of such an approach is that the internal representations involved, being partial, will not map neatly onto our public language contents. There are no internal representations of the world. Instead, the representation of the world is the pattern of relationships between all its partial representations (Arbib, 1993, p. 273; see also Minsky, 1985). Connectionists may thus need to view individual neural networks as the loci of multiple partial problem-solving competencies. Work on modular connectionist systems (e.g., Jacobs, Jordan, & Barto, 1991) represents a useful step in this direction.

Third, much more attention needs to be paid to issues concerning the role of innate knowledge and structure in promoting successful connectionist learning (see, e.g., the discussion in Clark, 1993, Chap. 9). Such studies should also address the issue of innate knowledge in large-scale networks of networks (see earlier and Arbib, 1993) and the important interplay between genetic evolution and processes of individual learning (see Ackley & Littman, 1992; Clark, 1993, Chap. 9).

Finally, and perhaps most significant, a deep issue concerning the distribution of intelligence between the organism and its environment (including its body) needs to be kept open. Natural intelligent systems are essentially environmentally situated. This condition, sadly marginalized by most work in both classical and connectionist AI, will have profound implications for the evolution and learning of problem-solving capacities. If we can reduce our internal processing load by exploiting real structure already present in the environment then why not do so? In Clark (1989) I cast this as the 007 principle; namely,

> The 007 Principle. In general, evolved creatures will neither store nor process information in costly ways when they can use the structure of the environment and their operations upon it as a convenient stand-in for the information-processing operations concerned. That is, know only as much as you need to know to get the job done. (Clark 1989, p. 64)

The moral is that we should always be suspicious of the heuristic device of studying intelligent systems independent of the complex structure of their natural environment. To do so is to risk putting into the modeled head what nature leaves to the world. Both connectionism and classical AI are exposed to this very real danger for essentially the same reason; both have tended to model fragments of human cognitive skills. But the complexities of human sensory transduction and motor skills are such as to render it impossible, as yet, to embed these computational models in anything approaching their natural environment (viz., the human body, with its vast sensory inputs and range of motor skills, located in the real world). One response to such a problem is to shift the cognitive scientific focus on to simpler things, which brings us to Section IV.

IV. ARTIFICIAL LIFE

Under this banner I mean to gather both work on real robotic systems such as Brooks's mobile robots (see later) and work on what I shall call *simulated artificial life;* that is, work that studies whole organism–environment interactions using not the real world but a simplified simulated environment. Work in both simulated and "real" artificial life is informed by the belief that we shall better understand the fundamental principles of cognition if we pitch our initial investigations at something akin to the kind of competence achieved by much lower animals (on this, see also Dennett, 1978).

"Real" artificial life attempts to create actual robots whose task is to achieve some goal in the real world. Examples include Genghis, a robot insect capable of clambering successfully around a room cluttered with obstacles, and Herbert, a coke-can collecting robot that functions in the changing and complex environment of a working laboratory (see Connell, 1989). Both projects (and there are many others; see, e.g., Levy, 1992; Meyer & Wilson, 1991), exploit variants of what Brooks (1991) dubs a *subsumption architecture.*

Subsumption architectures represent an attempt to effectively short-circuit what Malcolm, Smithers, and Hallam (1989) call the *sense–think–act cycle* of more classical approaches. Instead of having elaborate sensors that feed data to a kind of central planner which then deploys techniques such as means–end analysis to yield a blueprint for behaviors, the subsumption architecture aims to cut out the middle step—to achieve successful behavior without an intervening stage of planning in a symbolic code. In its place we are to put a bag of separately specified behavior-producing modules, each of which exploits a tight coupling between sensing and action. The idea is to effectively delegate a large chunk of the problem to the environment itself. The on-board equipment consists of layers of behavior-specific modules that cede control to each other according to simple rules. Thus, a walking behavior may continue unless it is interrupted, say, by hitting an obstacle. At that point a different behavior such as turning will take control. At the top end of such a hierarchy can be quite abstract behaviors such as exploration (walking with random turns) and so on. By choosing a well-adapted set of such behaviors, Brooks and others hope to achieve real-time, real-world success: to create robots whose canny use of very simple computational procedures in response to a complex environment yields robust emergent solutions to practical problems (walking, finding "food," avoiding obstacles, etc.).

The underlying vision here is radically different indeed. Orthodox methodology suggests that successful modeling involves realizing some body of knowledge in a set of symbolic structures, which are then the objects of complex computational operations [see Newell's (1982) description of the role of the "knowledge level" and the "symbol level"]. By contrast, subsumption-style work—or more generally, work in what Malcolm et al. (1989) call the *new robotics paradigm*—deliberately avoids treating the problem in those terms. In their view, action is what counts and the very idea of interposing symbol-manipulating processes between sensing and action is seen as potentially counterproductive. In this vein Brooks attacks the whole idea of what he calls an *abstraction barrier*—an intervening stage of information and processing in which a plan is formulated in some inner code. At every point, he believes, we have a choice between inserting a symbolic planner and inserting a program that just "does the right thing."

However, a gray space is somewhere hereabouts. Clearly, an important difference lies between invoking a central planner that "cogitates" in a symbolic inner code and invoking a special-purpose behavioral module. But it is not so clear that such modules will never themselves warrant description and explanation in representational terms. If, for example, a behavior-producing module consisted of a trained-up connectionist network, then it may well be quite proper and useful to consider it as a kind of mini-representational system. In particular, this will be essential to whatever degree the behaviors depend on the net's encoding of some similarity metric as described in Section III. Opposition to the classical vision of central planning and a single symbolic (quasi-sentential) code thus need not lead to total antirepresentationalism. Arbib's vision (Section III) of behavioral success as dependent on the cooperative (but not centrally controlled) activity of multiple networks encoding partial representations of the world preserves much of the biological flavor of the subsumption idea but clearly eschews any antirepresentationalist conclusion.

Real artificial life, I conclude, is methodologically laudable: in attempting to face both the problems and the opportunities provided by the complexities of the real world, it avoids several of the failings common to both connectionist and classical AI. But it is also in occasional danger of overreacting to such failings by completely rejecting the insights of representation-oriented AI.

Simulated artificial life presents yet another twist. The focus of attention here is (largely, these are just rough and ready categories) not so much on individual organisms as on whole ecosystems or populations of organisms. Ray (1992) investigated a virtual ecosystem named Tierra, in which digital "organisms" (each one a kind of small program) competed for CPU time. The organisms (or code fragments) were capable of reproducing (creating a copy of themselves) and were subject to some randomly introduced alterations (mutations) and genetic variation caused by occasionally inaccurate reproduction. The idea was to set up such a system (implemented in the memory of a digital computer) with an initial population of organisms and let (simulated) nature take its course. The resulting runs of simulated evolution could then be analyzed, and the characteristics of the evolving population displayed. This proved to be a fruitful exercise. Organisms evolved whose code contained elegant tricks to promote survival and reproduction. Yet Ray also observed that the way such tricks were algorithmically realized was often counterintuitive—robust, effective solutions which nonetheless offended against the ideals of neat, human programming techniques. In addition, a succession of successful survival strategies ensued, each one exploiting the characteristic weaknesses of the previously dominant strategy. Thus some organisms would evolve to exploit the instructions embodied in other organisms' code (parasites). Later still, organisms evolved which were capable of turning the tables on these: of diverting the CPU time belonging to a hopeful parasite to themselves, and so on.

Work such as the Tierra project provides useful insights both into the nature of evolutionary processes and the probably nonintuitive space of computational solutions which such a process can generate. But it appears distant, at first sight, from the mainstream concerns of cognitive science. To see what its value might be closer to home, recall the plea for greater attention to issues concerning innate knowledge entered at the close of Section III. One exciting possibility is to use simulated evolutionary processes to mold the initial states of more complex organisms—ones capable of individual learning and performing more obviously cognitive tasks. The opportunity now exists, as Ackley and Littman (1992) point out, to study cognition at multiple scales simultaneously; that is, to exploit the speed and power of modern computing resources to study both the long-term emergence of structures and knowledge caused by evolutionary change in an entire population and the short-term development of knowledge and responses characteristic of individual learning. The interplay between these factors is highly complex and important.

Just that interplay was the focus of a recent study (Ackley & Littman, 1992) that combined simulated genetic evolution with neural network learning in the context of a mini ecosystem. The "organisms" studied each consisted of two subnetworks. One subnetwork (the "action network") took in "sensory" input and yielded motor commands. The other (the "evaluation network") took sensory input and mapped it to a scalar judgment representing the "goodness" (desirability) of th current situation. The evaluation network changed only over evolutionary time and its weights were specified by a genetic code. The same code specified the initial weights of the "action network" and hence determined the "instinctual" (prior-to-learning) behaviors of the overall organism. But during its lifetime it would use a weight adjustment algorithm to modify itself, so as to increase its tendencies to move toward whatever the evaluation network was telling it were good situations. Genetic evolution proceeded by allowing the fittest organisms to reproduce; that is, to have their genetic code used (with some mutation and recombination) to generate the next generation of organisms. Fitness was determined by the success of the organism in surviving in a mini-world populated with some prespecified carnivores, plants, trees, and walls. The world consisted of a 100×100 array of cells within which the organisms could move. Sensory input consisted of a coding for the nearest objects in each direction, up to a maximum distance of four cells. The output of the action network determined movement within the world.

Several interesting results were obtained during runs of this system. One such result concerned evidence of the so-called Baldwin effect (Baldwin, 1986), in which evolved abilities to learn to achieve a goal transmute, over evolutionary time, into an innate (instinctual) ability to directly achieve the goal. This sounds Lamarckian; that is, it sounds as if, contrary to evolutionary theory, knowledge learned during an individual lifetime is somehow "getting back into the gene" and being passed on. But, in fact, a good Darwinian explanation exists. An organism that can learn to do X will be able to exploit any evolutionary changes (due to crossover or mutation) which make it quicker or easier to learn to do so, whereas beings unable to learn to do X would not have their fitness increased by such supportive adaptations. Over evolutionary time, a population that once was capable of learning to do X may thus be speeded on its way to becoming a population able to do X directly, courtesy of all these supportive adaptations. In the case at hand, the successful organisms in early generations turned out to have evolved evaluation networks that told them that plants (the source of energy for continued survival) were good. They thus trained their action networks to produce plant-approaching behavior and hence were fitter. Later in the simulation, plant-approaching behavior was seen to be directly coded in the action networks at birth—the organisms now know "instinctually" to head for plants. This is explained, by Ackley and Littman (1992, p. 16), as the Baldwin effect at work.

Even more interesting, Ackley and Littman later noted a kind of inverse Baldwin effect. For some time, the evaluation nets of these successful agents encoded a preference for situations in which carnivores were present! This was potentially disastrous, since if the action net was trained in this way the organisms would learn to approach carnivores and hence perish. Yet for a substantial period (over a million time steps) this evaluation persisted. How could it survive?

The answer was that at this late stage in the evolutionary process, the organisms' action networks had become so replete with good innate "instincts" that they would from the outset avoid carnivores and hence the potentially disastrous learning never had a chance to occur. As they put it, "the well-adapted action network apparently shielded the maladapted learning network from the fitness function" (Ackley & Littman, 1992, p. 18). In short, once the instincts were in place, the evolutionary pressure to preserve the good evaluations that would lead to appropriate learning was removed. That knowledge (hard won over evolutionary time) was then subject to gradual decay over succeeding generations, as there was no longer any pressure to keep it well-tuned. The upshot is what Ackley and Littman term *goal regression*. The original well-evolved goals (the situations judged "good" by the evaluation network) may speed the organisms (via the Baldwin effect) on to a state in which the target behaviors do not even need to be learned. At that point, the pressure on the evaluation network is lifted, and changes and mutations can occur without immediately affecting fitness. Hence, the original innate knowledge concerning goals decays, to be replaced by representations whose contents are unpredictable and can include "crazy" judgments.

Ackley and Littman's work is a step along an important road. It sheds some initial light on the complex interactions that can occur between individual and evolutionary learning. And it begins to illuminate the counterintuitive and unexpected ways in which systems exploiting multiple networks (two, in this case) may evolve to balance some of those networks against others. The computational and methodological resources are thus in place that would allow us to address some of the criticisms of existing neural networks research raised in Section III. To realize that potential, we shall need to investigate how evolution might distribute tasks and initial biases across a genuine multiplicity of inner resources and what kinds of harmonizations may evolve between such resources (on this, see the discussion in Clark, 1993, Chap. 9).

Artificial life (both "real" and simulated) is therefore best viewed (I claim) as adding important new tools to the repertoire of cognitive science. The lasting value of these tools may lie most of all in their ability to help augment and enrich the neural networks approach outlined in Section III. Such augmentation and enrichment may take many forms, but it will include essentially (1) recognition of the crucial role of the external environment for understanding both the form and scope of internal representations, (2) exploration of the important interplay between slow evolutionary change and processes of individual learning, and (3) investigation of the nature of innate knowledge and the particular forms it may take in the context of complex networks of networks and the capacity for individual learning.

V. THE WASTELAND

At the end of all that, the philosopher stands amid scenes of devastation. The relatively straightforward vision of the mind as at root a quasi-linguistic symbol system is now challenged by approaches whose ontology and methodology is much less well-defined and much more conceptually taxing.

Where once we had a reasonably clear idea of, for example, what a representation was supposed to be (a referring item occurring as a syntactic structure in the context of an overall symbol system), we now face puzzles. The physical vehicles of representation threaten to be much more complex than we imagined—more likely to involve distributed activity patterns (or long-term weights) in whole networks, or even in networks of networks, or even in embodied embedded networks of networks! Related notions such as explicit representation and structured representation are likewise subject to reappraisal (see Clark, 1993; Kirsh, 1991; Van Gelder, 1990). And visions of the nature of mental causation and the scientific vindication of folk psychology predicated on that same symbol system model (Fodor, 1987) look due for a full re-evaluation. As the conceptual distance between folk psychology and inner stories increases, our attitudes to folk psychology must themselves be re-examined. Unless we are willing to infer that the folk vision is simply false (P. M. Churchland, 1989, Chap. 1), we may need to recognize a fundamentally different kind of relationship between the mental realm (of beliefs, desires, etc.) and the cognitive scientific one (of activation vectors, partial representations, etc.). Equally, if talk of world-referring contents (and hence of operations upon the computational vehicles of such contents) turns out to be too limiting to display the nature and richness of the inner processing events, cognitive science may itself need to investigate new, non-content-based frameworks of description and explanation, such as dynamic systems theory (see, e.g., Abraham & Shaw, 1992; Beer, 1990).

Cognitive science, I conclude, has reached an important historical cross-roads. The complex of ideas that once defined the field is being challenged from several angles. The emerging alternative (a powerful combination of insights from neural networks and artificial life—see Clark (in press) for a detailed exploration) demands new conceptualizations of almost all the key terms. These conceptualizations are not yet fully formed, and their development will be driven as much by further practical model-building experience as by philosophical reflection. At the heart of this new understanding will be a much better appreciation of the delicate balance between initial structure,

external environment, and the dependable effects of bombardment by ecologically realistic stimuli. Understanding the details of that ancient bargain
remains the essence of cognitive science.

References

Abraham, R., & Shaw, C. (1992). *Dynamics—The geometry of behavior* (2nd ed.). Redwood
City, CA: Addison-Wesley.
Ackley, D., & Littman, M. (1992). Interactions between learning and evolution. In C. Lang-
ton, C. Taylor, D. Farmer, & S. Rasmussen (Eds.), *Artificial Life II* (Santa Fe Institute
studies in the sciences of complexity, Vol. 10, pp. 1–23). Reading, MA: Addison-Wesley.
Arbib, M. (1993). Review of Allen Newell 'Unified theories of cognition.' *Artificial Intelligence,
59*, 265–283.
Baldwin, J. (1896). A new factor in evolution. *American Naturalist, 30*, 536–553.
Beer, R. (1990). *Intelligence as adaptive behavior: An experiment in computational neuroethology.* San
Diego, CA: Academic Press.
Borst, C. V. (1970). *The mind/brain identity theory.* London: Macmillan.
Brooks, R. (1991). Intelligence without representation. *Artificial Intelligence, 47*, 139–159.
Churchland, P. M. (1989). *A neurocomputational perspective.* Cambridge, MA: MIT/Bradford
Books.
Churchland, P. S. (1978). Fodor on language and learning. *Synthese, 38*(1), 149–159.
Churchland, P. S., & Sejnowski, T. J. (1992). *The computational brain.* Cambridge, MA: MIT
Press.
Clark, A. (1989). *Microcognition: Philosophy, cognitive science and parallel distributed processing.*
Cambridge, MA: MIT/Bradford Books.
Clark, A. (1993). *Associative engines: Connectionism, concepts and representational change.* Cam-
bridge, MA: MIT Press.
Clark, A. (in press). *Being there: Putting brain, body & world together again.* Cambridge, MA:
MIT Press.
Connell, J. (1989). *A colony architecture for an artificial creature* (MIT AI Tech. Rep. No. 1151).
Cambridge, MA: Massachusetts Institute of Technology.
Dennett, D. (1978). Why not the whole iguana?.*Behavioral and Brain Sciences, 1*, 103–104.
Dennett, D. (1991a). Mother nature versus the walking encyclopedia. In W. Ramsey, S. Stich,
& D. Rumelhart (Eds.), *Philosophy and connectionist theory* (pp. 21–30). Hillsdale, NJ:
Erlbaum.
Dennett, D. (1991b). *Consciousness explained.* Boston: Little, Brown.
Fodor, J. (1975). *The Language of thought.* New York: Crowell.
Fodor, J. (1981). The present status of the innateness controversy. In J. Fodor (Ed.), *Representa-
tions: Philosophical essays on the foundations of cognitive science* (pp. 257–316). Brighton,
Sussex: Harvester Press.
Fodor, J. (1987). *Psychosemantics: The problem of meaning in the philosophy of mind.* Cambridge
MA: MIT Press.
Fodor, J., & Lepore, E. (1992). *Holism: A shopper's guide.* Oxford: Blackwell.
Fodor, J., & McLaughlin, B. (1991). Connectionism and the problem of systematicity: Why
Smolensky's solution doesn't work. In T. Horgan & J. Tienson (Eds.), *Connectionism and
the philosophy of mind* (pp. 331–354). Cambridge, MA: MIT Press.
Fodor, J., & Pylyshyn, Z. (1988). Connectionism and cognitive architecture: A critical analy-
sis. *Cognition, 28*, 3–71.

Haugeland, J. (1981). Semantic engines: An introduction to mind design. In J. Haugeland (Ed.), *Mind design* (pp. 1–34). Cambridge, MA: MIT Press.

Jacobs, R., Jordan, M., & Barto, A. (1991). "Task decomposition through competition in a modular connectionist architecture: The what and where visual tasks. *Cognitive Science, 15*, 219–250.

Karmiloff-Smith, A. (1992). Nature, nurture and PDP: Preposterous developmental postulates? [Special issue on Philosophical issues in connectionist modelling]. *Connection Science, 4*(3 & 4), 253–270.

Kirsh, D. (1991). When is information explicitly represented? In P. Hanson (Ed.), *Information, thought and content* (pp. 340–365). Vancouver: UBC Press.

Levy, S. (1992). *Artificial life: The quest for a new creation.* London: Jonathan Cape.

Lycan, W. (1990). *Mind and cognition: A reader.* Oxford: Blackwell.

Malcolm, C., Smithers, T., & Hallam, J. (1989). *An emerging paradigm in robot architecture* (Research Paper No. 447). Edinburgh: Edinburgh University, Department of Artificial Intelligence. (Presented at the Intelligent Autonomous Systems Two Conference)

Meyer, J., & Wilson, S. (Eds.). (1991). *From animals to animats: Proceedings of the first international conference on simulation of adaptive behavior.* Cambridge, MA: MIT Press/Bradford Books.

Minsky, M. (1985). *The society of mind.* New York: Simon & Schuster.

Newell, A. (1982). The knowledge level. *Artificial Intelligence, 18*, 87–127.

Newell, A., & Simon, H. (1976). Computer science as empirical enquiry. In J. Haugeland (Ed.), *Mind design* (pp. 35–66). Cambridge, MA: MIT Press.

Oaksford, M., & Chater, N. (1991). Against logicist cognitive science. *Mind and Language, 6*(1), 1–38.

Pinker, S., & Prince, A. (1988). On language and connectionism: Analysis of a parallel distributed processing model of language acquisition. *Cognition, 28*, 73–193.

Plunkett, K. (1993). Making nets work hard. Commentary on A. Clark & A. Karmiloff-Smith, The cognizer's innards: A psychological and philosophical perspective on the development of thought. *Mind and Language.* 8:4:p. 549–558.

Plunkett, K., & Marchman, V. (1991). U-shaped learning and frequency effects in a multi-layered perception: Implications for child language acquisition. *Cognition, 38*, 1–60.

Putnam, H. (1960). Minds and machines. Reprinted in H. Putnam (Ed.), *Mind, language and reality: Philosophical papers* (Vol. 2, pp. 362–385). Cambridge, UK: Cambridge University Press.

Ray, T. (1992). An approach to the synthesis of life. In C. Langton, C. Taylor, J. Farmer, & S. Rasmussen (Eds.), *Artificial Life II* Santa Fe Studies in the Sciences of Complexity Vol. 10 (pp. 371–408). Reading, MA: Addison-Wesley.

Rumelhart, D., & McClelland, J. (1986a). PDP Models and general issues in cognitive science. In D. Rumelhart, J. McClelland, & the PDP Research Group (Eds.), *Parallel distributed processing: Explorations in the microstructure of cognition* (Vol. 1, pp. 110–146). Cambridge, MA: MIT Press.

Rumelhart, D., & McClelland, J. (1986b). On learning the past tenses of English verbs. In D. Rumelhart, J. McClelland, & the PDP Research Group (Eds.), *Parallel distributed processing: Explorations in the microstructure of cognition* (Vol. 2, pp. 216–271). Cambridge, MA: MIT Press.

Sejnowski, T., & Rosenberg, C. (1987). Parallel networks that learn to pronounce English text. *Complex Systems, 1*, 145–166.

Smolensky, P. (1988). On the proper treatment of connectionism. *Behavioral and Brain Sciences, 2*, 1–74.

Smolensky, P. (1991). Connectionism, constituency and the language of thought. In B. Lower & G. Rey (Eds.), *Jerry Fodor and his critics* (pp. 201–229). Oxford: Blackwell.

Van Gelder, T. (1990). Compositionality: A connectionist variation on a classical theme. *Cognitive Science, 14,* 355–384.

Van Gelder, T. (1991). What is the 'D' in 'PDP'? A survey of the concept of distribution. In R. W. Ramsey, S. Stich, & D. Rumelhart (Eds.), *Philosophy and connectionist theory* (pp. 33–59). Hillsdale, NJ: Erlbaum.

CHAPTER 2

Planning and Problem Solving*

Robert Inder

In the AI literature, *planning* refers to determining a sequence of actions you know how to perform that will achieve a particular objective. *Problem solving* is finding a plan for a task in an abstract domain. A problem is hard if you do not know how to work out an appropriate sequence of steps and is solved once such a sequence has been found: actual execution is irrelevant.

Unlike many areas of AI, planning shows a clear line of researchers building on each other's work, and this chapter will describe some of the landmarks along the way. Section I discusses the overall planning task from an AI perspective and introduces some terminology. Section II then shows how these general principles are embodied in the seminal work on sequencing activities, Newell and Simon's General Problem Solver (GPS), which was inspired by investigating human problem solving. However, those working in robotics also quickly found the need to combine their robots' primitive operations—moving itself or its arm, grasping or releasing something, and so forth—to produce interesting behavior. Section III discusses the Stanford Research Institute Problem Solver, STRIPS, and the way it extended the ideas of GPS to the activities of a robot pushing boxes between

* The support of the Economic and Social Research Council for the Human Communication Research Centre is gratefully acknowledged. The author was supported by the UK Joint Councils Initiative in Cognitive Science and HCI, Grant G9018050.

Artificial Intelligence

rooms. Following STRIPS, planning for a robot in an idealized world to rearrange a handful of building blocks on a table soon became a standard task (see Figure 1). The blocks are named but usually otherwise identical, and the robot can lift and move only a single block that has nothing else on top of it.

From this "toy" domain, a thread of technology-oriented research has lead planning toward being able to tackle meaningful tasks. Section IV discusses the early attempts to address the problems caused by interactions between different parts of a plan. However, the limits of the "natural" representations adopted in GPS and STRIPS meant that large classes of tasks could not be planned effectively. In 1975, a system called NOAH demonstrated how to overcome these limitations by making a fundamental change of representation that allowed sequencing decisions to be delayed. NOAH, and some related systems, are described in Section V.

The work mentioned so far gave rise to a body of techniques that are now accepted practice, and planning systems that embody them are starting to be applied to tackle tasks of practical significance. Current work, though, is inevitably diverse, as researchers grapple with various ways of extending planning systems to deal with specific aspects of real world problems. Some of this work is outlined in Section VI. Section VII discusses some of the aspects of planning that are particularly relevant to cognitive science. Finally, the References offer some suggestions for further reading.

I. SOME BASIC IDEAS

To avoid having to cope with the complexities of the physical world, much early work in AI was directed toward abstract activities such as proving theorems, playing games like chess and checkers, or solving puzzles. To illustrate the discussion in this section, we will use the Tower of Hanoi (Hanoi), a puzzle involving three pegs, on which disks can be placed, and a set of disks of varying size (see Figure 2). The disks only can be moved, one at a time, between the pegs, and a disk must never be stacked on top of a smaller one. The problem is to transport the entire stack of disks to another peg.

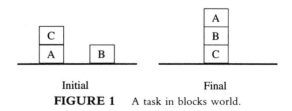

Initial   Final
FIGURE 1   A task in blocks world.

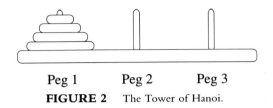

Peg 1   Peg 2   Peg 3

FIGURE 2   The Tower of Hanoi.

Reasoning about such a problem obviously requires representing states of the world and having some way of specifying the objective, or *goal*. These representations must be rich enough to embody all the aspects of the world that will be reasoned about. In particular, since planning is about changing things, every property that might be affected must be represented as dependent on time in some way. For Hanoi, this requires only an ability to represent sets of disks' positions as the disks are initially, as they are required to be eventually, and as they may be in between. A planner also needs to represent what can be done—such as the moves that can be made, as determined by the nature of the game or puzzle. There is a fundamental difference between an agent *executing an action,* and thus affecting the world, and a planning system manipulating representations to derive information about doing so, which we call *applying an operator.* Unfortunately, authors often rely on context to make their intentions clear when, for instance, they refer to operators by describing actions.

The representation of an action must provide a way of characterizing its effects, and the *level of abstraction* is vital, since it has a huge influence on the complexity of the planning task. If a robot were required to actually manipulate a stack of disks, it would be necessary to determine all the details of grasping a disk, lifting it off the peg, and so forth. But since we are interested only in solving the puzzle, we can treat moving a disk to be a single, atomic action, and thus remove the need to represent the world when the disk is half way between pegs, or when it is nearly but not quite off one. Ignoring such details makes the problem very much simpler. At this level of abstraction, 4-disk Hanoi has 24 possible operators: each of 4 disks can be moved from each of 3 initial pegs to either of 2 destination pegs: thus Disk 1 can be moved from Peg 1 to Peg 2, or Peg 2 to Peg 1, or Peg 1 to Peg 3, and so forth.

For interesting tasks, describing every possible operation in this way quickly gets unmanageable and is literally an infinite task for robots that might move to coordinates or dial telephone numbers. Further abstraction is required. Generalizing over the identity of the pegs and the disk can reduce Hanoi to a problem with just a single operator: move a disk d from one peg, $p1$, to another peg, $p2$. Note, though, that the result of this generalization does not represent an action that can actually be carried out: it is an abstraction of a family of operations, an operation *schema*. Whenever such an operation is included in a plan, the schema must be *instantiated:* it must be copied and modified to produce an executable operator that specifies the actual entities—blocks, pegs, or whatever—that the action will involve. It will often be possible to instantiate the same operation schema in more than one way in a single state, which simply indicates that there are several primitive operators that could be applied.

Unfortunately, describing the possible operators themselves is not enough. We cannot usually do any thing at any time: the world—or the rules of the game—imposes restrictions. For example we cannot start solving Hanoi by moving Disk 4 to Peg 3 because we are allowed to move only the topmost disk on any pile. If operators are to be selected sensibly, their descriptions must indicate any constraints on the situations in which the action can be carried out—its *preconditions*. If the preconditions for an operator are all satisfied by a state, it is *applicable* to that state.

Given a way of describing states and some operator schemata that specify the effects and the preconditions of actions, the task of the planner is to find a sequence of applicable actions that will transform the current situation into one that matches a goal. Unfortunately, this is not easy. Even where there are only a few choices in any situation, as the number of steps in the plan increases, the number of *combinations* of operators rises very quickly indeed—so quickly that any system attempting to reason about them all would soon be overwhelmed. Such a rapid rise in the number of options is called a *combinatorial explosion*.

Simple classes of problems can sometimes be analyzed to produce a way of determining how to proceed in any given situation. But for most situations of interest we have no effective way to tell what actions are appropriate. If we can determine how far any given state is from a solution—for Hanoi, we might count disks out of place or possibly sum their sizes—we can try applying operators that move "toward" a solution. But unfortunately, realistic domains have complex state descriptions, and because the range of applicable operators depends on *combinations* of features, there is no general way of assessing how difficult it is to get from one given state to another. Consider trying to drive from Rome to Athens, or New York to Panama, by going directly toward the destination. Although the distance gets smaller to start with, there comes a point where further progress is impossible: the remaining gap cannot be crossed because something about the situation (lack of roads, caused by depth of water) means the relevant operator just cannot be applied. In general, there is no way to know whether a particular approach will lead to such a dead end without following it through and building a plan that actually achieves the goal. Since the planner cannot reliably tell whether a decision is actually a step toward its objective, it can find a path only if it is prepared to *search*.

Much AI research has concerned ways of dealing with such situations by searching for solutions efficiently. The common way of thinking about such problems is in terms of a *search space,* an abstract space in which points correspond to possible states of the system being considered. Operators bring about moves from one position to another, and they are thought of as linking the points. One of the positions is the starting point for the task, and one or more others constitute completion or success. For Hanoi, states could be identified with a combination of an arrangement of disks and a record of how that arrangement was reached from the initial point (see Figure 3; note that the same arrangement of disks occurs in more than one state). Such a space has the structure of an infinite tree, and finding a plan involves finding a branch that reaches a state that has the desired configuration of disks. However, there are many ways of conceiving of a problem as a search space. The choice determines what must be considered while solving the problem and the range of solutions that can be found, and thus the difficulty of the task for either a machine or a human reasoner (see Newell, 1980). A specific change of search space, which has had a very significant effect on planning systems, will be discussed in Section V.

One obvious way to make searching for a plan easier would be to reduce

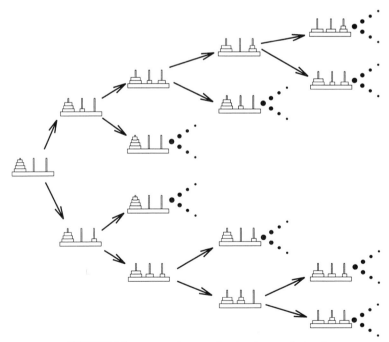

FIGURE 3   A search space for the Tower of Hanoi.

the size of the search space, by clever encoding of operators or something similar. However, the search space defines the set of plans that the system can make: reducing it makes searching simpler but does so by reducing the number of things the system can plan to do. This approach is fine for systems that always do nearly the same thing, such as inserting components into printed circuit boards. But for many types of agent—such as manufacturing robots, Mars probes, and indeed people—flexibility is paramount. Having a rich search space and searching it efficiently is what planning is all about.

II. THE GENERAL PROBLEM SOLVER

The previous section discussed planning and the idea of searching for a suitable sequence of operations and introduced some of the relevant terminology. This section describes how they are realized in one of the landmark systems in planning: GPS, the General Problem Solver. During its 10-year development, GPS was presented as relevant to both explaining human performance and achieving intelligent behavior from a machine. Newell and Simon (1961) present it as simulating human behavior on a theorem proving task, while some subsequent publications explicitly ignore psychological plausibility and present it purely as illustrating techniques for allowing a computer program to tackle a wide range of tasks.

GPS must obviously be given a specification of the particular problem it is to work on. Much of this is concerned with defining terms and abbreviations: these not only make the specification and subsequent output more comprehensible but also identify the structure of the objects involved in the problem. The rest of the specification describes the initial situation, the objective GPS is to seek and the operators it can use.

GPS works on "objects"—data structures that represent a state of the problem domain, which could be a mathematical expression being manipulated or a description of a physical situation. These objects are the points in the search space: the problem to be solved is given as an initial object and a (possibly partial) target object. GPS explores this search space, creating objects to represent the states that result from applying operators, until it finds one that matches the target object. The sequence of operators which produced that object then corresponds to a sequence of actions that will solve the problem.

Operators are specified as schemata with preconditions, effects, and variables that are instantiated to suit the object to which it is being applied. In particular, operators can be defined to be "move" operators, which to GPS means that the result of applying the operator to an object is a new object that contains a different arrangement of its substructures. The problem specification also contains the Table of Connections (TOC), an indication of when each operator is likely to be useful.

The heart of GPS, and an area where it has influenced almost every planning system since, is the way it chooses which operator to apply in any given state by using means–ends analysis (MEA). GPS's approach to a problem is driven by *goals*, data structures that contain three kinds of information:

- A target or objective, as indeed *goal* would normally suggest.
- An existing situation—that is, an object from which the target must be achieved.
- A history of previous attempts—this information allows GPS to return to a goal and try alternative ways of achieving it.

At any time, GPS's processing is controlled by a single, current goal, although as part of working on a goal, GPS will often create and start to work on a subgoal. Achieving a subgoal should either satisfy the goal itself, or result in a simplification of the goal—an object from which the objective of the goal can more easily be reached.

There are three kinds of goal: *transform* an object into another, *reduce* a difference between an object and a target, and *apply* a specified operator to an object. (Later versions have a fourth kind of goal, concerned with selecting the best element from a set.) The problem specification given to GPS must define an overall goal to transform an initial object into a desired object.

GPS tackles `transform` goals by comparing the two objects and giving itself the subgoal of trying to `reduce` the single biggest difference between them. If this subgoal succeeds, producing a new object with the biggest difference `reduced`, then GPS gives itself another new goal to `transform` this new object into the desired object. This continues until either no differences are left, in which case it has solved the problem, or one of the `reduce` goals cannot be dealt with, in which case it has failed.

The heart of GPS's problem solving is the interplay of its attempts to solve `reduce` and `apply` goals.

GPS tackles a goal to `reduce` a difference between two objects by using information in the TOC in the problem specification. This specifies which types of operator might be useful for which types of difference; that is, which operators to consider relevant *means* for achieving which *ends*. GPS picks such a relevant operator and creates a new goal to actually `apply` it to the current object. If that subgoal succeeds, so does the `reduce` goal itself, since the subgoal's results will be an object with the operator applied and thus the difference reduced. If the subgoal fails—if GPS cannot `apply` the operator—then it will try again with another relevant operator from the TOC, until there are no more operators, in which case the `reduce` goal itself has failed.

When working on a goal to `apply` an operator to an object, GPS starts by checking the operator's preconditions. If they are all satisfied, GPS simply constructs the new object in line with the operator definition, and the goal is finished. In general, though, the operator's preconditions will not match the object, and there will be a set of differences. GPS uses the definitions in the problem specification to rank these differences in order of importance and establishes a goal to r e d u c e the most significant of them. If this subgoal fails—the difference cannot be r e d u c e d—then the goal itself fails: the operator cannot be applied. If the subgoal succeeds, creating an object with the difference reduced, then a second subgoal is created to a p p l y the operator to that new object, with the result of that subgoal being the result of the goal itself.

MEA is a very powerful way of directing the process of plan generation by creating a hierarchy of subgoals and focusing on achieving each in turn. However, it is not perfect. An operator may not remove every difference of the kind the TOC shows it addresses; and even where it does, making progress toward one goal can easily block, or even undo, the achievement of another. To prevent this kind of interference between subgoals, GPS keeps a record of every goal and state that it has worked on. By checking these records whenever a goal or state is generated, GPS can detect when it is going round in circles and can thus abandon the approach that caused it. The problem description also includes heuristics for evaluating the difficulty of a goal. GPS checks that every subgoal is easier than the goal that invoked it. It also always tackles the hardest subgoal first. This means that the attempt to satisfy the goal is most likely to fail as soon as possible. It also allows GPS to check that it is making progress, by ensuring that each subsequent subgoal of a goal is easier than those that went before.

A. GPS in Action: The Tower of Hanoi

Having considered the operation of GPS in general terms, let us see how it handles the specific problem of Hanoi. The problem will be described in great detail, much more than will be given for subsequent work. This detail should convey precisely how GPS's "intelligent" behavior emerges as a result of describing a problem in a structured way so that a small set of straightforward algorithms can break it down further and further, until solving its parts becomes trivial.

States of the puzzle—disk configurations—are represented in a data structure that comprises three stack descriptions, one for each peg, each containing a token to indicate the presence of each disk that is on that peg. The single operator—for moving a disk from one peg to another—is shown in Figure 4. Given the discussion so far, the effort invested in making GPS's interactions "Englishlike" should make most of this comprehensible. The line following M O V E S specifies the operator's effects: it transforms an object into a new one by moving the token indicating the presence of D I S K from the stack description of F R O M - P E G to the stack description of T O - P E G .

```
MOVE-DISK = ( CREATION-OPERATOR
               VAR-DOMAIN
    1. THE TO-PEG IS AN EXCLUSIVE-MEMBER OF THE PEGS .
    2. THE FROM PEG IS AN EXCLUSIVE MEMBER OF THE PEGS .
    3. THE OTHER-PEG IS AN EXCLUSIVE MEMBER OF THE PEGS .
    4. THE DISK IS IN-THE-SET OF DISKS .
    PRETESTS
        1. X ON THE OTHER-PEG IS DEFINED FOR-ALL X SMALLER
           THAN THE PARTICULAR DISK .
    MOVES
        1. MOVE THE DISK ON THE FROM-PEG TO THE DISK ON THE TO-PEG
           )
```

FIGURE 4   Definition for the GPS MOVE-DISK operator.

The preconditions may be slightly surprising given the statement of the
problem. They do not say that DISK must be the top disk on FROM-
PEG, or that it must be smaller than the top disk on TO-PEG. Instead they
require all disks smaller than DISK to be on OTHER-PEG. Because there
are only three pegs, this single requirement is equivalent to the two in the
problem statement, although the reformulation is not without consequence,
as will be discussed later. Finally, the four lines following VAR-DOMAIN
specify that TO-PEG and FROM-PEG, which have obviously predictable
roles, and OTHER-PEG, which does not, are three different pegs, and that
DISK is a disk.

In addition to the initial and target objects and the operator schema, the
problem statement also includes some miscellaneous information: defining
which disks are smaller than which other ones, indicating the significant
kinds of differences between objects and their relative importance, and specifying that the MOVE-DISK operator is relevant for resolving any difference.

GPS starts with a goal to transform the initial state (all disks on Peg
1) into the target state (all disks on Peg 3). Comparing these states reveals
four differences: each of the four disks is in the wrong place. Because GPS
has been told that differences involving higher numbered disks are more
significant, it chooses the difference involving Disk 4 as the most important, and sets up a subgoal, Goal 2, to reduce that difference; that
is, to get Disk 4 onto Peg 3. By using the TOC, GPS discovers that the
only operator relevant to doing this is MOVE-DISK, with its DISK parameter instantiated to Disk 4 and its FROM-PEG and TO-PEG parameters instantiated to Peg 1 and Peg 3, respectively, thus determining the
OTHER-PEG parameter, too. So it now establishes Goal 3, to *apply* this
operator to the current (i.e., initial) state.

The preconditions of this operator indicate that it cannot be applied
because the other disks (3, 2, and 1) are in the wrong place. So GPS es-

tablishes Goal 4 to **reduce** the largest of these, the difference involving Disk 3. As before, the TOC suggests the MOVE-DISK operator, and GPS sets up a subgoal (Goal 5) to **apply** it to move Disk 3 to Peg 2. But again, there are unsatisfied preconditions: Disks 1 and 2 on Peg 1 rather than Peg 3. So GPS establishes another subgoal (Goal 6) to **reduce** the more significant of these (Disk 2) and thus yet another subgoal (Goal 7) to **apply** MOVE-DISK to do it. This still cannot be done, now because Disk 1 is on Peg 1 not Peg 2, so Goal 8 is set up to fix this, and Goal 9 to use MOVE-DISK to do so.

This time, one may be relieved to hear, the preconditions of MOVE-DISK are satisfied and the operator can be applied. Doing so satisfies both Goal 8 (reduce the difference involving Disk 1) and Goal 9 (do so using MOVE-DISK) and also creates a new object that describes the state after moving the disk. Now, with Goals 8 and 9 achieved, GPS shifts its attention back to Goal 7: solving Goal 6 by applying MOVE-DISK to Disk 2. Goal 8 should have reduced the differences that were stopping MOVE-DISK being applied, so GPS sets up a new goal (Goal 10) to **apply** it to the resulting state. Fortunately, moving Disk 1 left no differences to block the movement of Disk 2: the resulting state satisfies the preconditions for using MOVE-DISK to move Disk 2, so this operator can now be applied, satisfying Goal 10, 6, and 7, and creating a third object describing the situation after two moves.

Having now applied two operators, GPS returns to Goal 5: get Disk 3 to Peg 2 to by applying MOVE-DISK. Having succeeded in reducing the relevant differences, it creates a new goal (Goal 11) to **apply** the operator in the new state. However, in tacking this goal, it discovers a difference— Disk 1 is on Peg 2 when it should be on Peg 3. So . . .

So far, two move operators have been applied, moving two steps down the topmost branch in Figure 3, and GPS is working on getting Disk 1 to Peg 3 as a step toward getting Disk 3 to Peg 2, which in turn would be progress toward getting Disk 4 to Peg 3, Eventually, GPS will battle its way to an optimal solution: a sequence of 15 operators that will move the four disks from one peg to another. In doing so, it will have worked on 46 subgoals.

This example illustrates the two key features of GPS's approach that have been taken up by almost all work in the field:

- Selecting operators on the basis that they are identified as relevant to making some change to a particular state.
- Generating subgoals to bring about any unsatisfied preconditions of an operator that is to be applied.

This approach may look very powerful—a "general" approach to problem solving that efficiently produces optimal solutions. Unfortunately, such good performance is certainly not guaranteed, and the excellent performance in this case is a result of the precise way the problem domain was encoded—see page 37.

One further thing must be mentioned about this example—perhaps the most striking feature of all. Even though it illustrates an optimal search for a tiny task in a trivial domain, there is an astonishing amount of it! Yet, nothing is "wasted" or unnecessary: eliminating any operations would reduce flexibility and thus the power of the system. The descriptions of the operation of other systems that appear in subsequent sections will not go into anything like this much detail. They will highlight one or two features of the system, and this may give the impression that these mechanisms or kinds of operation generate plans simply or easily. This is deceptive. Our ability to grasp complex operations or information structures from a few simple sentences tends to obscure the complexity of what is being described and the amount of computation it can involve. Planning is hard.

III. STRIPS

Games and puzzles are a good starting point for work in AI because they involve only a very simple world, all the relevant features of which can be captured in a few, small data structures. GPS took advantage of this in the way it handled the effects of operators by creating a complete new description of the resulting state. Interesting planning, however, involves representations of many objects with complex properties and interrelationships. GPS's approach is not practical for such domains because the resources required for building, holding, and searching complex states quickly become prohibitive.

The program that has shaped the way planning techniques are applied to complex situations is STRIPS, which is described in Fikes and Nilsson (1971) and Cohen and Feigenbaum (1982). STRIPS generated plans for a robot, Shakey, that could move about between a number of rooms, pushing boxes around and carrying out a small number of other actions.

Like GPS, STRIPS used goals to guide its planning, considering operators on the basis of the effect required and generating subgoals to bring about their preconditions. It, too, searched for a path through a space of points, which it characterized by a combination of a state of the world and an ordered list of goals to be achieved.

It differed, though, in the nature of its state descriptions. Whereas GPS used a single data structure which captured all there was to say about a state of the world, STRIPS described states using a set of formulas in *first-order predicate calculus*. This is a standard logical formalism, in which a formula can represent either a statement about the properties of an object or class of objects or a rule for deriving new statements from existing ones. Therefore, a STRIPS state could contain statements to the effect that "Box 1 is in Room 1" or that "All boxes are in Room 1," but also rules along the lines of "If some object, A, is on top of some other object, B, then B is beneath A." To make correct use of all this information in working with state descriptions, STRIPS included a *theorem prover,* a program for manipulating logical statements to determine their consequences. This allowed STRIPS to tell whether something was true in a state even though it was not explicitly mentioned.

The main benefit of using predicate calculus is that state descriptions are broken up into independently meaningful parts, and there is a well-understood means for formulating and combining *partial* descriptions and, in particular, descriptions of state differences. This has two consequences. First, since most aspects of the world are unchanged by the plan—the same boxes, rooms, and doors will exist throughout—state descriptions can be very much smaller if they describe not the state itself but the way it differs from the initial state. Second, the effects of an operator can be naturally expressed as the changes it makes to the set of formulas describing the state in which it is applied. In particular, the effects of STRIPS operators are described in terms of two lists of statements: those to be added to the state description, and those to be deleted from it. The resulting state description is then interpreted as follows:

- If a statement is added by the operator, it is true of the resulting state.
- If a statement is true of the state to which the operator was applied and it is not deleted by the operator, then it is true of the resulting state.

This rule for passing information between states is known as the *STRIPS assumption.*

STRIPS's formulation of the effects of an operator allows the consequences of an action to be expressed very concisely. For example, an operator that moves something has the old location on its delete list and the new location on its add list. Applying this operator produces a state description that differs in the location of the object being moved, but is otherwise identical; that is, the STRIPS assumption implies that *nothing else has changed.* For the most part, this is a very good thing, since the number of things that are not affected by an action grows with the size and complexity of the state description. It means that the move operator specification need not explicitly state that the size of the disk being moved is unaltered, or that moving one disk does not alter the position of any other disk or indeed make it disappear altogether. Without an assumption of this kind, the size and complexity of every operator description would have to match that of a state description, since it would have to explicitly indicate everything that was not changed. Adopting this assumption is another aspect of STRIPS's attempt to remove the domain complexity limitations of GPS, where operators build complete state specifications.

In operation, STRIPS has much in common with GPS. It uses MEA to direct operator selection, although without needing anything like GPS's Table of Connections. Because their effects are represented explicitly, it suffices to check the operators' add and delete lists to identify those that are relevant. When trying to apply an operator, STRIPS checks its preconditions against the state description and creates subgoals to bring about any that do not hold. However, since its state representations can be the combination of a number of partial descriptions from previous operators and can include rules and class statements, STRIPS cannot simply check whether the required conditions are explicitly satisfied in the way GPS can. Instead, it must use its theorem prover to check whether the required conditions are implied by the state description: if it cannot prove that they are, it uses the partial proof to identify what extra conditions are required, and these are used to create subgoals.

STRIPS's larger, more complex state representations make both state matching and difficulty assessment problematical, and as a result it does not have GPS's mechanisms for monitoring the planning process that were described on page 29. This can greatly degrade planning performance, and not only when planning might go round in circles. If STRIPS were charged with planning to travel from Edinburgh to somewhere in Stirling, it might well decide to reduce the difference in city by using a "go by plane" operator. The preconditions for this operator could include the traveler being at an airport, and there being some sequence of flights that gets to the destination. STRIPS could well work out every detail of going to the station, boarding a bus, buying a ticket, and riding to Edinburgh airport before it noticed that it cannot satisfy the second precondition because Stirling does not actually have an airport. Unfortunately, by the time the problem becomes apparent, a lot of planning effort has been wasted: STRIPS falls victim to what Stefik dubbed the *tyranny of detail*.

To ensure an efficient planning process, it is important that, if an approach to a task is going to fail, this should become apparent as soon as possible. For this to happen, the planner must work first on the difficult goals and leave the "details" for later. The problem is that, although GPS's strategy of tackling differences in order of difficulty does roughly this, losing that mechanism left STRIPS with nothing at all that corresponds to the difference between "difficult goal" and "detail."

This weakness was addressed by the development of ABSTRIPS, Abstraction-Based STRIPS (Sacerdoti, 1974). This extended version of STRIPS was able to associate preconditions with some measure of their importance. As part of its preparation for planning, ABSTRIPS evaluates the *criticality* of each of the preconditions of each operator and then uses a criticality threshold during its planning activities to delay the consideration of unimportant (low criticality) preconditions. It bases its criticality values on information in the problem specification, but raises them for preconditions that represent important tasks, that is, those for which it either has no relevant operators, like a city having an airport, or is unable to generate a short plan.

ABSTRIPS prepares to build a plan for some set of goals by first creating a trivial plan to execute a dummy operator that has those goals as its preconditions. It also initializes its criticality threshold to its maximum value, which means that when it starts planning, ABSTRIPS will initially consider only those preconditions that it cannot affect.

ABSTRIPS plans by repeatedly reanalyzing its current plan using a progressively lower criticality threshold. This means that each pass takes account of preconditions of the operators in the plan which were not considered when it was built using a higher threshold. Where these preconditions are unsatisfied, they represent "gaps" between the operators in the plan. As the falling criticality threshold lets ABSTRIPS see these gaps, it builds new plans to bridge them. Whenever an operator in the plan is found to have unsatisfied preconditions, ABSTRIPS builds a new fragment of plan to achieve those preconditions, starting from the state in which the operator is meant to be applied. At the end of each pass, these new plan fragments are linked into the initial plan. The resulting plan includes all the operators of the original plan and additional steps that take account of the preconditions at the current criticality threshold. When the threshold reaches the minimum value, all preconditions will have been considered and satisfied, and planning is finished.

By incorporating these mechanisms, ABSTRIPS was able to perform substantially better than STRIPS on a number of tasks and thus demonstrated the importance of taking account of the structure of the domain. By demonstrating the application of MEA with state and operator representations that were much more powerful than the simple structures used in GPS, STRIPS itself became one of the most influential planning systems built. Its formulation of the effects of an operator—add lists and delete lists and the STRIPS assumption—has since been almost universally adopted in planning research.

IV. HANDLING INTERFERENCE

For all its success, STRIPS has a fundamental weakness (shared by GPS), which we can see by considering how it would handle a particular block stacking task known as the *Sussman anomaly*. The task, which was illustrated in Figure 1, is to achieve the two goals of having A on B, and B on C, simultaneously.

STRIPS would start by establishing a subgoal for achieving one of these. We will consider achieving A on B first, although tackling the goals in the other order leads to similar outcome. It would recognize that moving disk A is the appropriate operator, and that it is inapplicable because its precondition that A is clear is not satisfied. It would deal with this by establishing a subgoal to clear A, and satisfy it by moving C to the table, which would allow A to be moved onto B. This would give rise to the state shown in Figure 5(a), with only the goal of having B on C left to worry about. STRIPS would recognize that moving block B was an appropriate operator, but it would also recognize that it was inapplicable because B is not clear. It would address this problem by creating a subgoal to clear B, and satisfying that goal by moving block A to the table. This would mean that the problematic precondition was satisfied and B could be moved onto C, creating the situation shown in Figure 5(b). With no goals left to work on, the system would stop. STRIPS has fallen foul of an interaction between the two goals: achieving the second goal has falsified or undone the first (the technical term is *clobbered!*), but STRIPS has no mechanisms for dealing with this. Even if it noticed the unsatisfied goal, as GPS would, the best STRIPS could do would be to extend the plan to reachieve the first goal. The resulting plan would be valid but inefficient.

Notice that, although the multiple goals in the Sussman anomaly are explicit in the statement of the problem, they can also emerge as subgoals during the processing of a single goal. Recall (page 31) GPS's "slightly surprising" formulation of MOVE-DISK's preconditions in terms of OTHER-PEG. Were the preconditions specified in the most natural manner, the operator would have two independent constraints on where the smaller disks could be: not on FROM-PEG and not on TO-PEG. Crucially, GPS would be able—even likely—to spend effort satisfying one constraint in a way that did not satisfy the other. As a result, it would have to do substantial amounts of additional planning to rectify this and nevertheless quite possibly produce a suboptimal plan. Since GPS cannot handle interference between subgoals, it can tackle the problem effectively only

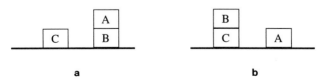

a   **b**

FIGURE 5   Problems with the Sussman anomaly.

because the preconditions of the operator have been reformulated to remove the potentially interfering subgoals.

Interfering subgoals can arise in any planning task, so handling them became a major focus for planning research. Most work was based on trying to build a plan to achieve one goal and *protect* that goal; that is, to note that certain features of a state were deliberately achieved and should not be undone. Once interference was detected, several approaches to removing it by reordering parts of the plan were tried. Some involved moving, or *regressing,* the conflicting action to progressively earlier points in the plan until it could be fitted in without interference. However, simply repositioning individual actions is not enough, since they must be kept with the steps that establish their preconditions. Instead, entire groups of related actions—complete subplans—need to be moved and their preconditions established in their new setting. To achieve this, some systems discard the unsatisfactory part of the plan, reorder some of the goals involved, and then plan to achieve them once again. Waldinger (1977) went one step further. He noted that a goal might hold in the state after an action if some other goal was achieved before it, and his system included regression rules that specified how to regress goals past each type of action. Unfortunately, the generality of the mechanisms involved is not clear.

These approaches are able to handle the Sussman anomaly. They would proceed along the same lines as STRIPS until the position shown in Figure 5(a), when, like STRIPS, they would recognize that the outstanding goal (B on C) cannot be achieved because B is not clear. But, unlike STRIPS, these systems would know that they cannot simply move A away from B because "A on top of B" would be *protected,* flagged as something that was achieved to satisfy a goal. Recognizing this, they would try to rearrange the parts of plan. Waldinger's system, for instance, would try to regress "B on C" and would find that it could simply insert an action to move B onto C at the point just before A is moved onto B. As a result of modifying the plan that had already been generated, the task is done.

V. NONLINEAR PLANNING

The planners discussed so far have similar limitations on their ability to handle interactions between goals. Sacerdoti (1975) introduced what he called a "deceptively simple idea," which showed how these limits could be surpassed by *nonlinear* planning. Unfortunately, planning can be "linear" in two distinct ways:

• The systems discussed so far all maintain, at every stage of operation, a fully specified ordering of the operators in the plan; that is, there is a *linear* arrangement of them. However, this is not essential: one can decide to read someone's letter immediately before phoning the person without deciding whether to phone before or after lunch. A system can therefore be "nonlinear" because it can reason about *partially ordered* plans.

- If a physical system is described by an equation that defines a straight line—that is, a linear equation—then its response to several simultaneous inputs is simply the sum of its responses to each alone. By analogy, planning systems can be called *linear* if they assume that the solution to the problem they are working on is the "sum" of the solutions to its parts; that is, subgoals are independent and therefore can be sequentially achieved in an arbitrary order. Conversely, a "nonlinear" planner avoids this assumption.

Both definitions are in common use, and it may not be obvious which meaning an author intends, since they are not unrelated.

Planning is hard because the assumption that subgoals are independent is false. Nevertheless, many planning systems make that assumption, and then try to repair the resulting problems, primarily by tailoring the order in which the steps of the solutions are carried out. Section IV described systems that develop fully ordered plans, which they then modify when interactions are detected. This means they have to work to regenerate parts of the plan every time anything is rearranged. The independence assumption still benefits these systems, even though they have to replan like this. There are $n!$ orderings of n subgoals, so assuming that one is as good as another brings about a huge reduction in the number of plans that have to be considered. Since some subgoal solutions *are* independent, then, at least for some tasks, having to consider far fewer options more than compensates for the effort of recovering from the problems.

Ideally, a planner should consider interactions as it builds the plan in the first place and sequence the various subplans only after it knows how they interact. Doing this involves constructing the various subplans without settling how they interrelate, something that requires a plan representation that allows the relative ordering of various parts to be unspecified; that is, a partially ordered plan. In other words, a planner that is nonlinear in the second sense is likely to also be nonlinear in the first.

In this chapter, the term will not be used at all: discussion will refer to systems that are fully or partially ordered and either do or do not assume the independence of subgoals.

With partially ordered plans, it is often impossible to determine certain features of a state, since they may depend on the way that as yet unordered actions are finally sequenced. For example, prior to deciding whether to deal with the mail before or after emptying the paper recycling box, one cannot tell whether the box will be empty when both jobs have been done: the mail will probably contain paper for recycling that, if (and only if) the box is emptied first, will be left in the box. Since state descriptions are undefined, it is hard to see the problem as searching a space of state descriptions. It must be viewed in a fundamentally different way: as searching a space of *partial plans*. Movement in this space represents not actions that can be done in the world, but changes that can be made to a plan, such as how a particular goal is tackled or whether it is achieved before or after another.

To minimize wasted work, a planning system should aim to detect problems with a plan as soon as possible—when as few details as possible have been determined. ABSTRIPS's approach is powerful, but it is fundamentally blind to any interactions between the preconditions, since they cannot be predicted without an understanding of the task domain. However, it can be extended. Thus far, planning has been presented as sequencing primitive actions, whereas we normally see the world in terms of higher level, more abstract activities. We naturally talk of telephoning someone as a single action, even though it actually involves picking up the receiver and dialing, and dialing itself involves pushing one button, then pushing another, and so forth. This approach can be adopted by a planning system if it can handle high-level actions; that is, actions which, if carried out, will actually involve a number of other actions. In addition to its effects and preconditions, the definition of such high-level actions must also include information about how to generate a subplan for the action in terms of simpler actions. Provided the preconditions and effects of the high-level operators are defined carefully, in the light of knowledge of the domain, they will ensure that a plan built with them will not suffer from interactions between whatever detailed actions they subsequently expand into. Because of the way actions are defined in terms of other, simpler, actions, these are known as *hierarchical* planning systems.

Like ABSTRIPS, hierarchical planners start with a trivial plan and then repeatedly refine it until it can be executed. However, whereas ABSTRIPS adds steps to achieve the preconditions of existing actions, hierarchical planners repeatedly replace a high-level action with a partially ordered set of lower level operations that specify in more detail how it is to be achieved. The process of refinement is continued until all the high-level actions have been expanded into executable actions. Where an expansion reveals a potential interaction with some other part of the plan, this is addressed immediately by, for instance, enforcing an ordering between the interacting actions.

The first system to embody these ideas was called *NOAH,* because it dealt with Nets of Action Hierarchies. It is described in Sacerdoti (1975) and in Cohen and Feigenbaum (1982, Chap. 15, Section D1.) As its name suggests, NOAH represents plans as nets of actions, with links between nodes indicating ordering requirements between actions. In such a formalism, it is easy to record partial orderings, and establishing an additional ordering is simply a matter of adding a link. Node expansions are specified by associating each high-level operator with a short program in a special language called *SOUP.* When executed, this program builds a subplan that can replace a specific occurrence of the high-level operator. This subplan must, therefore, refer to the same objects that the high-level operation is being applied to, although it may also refer to *formal objects,* objects that have no role outside the newly created subplan.

Each time an action is expanded, the resulting plan is evaluated by a set of three analysis procedures that, following HACKER (Sussman, 1974), are called *critics.* These recognize and correct specific misfeatures of the plan. One is responsible for finding ways of associating formal objects with actual objects. A second recognizes and rectifies situations where combining subplans has resulted in a single precondition being achieved twice. The third, and possibly most important, recognizes conflicts, places where one action deletes a precondition of another. If the ordering of the actions involved is unconstrained, the critic resolves the situation by ordering them, so that the action that needs the precondition must be carried out before the action that deletes it. If the ordering of the actions is determined, the critic instead creates a new goal to reachieve it.

To see how NOAH works, consider the Sussman anomaly once more (see Figure 1). Assume that the domain has been formalized in terms of a single primitive operation, *move to,* and two higher level operators, *put on* and *clear.* The operator (put B1 on B2) expands into (clear B1) and (clear B2), in either order, followed by (move B1 to B2). The operator (clear X) expands into (clear Y) and then (move Y to Z), where Y is whatever is on X, and Z is any location.

NOAH's initial plan simply involves the two operations (put A on B) and (put B on C), with no commitment to their relative ordering. At the next stage, it expands both of these, producing the plan shown in Figure 6(a). Notice that there is still no commitment to the ordering of these activities. Now, though, NOAH notices an interaction between the two operators shown in bold in Figure 6(a): (put A on B) conflicts with (clear B). This is an interaction between unordered activities, which NOAH's critics resolve by introducing an ordering to ensure that the precondition is "used" before it is violated—(put B on C) must come before (put A on B). This is shown in Figure 6(b), where the dashed line indicates this latest link. Once this ordering is imposed, another critic can notice (clear B) is unnecessarily being achieved twice and delete one of them.

Since B and C are clear in the initial state, nothing need be done to achieve them, so NOAH has only one nonprimitive action to attend to, (clear A). It expands this into (clear C) followed by (move C to somewhere), and this reveals another interaction: (put B on C) conflicts with (clear C). Once again, the critic for resolving conflicts is invoked. Since the actions involved are unordered, the critic can handle the situation by order-

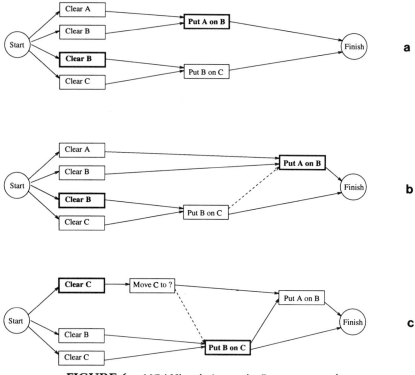

FIGURE 6   NOAH's solution to the Sussman anomaly.

ing them so that the action to (move C to somewhere) comes before the action to (put B on C). This situation is shown in Figure (c), where once again the dashed line indicates the latest link. The critic concerned with goals being reachieved will notice that (clear C) is being achieved twice and delete one. Finally, the critic handling the identities of formal objects will identify *somewhere* with the table, and the plan is finished.

NOAH has produced the optimal plan without wasting any computation as a result of making any wrong decisions and using methods that are efficient in more situations than regression. If it all looks easy, though, remember the caveat about apparent simplicity given in Section II. The level of detail of the presentation means that the substantial effort NOAH spends on inferring state descriptions and detecting interactions in the partially ordered plans is all invisible.

Since the first appearance of a partial-order plan representation in NOAH, its advantages have been widely recognized as outweighing the complexities of deducing the properties of states, and it now forms the basis of most planning systems. Yet, for all the sophistication of its approach to sequencing activities, NOAH and its various enhancements have a surprising limitation that significantly limits the domains to which they can be applied. They have no conception of time: they deal only with ordering, not timing.

This shortcoming was addressed in Deviser (Vere, 1983), which builds on NOAH's techniques to handle planning for activities with extended durations. Deviser's goals and actions have time windows and durations. A *time window* indicates the earliest and latest time at which a goal must be satisfied or an action started and thus defines a range of acceptable times. A *duration* indicates the time for which a goal must hold or the time an action will take. Goals have time windows and durations set by the problem statement. Actions' durations are specified in the operator schema, either as a constant or as a function of the particular instantiation of the schema, thus allowing, for example, the duration of a movement to depend on the speed and the start and end points involved. Although the schema can also carry a time window, this must usually be restricted when a specific instantiation is introduced into the plan: an action cannot start before a preceding action has finished, and must finish before the latest start time of the following goal or action, and its time window must be initialized to reflect this. Given that actions have a single, fixed duration, earliest and latest finish times can be straightforwardly derived from an action's (start) time window.

As planning proceeds and decisions are made about the relationships between actions, their time windows will be repeatedly narrowed; that is, the earliest and latest times are moved closer together. This can happen either when an ordering is specified for two previously unordered actions or when a duration is determined (once and for all) because some parameter has been set; for example, the speed for a "move" operation has been chosen. Crucially, whenever Deviser changes one time window, it also updates every other time window that is affected: delaying the earliest start of one action will delay the earliest start of every following action. If this process completely closes the window for some action—makes its earliest start time after its latest start time—then the current plan is impossible and Deviser must backtrack. Otherwise, planning continues until all high-level actions have been expanded, at which point Deviser picks specific start points within the time window of each action and the plan is complete.

Deviser has another feature missing from previous planning systems: because it handles time, it can handle *events;* that is, things that will happen at some point in the plan, outside the control of the planning system. Events are effectively actions, complete with time windows, which are part of the problem specification and cannot be altered.

VI. MORE SOPHISTICATED PLANNING

The previous sections have presented work that is more-or-less the mainstream of planning; that is, the systems that were first to embody ideas that have since come into widespread use. By making use of such representations and the phenomenal speed of modern machines, researchers are now able to build plans of considerable size for a wide range of tasks, such as fire fighting, space missions, and industrial plant overhaul. Planning theory has progressed beyond these systems, but it is not (yet) possible to identify which techniques will gain widespread acceptance. This section, therefore, contents itself with indicating a range of areas currently being worked on: the reader seeking more detail should consult the review articles in the References.

In Section V we looked at systems which were able to delay making ordering decisions until they had seen the interactions that affected them. This can be seen as an example of a general approach: express plans so planning that does not directly depend on a particular decision can continue without the decision having to be made. The plan notation used in partial-order planners allows parts of plans to be refined before their relative ordering is determined. Similarly, NOAH's formal objects and Deviser's delayed computation of durations allow planning to continue in the absence of information that is essential to finally completing the plan. Building a plan while delaying decisions for as long as possible is known *least commitment planning*.

Delaying decisions in this way is a very powerful technique. However, it can be significantly generalized: instead of some aspect of the plan going from "unknown" to "decided," some formalisms allow the planner to "spread out" a decision—to make, in a sense, a series of partial decisions. Deviser's time windows illustrate the idea: activity start times need not be simply decided, rather the range of possible values can be progressively reduced by successive adjustments of the window. A similar approach is often taken for nonnumeric decisions; for instance, an interior designer may well decide to reupholster a sofa to match the new curtains, but delay the actual choice of material until after a carpet has been chosen. There are mechanisms for formalizing such an approach, based on accumulating separate restrictions, or constraints, on the acceptable choices for something. Systems that use such mechanisms are known as *constraint-based systems*.

However, delaying decisions is not enough. If the consequences of the constraints and combinations of constraints are not determined immediately, the system can waste effort developing a plan that could never be finalized because it embodies inconsistent constraints. Therefore, when Deviser narrows the time window on an action, it propagates this throughout the plan and ensures that any other time window affected is also updated. In general, a constraint-based system must be able to do three things. It must be able to recognize when a constraint is appropriate and formulate it, to propagate its effects and combine them with other constraints, and to choose specific values to satisfy all the relevant constraints or recognize as early as possible that no such value exists.

Molgen (Stefik, 1981) used constraint propagation to control the planning of experiments in molecular genetics. Wilkins (1984) subsequently developed the use of domain-independent constraint-based techniques in SIPE, the System for Interactive Plan Execution and monitoring. SIPE supports the formulation of certain sorts of constraints on the various objects involved in a plan and then identifies specific objects that satisfy them. In particular, it is possible to constrain an object to be of a particular class, to satisfy some particular predicate, to be the same as some other object, or to have a particular value for some attribute. Constraints that are the opposite of these are also allowed. Whenever an object is constrained to be the same as another, all the constraints that apply to either object are combined. Whenever any additional constraint is imposed on any object, SIPE checks that there is at least one object that satisfies all the constraints now applicable. In this way, unsatisfiable constraints are identified as soon as possible.

Another active area of interest concerns the interleaving of planning and execution. The systems described so far have all been geared toward generating a plan, in every last detail, before any part of it is carried out. Unfortunately, this is not always possible: we cannot plan the details of paying for our shopping—which coins and notes should be tendered and so forth—until we know the price of our purchases. And even when a fully detailed plan is possible, it is seldom sufficient because things may well go wrong as it is executed. This may be because of a failure in actually carrying out an action, such as something may be dropped accidentally. Or it may be caused by an error in the planner's knowledge, either of the initial state of the world or of the actions being used; that is, the operator descriptions do not accurately reflect the preconditions and effects of the action. If nothing is done, the failure will pass unnoticed and plan execution will simply carry on regardless: who has not watched a vending machine pour a drink into its drip tray when a cup sticks in the chute?

It is obviously important to prevent such pointless and potentially expensive behavior. Where a specific problem can be anticipated, it can be tested for, and some sort of recovery procedure preplanned: many fax machines will redial if the receiving number is busy. But, in general, problems can occur at any point, and the whole execution of the plan needs to be monitored. This requires sensing how the world is and comparing it with how it *should* be.

Once a problem has been detected or reported, one must decide how to proceed. The simplest approach would be to update the planner's knowledge of the world to reflect the failure (and, ideally, its cause) and build a new plan. However, the effects of a problem will often be localized, so building a whole new plan would be inefficient because most of the original plan can be left unchanged. The problem is to identify which parts are affected and which goals need to be replanned. Some planning systems, such as SIPE, maintain records of the purposes and effects of the various parts of the plan at least in part to support this kind of activity.

There is another possible shortcoming of the planner's knowledge: it may be incomplete. Whereas incorrect knowledge becomes apparent only when the plan is executed, incomplete knowledge is obvious when the plan is being built, and the planner can make suitable allowances. One possibility is to make *conditional* plans; that is, to generate plans that, like computer programs, contain distinct branches appropriate to the different possible circumstances. In more complex situations, some planners have been used to plan to actively seek the information that is required, by, for instance, carrying out a measurement. Thus, for instance, a SIPE-based planner has been used to plan the processing of seismic signals, including specifying operations to measure the noise level in the signal, which then determines the filtering steps required. Finally, work is being done on systems to handle situations where the missing knowledge will significantly affect subsequent activity: such systems plan to plan once the relevant information has been gathered.

Another active field of research is planning in domains with more than one agent, where actions can therefore take place in parallel. Since actions will vary in duration, some will start or finish while others are in progress. This means that they cannot be regarded as simply transforming one state into another, because the planner needs to worry about states where some actions are in progress. Instead, systems have to adopt more complex representations that allow much finer division of time and the assignment of intervals to properties. Things get still more complicated when the agents involved are independent. Agents typically have limited communication capabilities and hence only limited, and possibly unreliable, information about the state and goals of the others. Therefore work toward solving an actual problem must be combined with communicating with other agents—recognizing the possibility of seeking their assistance, deciding what information should be shared with them, and assessing and responding, in a timely fashion, to requests from them. The particular problem of such distributed problem solving is discussed in Barr, Cohen, and Feigenbaum, 1989, Chap. 12.

Finally, it has long been recognized that one of the best ways to get a plan for something is not to build it, but to remember it—to recognize the task as being an example of something that has been done before. Later versions of STRIPS had mechanisms for pulling together the preconditions and consequences of a sequence of operators in a plan, thus allowing it to be stored and subsequently used as a single operator. Other systems try to generalize goal reorderings used to overcome conflicts. In addition, researchers are investigating *case-based* approaches, producing systems which recall a specific plan for something similar to the current objective and then modifying it appropriately.

One of the most ambitious attempts to incorporate learning into a problem-solving system and also to increase its flexibility with the aim of using it as a basis for psychological modeling is SOAR (Laird, Newell, & Rosenbloom, 1987). Like the other systems discussed in this chapter, SOAR is goal driven, working at any time on one goal and creating subgoals. However, SOAR's subgoals may concern not only subparts of the problem but also key steps in the actual problem solving or planning process: SOAR is able to tackle and learn about aspects of the planning task using the same mechanisms it uses for the problem itself. To do this, SOAR is able to support multiple problem spaces and, in principle, choose which to use to pursue any particular goal.

SOAR differs from the majority of the systems discussed in that, although the representations it offers are powerful enough for such things to be built, SOAR itself offers no facilities for handling constraints or delaying decisions. Instead, the emphasis in SOAR is on the ability to bring reasoning and knowledge to bear on making decisions correctly. It is a *production system,* which operates by continually matching the state of its "working memory" against a large set of independent rules, or productions. Each rule specifies one or more things that should be added to the working memory, together with a set of conditions for adding them: when the conditions in the rule are satisfied, the conclusions are added. No restriction is placed on the content of the conclusion, and in particular, although reasoning is always directed toward a particular goal, a rule's conclusions can satisfy, change, or even invalidate any higher level goal. Because of this, SOAR is able to vary the level of detail at which it reasons.

In operation, SOAR normally alternates between making a decision and elaborating its consequences; that is, inferring as many new facts as possible about the current state of the planning process. These new facts include "preferences," explicit representations concerning which decision should be made next, and what would be a satisfactory choice. If the preferences generated indicate a single best course of action, then SOAR simply takes it, refining its solution (plan) accordingly, with further consequences then being elaborated. Sometimes, though, the set of preferences does not indicate a clear decision, either because the preferences are not sufficient or because they are inconsistent. Either way, SOAR has reached an *impasse,* and it responds by creating a goal to make a decision.

Whenever a goal is satisfied, SOAR discards the "working" used to achieve it, but it generalizes both the goal and the solution found (a process known as *chunking*) and adds the result to its set of productions. Unlike GPS, which creates a goal for every thing that needs to be done, SOAR creates goals only when it is unable to reach a decision—when it needs to know how to create a preference that will let it proceed in a given situation. When a decision is reached, it is generalized and remembered so that it can be used when a related decision is required in future. Note that the impasse, and therefore learning, may occur either in the actual problem domain or at some stage of the planning process.

VII. PLANNING AND COGNITIVE SCIENCE

People plan at several "levels." At one extreme, professionals plan shopping centers and space missions; at the other we all continually plan the way we move our bodies, when walking over uneven terrain, grasping objects, or arranging the way we are carrying things. Cognitive factors affect the former by influencing the way explicit planning procedures are followed and the latter by directing the process. In between these two extremes, we have a host of things we want to achieve, and we shape our behavior accordingly. This section discusses the applicability of AI planning techniques to the cognitive planning of daily life.

Some researchers argue that much of our apparently goal-driven behavior is not produced by following a plan but by responding to our current situation in some (very sophisticated) way. There is undoubtedly some truth in this notion of "situated action"—as Suchman (1987) points out, a canoeist can plan a route through rapids only at the very highest level, with all the details being decidable only during the run when the precise position and velocity of the boat is apparent. Brooks (1991) reports a highly influential attempt to apply similar ideas to robotics by creating robots which produce complex behavior primarily by reacting to the state of the world.

Nevertheless, planning is still important: situated action alone cannot capture one of the most sophisticated features of human activity—the combination of activities directed toward a number of goals. There is nothing unusual about offering to buy something on the way to or from somewhere, but the apparent effortlessness of doing so obscures the amount and sophistication of the processing required. One must identify a suitable shop and how to get there, make sure enough money will be available and decide how the goods can be transported. But above all, one must determine how the errand can be integrated with existing work and travel plans. Volunteering to do something *en route* can be seen as situated action only if the "situation" includes having a plan to travel.

A major difference between human and machine planners concerns their goals. Planning systems are given a set of clearly specified goals which will normally all be consistent or even essential to a single higher level goal. People, in contrast, can and must determine their own goals and notice when something is possible or appropriate. As a result, people almost always have many independent, and often even conflicting, goals: not only things that must be achieved but also things that must be either avoided or maintained (see Wilensky, 1983). Therefore it is perfectly normal for someone to have the conflicting goals of going skiing, avoiding expense, and remaining warm and dry.

Another prominent feature of cognitive planning is that it deals not with some abstract domain but with the world itself. Our lives involve interactions with countless other agents, and we have only incomplete information, and often very limited time, with which to plan them as best we can. We should expect that things seldom go exactly as we plan. It is essential that we monitor the execution of our plans, and when things go awry, or when we discover something new, we must be able to reassess our situation. In simple cases, we need "only" devise a new plan to achieve our targets. But often, our new knowledge may change our understanding of the difficulty or the importance of our various objectives, so we must continually review which goals to pursue at any moment, which to leave in abeyance, and indeed, which to modify or abandon altogether.

Work has been done on relaxing constraints (goals) for scheduling. For instance, domain descriptions for ISIS (Fox & Smith, 1984) classify each requirement according to its importance and show how it can be weakened if necessary. If ISIS cannot build a schedule that satisfies every requirement, it uses this information to choose which constraint to relax, and how, so it can make the problem easy enough to solve. Similarly, researchers are investigating multiagent planning and planning for further planning and for plan failures. But in all these areas, the state of the art is a long way from matching human planners, who continually do these things without noticing.

The need to reason about the real world highlights one of the greatest limitations on planning systems: their ability to represent and reason about complex states of the world. The STRIPS formulation of the effects of an operator works extremely well for the "direct" consequences of an action, which can be expressed very concisely. However, as we reason about more complex domains, we need to worry more about the relationships and interactions between objects and about the ramifications—the indirect consequences—of an action. In a blocks world, for instance, moving an object may change the "liftability" of up to two other objects, but trying to reflect this in the STRIPS-type operator for move will make it much more complex. The "vanilla" (i.e., normally encountered, unadorned) blocks domain is so simple that this may not be obvious, but consider trying to maintain an explicit indication of which blocks can be lifted in a block stacking problem where blocks can support more than one other or where the robot can lift a stack of up to a certain size.

The standard answer to this is that the move operator should update only the position of the object being moved, and a theorem prover or other reasoning system should be used to deduce which other objects can or cannot be picked up. This approach is not straightforward, though, since the STRIPS assumption means that anything that holds in any previous state is true in the current one unless it is explicitly deleted, and specifying which derivable properties to delete is no easier than specifying which to assert. STRIPS tries to get around the problem by identifying a class of *primitive* predicates which are asserted or deleted by operators, and statements of other predicates may be derived only by the theorem prover. This, however, is not an adequate solution, since for some operations *in some circumstances,* primitive predicates may be indirectly affected. For example, moving a container changes the position of whatever is inside it. One could imagine extending the "move" operator to be sensitive to the presence of such an object and to update its positions as well. But this would get out of hand if one tried to take account of a number of contained objects or the fact that they could themselves be containers. Moreover, containment is not the only relationship that causes the position of one object to be affected by moving another: parts of assemblies move when the whole is moved, as do objects resting on the moving object, or attached to it, and as, indeed, do objects simply in the way of the movement.

People know these things: computers must be told. Trying to embody this kind of domain knowledge within the definition of individual operators, such as move, requires making the definition of every operator dependent on everything we know about the world. It would be far better to have some principles for determining the effects of each operation in a given situation. But, even though it is possible to specify what is relevant to doing this in any given situation, each situation is unique and may well require some additional aspect of the world to be considered. Delimiting the effects of an action potentially involves everything we know about the situation and the causal processes involved, and trying to formulate this in some general way is a notoriously hard problem—the *frame problem.*

It is not only the task that distinguishes cognitive planning from the activities of planning systems. Introspection rapidly highlights differences between the way people plan and the functioning of planning systems of the kind discussed in this chapter, and it is supported by experimental results. For example, Hayes-Roth and Hayes-Roth (1978) gave subjects a list of errands and a map of an imaginary town, asked them to think aloud as they planned their day, and then analyzed of the resulting protocols.

One major difference that this study highlighted concerns the overall approach to the task. Planning systems typically embody one approach to generating plans. It may be well thought-out—based, for instance, a gradual refinement from general to fine detail—and efficient, but it will be used in all circumstances. In contrast, people can adjust their approach, even within the making of a single plan. They often take an *opportunistic* (or, perhaps, "haphazard") approach, mixing refining abstract operations with fixing specific details that make some goal particularly easy to achieve. They can also be flexible about the point at which planning gives way to execution, something which is particularly important in situations where the time taken to plan is potentially significant.

Hayes-Roth and Hayes-Roth can account for this phenomenon because they discuss their subjects' performance in terms of a planning system based on a *blackboard* architecture. This architecture has been used in a range of systems where a flexible control structure is required (Barr et al., 1989, Chap. 11). It is so named to suggest an analogy with a collection of specialists collaborating on a problem written on a blackboard, each adding his or her own contributions to the blackboard on the basis of the person's own unique expertise. Within a computer system, the blackboard becomes a data structure that can be read or modified by a number of independent software "specialists." The specialists have indications of the type of information to which they respond, and there is a central executive that allows them to run when such information is added to the blackboard. The behavior of the system results from the way a contribution from one specialist enables further contributions from others and thus directs the focus of reasoning. The basic operation of such a system has much in common with production systems, such as SOAR (see Section VI). In both types of system, every rule or specialist is considered for activation at every state, without regard for the topic or level of its likely contribution. As a result, they can produce the observed flexibility of processing and switching between different aspects of the problem or levels of abstraction.

A second significant feature of the errand-planning protocols is that, in contrast to the importance of least commitment techniques in planning research, subjects worked mostly with a specific plan, which they then repaired or abandoned as problems came to light. Given that people do on occasion delay planning decisions—for example, by deciding to decorate using matching materials without choosing which—why do people achieve such high performance on planning tasks without using one of the most powerful techniques known?

Section VI pointed out that least commitment approaches are powerful because they minimize the work that must be revised or repeated when a bad decision comes to light. These advantages must be balanced against the fact that working with more fully specified situations and sequences facilitates simulating the plan in more detail and thus having a more detailed picture of future states. People have an enormous range of actions open to them in any situation. They can plan effectively only because they are very good at taking into account many aspects of the situation and effectively deciding which goals are the nub of the problem and which operations are both relevant and potentially applicable. While the mechanisms that allow this may be goal directed, they are obviously far more sophisticated than MEA, criticality factors or the other approaches used in planning systems.

They involve evaluating many aspects of a situation in the light of a huge and continuously growing body of knowledge, ranging from very general knowledge of the way the world behaves to cases of solving specific problems in the past. People plan so effectively the way they do because having richer state descriptions available to help make better decisions saves more effort than the early detection of those mistakes that are made.

Adopting this approach in a general purpose planning system on current machines would be a colossal task. Even if the frame problem could be solved, so that relevant knowledge could be delimited and formalized, and even if adequate learning techniques could be developed, the resulting knowledge base would be enormous. Identifying and acting on the relevant parts of such a body of knowledge is a daunting task, and one that brains appear to support much better than CPUs. Despite many years of algorithm development and phenomenally fast processors, such complex pattern matching cannot yet be achieved on anything like the required scale. Faced with such obstacles to giving a machine enough knowledge to get decisions right, planning research has concentrated on improving system capability by using the ability of digital computers to manipulate sophisticated representations to support more efficient search mechanisms.

The differences in the computational architectures involved have thus lead AI workers to emphasize quite different aspects of the task from those that appear to dominate cognitive planning. Nevertheless, their work increases our understanding of the problem and our appreciation of the reasoning that so often passes unnoticed. Moreover, as machines become increasingly able to take the processing load of supporting quite different computing architectures, like SOAR, the overlap between the approaches can only increase.

NOTES ON REFERENCES

There are introductions to planning and problem solving in most AI textbooks, and in Boden (1987, Chap. 12). Steel (1987), Barr and Feigenbaum (1981, Sections IIB and IIC), and Cohen and Feigenbaum (1982, Section XV) offer more advanced overviews. The analysis of techniques and the extensive reference list in Tate, Hendler, and Drummond (1990) or Hendler, Tate, and Drummond (1990) are also recommended. To facilitate further study, many references in this chapter have been chosen from Allen, Hendler, and Tate (1990), which is an excellent collection of reprints of nearly 50 key papers. The original sources are cited in the Reference section, but the page numbers in the collection are indicated thus: [AHT 1–10].

References

Allan, J., Hendler, J., & Tate, A. (1990). *Readings in planning*. San Mateo, CA: Morgan Kaufmann.

Barr, A., Cohen, P., & Feigenbaum, E. (1989). *Handbook of Artificial Intelligence* (Vol. 4). Reading, MA: Addison-Wesley.

Barr, A., & Feigenbaum, E. (1981). *Handbook of Artificial Intelligence* (Vol. 1). Los Altos, CA: William Kaufmann.

Boden, M. (1987). *Artificial intelligence and natural man* (2d ed.). London: MIT Press.

Brooks, R. (1991). Intelligence without representation. *Artificial Intelligence, 47,* 139–160.

Cohen, P., & Feigenbaum, E. (1982). *Handbook of Artificial Intelligence* (Vol. 3). Los Altos, CA: William Kaufmann.

Fikes, R., & Nilsson, N. (1971). STRIPS: A new approach to the application of theorem proving to problem solving. *Artificial Intelligence, 2,* 189–208. [AHT 88–97]

Fox, J., & Smith, S. (1984). ISIS: A knowledge-based system for factory scheduling. *Expert Systems, 1*(1), 25–49. [AHT 336–359]

Hayes-Roth, B., & Hayes-Roth, F. (1978). *Cognitive procedures in planning* (Report R-2366-ONR). Santa Monica, CA: Rand Corporation. [AHT 245–262]

Hendler, J., Tate, A., & Drummond, M. (1990, Summer). AI planning: Systems and techniques. *AI Magazine, 11*(2).

Laird, J., Newell, A., & Rosenbloom, P. (1987). SOAR: An architecture for general intelligence. *Artificial Intelligence, 33,* 1–64.

Newell, A. (1980). Reasoning, problem solving and decision processes: The problem space as a fundamental category. In R. Nickerson (Ed.), *Attention and Performance VIII* (pp. 693–718). Hillsdale, NJ: Erlbaum.

Newell, A., & Simon, H. (1961). GPS: A program that simulates human thought. In H. Billing (Ed.), *Lernende automaten* (pp. 109–124). Munich: Oldenbourg. [AHT 59–66]

Sacerdoti, E. (1974). Planning in a hierarchy of abstraction spaces. *Artificial Intelligence, 5,* 115–135. [AHT 98–108]

Sacerdoti, E. (1975). The nonlinear nature of plans. *International Joint Conference on Artificial Intelligence* (pp. 206–214).

Steel, S. (1987). The bread and butter of planning. *Artificial Intelligence Review, 1,* 159–181.

Stefik, M. (1981). Planning with constraints. *Artificial Intelligence, 16,* 111–140. [AHT 171–185]

Suchman, L. (1987). *Plans and situated actions*. Cambridge, UK: Cambridge University Press.

Sussman, G. (1974). The virtuous nature of bugs. *Proceedings of AISB-1, Brighton, 1974,* pp. 224–237. [AHT 111–117]

Tate, A., Hendler, J., & Drummond, M. (1990). A review of AI planning techniques. [AHT 26–49]

Vere, S. (1983). Planning in time: Windows and durations for activities and goals. *IEEE Transactions on Pattern Analysis and Machine Intelligence, PAMI-5*(3), 246–267. [AHT 297–318]

Waldinger, R. (1977). Achieving several goals simultaneously. In E. Elcock & D. Michie (Eds.), *Machine Intelligence 8*. Chichester: Ellis Horwood. [AHT 118–139]

Wilensky, R. (1983). *Planning and understanding*. Reading, MA: Addison-Wesley.

Wilkins, D. (1984). Domain independent planning: Representation and plan generation. *Artificial Intelligence, 22,* 269–301. [AHT 319–335]

CHAPTER 3

Representation of Knowledge*

Derek Partridge

I. REPRESENTATION AND KNOWLEDGE

In the context of AI and computational psychology, the term *knowledge* is used in a way quite unlike the way a philosopher—or a layperson—uses it. For current purposes, *knowledge* is information necessary to support intelligent reasoning. The topic of "knowledge representation" concerns the various ways in which collections of such information may be organized and processed. A collection of words, say, may be organized as, for example, a list or a set. In the former representation of this information, there will be a first word in the list and a last one. So, for any list of words we can inspect, delete, replace, copy, and so forth the first word in the list. By way of contrast, a set representation of the same collection of words does not admit any of these simple operations—the set representation (when interpreted strictly) does not embrace the notion of first and last elements. Set elements have no ordering; this is part of what makes a given grouping a set rather than a list. A set representation would, for example, admit the possibility of checking whether any given word is in the set or not.

---

* This chapter is based on material in Partridge, D. (1991). *A new guide to artificial intelligence.* Norwood, NJ: Ablex.

Artificial Intelligence

A. Representation as Structure and Function

The important point is that the notions of organization and processing are intertwined: the way that information is organized has an effect on the processes, or operations, that can (and cannot) be used to manipulate elements of the information; alternatively, the available operations begin to determine the organization. We have, quite simply, complementary ways to view any complex collection of items of information. Knowledge representation is thus a question of both structure (the static organizational viewpoint) and function (the dynamic operational viewpoint).

1. Process Models and Content Theories

McDermott's (1986) assault on the use of logic in AI claims that the logicist's goal is a "content theory" (i.e., a theory of what people know). It is a theory of knowledge in the form of logical axioms that are independent of any specific program to operate on them. All that logic offers as a process theory is logical deduction; thus, for McDermott, "there is an unspoken premiss [sic] in the argument that a significant amount of thought is deductive" and this premise (he tells us) is false.

Much work in AI is based on an intertangled content theory and process model; we shall see numerous examples later. One of the reasons for the use of logic-based schemes in knowledge representation is that logic goes a long way toward avoiding the structure–function entanglement. The use of logic-based schemes for knowledge representation is widespread. It is, in some quarters, taken as axiomatic that this is the only sensible course to take (e.g., Genesereth & Nilsson, 1987; Kowalski, 1980; McCarthy, 1986). But elsewhere, researchers are equally convinced that this is absolutely the wrong basis for knowledge representation (obviously McDermott, 1986, but also Chandrasekaran, 1990; Minsky, 1981). Partridge (1991) provides an extensive survey of this debate.

McDermott claims that "in most cases there is no way to develop a 'content theory' without a 'process model'" (i.e., an explanation of how this knowledge should be used). The content-theory style of knowledge representation is what we might term a *static theory* of knowledge; that is, structure without function. The elements of the theory are given meaning by tying them to a more basic theory, such as set theory or number theory. The meaning of a representation is given by what it "denotes" in the underlying, basic theory; and the soundness of the underlying theory guarantees a similar soundness in the representation of knowledge built on top. Such representations are said to have a *denotational semantics*.

Hence, Lenat, Prakash, and Shepherd (1986) CYC project is covered by McDermott's interdict. Lenat presents the CYC project in terms of the laudable goal of first constructing a rich information base (tens of thousands of pieces of knowledge, i.e., a machine-readable encylopedia), which ought to be sufficient to support commonsense reasoning, then thinking about designing systems to use the knowledge base. Quite justifiably, he charges the AI world with attempting to build fancy systems that have only a laughably small knowledge base at their disposal. If the widespread belief in the criticality of knowledge is correct, then these systems are crippled from the outset. Elaborate domain-specific heuristics can atone for some inadequacies of the available knowledge base, but they cannot provide total compensation. He plans to spend about 10 years building up this encylopedic knowledge base. But accumulation of a mass of "knowledge elements" (i.e., facts, etc.) with no associated functions for using the knowledge (i.e., no process model) is clearly an example of a pure content theory and as such falls under the same strictures as logicism. Accumulation of facts and so on, independent of any mechanism for using these facts, is an undirected and endless task. In McDermott's words, "You cannot start listing facts people know, expressed in logic or any other notation, without saying something about how you assume they will be used by a program, and hence what class of inferences you are trying to account for. . . . How will [you] . . . know when they are making progress?"

Another link back to the early days is provided by the *epistemic–heuristic distinction* propounded by McCarthy and Hayes (1969). It was a proposal that intelligence is most usefully separated into two components: the epistemic one, the logic-based one, which covers the essential details of what types of knowing are necessary for intelligent behavior; and the heuristic one, which takes care of how the necessary knowledge is to be represented and used with the requisite efficiency. In terms of the current context, the epistemic component is content theory and the heuristic component is largely a process model. McDermott is clearly challenging the validity of this widely accepted distinction as a model for the pursuance of AI goals.

Chandrasekaran (1990), who is similarly critical of the value of this distinction, frames his own challenge in terms of an unhelpful separation of representation and control. He prefers "generic functional theories" within which computational theorizing is an integral part of the overall effort; that is, the process model is included from the beginning.

The question of whether this separation is beneficial or not to the furtherance of attempts to model intelligent behavior occurs repeatedly in this field of research. The knowledge-based representational approach to AI, as exemplified in most expert systems work, is founded upon the conceptual simplification gained by separating a knowledge base (content theory) from the inference engine (process model). And we shall see later a similar strategy is manifest as the basis for the novel programming language Prolog.

B. Representational Choice

There are many different ways to represent knowledge in a computational framework, and the differences occur along a number of different dimensions. The builder of computational models needs an awareness of both the range and the scope of representational choice. Every choice embraces biases (both explicitly and implicitly), and the model builder needs to be fully aware of the inclusions and exclusions inextricably bundled up with the representational commitments he or she makes.

1. Viewpoint Level

There are various levels from which we can view any given knowledge representation. A set of words, for example, can be implemented (in a computer program) as a list of items, each item being one word. If this is the case then the set operations have to be implemented in terms of the basic list-processing operations. So the membership operation (i.e., is a given word in the current set or not) can be implemented, for example, by programming a loop structure that checks if the target word (the one we are looking for) is the first list word; if not, is it the second; if not, is it the third, and so forth? Then either the target word is found in the list, in which case the word is a member of the set, or the loop structure reaches the end of the current list without having found the target word, in which case it is not a member of the set. At an even lower level the basic list-processing operations of the chosen programming language will themselves have been composed from more primitive computational operations.

Similarly, we can move up levels: it may be that the collections of words demanded by some model of cognitive behavior are merely conveniently implemented as sets in the cognitive model or the set representation may be a crucial element of the model. This latter view could be the case if, for example, the cognitive behavior being modeled did not indicate (via response times, say) that the collections of words were processed according to some strict sequential ordering. For example, an early model of the lexical decision task—that is, response time for recognition of a target word after "priming" with an initial word—was described in terms of a *set* of potential target words that are "semantically related" to the priming word. The model then went on to describe how this set is processed in some order (determined by degree of semantic relatedness and similarity to visual features of the actual target word) to arrive at the final recognition decision. A central implication of this model involved response time as crucially influenced by the number of potential target words that had to be checked before the recognition threshold was exceeded—that is, before recognition was reported (rightly or wrongly). The proper representation of the collection of potential target words was, of course, a list and not a set.

One quite reasonable response to the foregoing example is that use of the word *set* in the description of a cognitive model rather than the more precisely accurate one, *list*, is an example of little more than excessive pedantry. However, although it may be granted that the example borders on the trivial, it still flags a significant issue when a computational model is to be built. In textual characterizations of cognitive models, the inherent imprecision of natural language sets a level below which further consideration of fine distinctions is likely to be unproductive. But when the move is made to computer models—characterizations in terms of the fixed and precisely defined elements of a programming language—these fine distinctions can no longer be ignored. Articulation of a cognitive model in terms of a programming language forces the modeler to think long and hard about previously rather fuzzy aspects of the textually described model.

This extra thought is directed mostly at producing decisions about how precisely to represent, in the programming language structures, various aspects of the textually described model. These representational decisions fall, roughly, into two categories: decisions about representing mechanisms (i.e., what control structures, such as *while* loops, and operations to program?) and decisions about representing data items (i.e., what data structure should be used to implement each abstract information structure in the theory?).

Hence, we see the emergence of a subtopic of AI, knowledge representation, which covers issues of both structure and function. In terms of programming effort, it is focused upon representational issues that completely cover the category of data-structure decisions, and (because of the inevitable intertwining of structure and function aspects) it also covers much of the control-structure decision category as well.

2. Representational Precision

This concern for representational specifics yields a variety of benefits for the psychologist, and particularly for the psychologist who contemplates building computational models.

Benefits with respect to representational issues center on the necessity to transform imprecise textual description into totally precise computationally acceptable characterization. Each such decision process focuses attention on an element of the theory, and each resultant choice (because it posits a well-defined component in the context of a well-defined framework) will immediately project further implications that the computational modeler must consider: they may turn out to be helpful new insights, awkward unforeseen implications, or theory-neutral repercussions. The point is that the theorizer is forced to consider them.

A further benefit of the resultant computational model is that it is an

active model: when the computer executes the program, inescapable consequences of the theory will automatically emerge, and these will fall into the
same three categories as the initial projections from the original representational decisions—helpful, awkward, and neutral. The point here is that,
with the inexorable logic of the computer churning out the implications of
the model, this active model provides a check on the theorizer's derived
implications of the theory, and the human predictions can be shown to be in
error.

For example, it was long accepted that the empirical evidence on human
habituation behaviors favored the class of dual-process theories rather than
single-process theories (the dual-process theories posited the interaction of
two processes, habituation and sensitization, to account for the observed
extinction of the orienting response when a stimulus is repeated; single-
process theories, touting the virtue of parsimony, posited only one). This
balance of favor rested on the supposed fact that single-process theories
could not account for a class of observed behaviors—incremental habituation behavior. However, a computational model of a single-process theory
clearly demonstrated that the appropriate incremental habituation behavior
could be derived from a single-process theory. The accepted fact (based on
human extrapolation of theoretical implications) was no fact at all, computational modeling revealed it to be an erroneous supposition (see Partridge,
Johnston, & Lopez, 1984, for full details).

There are a few drawbacks, however, with respect to computational
modeling, and curiously, these drawbacks are also based on the necessity for
high-precision representation in computational models. A computational
model is a computer program, and if it is to be runnable on a computer, its
detailed form must be that demanded by the chosen programming language. This strict requirement can force the cognitive model builder to
make a choice among representational specifics that goes far beyond anything that the basic psychological theory can support.

To return to the example of word recognition as a source of examples, a
well-known psychological theory of the lexical decision task, the Logogen
theory (Morton, 1969), maintains that recognition of a specific word is
triggered when the accumulated evidence (from semantic priming, visual
similarity, etc.) exceeds some threshold value. To construct a computational
model of the Logogen theory, it is necessary to program a specific representation of the accumulated evidence and a specific mechanism for adding new
evidence to increase the total. How do we represent elements of all the
varieties of evidence? How do we construct an accumulated total? Precisely
how to answer these questions is not determined in the theory, but precise
answers, in the guise of programming language specifics, must be found
before a computational model can be built. In fact, more or less arbitrary
decisions must be made, many such arbitrary decisions, before a complete

and executable computational model can be built. The danger then is that the behavior of the computational model, which is expected to be analogous (in some way) to the human behavior that the underlying theory purports to explain, is crucially, but not obviously, dependent upon one (or more) of the arbitrary decisions it contains. Specific examples of this problem of excessive representational precision, in the context of a computational model of a "novelty drive" theory, are given in Partridge (1990).

3. Representational Needs Driving Programming-Language Development

The desire to represent in computational models the cognitive structures and mechanisms posited by the psychologist has been a powerful influence on the development of new programming languages. The turn of the decade from the 1950s to the 1960s was the time of the first flush of high-level programming languages (i.e., machine-executable notations oriented toward the human programmers rather than toward the computer hardware). COBOL supported the business-oriented data-processing community, and FORTRAN gave the engineers and scientists the ability to represent numbers and numerical operations easily. But neither of these formal linguistic inventions was very much help to the psychologist, who typically needs to represent and manipulate symbol structures such as words, phrases, concepts, and the associations between them.

The recognition that high-level programming languages can be devised to represent and manipulate complex, nonnumeric (i.e., symbolic) data, coupled with the lack of such a language to service those whose domain of interest was cognitive models, led the cognitive modelers to design their own languages. Newell, Shaw, and Simon (1961) developed a series of "information processing languages," the most famous of which was IPL-V. This language was used as a representational basis for modeling a variety of human problem-solving tasks: chess, symbolic logic, and algebra-like puzzles (Newell & Simon, 1972). At much the same time, McCarthy at MIT designed the LISP language (McCarthy et al., 1965), which offered the cognitive modeler a simple but powerful (and well-defined) representational scheme primarily for the manipulation of symbol structures. The early anthologies of computational models, *Computers and Thought* (Feigenbaum & Feldman, 1963) and *Semantic Information Processing* (Minsky, 1968), were made possible by the availability of a suitable representational framework, the so-called list-processing languages: LISP, IPL-V, and FLPL (a list-processing extension of FORTRAN).

Just as the development of new programming languages to support computational interests across an ever-expanding frontier of possibilities has continued unabated during the last three decades, so some of this creative effort has opened new representational possibilities for the cognitive modeler. In particular, mention should be made of the language Prolog. For Prolog does not merely offer more, and different, representational vehicles within a familiar framework. Prolog offers a whole new representational framework, and moreover a framework which implements a central representational scheme in the field of knowledge representation—namely, logic. As mentioned earlier, logic is (virtually) a pure content theory with logical deduction as the only, but quite separate, process model. Prolog is an attempt to reproduce this disentanglement of the structure and function aspects of knowledge representation in a machine-executable language. And this is what sets it apart from most other programming languages, which offer these two aspects intertwined in most of their representational elements.

4. Representational Styles

Beyond the specific representational constraints of particular programming languages, there are the looser representational constraints (or better perhaps, opportunities) made available within what might be termed *styles* of computational modeling—and certain programming languages support certain representational styles better than others. (The word *style* is being used here to distinguish different general frameworks of computational mechanisms; the term *paradigm* will be reserved for more radical differences.)

Specifically, it should be noted that until the current decade most computational models were developed in the functional decomposition style. The models, and hence representational commitments, were based on a functional (or process-centered) view. First, the complex functions inherent in the theory were identified and decomposed into groups of simpler subfunctions. Next, the data elements were identified and organized to fit within the functional framework. So, the processes took precedence, and subsequently the data item representations were (to varying degrees) dictated by the prior functional framework. The resultant model is primarily a processing framework, a close reflection of the operations and mechanisms specified in the theory, together with separate blocks of data item representations. This functional core of the model then makes explicit reference to individual data items as necessary.

The latter half of the 1980s has seen the rise of an alternative style known as *object-oriented* modeling. The big difference introduced with the object-oriented style is that initial representational commitments are made, more or less equally, to both function and data. The two are identified, developed and combined on a more or less equal footing; neither has clear precedence. Furthermore, the computational model is based on representations of the "objects" identified in the theory. A widely used heuristic is to separate out all the nouns in a textual description of the theory and use this set as a first approximation to the set of computational "objects." Such an "object" is an integrated combination of functional representations (called *methods*) and data representations (called *instance variables*). A final characteristic of the object-oriented style is the *inheritance hierarchy:* specific objects are most conveniently represented as special cases of more general objects. Thus, an orange is a special case of fruit, apple is another. The big advantage, from a representational viewpoint, is that general objects (sometimes distinguished as "class objects") may be represented just once, and then a more specialized object (such as an "apple" object) need be represented by only its special properties (e.g., grows in temperate climate), both functional and data value. It will automatically *inherit* all the general properties of fruit (e.g., that it is perishable) from its class object, fruit. Similarly, individual varieties of apple may be represented as special cases of the apple object, and so on. A cognitive model, in the object-oriented style, is then represented by a collection of interacting objects, each with a well-defined position within an inheritance hierarchy. The functional core of the decomposition model has been dispersed among the set of "objects." Booch (1991) provides a comprehensive (and technical) guide to model design in the object-oriented style, whereas Yourdon (1990) contrasts this new style with the old.

By way of example, we might return to the Logogen theory. It posits a collection of Logogens, one for each individual word that is potentially recognizable, and a framework for perceptual evidence extraction, semantic priming, comparing total evidence accumulated to some threshold value, and so forth. A functional-decomposition representational scheme would concentrate on how a Logogen must behave if it is to be true to the psychological theory. The main question to be answered is, what functions characterize Logogen systems? Specific subfunctions would then be identified within the overall functionality. For instance, we might decide on a subfunction to "accumulate" the available evidence, a subfunction to compare the total evidence with a threshold value and determine whether the threshold was exceeded or not, and so on. Subsequent to this functional representation of the theory and dependent upon the chosen functional decomposition, representations for the necessary data elements would then be decided upon. The items of evidence might be represented as simple numeric values (which the "accumulation" subfunction could simply add together), or they might be given a more complex representation, which could accommodate visual feature evidence as well as semantic relatedness evidence (in which case the "accumulation" function might simply add 1 to the total for each new piece of evidence). Clearly, an interdependence lies between functional decisions and data-structure decisions but, in this representational style, functional decomposition generally takes precedence. The individual Logogens, one for each word the model is required to potentially recognize, would be represented by different blocks of data items—one data structure to store the total evidence for each individual Logogen, one to store its name, and so forth. But this is only the content representation for each Logogen, the process model is quite separate in this style of computational model. The Logogen process model would be represented by a collection of subfunctions in the functional core of the computational system; namely, the group of subfunctions that implement the general Logogen functionality.

An application of the object-oriented representational style to the Logogen theory gives a different emphasis. In this style, a Logogen is a "class object" in the representational scheme; it is specified in terms of both subfunctions and data items necessary to achieve the theoretical capabilities common to all Logogens. The two aspects of the representation come bundled together as one computational unit, no precedence is accorded to either aspect. Individual Logogens are then realized in the computational model as specific "objects" defined as special cases of the general "class object." Each Logogen is then a separate computational package that has the same representational structure as the class object (i.e., the same subfunctions and data items), but each is distinguished by individual differences. In this example, the major difference between these individual objects would be the name of the word that each Logogen represents. But there might be other differences, such as different recognition threshold values for different classes of word. The resultant computational model is then viewed as a population of separate Logogen "objects" that interact with each other and with other "objects." The wealth of apparent duplication—such as the same evidence-accumulation function in each individual Logogen—is illusory: each individual Logogen inherits most of its representational structure (both process and content) from the "class object." General structure and function is thus represented just once, but because of the inheritance-hierarchy mechanism, the population of individual Logogen "objects" behave as if there is massive duplication of representational decisions. Figure 1 is a schematic illustration of these two representational styles applied to three individual Logogens (those for the words *nurse, doctor,* and *lion*) within the Logogen theory.

These two representational schemes are rather different, but they are not totally different, and any intermediate scheme can be adopted. The main point is not to advocate one representational style over another, but just to show that these options exist and the choice made will "color" the experimenter's perception of the problem.

C. What Is Knowledge?

Before we wade into the ocean of concrete representational choice, we might briefly consider what we are aiming to represent. We need to consider

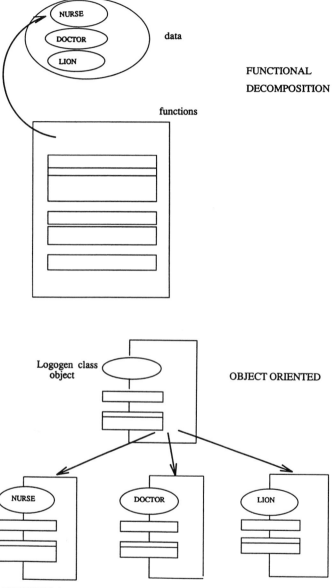

NURSE

DOCTOR

LION

data

FUNCTIONAL
DECOMPOSITION

functions

Logogen class
object

OBJECT ORIENTED

NURSE

DOCTOR

LION

FIGURE 1   A schematic illustration of two representational styles.

the vexed question, what is knowledge? For current purposes we can avoid the philosophical intricacies that a complete answer might demand and simply state that knowledge is data or information that appears to be necessary to support computational attempts to model, simulate, or reproduce aspects of intelligent behavior. It is not a well-defined quantity. It is simply the accepted parlance in AI and (to a lesser extent) in cognitive science. An implication of the use of the term *knowledge representation,* rather than *data representation* or *information structures,* is that we are dealing with quite complex collections of simple data items. So, in reality, the sets and lists used in the earlier examples are more properly called *data structures;* their basic simplicity does not warrant use of the term *knowledge representations.* All this, however, is really a question of attitude, and implication, not one of definitionally proper usage.

D. A Pair of Paradigms

The two paradigms to be distinguished are the classical AI one based on the notion of explicit searching of symbol structures—called the *symbolic search space paradigm* (Partridge, 1991), or *good old-fashioned AI,* GOFAI (Haugeland, 1985)—and the connectionist, neural network or parallel-distributed processing (PDP) one (the topic of Chapter 5).

Taken most broadly, connectionism is computing with a network of primitive processing elements, or units, where the links in the network (connecting one unit to another) have an associated "strength of connection," a *weight,* typically a numeric value associated with each link. Each unit accumulates and stores an *activity* level, which is passed along the connecting links (and moderated by each link's weight) from one unit to another. In addition, often some degree of parallel processing occurs; that is, activity values are passed simultaneously from one subset of units to another. (Chapter 5 gives this complex topic the full consideration that it requires.)

To distinguish a radically new representational paradigm, we need to focus on one subset of connectionist systems: those which exhibit distributed (or subsymbolic, e.g., Smolensky, 1988) representations. The crux of this distinction is that a unit in a distributed connectionist system has no simple representational status at the cognitive level; that is, at the level of conceptually meaningful elements of the problem being computed or the theory being modeled. The representations of these conceptually meaningful elements are found in subsets of units in which every unit has a high activity level—this is termed a *pattern of activation.* A single unit may thus participate in the representation of many different (but presumably related) concepts.

The way Fodor and Pylyshyn (1988) summarize the essential difference between "classicists and connectionists" is that connectionists assign semantic content (i.e., meaning) to nodes or aggregates of nodes and classicists assign meaning to "expressions," such as "The yellow dog" or "10 = 5 × 2." Further than this, connectionists "acknowledge *only causal connectedness* as a primitive relation among nodes; When you know how activation and inhibition flow among them, you know everything there is to know about how the nodes in a network are related. By contrast, Classical theories acknowledge not only causal relations . . . but also a range of structural relations, of which constituency is paradigmatic." (Chapter 1 examines this issue in detail.)

For Fodor and Pylyshyn, the connectionist paradigm is just a lower, and not very handy, representational level than the classical one. So they presumably would see little of deep significance in the specific representational schemes utilized by connectionists. There is, however, no general agreement that such a dismissive view is correct, and thus it is appropriate to give considerable space to a presentation of knowledge representation from a connectionist perspective.

Van Gelder (1990), for example, argues that, although connectionist representations may not be compositionally structured in the classical manner —that is, complex representations composed by concatenating atomic representational elements—they may still employ compositionally structured representations. He then defines a notion of "functional compositionality" which some connectionist representations exhibit. He contrasts classical, "concatenative compositionality" with "functional compositionality" and on the basis of this distinction demonstrates that representations can be compositional without being classical.

Chandrasekaran (1990) advocates a view somewhat similar to that of Fodor and Pylyshyn, and we can briefly examine the basis of his chosen viewpoint. He argues that "connectionist (and symbolic) approaches are both *realizations* of a more abstract level of description, namely the *information processing* (IP) level." He claims that belief in IP theory is almost universal among workers in AI; the belief is stated as, "Significant (all?) aspects of cognition and perception are best understood/modeled as *information processing activities on representations*." A key element in the foundation of this belief is that theorizing is best pursued in terms of conceptually meaningful units. The conceptual opacity of distributed representations prevents them from being units in an abstract theoretical framework; this necessarily restricts such representations to a lower, more implementational level.

IP theory is usually associated with Marr (1990). The idea is to examine the phenomenon of interest and "first, identify an information processing function with a clear specification about what kind of information is available for the function as input and what kind of information needs to be made available as output by the function. Then specify a particular IP theory for achieving this function by stating what kinds of information the theory proposes need to be represented at various stages in the processing." At this stage there is no commitment to specific algorithms for realizing the theory in a computational model. Hence, there is no commitment to either the connectionist or the classical representational paradigm. Subsequent implementations can go either way, or both ways. From this viewpoint the choice appears to be one of implementation strategy, and thus not a fundamental one.

II. CLASSICAL APPROACHES

In the classical approach to knowledge representation, units of our representation stand for clearly articulatable things, and the information that is moved and manipulated by the applicable operations is also comfortably meaningful at a useful conceptual level. Much information is readily available on this vast AI subfield—a chapter in every AI book, and various compilations (e.g., Brachman & Levesque, 1985).

As a general introduction I shall use the points singled out by Brachman and Levesque. There are two issues of overall adequacy:

1. Expressive adequacy—what can be represented? They ask if every representation language should be a notational variant of full first-order logic? And they complain of the lack of precise statements about what exactly can or is being represented.

2. Reasoning efficiency—can the representation support processing that generates results at an acceptable speed?

There are three more issues concerning basic questions about the limits and validity of conventional knowledge representation schemes.

1. Primitives—what are the primitive elements? For example, later we shall see Schank's attempt to lay out a set of primitive representational elements for natural language processing.

2. Metarepresentation—there appears to be a need for knowledge about knowledge, but there is no general agreement on the relationship of meta-knowledge to the basic-level knowledge.

3. Incompleteness—the problems of reasoning with knowledge that is known to be incomplete. This problem is aggravated by the customary use of logic-based reasoning which requires that *all* relevant information is in the knowledge representation—this is a difficult requirement to meet. But, as we shall see, in non-logic-based approaches (e.g., in Smolenksy's, 1987, connectionist circuit analysis system), incomplete knowledge representations are no longer such an important concern.

A. Semantic Networks

There has long been a persistent belief within the community of cognitive modelers that the basic representation of knowledge should be a richly interconnected structure, an aggregate of associated elements. Analysis of the human ability to reason invariably suggests that each element of our knowledge exists in a context of many different relationships to many other such elemental pieces of knowledge. This view seems to indicate that the basic representational structure is a network, and the generic name for this sort of representation is a *semantic network*. An example of early studies using the semantic network representation is the work of Collins and Quillian (1969). Their semantic-network model, known as the *teachable language comprehender* (TLC), attempted to simulate the human ability to comprehend and use language in a natural way.

Viewed formally, a semantic network is a graph structure for representing knowledge. Typically, the nodes of a semantic network represent concepts such as bird, robin, John. The arcs represent relations between these concepts, such as isa, father_of, belongs_to. Woods (1975) in his famous critique, "What's in a Link," states that "The major characteristic of the semantic networks that distinguishes them from other candidates is the characteristic notion of a link or pointer [arc] which connects individual facts into a total structure." Many problems are associated with semantic networks (see Woods's paper) but one strong point in their favor is that they are conceptually transparent.

In fact, semantic networks are too conceptually suggestive. So, this initially positive feature also forms the basis for one of the difficult problems that every computational modeler must grapple with; in this case, "the *Eliza* syndrome" (Partridge, 1986), overly suggestive naming of objects in computational models inevitably leads interested observers to make unwarranted grandiose assumptions about the model's scope and limitations. A label in a representational scheme is just that and no more. If a meaning (an interpretation in terms of the empirical world) is to be attached to the label, then that meaning must derive from the accompanying process model together with a mapping from representational scheme to real-world phenomena. McDermott (1976) first publicized this awkward representational problem within the AI community.

An example of a semantic network is given in Figure 2. This network appears to represent a small, but quite significant, amount of knowledge. Any system using this knowledge base will know about birds and that they have wings; it will know that robins are birds; it will know that John owns a robin, and in addition, that he loves Mary, and so forth.

In fact, it might be taken to be mildly impressive. And that is the root of the problem; for example, in the one-sentence survey of the knowledge captured, the piece of knowledge that John is male was slipped in. That information is not in the network; it is an implication that we draw all too readily from the name "John" and perhaps from the relationship "loves" with a node named "Mary." Without further information as to the implementation details that support reasoning with this network, the presence of

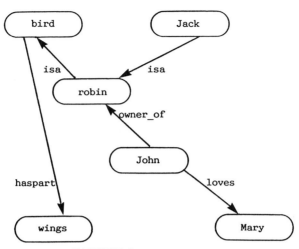

FIGURE 2   A semantic network.

the relationship "John loves Mary" tells us nothing more than that there is some binary relation between two objects; "A × B" is equivalent but far less impressive (read it as A ×es B).

Once more, we see that the process model is crucial. For what knowledge has indeed been captured by a semantic network is determined largely by the program details for reasoning with the nodes and links (i.e., the process model); it is not determined by the wealth of implications that you or I or anyone else brings to mind when we see the node and link labels. The sort of information that might be represented in this particular semantic network could support intelligent reasoning by, for example, being used to generate answers to questions: such as, "Is Jack a robin?" or "Do all birds have wings?" It is not clear from the semantic network alone what the answers to these questions ought to be; that depends on exactly how the arc properties have been implemented. Typically, the implementation will be very specific; it will behave reliably (and reasonably) only for this particular network when queried with just the very limited types of questions that the implementor had in mind at the time. Brachman (1985) exposes the basic weaknesses of representational schemes using "isa" links and property-inheritance strategies; for example, if Figure 2 has represented the information that a "robin haspart wings," it can be only because the node "robin" has inherited this property from its super-class node "bird."

Hayes (1979), in a searching examination of knowledge representation, addresses this problem in terms of the "fidelity" of a formalization. "It is perilously easy to think that one's formalization has captured a concept (because one has used a convincing-sounding token to stand for it, for example), when in fact, for all the formalization knows, the token might denote something altogether more elementary."

Brachman (1985) goes further than this: he argues that efforts to represent common sense knowledge (e.g., that a three-legged elephant is still an elephant even though elephants have four legs) has led to a chaotic situation in semantic-network representation: ad hoc and simplistic special practices and representations that miss important basic facts.

Figure 3 is a part of the semantic network illustrated earlier (Figure 2); it will provide a basis for illustrating some of the representational problems. One of the representational efficiency gains to be made with this knowledge representation is the ability to represent, just once, a specific property which is common to all individuals of a class (e.g., all individual birds have wings). This is achieved by attaching the general property to the class node, in this case "bird," and all specific birds that are represented can *inherit* this property automatically. Such inheritance schemes are an integral part of many representations of information that are designed to support cognitive models. Now these inheritance structures work fine if the property to be represented is a *defining* feature of the class. So "four sided" works fine as an inheritable property of the class "quadrilaterals." But for natural classes, such as "bird," problems arise.

It may be true that the property of "having wings" is partially what defines a bird. However, a wingless robin is gruesome but nevertheless quite plausible in a way that a three-sided quadrilateral is not. The resultant problem for the inheritance strategy is that the property is sort-of-defining, normally true, typically true, or to be assumed true in the absence of evidence to the contrary—the possible interpretations are many and they are all ill-defined. How is this to be addressed in a formal representation scheme? If we are to represent information that can support intelligent reasoning then we have to be able to represent the notion that birds have

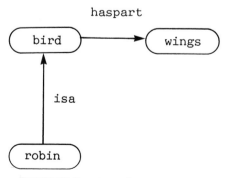

FIGURE 3   A small semantic network.

wings but that any poor robin who happens, as a result of some ghastly accident, to have been separated from its appendages for flight is still indisputably a bird. We need to represent the notion that birds *typically* have wings, but that any individual need not *necessarily* have them.

The standard solution is to introduce a means of overriding properties that instances of a general class would normally inherit—a "cancel link" in effect. So the poor grounded robin, called Joe, can be represented in the network as illustrated in Figure 4. Thus, the casual interpretation of the "bird–wings" relationship, that is, "every bird has wings," is not accurate. Having wings is a default property—we assume that every bird has wings unless we have direct evidence to the contrary. A better interpretation of the relationship in question is that "birds typically have wings," or "birds usually have wings." But, then, what is the precise meaning of *typically* or of *usually,* the meaning to be formally specified in the appropriate part of the process model?

There is none. And once absolute definitional status is abandoned, we are catapulted into a limbo world of hazy meaning and multiple interpretations. The plausible descriptions of what the network represents is just a hedge because "every" is clearly not correct. Thus, such structures in semantic networks (and default slots in frames; Section B) do not define *necessary* conditions and will not support reasoning based on unequivocal, universal statements, such as that every A has a B. The rules are made to be broken— sometimes. And here is the crunch. We need to distinguish in our represen-

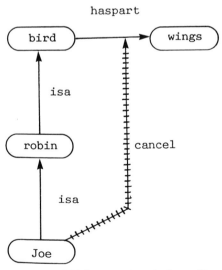

FIGURE 4   Joe, the wingless robin.

tations between relationships that are "typically" true and those that must always be true, that is, those that are definitional—a square always has four sides, and a robin is always a bird. Such relationships are not candidates for cancellation. As Brachman (1985) concludes: "The call to arms sounded by Fahlman (1979) and Minsky (in Kolata, 1982) for the need to represent three-legged elephants and dead ducks (or those with their feet set in concrete), while crucially important if AI is ever to get a hold of 'common sense', has led to naive mechanisms that both admit arbitrary, bizarre representations and force the ignorance of crucial, obvious facts."

The form of inheritance just mentioned is called *downward inheritance;* it exploits the fact that specific instances of a class share many features in common and thus these features need be represented only once, in association with the class node (compare the object-oriented style; Section I.B.4). In addition, the examples have been restricted to inheritance between objects. What else could we want to represent?

In some models there is a need to represent actions. Can this be done while continuing to exploit an inheritance mechanism? Therefore, "moving relocates an object" and "walking is a type of moving," so we might want walking to inherit the "relocation" property. Alternatively, we might want a strategy for *upward inheritance,* a basis for reasoning from the particular to the general. Returning to the earlier example of Joe, the robin, we might know that "Joe preens his feathers" and as "Joe is a bird" a mechanism of upward inheritance might allow us to reason that "birds preen their feathers."

The possibilities for storing information in one place and transferring it through the network to support reasoning elsewhere are many and varied and mostly fraught with danger. For example, it is necessary to distinguish between the properties of a set and the properties of elements of the set. Consider how a failure to observe this distinction can lead to error: "birds are found on every continent" and "a robin is a bird" should not permit us to reason that "robins are found on every continent." Touretzky (1986) provides a treatment of the mathematical foundations of inheritance systems.

Many researchers believe that first-order logic (i.e., predicate logic) is the proper framework for building these networks on a well-defined, and hence firm, foundation. That many knowledge representation problems do not appear to fit into the framework of such logical schemes (e.g., they resist useful approximation as a collection of context-free elements) may be more a reflection of our misconception of the problems than a limitation inherent in first-order logics. In addition, a variety of ways can be used to extend the expressive power of first-order logic, and much research effort is directed toward the exploration of these more elaborate, formal systems.

Others, however, believe logic to be inadequate for the description of many aspects of human knowledge; for example, the inability to cope with the inconsistencies characteristic of much human knowledge (see Hewitt's, 1990, criticism).

A second route to placing semantic network representations on firmer foundations is to base them on empirical data. In this case, the node and arc names will be labels for quantities derived from a statistical analysis, perhaps. In any event the "meaning" of any particular network will be founded on an interpretation of the underlying analysis and data; it may well be questionable, but it will be explicit—that is the important thing. Schvaneveldt (1990) presents such a basis for his link-weighted semantic networks.

B. Frames, Scripts, and Schemata

In keeping with the accepted view that intelligence is based upon the associationistic properties of knowledge—that is, that one thing always leads to another—the units of most knowledge representations tend to be not elementary facts but cohesive clusters of related facts. The term *frame,* due to Minsky (1975), is perhaps the most common name for such collections of knowledge. Schank's *scripts* are designed to capture the sequencing of events (such as enter–sit–order–eat–pay–leave in the famous restaurants script) as well as collect together the related facts (the props like chairs and tables, and the actors like waitresses and managers). Scripts were designed for, and have been primarily used in, representations of knowledge to support models of natural-language processing.

The term *schema* is used more by psychologists and cognitive scientists than by AI researchers. A schema may also be more of an abstract knowledge representation structure whereas frames tend to be more concrete, even if they are not always part of an implemented and working system.

To complicate the issues further, there are structured units of knowledge called *objects* (as mentioned earlier in the context of the object-oriented style of knowledge representation; Section I.B.4). Both frames and objects can be implementation-level structures offered by a programming language. They can also be used as abstractions in the design of a knowledge representation, and then be implemented in terms of primitive procedural and declarative features of a given programming language. This brings in again the question of viewpoint level when considering representations of knowledge. In this particular case, the use of, say, frames in a representation scheme may be primarily at an abstract level of representation, if the implementation language does not happen to provide direct support for frames (in which case the abstract frames will have to be simulated and approximated using the features that the chosen programming language offers). Alternatively, the abstract representation might be designed in terms of objects and then implemented (and approximated) using framelike features of an implementation language which does not directly support objects. So, frames, for example, might be the fundamental elements of a representation of knowledge, but only at some abstract level, or they might be primarily a result of implementation-level constraints with little significance at the level of abstract analysis.

A frame is an elaboration of the computer science data structure known as a record—a structure for grouping related pieces of information, such as an employee record might contain name, salary, job title, and so on. But a frame is not only a collection of data items that possess some similarity, all related to, say, the concept of a chair (to pick a concept at random). The chair record might be a collection of data items such as color, seat covering material, height of seat from floor. The notion of a chair frame is a major development of this general idea. And it is, moreover, a development that explicitly recognizes the process-model aspect of knowledge representation.

A chair frame will, in addition to a collection of relevant facts, contain links to more general concepts such as furniture; that is, a chair is a "type of" furniture (the "is a" link in semantic networks). The point of this so-called superordinate link is that the chair frame can inherit properties of the furniture frame without having to repeat all of these properties within the chair frame (and every other type-of-furniture frame). One such inherited property might be "typically found in houses," this is characteristic of all furniture and thus of chairs. A frame may also have links down to more specialized frames such as an armchair frame and a deck-chair frame. This results in a structure very like the inheritance hierarchy that is characteristic of the object-oriented style of representation (Section I.B.4).

Stored explicitly within the chair frame are various categories of data item. These items are usually associated with frame *slots;* that is, a place for a specific piece of information which may, or may not, be filled in any particular frame. Some slots for the chair frame will be purely optional, such as a chair-owner slot will have a value if we happen to know the owner of the current chair, otherwise it will be empty. Some will perhaps always have to be filled, such as the number of legs (if this is considered to be an important characteristic of chairs). For these nonoptional slots *default values* may be supplied. That is to say, if, when a particular chair frame is constructed, we have no explicit statement of how many legs this particular chair has then a default value of "four" may be automatically filled in. This use of default values is particularly useful with data structures to support intelligent reasoning because it is a mechanism for utilizing implicit information. If we are reasoning about a particular chair we are likely to assume, in the absence of any information to the contrary, that it has four legs. The frame data structure offers us a mechanism with which to begin to mimic this human ability.

Despite all their admirable qualities frames and schemata have many unsatisfactory properties when considered as the basic elements of knowledge representation to support intelligent reasoning. Their major drawback stems perhaps from the very fact that the idea of a frame or schema is to encapsulate knowledge. Neat packages of knowledge (even with the odd links to other packages) are great for the management of complexity but they jar with the (apparent) fluidity of intelligent reasoning.

In a frame-based system there are always awkward problems of situations that fall between frames or schemata and questions of when to change frames or schemata. Similarly, there are always situations that do not fit any particular frame or schema very comfortably. If I sit on a log, it becomes, to some extent, a chair (therefore, a friend might say, "Can I share your chair?"). But this possibility is unlikely to be in any chair frame. As another example, is a large canopy on the lawn to be reasoned about using a room schema (rooms do not usually have grass on the floor, but they do have tables and chairs in and a ceiling overhead)?

"Objects" (introduced in Section I.B.4) can be considered the result of further development of the process model in composite representational elements. Frames have a rudimentary process model associated with inheritance properties and the provision of default slot values. Objects have procedural components, called *methods,* on a par with the traditional static data values, called *instance variables.* In addition, objects exist within an inheritance structure that permits individual objects to represent complex phenomena succinctly: general instance variables and methods are explicitly represented once and, through automatic inheritance, each individual object behaves as if these general components of process model and content theory were explicitly repeated within it.

Examples of script-based natural-language understanding (NLU) can be found in the SAM (script applier mechanism) system (Schank & Abelson, 1977). Hendrix and Sacerdoti (1981) state that this approach to NLU was one of the first that attempted to deal with structured sequences of actions (i.e., discourse analysis rather than single sentence analysis). They list three limitations of the SAM system.

1. Players and props are limited to single objects. Therefore, stories involving more than one customer or table, for example, are too complex. This limitation allows the tricky NLU problem of reference (i.e., which object in the world is referred to by some element of the text) to be eliminated: "the table" refers to the only table under consideration.

2. Scripted actions follow a strict linear sequence (and later a few strictly limited alternative sequences). This limits allowable stories to just those which follow a particular script.

3. A further limitation is one of selecting the appropriate script for a given story. This is a largely unaddressed problem which we have encoun-

tered already (in the guise of selecting the "right" frame for a given situation).

Subsequent to SAM there was PAM (plan applier mechanism), which attempts to understand stories by matching the actions of the story with methods that it knows will achieve the goals of a generated goal plan. A review of the ideas underlying these systems is provided by Schank (1980).

A significant part of Schank's early achievements in NLU rested on his attempts to devise a canonical notation that was both necessary and sufficient to represent the conceptual structures underlying English text.

1. Representational Primitives

A major weakness of the non–logic-based semantic-network representations is the lack of any accepted standard set of well-defined node labels and link properties. Each cognitive modeler was free to devise whatever node concepts and associative relations that he or she found most convenient. One way to address the resultant unhelpful diversity and absence of simple correspondence between one person's semantic network and another's is to found the representation on logic (which has already been considered). Another is to devise a well-defined, standard set of concepts and relations. This latter option has been most vigorously pursued by workers associated with NLU.

In an effort to address the problem of a proliferation of representations designed to capture the meaning of natural language text Schank proposed the *conceptual dependency* (CD) notation.

The CD notation was designed to represent the "meaning" of natural-language stories, independent of the specific concepts (and particular surface language) involved in the text. Furthermore, it was meant to be something approaching a complete notation; that is, the elements of the notation should be sufficient to represent the meaning in any (reasonable) piece of text. The language-independence claim of CD theory makes it a potential interlingua (an intermediate language as used in some machine-translation work).

The CD notation is composed of a small number of semantic primitives, both primitive acts and primitive states. Some examples of primitive acts are

PTRANS. The transfer of the physical location of an object. For example, the verb *put* would typically be represented as a PTRANS act.

MTRANS. The transfer of mental information. For example, use of the verb *tell* would be likely to be represented as an MTRANS of information from one person to another.

"There exist formally defined dependency relations between categories of concepts" (Schank, 1973). They are listed, explained, and exampled by

Schank (1973). Each such dependency has a graphical symbol, usually a sort of arrow. Then arrowy diagrams become the visual representations of meanings in CD theory. The canonical example, in the canonical form is "John gave Mary a book," which is illustrated in Figure 5.

The *p* signifies past tense; *o*, objective dependency; and *R*, a recipient–donor dependency. In addition, the three "arrow" structures all have interpretations within the CD notation.

The small, well-defined number of elements in CD theory was always a laudable goal but not very realistic. As with almost any firm principle concerning natural language, once the principle is stated clearly, a counterexample is produced.

Subsequent to CD theory, Schank (1982) introduced MOPs (memory organization packets) and TOPs (thematic organization packets) coupled with the claim that "expectations are the key to understanding." Scripts are then viewed as a source of expectations, and expectation failures drive memory development and organization. This limited view of the notion of input-expectation discrepancy reduction that Schank calls *expectation failure* has been criticized in detail elsewhere (Partridge, 1985). Wilks (1977) reviews and criticizes many of the basic ideas on semantic primitives—the representational primitives for natural-language processing.

C. Logic-Based Representations

A simple logic-based representation of the semantic network illustrated earlier might be the following set of predicates:

    isa(robin, bird)
    haspart(bird, wings)
    isa(Jack, robin)
    owner_of(John, robin)
    loves(John, Mary)

These explicit facts, together with some explicit implication rules, will enable a process of logical deduction to generate more facts. An implication rule might be

$$\text{isa}(A,B) \text{ AND } \text{isa}(B,C) \rightarrow \text{isa}(A,C)$$

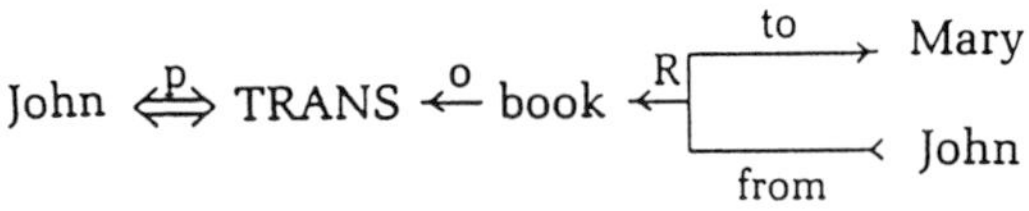

FIGURE 5   A CD representation of "John gave Mary a book."

which can be read as "if an A is a B, and a B is a C, then an A is a C." Given this implication rule and the two facts that "isa(Jack, robin)" and "isa(robin, bird)," we can deduce that "isa(Jack, bird)" is also true.

So what has changed (other than the syntax)? The point to make with this representation is not that it looks different but that each of its elements has a well-defined meaning, a denotational meaning in the predicate calculus. Now, a well-defined formalism determines precisely how this representation can be manipulated and how the elements can interact. The process model (logical deduction operating through the implication rules) is explicit, although severely limited in scope.

This representation, however, does not define anything to do with the relationships between the primitive knowledge elements, such as "owner _of" and "bird," and the real-world concepts these labels appear to identify. Therefore, a crucial part of the task of constructing such a knowledge representation is to argue for the validity of the various associations between the elements of the formal representation and "things" in some real world. Such an argument would have to be based on analogies between the similarities of scope and limitations of the formal representational elements and elements of the empirical world. This is a difficult problem, and it is not peculiar to formal representations of knowledge. It is, of course, a problem to be faced with all abstract representations and the world that is being represented in the knowledge.

1. Knowledge Bases

The blossoming subfield of knowledge-based systems (KBSs) or expert systems (ESs) (the topic of Chapter 6) is fundamentally based on a logic-based representational commitment. The basic belief is that high-quality reasoning, over a limited domain (i.e., something like human expertise), can be generated by a computational system in which the basic information is represented by a set of logical propositions and the process model is based on logical inference. In terms of ES terminology, we have a knowledge base and an inference engine, respectively.

The following simple example illustrates a popular approach to knowledge-base representation in the Prolog programming language:

```
F1 hobbit(bilbo).
F2 uncleof(frodo,bilbo).
R1 nephewof(X,Y):=uncleof(Y,X).
R2 hobbit(X):=uncleof(X,Y),hobbit(Y).
```

Four entries constitute this knowledge base: two facts, F1 and F2; and two rules, R1 and R2. In the Prolog notation, implication rules are written backwards: thus R1 is read 'if uncleof Y is X, then nephewof X is Y'.

Notice also (in R2) that the logical AND is written as a comma in Prolog. The two facts are the given "truths" of the system, and in combination with the rules they allow us to deduce further true statements. Thus, if we take R1 and instantiate X as "frodo" and Y as "bilbo," the truth of the resultant condition "uncleof(frodo, bilbo)," given by F2, enables us to infer the conclusion "nephewof(bilbo, frodo)" and so on.

Specific knowledge may be stored as facts; general knowledge may be stored as rules; and by combining the two (and invoking the process model of logical deduction), we can generate many new facts.

An important advantage of such a representation of knowledge is that it is modular, which means that a given knowledge base can be expanded (or reduced) by the addition (or deletion) of small, independent chunks. For example, the hobbit knowledge base could be extended to include further defining characteristics of hobbits, say the fact that they have hairy feet and live in middle-earth. The additional rule might be

$$hobbit(X) := hairyfeet(X), home(X, middle\text{-}earth).$$

This new rule may simply be added to the hobbit knowledge base, and its representational scope has been significantly and easily extended.

The well-defined nature of the basic logical operations is obtained at the cost of severe limitations on applicability in representations of the empirical world. Some problematic areas are incremental acquisition of knowledge, beliefs about truth rather than truth in some absolute sense, temporal aspects of knowledge, and the combination of general assumptions with exceptional situations that may override the normal assumption.

Many of these awkward characteristics of empirical knowledge and its use to support intelligent behavior can be reduced to the necessity to be able to add new knowledge that may then alter the truth of some current knowledge. In logical terms this leads us into a less well-understood logical world, the domain of nonmonotonic logic.

A further problem is that a process model which treats failure to prove truth as falsity must rest on the assumption that all the relevant knowledge is represented (otherwise there might be a way to prove the truth of the supposed negative fact in information that is not in the knowledge base). This crucial requirement is known in logic as the *closed world assumption*.

A common general criticism of most current knowledge bases is that the knowledge represented does not embody a deep understanding of the domain; it is instead a collection of "pattern → action" rules—a representation of superficial knowledge that excludes the possibility of using such knowledge to solve hard problems. The underlying principles are absent and so cannot be used to support deep reasoning.

Chandrasekaran and Mittal (1983) provide a lucid examination of this contention, which on the whole they support. But they do stress that, despite the many calls for more deep knowledge, there is no general agreement on the form and content of these deeper structures. In particular they illustrate that the popular belief that "causal" knowledge is deep knowledge, does not stand up to close scrutiny—in a nutshell, substituting "pattern *causes* action" for "pattern → action" is no guarantee that deeper knowledge has been encoded.

Mylopoulos and Levesque (1984) provide a concise and informative overview of logic-based knowledge representation. They characterize two other classes of schemes as procedural and semantic network representations. Having considered semantic networks earlier, this leaves us with only procedural representations to examine.

D. Procedural Representations

In a procedural scheme, knowledge is represented as a set of processes. One or more processes is activated by certain states and the execution of the activated process(es) transforms the current state into a new one, and so on. We can view this approach to knowledge representation as process–model centered, which is, of course, a point of contrast with the content-theory bias of logic-based representation.

1. Production Systems

Production systems are an important type of procedural knowledge representation. The bones of a production-system architecture can be laid out as illustrated in Figure 6. The major components of a production system are a collection of rules, each of which is composed of a condition and an action; a working memory (WM), which contains information that defines the current state of the system; and a control loop, which cycles continually from the rule set to WM and back again.

The operation of a production system is to match the conditions of the rules against the information in the WM and to *fire* a rule that matches; that is, a rule whose condition evaluates as true given the values in the WM. What if more than one rule matches the current WM? The typical strategy is to select just one of the rules that can be fired from the subset that could possibly be fired. This selection process, called *conflict resolution*, usually involves heuristic strategies and is thus a major focus of the creative effort when designing a production system representation (the other such focus is the rules themselves). It is time for an example.

The earlier logical knowledge base might be represented by the following productions:

P1: (UNCLEOF X Y) → (NEPHEWOF Y X)
P2: (UNCLEOF X Y) AND (HOBBIT Y) → (HOBBIT X)

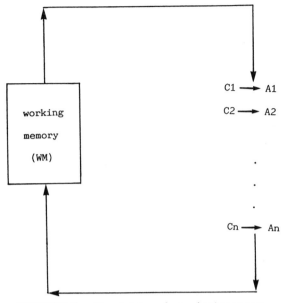

FIGURE 6   The skeleton of a production system.

and the current state, or working memory, which is given by the facts:

F1: (HOBBIT BILBO)
F2: (UNCLEOF FRODO BILBO)

With this rather limited example, we would find that the condition parts of both P1 and P2 will match the WM. Conflict resolution is thus required to decide which of the two matching rules to actually fire. A trivial strategy for conflict resolution is this: assuming that the control regime attempts to match rule conditions against the WM sequentially from top to bottom in the list of rules, then fire the first rule that matches.

Therefore, in the current situation, production rule P1 will fire. Typically, execution of the action part of a rule (i.e., firing the rule) will change the state of the WM by adding or deleting information or both. In addition, the action part may generate some information that is external to the production system proper. Thus an action part may output a message, for example. So, in the current example, the firing of P1 will cause the fact (NEPHEWOF BILBO FRODO) to be added to the WM.

Now, although the proposed conflict resolution strategy contains no heuristics and is painfully simple, several nonobvious features about the production system follow. Control structure is now contained in the *ordering* of the rules. Different rule orderings will give different results on exactly the same problem. In effect, hidden constraints are contained in the condition parts of the rules. This is obvious if you consider that the second rule can fire only if its condition part matches the WM and *the condition of the first rule does not match*. In fact, the second rule can *never* fire. Any state of the WM that matches P2 will also match P1, which will thus be fired in preference under the conflict resolution scheme proposed. The second rule is in effect:

R2: (UNCLEOF X Y) AND (HOBBIT Y) AND
(NOT(UNCLEOF X Y)) → (HOBBIT X)

Clearly, this is not a sensible rule: its effective condition can never be met. The point that I want to make is that the problem is not a problem with rule P2 itself, but a problem generated by my conflict resolution strategy and a rule that precedes P2: P1. So, even with this ludicrously simple example, we already see problems arising due to the interaction of several elements of the system. This provides a good example of the intertwining of process model and content theory with a representation: the control regime and conflict resolution strategy (process–model aspects) interact in subtle ways so as to change the effective rule structures (a content–theory aspect).

The production system architecture, as a basis for knowledge representation, has proven its worth in many sophisticated and diverse models of cognitive phenomena [e.g., the ACT* system of Anderson (1987), which models human skill acquisition, and many applications of the SOAR system of Rosenbloom, Laird, and Newell (1987), which is production–system based]. But the construction of a major production–system based model is not without its headaches.

Building control information into the set of production rules can eliminate much of the searching that plagues logical schemes. The introduction of these context dependencies does, of course, aggravate the problem of understanding and modifying production systems. The general trade-off here is that between searching context-free representations and providing guidance at the cost of introducing context dependencies.

Anderson (1987) feels that the production system architecture has several advantages over alternative knowledge representations. Like a successful politician, he wants to claim the vast middle ground between extremist architects of micro or macro schools. Production system rules are relatively well structured, simple and homogeneous, and independent of one another. *Well structured* is a somewhat fuzzy term, but it seems undeniable that, in contrast to connectionist networks, it is easier to understand what is learned and probably easier to predict consequences such as transfer of a learned skill from one domain to another. In being simple and homogeneous, productions contrast with the more macro symbolic representations such as schemata (e.g., Schank & Abelson, 1977) and frames. Therefore, it should be easier to implement a simple learning mechanism to construct new production rules compared with new schemata. Independence of production rules allows for incremental learning as productions are added (or deleted). It may also permit graceful degradation, which is touted as a characteristic virtue of the distributed representations that are considered next.

Touretzky and Hinton (1986) describe a connectionism–based production system model. On a small scale, they demonstrate that it is feasible for connectionist systems to reproduce certain constituents of symbolic models (e.g., consistent variable binding, so that if a variable X gets the value "A" in the condition part of the rule then any X in the action part also picks up this "A" value) and that such distributed models exhibit a number of interesting emergent properties (e.g., damage resistance).

E. Analogical and Iconic Representation

A further class of representations, which hold particular significance for the designer of cognitive models, is that of analogical or iconic representations. This type of representation can be contrasted with the linguistic, symbolic, or Fregean type of representation. A semantic network representation may well be an analogical one, whereas a logical representation, couched in the predicate calculus, is a Fregean representation.

These two classes are not well-defined, however, and we find different authors propounding rather different characterizations of them. Boden (1988) takes up this point; she states that a common element of all uses "is some (not necessarily well-defined) notion of *similarity* between the analogue-representation and the thing represented" (p. 29). From the process-model aspect, there is a tacit assumption that the similarity will play a significant role in the interpretation of the representation.

Sloman (1978) discusses at length the differences between these two classes of representation (he labels them *analogical* and *Fregean*). He maintains that this use of the term *analogue* carries no implication of a continuous (rather than discrete) structuring of the representation. He defines an analogical representation as one in which there is an interpretative mapping or significant isomorphism between the structure of the representation and the structure of what it is representing.

One of his main aims is to show that inferences made by manipulating non-Fregean representations may be perfectly valid. We can, and often do, use analogical representations to check or even as a basis for agreement to a Fregean inference claim. In set theory, it is common practice to use circles, juxtaposed and superimposed. In number theory, lines can be used to represent numeric values with direction and orientation as analogical representations of operations on these values.

As a specific example, the semantic network illustrated in Figure 2 is an analogical alternative to the Fregean one composed of logical predicates in

Section II.C. The essential trade-off between these two options was presented as one of ease of perception of what (in general) is being represented versus well definition of what is actually represented.

Funt (1980) describes an example of the advantages to be gained by a problem-solving system when aided by diagrammatic representations. The problem-solving domain is that of predicting the sequence of events that will occur when a blocksworld structure collapses; that is, a structure built from blocks, wedges, and so forth. He found that the diagrammatic representations enabled the conventional problem-solving system to "work with objects of arbitrary shape, detect collisions and other motion discontinuities, discover coincidental alignments, and easily update its world model after a state change."

For present purposes, the main point to be made is not one of relative perceptual merits or relative cognitive validity, it is merely one of range of choice: among the many representational choices open to the builder of a computational model, there is one of analogical versus Fregean.

The basic representational medium for computational models (i.e., programming languages) is, of course, linguistic or Fregean. And, although this may indeed facilitate the construction of similarly Fregean representations in computational models, it by no means excludes the possibility of constructing analogical representations at some higher level.

References

Anderson, J. R. (1987). Skill acquisition: Compilation of weak-method problem solutions. *Psychological Review, 94,* 192–210.

Boden, M. A. (1988). *Computer models of mind: Computational approaches in theoretical psychology.* Cambridge, UK: Cambridge University Press.

Booch, G. (1991). *Object-oriented design with applications.* Redwood City, CA: Benjamin Cummings.

Brachman, R. J. (1985). I lied about the trees. *AI Magazine, 6*(3), 80–93.

Brachman, R. J., & Levesque, H. J. (Eds.). (1985). *Readings in knowledge representation.* Los Altos, CA: Morgan Kaufmann.

Chandrasekaran, B. (1990). What kind of information processing is intelligence? In D. Partridge & Y. Wilks (Eds.), *The foundations of AI: A sourcebook* (pp. 14–46). Cambridge, UK: Cambridge University Press.

Chandrasekaran, B., & Mittal, S. (1983). Deep versus compiled knowledge approaches to diagnostic problem-solving. *International Journal of Man–Machine Studies, 19,* 425–336.

Collins, A. M., & Quillian, M. R. (1969). Retrieval time from semantic memory. *Journal of Verbal Learning and Verbal Behavior, 8,* 240–247.

Fahlman, S. E. (1979). *NETL: A system for representing and using real-world knowledge.* Cambridge, MA: MIT Press.

Feigenbaum, E. A., & Feldman, J. (Eds.). (1963). *Computers and thought.* New York: McGraw-Hill.

Fodor, J. A., & Pylyshyn, Z. W. (1988). Connectionism and cognitive architecture: A critical analysis. *Cognition, 28,* 3–71.

Funt, B. V. (1980). Problem-solving with diagrammatic representations. *Artificial Intelligence, 13,* 201–230.

Genesereth, M. R., & Nilsson, N. J. (1987). *Logical foundations of AI.* Los Altos, CA: Morgan Kaufmann.

Haugeland, J. (1985). *Artificial Intelligence: The very idea.* Cambridge, MA: MIT Press.

Hayes, P. J. (1979). The naive physics manifesto. In D. Michie (Ed.), *Expert systems in the electronic age* (pp. 242–270). Edinburgh: Edinburgh University Press.

Hendrix, G. G., & Sacerdoti, E. D. (1981, September). Natural-language processing: The field in perspective. *BYTE,* pp. 304–352.

Hewitt, C. (1990). The challenge of open systems. In D. Partridge & Y. Wilks (Eds.), *The foundations of AI: A sourcebook* (pp. 383–395). Cambridge, UK: Cambridge University Press.

Kolata, G. (1982). How can computers get common sense? *Science, 217,* 1237–1238.

Kowalski, R. (1980). Reply to questionnaire [Special issue on Knowledge representation]. *SIGART Newsletter* No. 70.

Lenat, D. B., Prakash, M., & Shepherd, M. (1986). CYC: Using common sense knowledge to overcome brittleness and knowledge acquisition bottlenecks, *AI Magazine, 6*(4), 65–85.

Marr, D. (1990). AI: A personal view. In D. Partridge & Y. Wilks (Eds.), *The foundations of AI: A sourcebook* (pp. 97–107). Cambridge, UK: Cambridge University Press.

McCarthy, J. (1986). AI reasoning should be logic with extensions. In D. Partridge (Ed.), Preprints for the workshop on the foundations of AI, Computing Research Laboratory, Las Cruces, NM, pp. 31–32.

McCarthy, J., & Hayes, P. J. (1969). Some philosophical problems from the standpoint of AI. In B. Meltzer & D. Michie (Eds.), *Machine Intelligence 4* (pp. 463–502). Edinburgh: Edinburgh University Press.

McCarthy, J., Abrahams, P. W., Edwards, D. J., Hart, T. P., & Levin, M. I. (1965). *LISP 1.5 programmer's manual* (2nd ed.). Cambridge, MA: MIT Press.

McDermott, D. (1976). Artificial Intelligence meets natural stupidity. *SIGART Newsletter,* No. 57, pp. 4–9.

McDermott, D. (1986). *A critique of pure reason* (Research Report YALEU/CSD/RR No. 480). New Haven, CT: Yale University, Computer Science Department.

Minsky, M. (Ed.). (1968). *Semantic information processing.* Cambridge, MA: MIT Press.

Minsky, M. (1975). A framework for representing knowledge. In P. H. Winston (Ed.), *The psychology of computer vision* (pp. 211–277). New York: McGraw-Hill.

Minsky, M. (1981). A framework for representing knowledge. In J. Haugeland (Ed.), *Mind design* (pp. 95–128). Cambridge, MA: MIT Press.

Morton, J. (1969). Interaction of information in word recognition. *Psychological Review, 76,* 165–178.

Mylopoulos, J., & Levesque, H. J. (1984). An overview of knowledge representation. In M. L. Brodie, J. Mylopoulos & J. W. Schmidt (Eds.), *On conceptual modelling* (pp. 3–17). New York: Springer-Verlag.

Newell, A., Shaw, J. C., & Simon, H. A. (1961). *Information processing language V manual.* Englewood Cliffs, NJ: Prentice-Hall.

Newell, A., & Simon, H. A. (1972). *Human problem solving.* Englewood Cliffs, NJ: Prentice-Hall.

Partridge, D. (1985). Input-expectation discrepancy reduction: A ubiquitous mechanism. *Proceedings of the Ninth International Joint Conference on AI, Los Angeles,* pp. 267–273.

Partridge, D. (1986). *AI: Applications in the future of software engineering.* Chichester, UK: Ellis Horwood/Wiley.

Partridge, D. (1990). What's in an AI program? In D. Partridge & Y. Wilks (Eds.), *The foundations of AI: A sourcebook* (pp. 112–118). Cambridge, UK: Cambridge University Press.

Partridge, D. (1991). *A new guide to artificial intelligence.* Norwood, NJ: Ablex.

Partridge, D., Johnston, V. S., & Lopez, P. D. (1984). Computer programs as theories in biology. *Journal of Theoretical Biology, 108,* 539–564.

Rosenbloom, P. S., Laird, J. E., & Newell, A. (1987). Knowledge level learning in Soar. *Proceedings of the American Association for AI,* AAAI-87, pp. 499–504.

Schank, R. (1973). Identification of conceptualizations underlying natural language. In R. Schank & K. M. Colby (Eds.), *Computer models of thought and language* (pp. 187–247). San Francisco: Freeman.

Schank, R. (1980). Language and memory. *Cognitive Science, 4,* 243–284.

Schank, R. (1982). *Dynamic memory.* Cambridge, UK: Cambridge University Press.

Schank, R., & Abelson, R. (1977). *Scripts, plans, goals, and understanding.* Hillsdale, NJ: Erlbaum.

Schvaneveldt, R. W. (1990). *Pathfinder associative networks: Studies in knowledge organization.* Norwood, NJ: Ablex.

Sloman, A. (1978). *The computer revolution in philosophy.* Brighton, UK: Harvester Press.

Smolensky, P. (1987). Connectionist AI, symbolic AI, and the brain. *Artificial Intelligence Review, 1*(2), 95–109.

Smolensky, P. (1988). On the proper treatment of connectionism. *Behavior and Brain Sciences, 11*(1), 1–23, 59–74.

Touretzky, D. S. (1986). *The mathematics of inheritance systems.* Los Altos, CA: Morgan Kaufmann.

Touretzky, D. S., & Hinton, G. E. (1986). *A distributed connectionist production system* (Report No. CMU-CS-86-172). Pittsburgh: Carnegie Mellon University, Computer Science Department.

Van Gelder, T. (1990). Compositionality: A connectionist variation on a classical theme. *Cognitive Science, 14,* 355–384.

Wilks, Y. (1977). *Good and bad arguments for semantic primitives* (Report No. 42). Edinburgh: University of Edinburgh, Department of AI.

Woods, W. A. (1975). What's in a link?: Foundations for semantic networks. In D. G. Bobrow & A. Collins (Eds.), *Representation and understanding* (pp. 35–82). New York: Academic Press.

Yourdon, E. (1990). Auld lang syne. *BYTE, 15*(10), 257–262.

CHAPTER 4

Machine Learning

Stuart Russell

I. INTRODUCTION

Machine learning is the subfield of AI concerned with intelligent systems that learn. To understand machine learning, it is helpful to have a clear notion of intelligent systems. This chapter adopts a view of intelligent systems as *agents*—systems that perceive and act in an environment; an agent is intelligent to the degree that its actions are successful. Intelligent agents can be natural or artificial; here we shall be concerned primarily with artificial agents.

Machine learning research is relevant to the goals of both artificial intelligence and cognitive psychology. At present, humans are much better learners, for the most part, than either machine learning programs or psychological models. Except in certain artificial circumstances, the overwhelming deficiency of current psychological models of learning is their complete incompetence as learners. Since the goal of machine learning is to make better learning mechanisms and to understand them, results from machine learning will be useful to psychologists at least until machine learning systems approach or surpass humans in their general learning capabilities. All of the issues that come up in machine learning—generalization ability, handling noisy input, using prior knowledge, handling complex environments, forming new concepts, active exploration, and so on—are also issues in the psychology of learning and development. Theoretical results on the computational (in)tractability of certain learning tasks apply equally to machines and humans. Finally, some AI system designs, such as Newell's SOAR architecture, are also intended as cognitive models. We will see, however, that it is often difficult to interpret human learning performance in terms of specific mechanisms.

Learning is often viewed as the most fundamental aspect of intelligence, as it enables the agent to become independent of its creator. It is an essential component of an agent design whenever the designer has incomplete knowledge of the task environment. Therefore, learning provides *autonomy* in that the agent is not dependent on the designer's knowledge for its success and can free itself from the assumptions built into its initial configuration. Learning may also be the only route by which we can construct very complex intelligent systems. In many application domains, the best systems are constructed by a learning process rather than by traditional programming or knowledge engineering.

Machine learning is a large and active field of research. This chapter provides only a brief sketch of the basic principles, techniques, and results and only brief pointers to the literature rather than full historical attributions. A few mathematical examples are provided to give a flavour of the analytical techniques used, but these can safely be skipped by the nontechnical reader (although some familiarity with the material in Chapter 3 will be useful). A more complete treatment of machine learning algorithms can be found in the text by Weiss and Kulikowski (1991). Collections of significant papers appear in Michalski, Carbonell, and Mitchell (1983–1990) and Shavlik and Dietterich (1990). Current research is published in the annual proceedings of the International Conference on Machine Learning, in the journal *Machine Learning,* and in mainstream AI journals.

A. A General Model of Learning

Learning results from the interaction between the agent and the world and from observation of the agent's own decision-making processes. Specifically, it involves making changes to the agent's internal structures to improve its performance in future situations. Learning can range from rote memorization of experience to the creation of scientific theories.

A learning agent has several conceptual components (Figure 1). The most important distinction is between the *learning element,* which is responsible for making improvements, and the *performance element,* which is responsible for selecting external actions. The design of the learning element of an agent depends very much on the design of the performance element. When trying to design an agent that learns a certain capability, the first

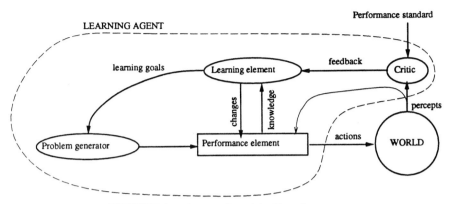

FIGURE 1   A general model of learning agents.

question is not, "how am I going to get it to learn this?" but "what kind of performance element will my agent need to do this once it has learned how?" For example, the learning algorithms for producing rules for logical planning systems are quite different from the learning algorithms for producing neural networks.

Figure 1 also shows some other important aspects of learning. The *critic* encapsulates a fixed standard of performance, which it uses to generate feedback for the learning element regarding the success or failure of its modifications to the performance element. The performance standard is necessary because the percepts themselves cannot suggest the desired direction for improvement. (The *naturalistic fallacy,* a staple of moral philosophy, suggests that one can deduce what ought to be from what is.) It is also important that the performance standard is fixed, otherwise the agent could satisfy its goals by adjusting its performance standard to meet its behavior.

The last component of the learning agent is the *problem generator.* This is the component responsible for deliberately *generating* new experiences, rather than simply watching the performance element as it goes about its business. The point of doing this is that, even though the resulting actions may not be worthwhile in the sense of generating a good outcome for the agent in the short term, they have significant value because the percepts they generate will enable the agent to learn something of use in the long run. This is what scientists do when they carry out experiments.

As an example, consider an automated taxi that must first learn to drive safely before being allowed to take fare-paying passengers. The performance element consists of a collection of knowledge and procedures for selecting its driving actions (turning, accelerating, braking, honking, and so on). The taxi starts driving using this performance element. The critic observes the ensuing bumps, detours, and skids; and the learning element formulates the goals to learn better rules describing the effects of braking and accelerating, to learn the geography of the area, to learn about wet roads, and so on. The taxi might then conduct experiments under different conditions, or it might simply continue to use the percepts to obtain information to fill in the missing rules. New rules and procedures can be added to the performance element (the *changes* arrow in the figure). The knowledge accumulated in the performance element can also be used by the learning element to make better sense of the observations (the *knowledge* arrow).

The learning element is also responsible for improving the *efficiency* of the performance element. For example, given a map of the area, the taxi might take a while to figure out the best route from one place to another. The next time the same trip is requested, the route-finding process should be much faster. This, called *speedup learning,* is dealt with in Section V.

B. Types of Learning Systems

The design of the learning element is affected by three major aspects of the learning setup:

- Which components of the performance element are to be improved.
- How those components are represented in the agent program.
- What prior information is available with which to interpret the agent's experience.

It is important to understand that learning agents can vary more or less independently along each of these dimensions.

The performance element of the system can be designed in several different ways. Its components can include (1) a set of "reflexes" mapping from conditions on the current state to actions, perhaps implemented using *condition–action rules* or *production rules* (see Chapter 6); (2) a means to infer relevant properties of the world from the percept sequence, such as a visual perception system (Chapter 7); (3) information about the way the world evolves; (4) information about the results of possible actions the agent can take; (5) *utility* information indicating the desirability of world states; (6) *action-value* information, indicating the desirability of particular actions in particular states; and (7) *goals* that describe classes of states whose achievement maximizes the agent's utility.

Each of these components can be learned, given the appropriate feedback. For example, if the agent does an action and then perceives the resulting state of the environment, this information can be used to learn a description of the results of actions (item 4 on the list). Thus, if an automated taxi exerts a certain braking pressure when driving on a wet road, then it will soon find out how much actual deceleration is achieved. Similarly, if the critic can use the performance standard to deduce utility values from the percepts, then the agent can learn a useful representation of its utility function (item 5 on the list). Thus, a taxi that receives no tips from passengers who have been thoroughly shaken up during the trip can learn a useful component of its overall utility function. In a sense, the performance standard can be seen as defining a set of *distinguished percepts* that will be interpreted as providing direct feedback on the quality of the agent's behavior. Hardwired performance standards such as pain and hunger in animals can be understood in this way.

Note that, for some components, such as the component for predicting the outcome of an action, the available feedback generally tells the agent what the correct outcome is, as in the braking example. On the other hand, in learning the condition–action component, the agent receives some evaluation of its action, such as a hefty bill for rear-ending the car in front, but usually is not told the correct action; namely, to brake more gently and much earlier. In some situations, the environment will contain a *teacher,* who can provide information as to the correct actions and also supply useful experiences in lieu of a problem generator. Section III examines the general problem of constructing agents from feedback in the form of percepts and utility values or rewards.

Finally, we come to prior knowledge. Most learning research in AI, computer science and psychology has studied the case where the agent begins with no knowledge at all concerning the function it is trying to learn. It has access to only the examples presented by its experience. Although this is an important special case, it is by no means the general case. Most human learning takes place in the context of a good deal of background knowledge.

Eventually, machine learning (and all other fields studying learning) must present a theory of *cumulative* learning, in which knowledge already learned is used to help the agent in learning from new experiences. Prior knowledge can improve learning in several ways. First, one can often rule out a large fraction of otherwise possible explanations for a new experience, because they are inconsistent with what is already known. Second, prior knowledge can often be used to directly suggest the general form of a hypothesis that might explain the new experience. Finally, knowledge can be used to *reinterpret* an experience in terms that make clear some regularity that might otherwise remain hidden. As yet, there is no comprehensive understanding of how to incorporate prior knowledge into machine learning algorithms, and this is an important ongoing research topic (see Section II.B.3 and Section V).

II. KNOWLEDGE-FREE INDUCTIVE LEARNING SYSTEMS

The basic problem studied in machine learning has been that of inducing a representation of a *function*—a systematic relationship between inputs and outputs—from examples. This section examines four major classes of function representations, and describes algorithms for learning each of them.

Looking again at the list of components of a performance element, given previously, one sees that each component can be described mathematically as a function. For example, information about the way the world evolves can be described as a function from a world state (the current state) to a world state (the next state or states); a goal can be described as a function from a state to a Boolean value (0 or 1), indicating whether or not the state satisfies the goal. The function can be *represented* using any of a variety of representation languages.

In general, the way the function is learned is that the feedback is used to indicate the correct (or approximately correct) value of the function for particular inputs, and the agent's representation of the function is altered to try to make it match the information provided by the feedback. Obviously, this process will vary depending on the choice of representation. In each case, however, the generic task—to construct a good representation of the desired function from correct examples—remains the same. This task is commonly called *induction* or *inductive inference*. The term *supervised learning* is also used, to indicate that correct output values are provided for each example.

To specify the task formally, we need to say exactly what we mean by an *example* of a function. Suppose that the function f maps from domain X to range Y (that is, it takes an X as input and outputs a Y). Then, an example of f is a pair (x,y) where $x \in X$, $y \in Y$ and $y = f(x)$. In English, an example is an input/output pair for the function.

Now we can define the task of *pure inductive inference*: given a collection of examples of f, return a function h that approximates f as closely as possible. The function returned is called a *hypothesis*. A hypothesis is *consistent* with a set of examples if it returns the correct output for each example, given the input. We say that h *agrees* with f on the set of examples. A hypothesis is *correct* if it agrees with f on all possible examples.

To illustrate this definition, suppose we have an automated taxi that is learning to drive by watching a teacher. Each example includes not only a description of the current state, represented by the camera input and various measurements from sensors, but also the correct action to do in that state, obtained by "watching over the teacher's shoulder." Given sufficient examples, the induced hypothesis provides a reasonable approximation to a driving function that can be used to control the vehicle.

So far, we have made no commitment as to the way in which the hypothesis is represented. In the rest of this section, we shall discuss four basic categories of representations:

- *Attribute-based representations.* This category includes all *Boolean functions*—functions that provide a yes/no answer based on logical combinations of yes/no input attributes (Section II.A). Attributes can also have multiple values. *Decision trees* are the most commonly used attribute-based representation. Attribute-based representations could also be said to include neural networks and belief networks.

- *First-order logic.* This is a much more expressive logical language, including quantification and relations, allowing definitions of almost all commonsense and scientific concepts (Section II.B).

- *Neural networks.* These are continuous, nonlinear functions represented by a parameterized network of simple computing elements (Section II.C and Chapter 5).

- *Probabilistic functions.* These return a *probability distribution* over the possible output values for any given input, and are suitable for problems where there may be uncertainty as to the correct answer (Section II.D). *Belief networks* are the most commonly used probabilistic function representation.

The choice of representation for the desired function is probably the most important choice facing the designer of a learning agent. It affects both the nature of the learning algorithm and the feasibility of the learning problem. As with reasoning, in learning there is a fundamental trade-off between *expressiveness* (is the desired function representable in the representation language?) and *efficiency* (is the learning problem going to be tractable for a given choice of representation language?). If one chooses to learn sentences in an expressive language such as first-order logic, then one may have to pay a heavy penalty in terms of both computation time and the number of examples required to learn a good set of sentences.

In addition to a variety of function representations is a variety of algorithmic approaches to inductive learning. To some extent, these can be described in a way that is independent of the function representation. Because such descriptions can become rather abstract, we shall delay detailed discussion of the algorithms until we have specific representations with which to work. There are, however, some worthwhile distinctions to be made at this point:

- *Batch* versus *incremental* algorithms. A batch algorithm takes as input a set of examples and generates one or more hypotheses from the entire set; an incremental algorithm maintains a *current* hypothesis, or set of hypotheses, and *updates* it for each new example.

- *Least commitment* versus *current-best-hypothesis* (CBH) algorithms. A least commitment algorithm prefers to avoid committing to a particular hypothesis unless forced to by the data (Section II.B.2), whereas a CBH algorithm chooses a single hypothesis and updates it as necessary. The updating method used by CBH algorithms depends on their function representation. With a *continuous* space of functions (where hypotheses are partly or completely characterized by continuous-valued parameters) a *gradient descent* method can be used. Such methods attempt to reduce the inconsistency between hypothesis and data by gradual adjustment of parameters (Sections II.C and II.D). In a discrete space, methods based on *specialization* and *generalization* can be used to restore consistency (Section II.B.1).

A. Learning Attribute-Based Representations

Attribute-based representations are quite restricted, but they provide a good introduction to the area of inductive learning. We begin by showing how attributes can be used to describe examples and then cover the main methods used to represent and learn hypotheses.

In attribute-based representations, each example is described by a set of *attributes*, each of which takes on one of a fixed range of values. The *target attribute* (also called the *goal concept*) specifies the output of the desired function, also called the *classification* of the example. Attribute ranges can be *discrete* or *continuous*. Attributes with discrete ranges can be *Boolean* (two-valued) or *multivalued*. In cases with Boolean outputs, an example with a "yes" or "true" classification is called a *positive* example; an example with a "no" or "false" classification is called a *negative* example.

Consider the familiar problem of whether or not to wait for a table at a restaurant. The aim here is to learn a definition for the target attribute *WillWait*. In setting this up as a learning problem, we first have to decide what attributes are available to describe examples in the domain. Suppose we decide on the following list of attributes:

1. *Alternate*—whether or not there is a suitable alternative restaurant nearby.
2. *Bar*—whether or not there is a comfortable bar area to wait in.
3. *Fri/Sat*—true on Fridays and Saturdays.
4. *Hungry*—whether or not we are hungry.
5. *Patrons*—how many people are in the restaurant (values are None, Some, and Full).
6. *Price*—the restaurant's price range ($, $$, $$$).
7. *Raining*—whether or not it is raining outside.
8. *Reservation*—whether or not we made a reservation.
9. *Type*—the kind of restaurant (French, Italian, Thai, or Burger).
10. *WaitEstimate*—as given by the host (values are 0–10 minutes, 10–30, 30–60, >60).

Notice that the input attributes are a mixture of Boolean and multivalued attributes, whereas the target attribute is Boolean.

We'll call the 10 listed attributes $A_1 \ldots A_{10}$ for simplicity. A set of examples $X_1 \ldots X_m$ is shown in Table 1. The set of examples available for

TABLE 1   Examples for the Restaurant Domain

Example	A_1	A_2	A_3	A_4	A_5	A_6	A_7	A_8	A_9	A_{10}	Will Wait
X_1	Yes	No	No	Yes	Some	$$$	No	Yes	French	0–10	Yes
X_2	Yes	No	No	Yes	Full	$	No	No	Thai	30–60	No
X_3	No	Yes	No	No	Some	$	No	No	Burger	0–10	Yes
X_4	Yes	No	Yes	Yes	Full	$	No	No	Thai	10–30	Yes
X_5	Yes	No	Yes	No	Full	$$$	No	Yes	French	>60	No
X_6	No	Yes	No	Yes	Some	$$	Yes	Yes	Italian	0–10	Yes
X_7	No	Yes	No	No	None	$	Yes	No	Burger	0–10	No
. . .											

learning is called the *training set*. The induction problem is to take the training set, find a hypothesis that is consistent with it, and use the hypothesis to predict the target attribute value for new examples.

1. Decision Trees

Decision tree induction is one of the simplest and yet most successful forms of learning algorithm and has been extensively studied in both AI and statistics (Breiman, Friedman, Olshen, & Stone, 1984; Quinlan, 1986). A decision tree takes as input an example described by a set of attribute values and produces as output a Boolean or multivalued "decision." For simplicity we shall stick to the Boolean case. Each internal node in the tree corresponds to a test of the value of one of the properties, and the branches from the node are labeled with the possible values of the test. For a given example, the output of the decision tree is calculated by testing attributes in turn, starting at the root and following the branch labeled with the appropriate value. Each leaf node in the tree specifies the value to be returned if that leaf is reached. One possible decision tree for the restaurant problem is shown in Figure 2.

2. Expressiveness of Decision Trees

Like all attribute-based representations, decision trees are rather limited in what sorts of knowledge they can express. For example, we could not use a decision tree to express the condition

$$\exists s\; Nearby(s, r) \wedge Price(s, ps) \wedge Price(r, pr) \wedge Cheaper(ps, pr)$$

(is there a cheaper restaurant nearby?). Obviously, we can add the attribute *CheaperRestaurantNearby*, but this cannot work in general because we would have to precompute hundreds or thousands of such "derived" attributes.

Decision trees are fully expressive within the class of attribute-based languages. This can be shown trivially by constructing a tree with a differ-

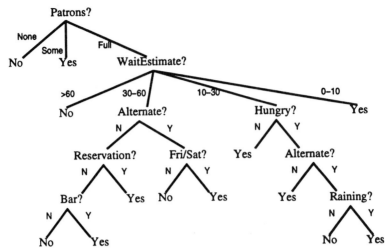

FIGURE 2   A decision tree for deciding whether or not to wait for a table.

ent path for every possible combination of attribute values, with the correct value for that combination at the leaf. Such a tree would be exponentially large in the number of attributes, but usually a smaller tree can be found. For some functions, however, decision trees are not good representations. Standard examples include *parity* functions and *threshold* functions.

Is any kind of representation efficient for all kinds of functions? Unfortunately, the answer is no. It is easy to show that with n descriptive attributes, there are 2^{2^n} distinct Boolean functions based on those attributes. A standard information–theoretic argument shows that almost all of these functions will require at least 2^n bits to represent them, *regardless of the representation chosen*. The figure of 2^{2^n} means that hypothesis spaces are very large. For example, with just 5 Boolean attributes, there are about 4 billion different functions to choose from. We shall need some ingenious algorithms to find consistent hypotheses in such a large space. One such algorithm is Quinlan's ID3, which we describe in the next section.

3. Inducing Decision Trees from Examples

There is, in fact, a trivial way to construct a decision tree that is consistent with all the examples. We simply add one complete path to a leaf for each example, with the appropriate attribute values and leaf value. This trivial tree fails to extract any pattern from the examples and so we cannot expect it to be able to extrapolate to examples it has not seen.

Finding a pattern means being able to describe a large number of cases in a concise way; that is, finding a small, consistent tree. This is an example of a general principle of inductive learning often called *Ockham's razor: the most likely hypothesis is the simplest one that is consistent with all observations.* Unfortunately, finding the *smallest* tree is an intractable problem, but with some simple heuristics we can do a good job of finding a smallish one.

The basic idea of decision-tree algorithms such as ID3 is to test the most important attribute first. By *most important,* we mean the one that makes the most difference to the classification of an example. [Various measures of "importance" are used, based on either the *information gain* (Quinlan, 1986) or the *minimum description length* criterion (Wallace & Patrick, 1993).] In this way, we hope to get to the correct classification with the smallest number of tests, meaning that all paths in the tree will be short and the tree will be small. ID3 chooses the best attribute as the root of the tree, then splits the examples into subsets according to their value for the attribute. Each of the subsets obtained by splitting on an attribute is essentially a new (but smaller) learning problem in itself, with one fewer attributes to choose from. The subtree along each branch is therefore constructed by calling ID3 recursively on the subset of examples.

The recursive process usually terminates when all the examples in the subset have the same classification. If some branch has no examples associated with it, that simply means that no such example has been observed, and we use a default value calculated from the majority classification at the node's parent. If ID3 runs out of attributes to use and there are still examples with different classifications, then these examples have exactly the same description, but different classifications. This can be caused by one of three things. First, some of the data are incorrect. Called *noise,* this occurs in either the descriptions or the classifications. Second, the data are correct, but the relationship between the descriptive attributes and the target attribute is genuinely nondeterministic and additional relevant information is lacking. Third, the set of attributes is insufficient to give an unambiguous classification. All the information is correct, but some relevant aspects are missing.

In a sense, the first and third cases are the same, because noise can be viewed as produced by an outside process that does not depend on the available attributes; if we could describe the process we could learn an exact function. As for what to *do* about the problem, one can use a majority vote for the leaf node classification or one can report a probabilistic prediction based on the proportion of examples with each value.

4. Assessing the Performance of the Learning Algorithm

A learning algorithm is good if it produces hypotheses that do a good job of predicting the classifications of unseen examples. In Section IV, we shall see how prediction quality can be assessed in advance. For now, we shall look at a methodology for assessing prediction quality after the fact. We can assess the quality of a hypothesis by checking its predictions against the correct classification once we know it. We do this on a set of examples known as the *test set*. The following methodology is usually adopted:

1. Collect a large set of examples.
2. Divide it into two disjoint sets U (training set) and V (test set).
3. Use the learning algorithm with examples U to generate a hypothesis H.
4. Measure the percentage of examples in V that are correctly classified by H.
5. Repeat steps 2 to 4 for different randomly selected training sets of various sizes.

The result of this is a set of data that can be processed to give the average prediction quality as a function of the size of the training set. This can be plotted on a graph, giving what is called the *learning curve* (sometimes called a *happy graph*) for the algorithm on the particular domain. The learning curve for ID3 with 100 restaurant examples is shown in Figure 3. Notice that, as the training set grows, the prediction quality increases. This is a good sign that there is indeed some pattern in the data and the learning algorithm is picking it up.

5. Noise, Overfitting, and Other Complications

We saw previously that, if two or more examples have the same descriptions but different classifications, then the ID3 algorithm must fail to find a

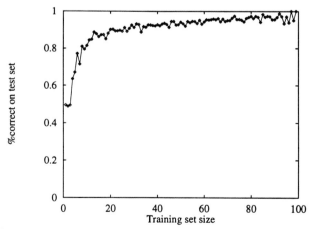

FIGURE 3   Graph showing the predictive performance of the decision tree algorithm on the restaurant data, as a function of the number of examples seen.

decision tree consistent with all the examples. In many real situations, some relevant information is unavailable and the examples will give the appearance of being "noisy." The solution we mentioned is to have each leaf report either the majority classification for its set of examples or the estimated probabilities of each classification using the relative frequencies.

Unfortunately, this is far from the whole story. It is quite possible, and in fact likely, that even when vital information is missing, the decision tree learning algorithm will find a decision tree consistent with all the examples. This is because the algorithm can use the *irrelevant* attributes, if any, to make spurious distinctions among the examples. Consider an extreme case: trying to predict the roll of a die. If the die is rolled once per day for 10 days, it is a trivial matter to find a spurious hypothesis that exactly fits the data if we use attributes such as *DayOfWeek, Temperature,* and so on. What we would like instead is that ID3 return a single leaf with probabilities close to $1/6$ for each roll, once it has seen enough examples.

This is a very general problem and occurs even when the target function is not at all random. Whenever there is a large set of possible hypotheses, one has to be careful not to use the resulting freedom to overfit the data. A complete mathematical treatment of overfitting is beyond the scope of this chapter. Here we present two simple techniques called *decision-tree pruning* and *cross-validation* that can be used to generate trees with an appropriate trade-off between size and accuracy.

Pruning works by preventing recursive splitting on attributes that are not clearly relevant. The question is, how do we detect an irrelevant attribute? Suppose we split a set of examples using an irrelevant attribute. Generally speaking, we would expect the resulting subsets to have roughly the same proportions of each class as the original set. A significant deviation from these proportions suggests that the attribute is significant. A standard statistical test for significance, such as the χ^2 test, can be used to decide whether or not to add the attribute to the tree (Quinlan, 1986). With this method, noise can be tolerated well. Pruning yields smaller trees with higher predictive accuracy, even when the data contains a large amount of noise.

The basic idea of cross-validation (Breiman et al., 1984) is to try to estimate how well the current hypothesis will predict unseen data. This is done by setting aside some fraction of the known data and using it to test the prediction performance of a hypothesis induced from the rest of the known data. This can be done repeatedly with different subsets of the data, with the results averaged. Cross-validation can be used in conjunction with any tree-construction method (including pruning) to select a tree with good prediction performance.

A number of additional issues have been addressed to broaden the applicability of decision-tree learning. These include missing attribute values, attributes with large numbers of values, and attributes with continuous values. The C4.5 system (Quinlan, 1993), a commercially available induction program, contains partial solutions to each of these problems. Decision trees have been used in a wide variety of practical applications, in many cases yielding systems with higher accuracy than that of human experts or hand-constructed systems.

B. Learning General Logical Representations

This section covers learning techniques for more general logical representations. We begin with a current-best-hypothesis algorithm based on specialization and generalization and then briefly describe how these techniques can be applied to build a least commitment algorithm. We then describe the algorithms used in inductive logic programming, which provide a general method for learning first-order logical representations.

1. Specialization and Generalization in Logical Representations

Many learning algorithms for logical representations, which form a discrete space, are based on the notions of specialization and generalization. These, in turn, are based on the idea of the *extension* of a predicate—the set of all examples for which the predicate holds true. *Generalization* is the process of altering a hypothesis to increase its extension. Generalization is an appropriate response to a *false negative* example—an example that the hypothesis predicts to be negative but is in fact positive. The converse operation, called *specialization,* is an appropriate response to a *false positive.*

These concepts are best understood by means of a diagram. Figure 4 shows the extension of a hypothesis as a "region" in space encompassing all examples predicted to be positive; if the region includes all the *actual* positive examples (shown as plus signs) and excludes the actual negative examples, then the hypothesis is consistent with the examples. In a current-best-

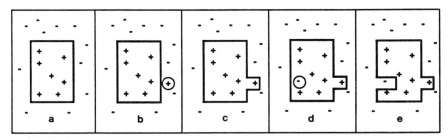

FIGURE 4   (a) A consistent hypothesis. (b) A false negative. (c) The hypothesis is generalized. (d) A false positive. (e) The hypothesis is specialized.

hypothesis algorithm, the process of adjustment shown in the figure continues incrementally as each new example is processed.

We have defined *generalization* and *specialization* as operations that change the *extension* of a hypothesis. In practice, they must be implemented as syntactic operations that change the hypothesis itself. Let us see how this works on the restaurant example, using the data in Table 1. The first example X_1 is positive. Since $Alternate(X_1)$ is true, let us assume an initial hypothesis

H_1: $\forall x$ $WillWait(x) \Leftrightarrow Alternate(x)$

The second example X_2 is negative. H_1 predicts it to be positive, so it is a false positive. We therefore need to specialize H_1. This can be done by adding an extra condition that will rule out X_2. One possibility is

H_2: $\forall x$ $WillWait(x) \Leftrightarrow Alternate(x) \wedge Patrons(x, Some)$

The third example H_3 is positive. H_2 predicts it to be negative, so it is a false negative. We therefore need to generalize H_2. This can be done by dropping the *Alternate* condition, yielding

H_3: $\forall x$ $WillWait(x) \Leftrightarrow Patrons(x, Some)$

The fourth example X_4 is positive. H_3 predicts it to be negative, so it is a false negative. We therefore need to generalize H_3. We cannot drop the *Patrons* condition, because that would yield an all-inclusive hypothesis that would be inconsistent with X_2. One possibility is to add a disjunct:

H_4: $\forall x$ $WillWait(x) \Leftrightarrow Patrons(x, Some) \vee [Patrons(x, Full) \wedge Fri/Sat(x)]$

Already, the hypothesis is starting to look reasonable. Obviously, there are other possibilities consistent with the first four examples, such as

H_4': $\forall x$ $WillWait(x) \Leftrightarrow Patrons(x, Some) \vee [Patrons(x, Full) \wedge WaitEstimate(x, 10-30)]$

At any point there may be several possible specializations or generalizations that can be applied. The choices made will not necessarily lead to the simplest hypothesis and may lead to an unrecoverable situation where no simple modification of the hypothesis is consistent with all of the data. In such cases, the program must backtrack to a previous choice point and try a different alternative. With a large number of instances and a large space, however, some difficulties arise. First, rechecking all the previous instances for each modification is very expensive. Second, backtracking in a large hypothesis space can be computationally intractable.

2. A Least Commitment Algorithm

Current best hypothesis algorithms are often inefficient because they must commit to a choice of hypothesis even when sufficient data are lacking; such choices must often be revoked at considerable expense. A *least commitment* algorithm can maintain a representation of *all* hypotheses consistent with the examples; this set of hypotheses is called a *version space*. When a new example is observed, the version space is updated by eliminating those hypotheses inconsistent with the example.

A compact representation of the version space can be constructed by taking advantage of the partial order imposed on the version space by the specialization/generalization dimension. A set of hypotheses can be represented by its most general and most specific *boundary sets,* called the *G-set* and *S-set*. Every member of the G-set is consistent with all observations so far, and there are no more general such hypotheses. Every member of the S-set is consistent with all observations so far, and there are no more specific such hypotheses.

When no examples have been seen, the version space is the entire hypothesis space. It is convenient to assume that the hypothesis space includes the all-inclusive hypothesis $Q(x) \Leftrightarrow True$ (whose extension includes all examples), and the all-exclusive hypothesis $Q(x) \Leftrightarrow False$ (whose extension is empty). Then, to represent the entire hypothesis space, we initialize the G-set to contain just *True,* and the S-set to contain just *False*. After initialization, the version space is updated to maintain the correct S- and G-sets, by specializing and generalizing their members as needed.

There are two principal drawbacks to the version-space approach. First, the version space will always become empty if the domain contains noise or if there are insufficient attributes for exact classification. Second, if we allow unlimited disjunction in the hypothesis space, the S-set will always contain a single most specific hypothesis; namely, the disjunction of the descriptions of the positive examples seen to date. Similarly, the G-set will contain just the negation of the disjunction of the descriptions of the negative examples. To date, no completely successful solution has been found for the problem of noise in version space algorithms. The problem of disjunction can be addressed by allowing limited forms of disjunction or including a *generalization hierarchy* of more general predicates. For example, instead of using the disjunction *WaitEstimate*$(x,$ 30–60$) \lor$ *WaitEstimate*$(x, >60)$, we might use the single literal *LongWait*(x).

The pure version space algorithm was first applied in the MetaDendral system, which was designed to learn rules for predicting how molecules would break into pieces in a mass spectrometer (Buchanan & Mitchell, 1978). MetaDendral was able to generate rules that were sufficiently novel to warrant publication in a journal of analytical chemistry—the first real scientific knowledge generated by a computer program.

3. Inductive Logic Programming

Inductive logic programming (ILP) is one of the newest subfields in AI. It combines inductive methods with the power of first-order logical representations, concentrating in particular on the representation of theories as logic programs. Over the last five years it has become a major part of the research agenda in machine learning. This has happened for two reasons. First, it offers a rigorous approach to the general induction problem. Second, it offers complete algorithms for inducing general, first-order theories from examples—algorithms that can learn successfully in domains where attribute-based algorithms fail completely. ILP is a highly technical field, relying on some fairly advanced material from the study of computational logic. We therefore cover only the basic principles of the two major approaches, referring the reader to the literature for more details.

a. An Example

The general problem in ILP is to find a hypothesis that, together with whatever background knowledge is available, is sufficient to explain the observed examples. To illustrate this, we shall use the problem of learning family relationships. The observations will consist of an extended family tree, described in terms of *Mother, Father,* and *Married* relations, and *Male* and *Female* properties. The target predicates will be such things as *Grandparent, BrotherInLaw,* and *Ancestor.*

The example descriptions include facts such as

Father(Philip, Charles)	Father(Philip, Anne)	. . .
Mother(Mum, Margaret)	Mother(Mum, Elizabeth)	. . .
Married(Diana, Charles)	Married(Elizabeth, Philip)	. . .
Male(Philip)	Female(Anne)	. . .

If Q is *Grandparent,* say, then the example classifications are sentences such as

Grandparent(Mum, Charles)	Grandparent(Elizabeth, Beatrice) . . .
¬Grandparent(Mum, Harry)	¬Grandparent(Spencer, Peter)

Suppose, for a moment, that the agent has no background knowledge. One possible hypothesis that explains the example classification is

$$Grandparent(x, y) \Leftrightarrow [\exists z\, Mother(x, z) \land Mother(z, y)]$$
$$\lor [\exists z\, Mother(x, z) \land Father(z, y)]$$
$$\lor [\exists z\, Father(x, z) \land Mother(z, y)]$$
$$\lor [\exists z\, Father(x, z) \land Father(z, y)]$$

Notice that attribute-based representations are completely incapable of representing a definition for *Grandfather,* which is essentially a *relational* concept. One of the principal advantages of ILP algorithms is their applicability to a much wider range of problems.

ILP algorithms come in two main types. The first type is based on the idea of *inverting* the reasoning process by which hypotheses explain observations. The particular kind of reasoning process that is inverted is called *resolution*. An inference such as

> *Cat* $\Rightarrow$ *Mammal* and *Mammal* $\Rightarrow$ *Animal*
>
> therefore *Cat* $\Rightarrow$ *Animal*

is a simple example of one step in a resolution proof. Resolution has the property of *completeness:* any sentence in first-order logic that follows from a given knowledge base can be proved by a sequence of resolution steps. Thus, if a hypothesis *H* explains the observations, then there must be a resolution proof to this effect. Therefore, if we start with the observations and apply *inverse resolution* steps, we should be able to find all hypotheses that explain the observations. The key is to find a way to run the resolution step backward—to generate one or both of the two premises, given the conclusion and perhaps the other premise (Muggleton & Buntine, 1988). Inverse resolution algorithms and related techniques (Muggleton, 1991) can learn the definition of *Grandfather* and even recursive concepts such as *Ancestor*. They have been used in a number of applications, including predicting protein structure and identifying previously unknown chemical structures in carcinogens.

The second approach to ILP is essentially a generalization of the techniques of decision-tree learning to the first-order case. Rather than starting from the observations and working backward, we start with a very general rule and gradually specialize it so that it fits the data. This is essentially what happens in decision-tree learning, where a decision tree is gradually grown until it is consistent with the observations. In the first-order case, we use predicates with variables, instead of attributes, and the hypothesis is a set of logical rules instead of a decision tree. FOIL (Quinlan, 1990) was one of the first programs to use this approach.

Given the discussion of prior knowledge in the introduction, the reader will certainly have noticed that a little bit of background knowledge would help in the representation of the *Grandparent* definition. For example, if the agent's knowledge base included the sentence

> *Parent*(x, y) $\Leftrightarrow$ [*Mother*(x, y) $\lor$ *Father*(x, y)]

then the definition of Grandparent would be reduced to

> *Grandparent*(x, y) $\Leftrightarrow$ [$\exists z$ *Parent*(x, z) $\land$ *Parent*(z, y)]

This shows how background knowledge can dramatically reduce the size of hypothesis required to explain the observations, thereby dramatically simplifying the learning problem.

C. Learning Neural Networks

The study of so-called artificial neural networks is one of the most active areas of AI and cognitive science research (see Hertz, Krogh, & Palmer, 1991 for a thorough treatment, and Chapter 5 of this volume). Here, we provide a brief note on the basic principles of neural network learning algorithms.

Viewed as a performance element, a neural network is a nonlinear function with a large set of parameters called *weights*. Figure 5 shows an example network with two inputs (a_1 and a_2, the activation levels of nodes I_1 and I_2) that calculates the following function:

$$a_5 = g_5(w_{35}a_3 + w_{45}a_4)$$
$$= g_5[w_{35}g_3(w_{13}a_1 + w_{23}a_2) + w_{45}g_4(w_{14}a_1 + w_{24}a_2)]$$

where g_i is the activation function and a_i is the output of node i. Given a training set of examples, the output of the neural network on those examples can be compared with the correct values to give the *training error*. The total training error can be written as a function of the weights and then differentiated with respect to the weights to find the *error gradient*. By making changes in the weights to reduce the error, one obtains a *gradient descent* algorithm. The well-known *back-propagation* algorithm (Bryson & Ho, 1969) shows that the error gradient can be calculated using a local propagation method.

Like decision-tree algorithms, neural network algorithms are subject to overfitting. Unlike decision trees, the gradient descent process can get stuck in local minima in the error surface. This means that the standard back-propagation algorithm is not guaranteed to find a good fit to the training examples even if one exists. Stochastic search techniques such as *simulated annealing* can be used to guarantee eventual convergence.

The preceding analysis assumes a fixed structure for the network. With a

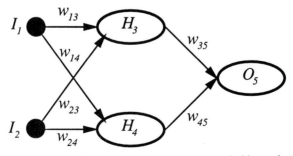

FIGURE 5.   A simple neural network with two inputs, two hidden nodes, and one output node.

sufficient, but sometimes prohibitive, number of hidden nodes and connections, a fixed structure can learn an arbitrary function of the inputs. An alternative approach is to construct a network incrementally with the minimum number of nodes that allows a good fit to the data, in accordance with Ockham's razor.

D. Learning Probabilistic Representations

Over the last decade, probabilistic representations have come to dominate the field of *reasoning under uncertainty,* which underlies the operation of most expert systems and any agent that must make decisions with incomplete information. *Belief networks* (also called *causal networks* and *Bayesian networks*) are currently the principal tool for representing probabilistic knowledge (Pearl, 1988). They provide a concise representation of general probability distributions over a set of propositional (or multivalued) random variables. The basic task of a belief network is to calculate the probability distribution for the unknown variables, given observed values for the remaining variables. Belief networks containing several thousand nodes and links have been used successfully to represent medical knowledge and to achieve high levels of diagnostic accuracy (Heckerman, 1990), among other tasks.

The basic unit of a belief network is the *node,* which corresponds to a single random variable. Associated with each node is a *conditional probability table* (CPT), which gives the conditional probability of each possible value of the variable, given each possible combination of values of the parent nodes. Figure 6(a) shows a node *C* with two Boolean parents *A* and *B.* Figure 6(b) shows an example network. Intuitively, the topology of the network reflects the notion of *direct causal influences:* the occurrence of an

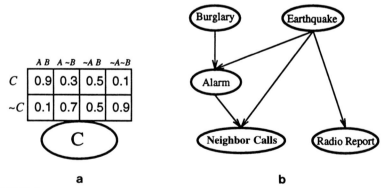

a   b

FIGURE 6   (a) A belief network node with associated conditional probability table. The table gives the conditional probability of each possible value of the variable, given each possible combination of values of the parent nodes. (b) A simple belief network.

earthquake or burglary directly influences whether or not a burglar alarm goes off, which in turn influences whether or not your neighbor calls you at work to tell you about it. Formally speaking, the topology indicates that a node is conditionally independent of its ancestors given its parents; for example, given that the alarm has gone off, the probability that the neighbor calls is independent of whether or not a burglary has taken place.

The probabilistic, or Bayesian, approach to learning views the problem of constructing hypotheses from data as a question of finding the most probable hypotheses, given the data. Predictions are then made from the hypotheses, using the posterior probabilities of the hypotheses to weight the predictions. In the worst case, full Bayesian learning may require enumerating the entire hypothesis space. The most common approximation is to use just a single hypothesis—that most probable given the observations. This is often called a *MAP* (maximum a posteriori) *hypothesis*.

According to Bayes's rule, the probability of a hypothesis H_i given data D is proportional to both the *prior probability* of the hypothesis and the *probability of the data given the hypothesis:*

$$P(H_i|D) \propto P(H_i)P(D|H_i) \tag{1}$$

The term $P(D|H_i)$ describes how good a "fit" there is between hypothesis and data. Therefore, this equation prescribes a trade-off between the degree of fit and the prior probability of the hypothesis. Hence, a direct connection is made between the prior and the intuitive preference for simpler hypotheses (Ockham's razor). In the case of belief networks, a *uniform* prior is often used. With a uniform prior, we need choose an H_i that only maximizes $P(D|H_i)$—the hypothesis that makes the data most likely. This is called a *maximum likelihood* (ML) *hypothesis.*

The learning problem for belief networks comes in several varieties. The structure of the network can be *known* or *unknown* and the variables in the network can be *observable* or *hidden*.

• *Known structure, fully observable.* In this case, the only learnable part is the set of CPTs. These can be estimated directly using the statistics of the set of examples (Spiegelhalter & Lauritzen, 1990).

• *Unknown structure, fully observable.* In this case the problem is to reconstruct the topology of the network. An MAP analysis of the most likely network structure given the data has been carried out by Cooper and Herskovits (1992), among others. The resulting algorithms are capable of recovering fairly large networks from large data sets with a high degree of accuracy.

• *Known structure, hidden variables.* This case is analogous to, although more general than, neural network learning. The "weights" are the entries in the conditional probability tables, and (in the ML approach) the object is to find the values that maximize the probability of the observed data. This probability can be written as a mathematical function of the CPT values and differentiated to find a gradient, thus providing a gradient descent learning algorithm (Neal, 1992; Russell, Binder, Koller, & Kanazawa, 1995).

- *Unknown structure, hidden variables.* When some variables are sometimes or always unobservable, the techniques just mentioned for recovering structure become difficult to apply, because they essentially require averaging over all possible combinations of values of the unknown variables. At present no good, general algorithms are known for this problem.

Belief networks provide many of the advantages of neural networks—a continuous function space, gradient descent learning using local propagation, massively parallel computation, and so on. They possess additional advantages because of the clear probabilistic semantics associated with individual nodes. In future years, one expects to see a fusion of research in the two fields.

III. LEARNING IN SITUATED AGENTS

Section II addressed the problem of learning to predict the output of a function from its input, given a collection of examples with known inputs and outputs. This section covers the possible kinds of learning available to a "situated agent," for which inputs are percepts and outputs are actions. In some cases, the agent will have access to a set of correctly labeled examples of situations and actions. This is usually called *apprenticeship learning,* since the learning system is essentially "watching over the shoulder" of an expert. Pomerleau's work on learning to drive essentially uses this approach, training a neural network to control a vehicle by watching many hours of video input with associated steering actions as executed by a human driver (Pomerleau, 1993). Sammut, Hurst, Kedzier, and Michie (1992) used a similar methodology to train an autopilot using decision trees.

Typically, a collection of correctly labeled situation–action examples will not be available, so the agent needs some capability for *unsupervised learning.* It is true that all environments provide percepts, so that an agent can eventually build a predictive model of its environment. However, this is not enough for choosing actions. In the absence of knowledge of the utility function, the agent must at least receive some sort of *reward* or *reinforcement* that enables it to distinguish between success and failure. Rewards can be received during the agent's activities in the environment or in terminal states that correspond to the end of an episode. For example, a program that is learning to play backgammon can be told when it has won or lost (terminal states), but it can also be given feedback during the game as to how well it is doing. Rewards can be viewed as percepts of a sort, but the agent must be "hardwired" to recognize that percept as a reward rather than as just another sensory input. Thus animals seem to be hardwired to recognize pain and hunger as negative rewards and pleasure and food as positive rewards.

The term *reinforcement learning* is used to cover all forms of learning from rewards. In many domains, this may be the only feasible way to train a program to perform at high levels. For example, in game playing, it is very hard for human experts to write accurate functions for position evaluation. Instead, the program can be told when it has won or lost and can use this information to learn an evaluation function that gives reasonably accurate estimates of the probability of winning from any given position. Similarly, it is extremely hard to program a robot to juggle; yet given appropriate rewards every time a ball is dropped or caught, the robot can learn to juggle by itself.

Reinforcement learning can occur in several possible settings:

• The environment can be fully observable or only partially observable. In a fully observable environment, states can be identified with percepts; whereas in a partially observable environment the agent must maintain some internal state to try to keep track of the environment.

• The environment can be *deterministic* or *stochastic*. In a deterministic environment, actions have only a single outcome; whereas in a stochastic environment, they can have several possible outcomes.

• The agent can begin with a *model*—knowledge of the environment and the effects of its actions—or it may have to learn this information as well as utility information.

• Rewards can be received only in terminal states or in any state.

Furthermore, as we mentioned in Section I, there are several different basic designs for agents. Since the agent will be receiving rewards that relate to utilities, there are two basic designs to consider. *Utility-based* agents learn a utility function on states (or state histories) and use it to select actions that maximize the expected utility of their outcomes. *Action-value* or Q-learning agents (Watkins & Dayan, 1993) learn the expected utility of taking a given action in a given state.

An agent that learns utility functions must also have a model of the environment to make decisions, since it must know the states to which its actions will lead. For example, to use a backgammon evaluation function, a backgammon program must know what are its legal moves and *how they affect the board position*. Only in this way can it apply the utility function to the outcome states. An agent that learns an action–value function, on the other hand, need not have such a model. As long as it knows the allowable actions, it can compare their values directly without having to consider their outcomes. Action-value learners can therefore be slightly simpler in design than utility learners. On the other hand, because they do not know where their actions lead, they cannot look ahead; this can seriously restrict their ability to learn.

Reinforcement learning usually takes place in stochastic environments, so we begin with a brief discussion of how such environments are modeled, how such models are learned, and how they are used in the performance element. Section III.B addresses the problem of learning utility functions, which has been studied in AI since the earliest days of the field. Section III.C discusses the learning of action-value functions.

A. Learning and Using Models of Uncertain Environments

In reinforcement learning, environments are usually conceived of as being in one of a discrete set of *states*. Actions cause transitions between states. A complete model of an environment specifies the probability that the environment will be in state j if action a is executed in state i. This probability is denoted by M_{ij}^a. The most basic representation of a model M is as a table, indexed by a pair of states and an action. If the model is viewed as a function, from the state pair and the action to a probability, then obviously it can be represented by any suitable representation for probabilistic functions, such as belief networks or neural networks. The environment description is completed by the *reward $R(i)$* associated with each state. Together, M and R specify what is technically known as a *Markov decision process* (MDP). There is a huge literature on MDPs and the associated methods of *dynamic programming,* beginning in the late 1950s with the work of Bellman and Howard (see Bertsekas, 1987, for a thorough introduction). Although the definitions might seem rather technical, these models capture many general problems such as survival and reproduction, game playing, foraging, hunting, and so on.

Figure 7(a) shows a simple example of a stochastic environment on a 3 × 3 grid. When the agent tries to move to a neighboring state (arrows from each of the four segments of the state show motion in each of four directions), it reaches that state with probability 0.9. With probability 0.1, perhaps due to a sticky right wheel, the agent ends up 90 degrees to the right of where it was headed. Actions attempting to "leave" the grid have no effect (think of this as "bumping into a wall"). The terminal states are shown with rewards ±1, and all other states have a reward of −0.01; that is, there is a small cost for moving or sitting still.

It is normally stipulated that the ideal behavior for an agent is that which maximizes the expected total reward until a terminal state is reached. A *policy* assigns an action to each possible state, and the *utility* of a state is

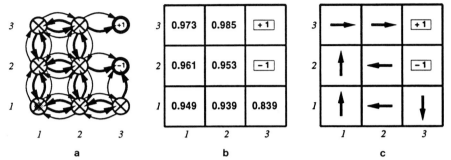

FIGURE 7   (a) A simple stochastic environment, with transitions shown. Heavy arrows correspond to a probability of 0.9, light arrows 0.1. Transitions to the same state are not shown. Each state has an associated reward of −0.01, except the terminal states (3, 3) and (3, 2) which have rewards of +1 and −1. The start state is (1, 1). (b) The exact utility values, as calculated in the text. (c) The optimal policy.

defined as the expected total reward until termination, starting at that state and using an optimal policy. If $U(i)$ is the utility of state i, then the following equation relates the utilities of neighboring states:

$$U(i) = R(i) + \max_a \sum_j M^a_{ij} U(j) \qquad (2)$$

In English, this says that the utility of a state is the reward for being in the state plus the expected total reward from the next state onward, given an optimal action. Figure 7(b) shows the utilities of all the states, and Figure 7(c) shows the optimal policy. Notice that the agent must carefully balance the need to get to the positive-reward terminal state as quickly as possible against the danger of falling accidentally into the negative-reward terminal state. With a low per-step cost of 0.01, the agent prefers to avoid the −1 state at the expense of taking the long way around. If the per-step cost is raised to 0.1, it turns out to be better to take the shortest path and risk death.

   Value iteration and *policy iteration* are the two basic methods for finding solutions to Eq. (2) in fully observable environments. Briefly, value iteration begins with randomly assigned utilities and iteratively updates them using the update equation

$$U(i) \leftarrow R(i) + \max_a \sum_j M^a_{ij} U(j) \qquad (3)$$

Policy iteration works similarly, except that it updates the policy instead of the utility estimates. Both techniques can be shown to converge on optimal values except in pathological environments.

When the environment is not fully observable, the problem (now a partially observable Markov decision process, or POMDP) is still more difficult. For example, suppose the agent has sensors that detect only an adjacent wall in the up and down directions and nothing else. In that case, the agent can distinguish only three states (top, middle, and bottom) and can easily get lost since its actions have stochastic effects. Exact solution of even medium-sized POMDPs is generally considered infeasible.

The next question is how to learn the model. In each *training sequence,* the agent executes a series of actions and receives a series of percepts, eventually reaching a terminal state. Considering the environment in Figure 7(a), a typical set of training sequences might look like this:

$$(1,1)\xrightarrow{U}(1,2)\xrightarrow{U}(1,3)\xrightarrow{R}(1,2)\xrightarrow{U}(1,3)\xrightarrow{R}(1,2)\xrightarrow{R}(1,1)\xrightarrow{U}(1,2)\xrightarrow{U}(2,2)\xrightarrow{U}(3,2)\underline{-1}$$
$$(1,1)\xrightarrow{U}(1,2)\xrightarrow{U}(1,3)\xrightarrow{R}(2,3)\xrightarrow{R}(2,2)\xrightarrow{L}(2,3)\xrightarrow{R}(3,3)\underline{+1}$$
$$(1,1)\xrightarrow{U}(2,1)\xrightarrow{L}(1,1)\xrightarrow{U}(2,1)\xrightarrow{L}(2,2)\xrightarrow{U}(2,3)\xrightarrow{R}(2,2)\xrightarrow{U}(3,2)\underline{-1}$$
$$\cdots$$

where *U, D, L, R* are the four possible directions of action.

When the environment is fully observable, the agent knows exactly what state it is in, which action it executes and which state it reaches as a result. It can therefore generate a set of labeled examples of the transition function M simply by moving around in the environment and recording its experiences. A tabular representation of M can be constructed by keeping statistics on each entry in the table. Over time, these will converge to the correct values. In an environment with more than a few states, however, this will require far too many examples. Instead, the agent can use a standard inductive algorithm to process the examples, using a more general representation of M such as a neural network, belief network, or set of logical descriptions. In this way, it is possible to build a fairly accurate approximation to M from a small number of examples.

Notice that the agent's own actions are responsible for its experiences. The agent therefore has two conflicting goals: maximizing its rewards over some short-term horizon and learning more about its environment so that it can gain greater rewards in the long term. This is the classical *exploration* versus *exploitation* trade-off. Formal models of the problem, known as *bandit problems,* can be solved only when there is some prior assumption about the kinds of environments one might expect to be in and the levels of reward one might expect to find in unexplored territory (Berry & Fristedt, 1985). In practice, approximate techniques are used, such as assuming that unknown states carry a large reward or adding a stochastic element to the action selection process so that eventually all states are explored.

When the environment is only partially observable, the learning problem is much more difficult. Although the agent has access to examples of the form "current percept $\xrightarrow{A}$ new percept," each percept does not identify the state. If actions are omitted from the problem, so that the agent passively observes the world going by, we have what is called a *Hidden Markov model* (HMM) learning problem. The classical Baum–Welch algorithm for this problem is described in Baum, Petrie, Soules, & Weiss (1970), with recent contributions by Stolcke and Omohundro (1994). HMM learning systems are currently the best available methods for several tasks, including speech recognition and DNA sequence interpretation.

B. Learning Utilities

There are two principal approaches to learning utilities in the reinforcement learning setting. The "classical" technique simply combines the value iteration algorithm, Eq. (3), with a method for learning the transition model for the environment. After each new observation, the transition model is updated, then value iteration is applied to make the utilities consistent with the model. As the environment model approaches the correct model, the utility estimates will converge to the correct utilities.

The classical approach makes the best possible use of each observation, but full value iteration after each observation can be very expensive. The key insight behind *temporal difference learning* (Sutton, 1988) is to use the *observed* transitions to gradually adjust the utility estimates of the observed states so that they agree with Eq. (2). In this way, the agent avoids excessive computation dedicated to computing utilities for states that may never occur.

Suppose that the agent observes a transition from state i to state j, where currently $U(i) = -0.5$ and $U(j) = +0.5$. This suggests that we should consider increasing $U(i)$ a little, to make it agree better with its successor. This can be achieved using the following updating rule:

$$U(i) \leftarrow U(i) + \alpha[R(i) + U(j) - U(i)] \tag{4}$$

where α is the *learning rate* parameter. Because this update rule uses the difference in utilities between successive states, it is often called the *temporal-difference* or TD equation.

The basic idea of all temporal-difference methods is to first define the conditions that hold locally when the utility estimates are correct and then to write an update equation that moves the estimates toward this ideal "equilibrium" equation. It can be shown that Eq. (4) does in fact cause the agent to reach the equilibrium given by Eq. (2) (Sutton, 1988). The classical and temporal-difference approaches are actually closely related. Both try to make local adjustments to the utility estimates in order to make each state

"agree" with its successors. Moore and Atkeson (1993) analyze the relationship in depth and propose effective algorithms for large state spaces.

C. Learning the Value of Actions

An agent that learns utilities and a model can use them to make decisions by
choosing the action that maximizes the expected utility of the outcome
states. Decisions can also be made using a direct representation of the value
of each action in each state. This is called an *action-value* function or *Q-value*.
We shall use the notation $Q(a, i)$ to denote the value of doing action a in state i.
Q-values play an important role in reinforcement learning for two reasons:
first, like condition–action rules, they suffice for decision making without
the use of a model; second, unlike condition–action rules, they can be
learned directly from reward feedback.

As with utilities, we can write an equation that must hold at equilibrium
when the Q-values are correct:

$$Q(a, i) = R(i) + \sum_j M_{ij}^a \max_{a'} Q(a', j) \qquad (5)$$

By analogy with value iteration, a Q-iteration algorithm can be constructed
that calculates exact Q-values given an estimated model. This does, however, require that a model be learned as well. The temporal-difference approach, on the other hand, requires no model. The update equation for TD
Q-learning is

$$Q(a, i) \leftarrow Q(a, i) + \alpha[R(i) + \max_{a'} Q(a', j) - Q(a, i)] \qquad (6)$$

which is calculated after each transition from state i to state j.

One might wonder why one should bother with learning utilities and
models, when Q-learning has the same effect without the need for a model.
The answer lies in the compactness of the representation. For many environments, the size of the model + utility representation is much smaller
than the size of a Q-value representation of equal accuracy. This means that
it can be learned from many fewer examples. This is perhaps the most
important reason why intelligent agents, including humans, seem to work
with explicit models of their environments.

D. Generalization in Reinforcement Learning

We have already mentioned the need to use generalized representations of
the environment model to handle large state spaces. The same considerations apply to learning U and Q. Consider, for example, the problem of
learning to play backgammon. The game is only a tiny subset of the real

world, yet contains approximately 10^{50} states. By examining only 1 in 10^{44} of the possible backgammon states, however, it is possible to learn a utility function that allows a program to play as well as any human (Tesauro, 1992). Reinforcement learning methods that use inductive generalization over states are said to do *input generalization*. Any of the learning methods in Section II can be used.

Let us now consider exactly how the inductive learning problem should be formulated. In the TD approach, one can apply inductive learning directly to the values that would be inserted into the U or Q tables by the update rules, Eqs. (4) and (6). These can be used instead as labeled examples for a learning algorithm. Since the agent will need to use the learned function on the next update, the learning algorithm will need to be incremental.

One can also take advantage of the fact that the TD update rules provide small changes in the value of a given state. This is especially true if the function to be learned is characterized by a vector of weights $\mathbf{w}$ (as in neural networks). Rather than update a single tabulated value of U, as in Eq. (4), we simply adjust the weights to try to reduce the temporal difference between successive states. Suppose that the parameterized utility function is $U_{\mathbf{w}}(i)$. Then after a transition $i \rightarrow j$, we apply the following update rule:

$$\mathbf{w} \leftarrow \mathbf{w} + \alpha[r + U_{\mathbf{w}}(j) - U_{\mathbf{w}}(i)]\nabla_{\mathbf{w}}U_{\mathbf{w}}(i) \qquad (7)$$

This form of updating performs gradient descent in weight space, trying to minimize the observed local error in the utility estimates. A similar update rule can be used for Q-learning. Since the utility and action-value functions typically have real-valued outputs, neural networks and other algebraic function representations are an obvious candidate for the performance element. Decision-tree learning algorithms can also be used as long as they provide real-value output, but they cannot use the gradient descent method.

The most significant applications of reinforcement learning to date have used a known, generalized model and learned a generalized representation of the utility function. The first significant application of reinforcement learning was also the first significant learning program of any kind—Samuel's checker player (Samuel, 1963). Samuel first used a weighted linear function for the evaluation of positions, using up to 16 terms at any one time. He applied Eq. (7) to update the weights. The program was provided with a model in the form of a legal-move generator for checkers.

Tesauro's TD-gammon system (Tesauro, 1992) forcefully illustrates the potential of reinforcement learning techniques. In earlier work, he had tried to learn a neural network representation of $Q(a, i)$ directly from examples of moves labeled with relative values by a human expert. This resulted in a program, called *Neurogammon,* that was strong by computer standards but not competitive with human experts. The TD-gammon project, on the other hand, was an attempt to learn from self-play alone. The only reward signal was given at the end of each game. The evaluation function was represented by a neural network. Simply by repeated application of Eq. (7) over the course of 200,000 games, TD-gammon learned to play considerably better than Neurogammon, even though the input representation contained just the raw board position with no computed features. When precomputed features were added to the input representation, a larger network was able, after 300,000 training games, to reach a standard of play comparable with the top three human players worldwide.

Reinforcement learning has also been applied successfully to robotic control problems. Beginning with early work by Michie and Chambers (1968), who developed an algorithm that learned to balance a long pole with a moving support, the approach has been to provide a reward to the robot when it succeeds in its control task. The main difficulty in this area is the continuous nature of the problem space. Sophisticated methods are needed to generate appropriate partitions of the state space so that reinforcement learning can be applied.

IV. THEORETICAL MODELS OF LEARNING

Learning means behaving better as a result of experience. We have shown several algorithms for inductive learning and explained how they fit into an agent. The main unanswered question was posed in Section II: how can one possibly know that one's learning algorithm has produced a theory that will correctly predict the future? In terms of the definition of inductive learning, how do we know that the hypothesis h is close to the target function f if we do not know what f is?

These questions have been pondered for several centuries, but unless we find some answers machine learning will, at best, be puzzled by its own success. This section briefly explains the three major approaches taken. *Identification in the limit* refers to the capability of a learning system to eventually converge on the correct model of its environment. It is shown that for some classes of environment this is not possible. *Kolmogorov complexity* provides a formal basis for Ockham's razor—the intuitive preference for simplicity. *Computational learning theory* is a more recent theory that attempts to address three questions. First, can it be shown that any particular hypothesis has *predictive* power? Second, how many examples need be observed before a learning system can predict correctly with high probability? Third, what limits does computational complexity place on the kinds of things that can be learned? This section will focus mainly on these questions.

A. Identification of Functions in the Limit

Early work in computer science on the problem of induction was strongly influenced by concepts from the philosophy of science. Popper's theory of falsificationism (Popper, 1962, Chap. 10) held that "we can learn from our mistakes—in fact, *only* from our mistakes." A scientific hypothesis is just a hypothesis; when it is proven incorrect, we learn something because we can generate a new hypothesis that is better than the previous one (see the current-best-hypothesis algorithm described earlier). One is naturally led to ask whether this process terminates with a true theory of reality. Gold (1967) turned this into the formal, mathematical question of *identification in the limit*. The idea is to assume that the true theory comes from some class of theories and to ask whether any member of that class will eventually be identified as correct, using a Popperian algorithm in which all the theories are placed in a fixed order (usually "simplest first") and falsified one by one. A thorough study of identification algorithms and their power may be found in Osherson, Stob, and Weinstein (1986). Unfortunately, the theory of identification in the limit does not tell us much about the predictive power of a given hypothesis; furthermore, the numbers of examples required for identification are often astronomical.

B. Simplicity and Kolmogorov Complexity

The idea of simplicity certainly seems to capture a vital aspect of induction. If an hypothesis is very simple but explains a large number of different observations, then it is reasonable to suppose that it has captured some regularity in the underlying environment. This insight resisted formalization for centuries because the measure of simplicity seems to depend on the particular language chosen to express the hypothesis. Early work by Solomonoff in the 1950s and 1960s, and later (independent) work by Kolmogorov and Chaitin used universal Turing machines (UTMs) to provide a mathematical basis for the idea. In this approach, an hypothesis is viewed as a *program* for a UTM, and observations are viewed as *output* from the execution of the program. The best hypothesis is the *shortest* program for the UTM that produces the observations as output. Although there are many different UTMs, each of which might have a different shortest program, this can make a difference of at most a *constant* amount in the length of the shortest program, since any UTM can encode any other with a program of finite length. Because this is true *regardless* of the number of observations, the theory shows that any bias in the simplicity measure will eventually be overcome by the regularities in the data, so that all the shortest UTM programs will make essentially the same predictions. This theory, variously called *descriptional complexity, Kolmogorov complexity,* or *minimum description length* (MDL) theory, is discussed in depth in Li and Vitanyi (1993).

In practice, the formal definition just given is relaxed somewhat, because the problem of finding the shortest program is undecidable. In most applications, one attempts to pick an encoding that is "unbiased," in that it does not include any special representations for particular hypotheses, but that allows one to take advantage of the kinds of regularities one expects to see in the domain. For example, in encoding decision trees, one often expects to find a subtree repeated in several places in the tree. A more compact encoding can be obtained if one allows the subtree to be encoded by the same, short name for each occurrence.

A version of descriptional complexity theory can be obtained by taking the log of Eq. (1):

$$\log P(H_i|D) = \log P(D|H_i) + \log P(H_i) + c \equiv L(D|H_i) + L(H_i) + c$$

where $L(\cdot)$ is the length (in bits) of a Shannon encoding of its argument, and $L(D|H_i)$ is the additional number of bits needed to describe the data given the hypothesis. This is the standard formula used to choose an MDL hypothesis. Notice that rather than simply choosing the shortest hypothesis, the formula includes a term that allows for some error in predicting the data [$L(D|H_i)$ is taken to be 0 when the data is predicted perfectly]. By balancing the length of the hypothesis against its error, MDL approaches can prevent the problem of overfitting described previously. Notice that the choice of an encoding for hypotheses corresponds exactly to the choice of a prior in the Bayesian approach: shorter hypotheses have a higher prior probability. Furthermore, the approach produces the same choice of hypothesis as the Popperian identification algorithm if hypotheses are enumerated in order of size.

C. Computational Learning Theory

Unlike the theory of identification in the limit, computational learning theory does not insist that the learning agent find the "one true law" governing its environment but instead that it find a hypothesis with a certain degree of predictive accuracy. It also brings sharply into focus the trade-off between the expressiveness of the hypothesis language and the complexity of learning. Computational learning theory was initiated by the seminal work of Valiant (1984), but also has roots in the subfield of statistics called *uniform convergence theory* (Vapnik, 1982). The underlying principle is the following: any hypothesis that is seriously wrong will almost certainly be "found out" with high probability after a small number of examples, because it will make an incorrect prediction. Thus any hypothesis that is consistent with a sufficiently large set of training examples is unlikely to be seriously wrong; that is, it must be probably approximately correct (PAC). For this reason, computational learning theory is also called *PAC learning*.

The preceding argument contains some subtleties. The main question is the connection between the training and the test examples—after all, we want the hypothesis to be approximately correct on the test set, not just on the training set. The key assumption, introduced by Valiant, is that the training and test sets are drawn randomly from the same population of examples using the same probability distribution. This is called the *stationarity assumption*. Without this assumption, the theory can make no claims at all about the future because there would be no necessary connection between future and past. The stationarity assumption amounts to supposing that the process that selects examples is not malevolent. Obviously, if the training set consists only of weird examples—two-headed dogs, for instance—then the learning algorithm cannot help but make unsuccessful generalizations about how to recognize dogs.

To put these insights into practice, we shall need some notation. Let $\mathbf{X}$ be the set of all possible examples; D, be the distribution from which examples are drawn; $\mathbf{H}$, be the set of possible hypotheses; and m, be the number of examples in the training set. Initially we shall assume that the true function f is a member of $\mathbf{H}$. Now we can define the *error* of an hypothesis h with respect to the true function f given a distribution D over the examples:

$$\text{error}(h) = P[h(x) \neq f(x) \mid x \text{ drawn from } D]$$

Essentially this is the same quantity being measured experimentally by the learning curves shown earlier.

An hypothesis h is called *approximately correct* if $\text{error}(h) \leq \epsilon$, where ϵ is a small constant. The plan of attack is to show that, after seeing m examples, with high probability all consistent hypotheses will be approximately correct. One can think of an approximately correct hypothesis as being "close" to the true function in hypothesis space—it lies inside what is called the ϵ-*ball* around the true function f. The set of functions in $\mathbf{H}$ but outside the ϵ-ball is called $\mathbf{H}_{\text{bad}}$.

We find the probability that a "seriously wrong" hypothesis $h_b \in \mathbf{H}_{\text{bad}}$ is consistent with the first m examples as follows. We know that error $(h_b) > \epsilon$. Thus, the probability that it agrees with any given example is $\leq (1 - \epsilon)$. Hence,

$$P(h_b \text{ agrees with } m \text{ examples}) \leq (1 - \epsilon)^m$$

For $\mathbf{H}_{\text{bad}}$ to contain a consistent hypothesis, at least one of the hypotheses in $\mathbf{H}_{\text{bad}}$ must be consistent. The probability of this occurring is bounded by the sum of the individual probabilities; hence,

$$P(\mathbf{H}_{\text{bad}} \text{ contains a consistent hypothesis}) \leq |\mathbf{H}_{\text{bad}}|(1 - \epsilon)^m \leq |\mathbf{H}| (1 - \epsilon)^m$$

We would like to reduce the probability of this event below some small number δ. To achieve this, we need $|\mathbf{H}|(1 - \epsilon)^m \leq \delta$, which is satisfied if we train on a number of examples m such that

$$m \geq \frac{1}{\epsilon} \left(\ln \frac{1}{\delta} + \ln |\mathbf{H}|\right) \tag{8}$$

Thus, if a learning algorithm returns a hypothesis that is consistent with this many examples, then with probability at least $1 - \delta$, it has error at most ϵ; that is, it is probably approximately correct. The number of required examples, as a function of ϵ and δ, is called the *sample complexity* of the hypothesis space.

Apparently, the key question, then, is the size of the hypothesis space. As we saw earlier, if **H** is the set of all Boolean functions on n attributes, then $|\mathbf{H}| = 2^{2^n}$. Thus the sample complexity of the space grows as 2^n. Since the number of possible examples is also 2^n, this says that any learning algorithm for the space of all Boolean functions will do no better than a lookup table, if it merely returns a hypothesis that is consistent with all known examples. Another way to see this is to observe that, for any unseen example, the hypothesis space will contain as many consistent hypotheses predicting a positive outcome as predict a negative outcome.

The dilemma we face, then, is that if we do not restrict the space of functions the algorithm can consider, it will not be able to learn; but if we do restrict the space, we may eliminate the true function altogether. There are two ways to "escape" this dilemma. The first way is to insist that the algorithm returns not just any consistent hypothesis but preferably the simplest one—Ockham's razor again. Board and Pitt (1992) have shown that PAC learnability is *formally equivalent* to the existence of a consistent hypothesis that is significantly shorter than the observations it explains. The second approach is to focus on learnable subsets of the entire set of Boolean functions. The idea is that in most cases we do not need the full expressive power of Boolean functions and can get by with more restricted languages.

The first positive learnability results were obtained by Valiant (1984) for conjunctions of disjunctions of bounded size (the so-called k-CNF language). Since then, both positive and negative results have been obtained for almost all known classes of Boolean functions, for neural networks (Judd, 1990), for sets of first-order logical sentences (Dzeroski, Muggleton, & Russell, 1992), and for probabilistic representations (Haussler, Kearns, & Schapire, 1994). For continuous function spaces, in which the aforementioned hypothesis-counting method fails, one can use a more sophisticated measure of effective hypothesis space size called the *Vapnik–Chervonenkis dimension* (Vapnik, 1982; Blumer, Ehrenfeucht, Haussler, & Warmuth, 1989). Recent texts by Natarajan (1991) and Kearns and Vazirani (1994) summarize these and other results, and the annual ACM Workshop on Computational Learning Theory publishes current research.

To date, results in computational learning theory show that the pure inductive learning problem, where the agent begins with no prior knowledge about the target function, is *computationally* infeasible in the worst case. Section II.B.3 discussed the possibility that the use of prior knowledge to guide inductive learning can enable successful learning in complex environments.

V. LEARNING FROM SINGLE EXAMPLES

Many apparently rational cases of inferential behavior in the face of observations clearly do not follow the simple principles of pure induction. In this section, we study varieties of inference from a single example. *Analogical* reasoning occurs when a fact observed in one case is transferred to a new case on the basis of some observed similarity between the two cases. *Single-instance generalization* occurs when a general rule is extracted from a single example. Each of these kinds of inference can occur either with or without the benefit of additional background knowledge. One particularly important form of single-instance generalization, called *explanation-based learning*, involves the use of background knowledge to construct an explanation of the observed instance, from which a generalization can be extracted.

A. Analogical and Case-Based Reasoning

Introspection and psychological experiments suggest that analogical reasoning is an important component of human intelligence. With the exception of early work by Evans and Kling, however, AI paid little attention to analogy until the early 1980s. Since then, there have been several significant developments. An interesting interdisciplinary collection appears in Helman (1988).

Analogical reasoning is defined as an inference process in which a similarity between a source and target is inferred from the presence of known similarities, thereby providing new information about the target when that information is known about the source. For example, one might infer the presence of oil in a particular place (the target) after noting the similarity of the rock formations to those in another place (the source) known to contain oil deposits.

Three major types of analogy are studied. *Similarity-based analogy* uses a syntactic measure of the amount of known similarity to assess the suitability of a given source. *Relevance-based analogy* uses prior knowledge of the relevance of one property to another to generate sound analogical inferences. *Derivational analogy* uses knowledge of how the inferred similarities are derived from the known similarities to speed up analogical problem solving. Here we discuss the first two; derivational analogy is covered under explanation-based learning.

1. Similarity-Based Analogy

In its simplest form, similarity-based analogy directly compares the representation of the target to the representations of a number of candidate sources, computes a degree of similarity for each, and copies information to the target from the most similar source.

When objects are represented by a set of numerical attributes, similarity-based analogy is identical to the nearest neighbor classification technique used in pattern recognition (see Aha, Kibler, & Albert, 1991, for a recent summary). Russell (1986) and Shepard (1987) have shown that analogy by similarity can be justified probabilistically by assuming the existence of an unknown set of relevant attributes: the greater the observed similarity, the greater the likelihood that the relevant attributes are included. Shepard provides experimental data confirming that, in the absence of background information, animals and humans respond similarly to similar stimuli to a degree that drops off exponentially with the degree of similarity.

With more general, relational representations of objects and situations, more refined measures of similarity are needed. Influential work by Gentner and colleagues (e.g., Gentner, 1983) has proposed a number of measures of relational similarity concerned with the coherence and degree of interconnection of the nexus of relations in the observed similarity, with a certain amount of experimental support from human subjects. All such techniques are, however, *representation dependent.* Any syntactic measure of similarity is extremely sensitive to the *form* of the representation, so that semantically identical representations may yield very different results with analogy by similarity.

2. Relevance-Based Analogy and Single-Instance Generalization

Analogy by similarity is essentially a knowledge-free process: it fails to take account of the *relevance* of the known similarities to the observed similarities. For example, one should avoid inferring the presence of oil in a target location simply because it has the same place name as a source location known to contain oil. The key to relevance-based analogy is to understand precisely what *relevance* means. Work by Davies (1985) and Russell (1989) has provided a logical analysis of relevance and developed a number of related theories and implementations.

Many cases of relevance-based analogy are so obvious as to pass unnoticed. For example, a scientist measuring the resistivity of a new material might well infer the same value for a new sample of the same material at the same temperature. On the other hand, the scientist does not infer that the new sample has the same mass, unless it happens to have the same volume. Clearly, knowledge of relevance is being used, and a theory based on similarity would be unable to explain the difference. In the first case, the scientist knows that the material and temperature determine the resistivity, whereas in the second case the material, temperature, and volume determine the mass. Logically speaking, this information is expressed by sentences called *determinations,* written as

$$\text{Material}(x, m) \wedge \text{Temperature}(x, t) > \text{Resistivity}(x, \rho)$$
$$\text{Material}(x, m) \wedge \text{Temperature}(x, t) \wedge \text{Volume}(x, v) > \text{Mass}(x, w)$$

where the symbol $>$ has a well-defined logical semantics. Given a suitable determination, analogical inference from source to target is *logically sound*. One can also show that a sound single-instance generalization can be inferred from an example; for instance, from the observed resistivity of a given material at a given temperature one can infer that all samples of the material will have the same resistivity at that temperature.

Finally, the theory of determinations provides a means for autonomous learning systems to construct appropriate hypothesis spaces for inductive learning. If a learning system can infer a determination whose right-hand side is the target attribute, then the attributes on the left-hand side are guaranteed to be sufficient to generate a hypothesis space containing a correct hypothesis (Russell & Grosof, 1987). This technique, an example of *declarative bias,* can greatly improve the efficiency of induction compared to using all available attributes (Russell, 1989; Tadepalli, 1993).

B. Learning by Explaining Observations

The cartoonist Gary Larson once depicted a bespectacled caveman roasting a lizard on the end of a pointed stick. He is watched by an amazed crowd of his less intellectual contemporaries, who have been using their bare hands to hold their victuals over the fire. The legend reads "Look what Zog do!" Clearly, this single enlightening experience is enough to convince the watchers of a general principle of painless cooking.

In this case, the cavemen generalize by *explaining* the success of the pointed stick: it supports the lizard while keeping the hand intact. From this explanation they can infer a general rule: that any long, thin, rigid, sharp object can be used to toast small, soft-bodied edibles. This kind of generalization process has been called *explanation-based learning,* or EBL (Mitchell, Keller, & Kedar-Cabelli, 1986). Notice that the general rule *follows logically* (or at least approximately so) from the background knowledge possessed by the cavemen. Since it requires only one example and produces correct generalizations, EBL was initially thought to be a better way to learn from examples. But the background knowledge must be sufficient to explain the general rule, which in turn must explain the observation, so an EBL agent does not actually learn anything *factually new* from the observation. A learning agent using EBL *could have* derived the example from what it already knew, although that might have required an unreasonable amount of computation. EBL is now viewed as a method for converting first-principles theories into useful special-purpose knowledge—a form of *speedup learning.*

The basic idea behind EBL is first to construct an explanation of the observation using prior knowledge and then to establish a definition of the class of cases for which the same explanation structure can be used. This definition provides the basis for a rule covering all of the cases. More specifically, the process goes as follows:

• Construct a derivation showing that the example satisfies the property of interest. In the case of lizard toasting, this means showing that the specific process used by Zog results in a specific cooked lizard without a cooked hand.

• Once the explanation is constructed, it is generalized by replacing constants with variables wherever specific values are not needed for the explanation step to work. Since the same proof goes through with any old small lizard and for any chef, the constants referring to Zog and the lizard can be replaced with variables.

• The explanation is then *pruned* to increase its level of generality. For example, part of the explanation for Zog's success is that the object is a lizard and therefore small enough for its weight to be supported by hand on one end of the stick. One can remove the part of the explanation referring to lizards, retaining only the requirement of smallness and thereby making the explanation applicable to a wider variety of cases.

• All of the necessary conditions in the explanation are gathered up into a single rule, stating in this case that any long, thin, rigid, sharp object can be used to toast small, soft-bodied edibles.

It is important to note that EBL generalizes the example in three distinct ways. Variablization and pruning have already been mentioned. The third mechanism occurs as a natural side effect of the explanation process: details of the example that are not needed for the explanation are automatically excluded from the resulting generalized rule.

We have given a very trivial example of an extremely general phenomenon in human learning. In the SOAR architecture, one of the most general models of human cognition, a form of explanation-based learning, called *chunking,* is the only built-in learning mechanism. It is used to create general rules from every nontrivial computation done in the system (Laird, Rosenbloom, & Newell, 1986). A similar mechanism, called *knowledge compilation,* is used in Anderson's ACT* architecture (Anderson, 1983). STRIPS, one of the earliest problem-solving systems in AI, used a version of EBL to construct generalized plans, called *macro operators,* that could be used in a wider variety of circumstances than the plan constructed for the problem at hand (Fikes, Hart, & Nilsson, 1972).

Successful EBL systems must resolve the trade-off between *generality* and *operationality* in the generalized rules. For example, a very general rule might be "any edible object can be safely toasted using a suitable support device." Obviously, this rule is not operational because it still requires a lot of work to determine what sort of device might be suitable. On the other hand, overly specific rules such as "geckos can be toasted using Zog's special stick" are also undesirable.

EBL systems are also likely to render the underlying problem-solving system slower rather than faster, if care is not taken in adding the generalized rules to the system's knowledge base. Additional rules increase the number of choices available to the reasoning mechanism, thus enlarging the search space. Furthermore, rules with complex preconditions can require exponential time just to check if they are applicable. Current research on EBL is focused on methods to alleviate these problems (Minton, 1988; Tambe, Newell, & Rosenbloom, 1990). With careful pruning and selective generalization, however, performance can be impressive. Samuelsson and Rayner (1991) have obtained a speedup of over three orders of magnitude by applying EBL to a system for real-time translation from spoken Swedish to spoken English.

VI. FORMING NEW CONCEPTS

The inductive learning systems described in Section II generate hypotheses expressed using combinations of existing terms in their vocabularies. It has long been known in mathematical logic that some concepts *require* the addition of new terms to the vocabulary to make possible a finite, rather than infinite, definition. In the philosophy of science, the generation of new *theoretical terms* such as *electron* and *gravitational field,* as distinct from *observation terms* such as *blue spark* and *falls downward,* is seen as a necessary part of scientific theory formation. In ordinary human development, almost our entire vocabulary consists of terms that are "new" with respect to our basic sensory inputs. In machine learning, what have come to be called *constructive induction systems* define and use new terms to simplify and solve inductive learning problems and incorporate those new terms into their basic vocabulary for later use. The earliest such system was AM (Lenat, 1977), which searched through the space of simple mathematical definitions, generating a new term whenever it found a definition that seems to participate in interesting regularities. Other *discovery systems,* such as BACON (Bradshaw, Langley, & Simon, 1983), have been used to explore, formalize, and recapitulate the historical process of scientific discovery. Modern constructive induction systems fall roughly into two main categories: inductive logic programming systems (see Section II.B.3) and concept formation systems, which generate definitions for new categories to improve the classification of examples.

A. Forming New Concepts in Inductive Learning

In Section II.B.3, we saw that prior knowledge can be useful in induction. In particular, we noted that a definition such as

$$Parent(x, y) \Leftrightarrow [Mother(x, y) \lor Father(x, y)]$$

would help in learning a definition for *Grandparent* and many other family relationships also. The purpose of constructive induction is to generate such new terms automatically. This example illustrates the benefits: the addition of new terms can allow more compact encodings of explanatory hypotheses and hence reduce the sample complexity and computational complexity of the induction process.

A number of explicit heuristic methods for constructive induction have been proposed, most of which are rather ad hoc. However, Muggleton and Buntine (1988) have pointed out that construction of new predicates occurs automatically in inverse resolution systems without the need for additional mechanisms. This is because the resolution inference step removes elements of the two sentences it combines on each inference step. The inverse process must regenerate these elements, and one possible regeneration naturally involves a predicate not used in the rest of the sentences, that is, a new predicate. Since then, general-purpose ILP systems have been shown to be capable of inventing a wide variety of useful predicates, although as yet no large-scale experiments have been undertaken in cumulative theory formation of the kind envisaged by Lenat.

B. Concept Formation Systems

Concept formation systems are designed to process a training set, usually of attribute-based descriptions, and generate new *categories* into which the examples can be placed. Such systems usually use a quality measure for a given categorization based on the usefulness of the category in predicting properties of its members and distinguishing them from members of other categories (Gluck & Corter, 1985). Essentially, this amounts to finding *clusters* of examples in attribute space. Cluster analysis techniques from statistical pattern recognition are directly applicable to the problem. The AUTOCLASS system (Cheeseman et al., 1988) has been applied to very large training sets of stellar spectrum information, finding new categories of stars previously unknown to astronomers. Algorithms such as COBWEB (Fisher, 1987) can generate entire taxonomic hierarchies of categories. They can be used to explore and perhaps explain psychological phenomena in categorization. Generally speaking, the vast majority of concept formation work in both AI and cognitive science has relied on attribute-based representations. At present, it is not clear how to extend concept formation algorithms to more expressive languages such as full first-order logic.

VII. SUMMARY

Learning in intelligent agents is essential both as a construction process and as a way to deal with unknown environments. Learning agents can be divided conceptually into a performance element, which is responsible for selecting actions, and a learning element, which is responsible for modifying the performance element. The nature of the performance element and the kind of feedback available from the environment determine the form of the learning algorithm. Principal distinctions are between discrete and continuous representations, attribute-based and relational representations, supervised and unsupervised learning, and knowledge-free and knowledge-guided learning. Learning algorithms have been developed for all of the possible learning scenarios suggested by these distinctions and have been applied to a huge variety of applications, ranging from predicting DNA sequences through approving loan applications to flying airplanes.

Knowledge-free inductive learning from labeled examples is the simplest kind of learning and the best understood. Ockham's razor suggests choosing the simplest hypothesis that matches the observed examples, and this principle has been given precise mathematical expression and justification. Furthermore, a comprehensive theory of the *complexity* of induction has been developed, which analyzes the inherent difficulty of various kinds of learning problems in terms of sample complexity and computational complexity. In many cases, learning algorithms can be proven to generate hypotheses with good predictive power.

Learning with prior knowledge is less well understood, but certain techniques (inductive logic programming, explanation-based learning, analogy and single-instance generalization) have been found that can take advantage of prior knowledge to make learning feasible from small numbers of examples. Explanation-based learning in particular seems to be a widely applicable technique in all aspects of cognition.

A number of developments can be foreseen, arising from current research needs:

• The role of prior knowledge is expected to become better understood. New algorithms need to be developed that can take advantage of prior knowledge to *construct* templates for explanatory hypotheses, rather than using the knowledge as a filter.

• Current learning methods are designed for representations and performance elements that are very restricted in their abilities. As well as increasing the scope of the representation schemes used by learning algorithms (as done in inductive logic programming), current research is exploring how learning can be applied within more powerful decision-making architectures such as AI planning systems.

• In any learning scheme, the possession of a good set of descriptive terms that render the target easily expressible is paramount. Constructive induction methods that address this problem are still in their infancy.

• Recent developments suggest that a broad fusion of probabilistic and neural network techniques is taking place. One key advantage of probabilistic schemes is the possibility of applying prior knowledge within the learning framework.

One of the principal empirical findings of machine learning has been that knowledge-free inductive learning algorithms have roughly the same predictive performance, whether the algorithms are based on logic, probability, or neural networks. Predictive performance is limited largely by the data. Clearly, therefore, empirical evidence of human learning performance, and its simulation by a learning program, does not constitute evidence that humans are using a specific learning mechanism. Computational complexity considerations must also be taken into account, although mapping these onto human performance is extremely difficult.

One way to disambiguate the empirical evidence is to examine how human inductive learning is affected by different kinds of prior knowledge. Presumably, different mechanisms should respond to different information in different ways. As yet, little experimentation of this nature seems to have taken place, perhaps because of the difficulty of controlling the amount and nature of knowledge possessed by subjects. Until such issues are resolved, however, studies of human learning may be somewhat limited in their general psychological significance.

References

Aha, D. W., Kibler, D., & Albert, M. K. (1991). Instance-based learning algorithms. *Machine Learning, 6*, 37–66.

Anderson, J. R. (1983). *The architecture of cognition.* Cambridge, MA: Harvard University Press.

Baum, L. E., Petrie, T., Soules, G., & Weiss, N. (1970). A maximization technique occurring in the statistical analysis of probabilistic functions in Markov chains. *Annals of Mathematical Statistics, 41*, 164–171.

Berry, D. A., & Fristedt, B. (1985). *Bandit problems: Sequential allocation of experiments.* London: Chapman & Hall.

Bertsekas, D. P. (1987). *Dynamic programming: Deterministic and stochastic models.* Englewood Cliffs, NJ: Prentice-Hall.

Blumer, A., Ehrenfeucht, A., Haussler, D., & Warmuth, M. K. (1989). Learnability and the Vapnik–Chervonenkis dimension. *Journal of the Association for Computing Machinery, 36*, 929–965.

Board, R., & Pitt, L. (1992). On the necessity of Occam algorithms. *Theoretical Computer Science, 100*, 157–184.

Bradshaw, G. F., Langley, P. W., & Simon, H. A. (1983). Studying scientific discovery by computer simulation. *Science, 222*, 971–975.

Breiman, L., Friedman, J., Olshen, F., & Stone, J. (1984). *Classification and regression trees.* Belmont, CA: Wadsworth.

Bryson, A. E., & Ho, Y.-C. (1969). *Applied optimal control.* New York: Blaisdell.

Buchanan, B. G., & Mitchell, T. M. (1978). Model-directed learning of production rules. In D. A. Waterman & F. Hayes-Roth (Eds.), *Pattern-directed inference systems* (pp. 297–312). New York: Academic Press.

Cheeseman, P., Kelly, J., Self, M., Stutz, J., Taylor, W., & Freeman, D. (1988). AutoClass: A Bayesian classification system. In *Proceedings of the Fifth International Conference on Machine Learning.* San Mateo, CA: Morgan Kaufmann.

Cooper, G., & Herskovits, E. (1992). A Bayesian method for the induction of probabilistic networks from data. *Machine Learning, 9,* 309–347.

Davies, T. (1985). *Analogy* (Informal Note No. IN-CSLI-85-4). Stanford, CA: Center for the Study of Language and Information.

Dzeroski, S., Muggleton, S., & Russell, S. (1992). PAC-learnability of determinate logic programs. In *Proceedings of the Fifth ACM Workshop on Computational Learning Theory.* Pittsburgh, PA: ACM Press.

Fikes, R. E., Hart, P. E., & Nilsson, N. J. (1972). Learning and executing generalized robot plans. *Artificial Intelligence, 3,* 251–288.

Fisher, D. H. (1987). Knowledge acquisition via incremental conceptual clustering. *Machine Learning, 2,* 139–172.

Gentner, D. (1983). Structure mapping: A theoretical framework for analogy. *Cognitive Science, 7,* 155–170.

Gluck, M. A., & Corter, J. E. (1985). Information, uncertainty and the utility of categories. In *Proceedings of the Seventh Annual Conference of the Cognitive Science Society* (pp. 283–287). Irvine, CA: Cognitive Science Press.

Gold, E. M. (1967). Language identification in the limit. *Information and Control, 10,* 447–474.

Haussler, D., Kearns, M., & Schapire, R. E. (1994). Bounds on the sample complexity of Bayesian learning using information theory and the VC dimension. *Machine Learning, 14,* 83–113.

Heckerman, D. (1990). *Probabilistic similarity networks.* Cambridge, MA: MIT Press.

Helman, D. (Ed.). (1988). *Analogical reasoning.* Boston: Reidel.

Hertz, J., Krogh, A., & Palmer, R. (1991). *Introduction to the theory of neural computation.* Redwood City, CA: Addison-Wesley.

Judd, J. S. (1990). *Neural network design and the complexity of learning.* Cambridge, MA: MIT Press.

Kearns, M., & Vazirani, U. (1994). *An introduction to computational learning theory.* Cambridge, MA: MIT Press.

Laird, J. E., Rosenbloom, P. S., & Newell, A. (1986). Chunking in Soar: The anatomy of a general learning mechanism. *Machine Learning, 1,* 11–46.

Lenat, D. B. (1977). The ubiquity of discovery. *Artificial Intelligence, 9,* 257–285.

Li, M., & Vitanyi, V. (1993). *An introduction to Kolmogorov complexity and its applications.* New York: Springer-Verlag.

Michalski, R., Carbonell, J., & Mitchell, T. (Eds). (1983–1990). *Machine learning: An artificial intelligence approach* (Vols. 1–3). San Mateo, CA: Morgan Kaufmann.

Michie, D., & Chambers, R. A. (1968). BOXES: An experiment in adaptive control. In E. Dale & D. Michie (Eds.), *Machine Intelligence 2* (pp. 125–133). Amsterdam: Elsevier.

Minton, S. (1988). Quantitative results concerning the utility of explanation-based learning. In *Proceedings of the Seventh National Conference on Artificial Intelligence.* San Mateo, CA: Morgan Kaufmann.

Mitchell, T., Keller, R., & Kedar-Cabelli, S. (1986). Explanation-based generalization: A unifying view. *Machine Learning, 1,* 47–80.

Moore, A. W., & Atkeson, C. G. (1993). Prioritized sweeping—reinforcement learning with less data and less time. *Machine Learning, 13,* 103–130.

Muggleton, S. (1991). Inductive logic programming. *New Generation Computing, 8,* 295–318.

Muggleton, S., & Buntine, W. (1988). Machine invention of first-order predicates by inverting resolution. In *Proceedings of the Fifth International Conference on Machine Learning.* San Mateo, CA: Morgan Kaufmann.

Natarajan, B. K. (1991). *Machine learning: A theoretical approach.* San Mateo, CA: Morgan Kaufmann.

Neal, R. M. (1992). Connectionist learning of belief networks. *Artificial Intelligence, 56,* 71–113.

Osherson, D., Stob, M., & Weinstein, S. (1986). *Systems that learn: An introduction to learning theory for cognitive and computer scientists.* Cambridge, MA: MIT Press.

Pearl, J. (1988). *Probabilistic reasoning in intelligent systems: Networks of plausible inference.* San Mateo, CA: Morgan Kaufmann.

Pomerleau, D. A. (1993). *Neural network perception for mobile robot guidance.* Dordrecht: Kluwer.

Popper, K. R. (1962). *Conjectures and refutations: The growth of scientific knowledge.* New York: Basic Books.

Quinlan, J. R. (1986). Induction of decision trees. *Machine Learning, 1,* 81–106.

Quinlan, J. R. (1990). Learning logical definitions from relations. *Machine Learning, 5,* 239–266.

Quinlan, J. R. (1993). *C4.5: Programs for machine learning.* San Mateo, CA: Morgan Kaufmann.

Russell, S. (1986). A quantitative analysis of analogy by similarity. In *Proceedings of the Fifth National Conference on Artificial Intelligence.* San Mateo, CA: Morgan Kaufmann.

Russell, S. (1989). *The use of knowledge in analogy and induction.* London: Pitman.

Russell, S., & Grosof, B. (1987). A declarative approach to bias in concept learning. In *Proceedings of the Sixth National Conference on Artificial Intelligence.* Seattle, WA: Morgan Kaufmann.

Russell, S., Binder, J., Koller, D., & Kanazawa, K. (1995). Local learning in probabilistic networks with hidden variables. In *Proceedings of the Fourteenth International Joint Conference on Artificial Intelligence.* Montreal, Canada, 1995.

Sammut, C., Hurst, S., Kedzier, D., & Michie, D. (1992). Learning to fly. In *Proceedings of the Ninth International Conference on Machine Learning.* San Mateo, CA: Morgan Kaufmann.

Samuel, A. (1963). Some studies in machine learning using the game of checkers. In E. A. Feigenbaum & J. Feldman (Eds.), *Computers and thought* (pp. 71–105). New York: McGraw-Hill.

Samuelsson, C., & Rayner, M. (1991). Quantitative evaluation of explanation-based learning as an optimization tool for a large-scale natural language system. In *Proceedings of the 12th International Joint Conference on Artificial Intelligence* (pp. 609–615). San Mateo, CA: Morgan Kaufmann.

Shavlik, J., & Dietterich, T. (Eds.). (1990). *Readings in machine learning.* San Mateo, CA: Morgan Kaufmann.

Shepard, R. N. (1987). Toward a universal law of generalization for psychological science. *Science, 237,* 1317–1323.

Spiegelhalter, D. J., & Lauritzen, S. L. (1990). Sequential updating of conditional probabilities on directed graphical structures. *Networks, 20,* 579–605.

Stolcke, A., & Omohundro, S. (1994). *Best-first model merging for hidden Markov model induction* (Report No. TR-94-003). Berkeley, CA: International Computer Science Institute.

Sutton, R. S. (1988). Learning to predict by the methods of temporal differences. *Machine Learning, 3,* 9–44.

Tadepalli, P. (1993). Learning from queries and examples with tree-structured bias. In *Proceedings of the 10th International Conference on Machine Learning.* San Mateo, CA: Morgan Kaufmann.

Tambe, M., Newell, A., & Rosenbloom, P. S. (1990). The problem of expensive chunks and its solution by restricting expressiveness. *Machine Learning, 5,* 299–348.

Tesauro, G. (1992). Temporal difference learning of backgammon strategy. In *Proceedings of the Ninth International Conference on Machine Learning.* San Mateo, CA: Morgan Kaufmann.

Valiant, L. (1984). A theory of the learnable. *Communications of the ACM, 27,* 1134–1142.

Vapnik, V. (1982). *Estimation of dependences based on empirical data.* New York: Springer-Verlag.

Wallace, C. S., & Patrick, J. D. (1993). Coding decision trees. *Machine Learning, 11,* 7–22.

Watkins, C. J. C. H., & Dayan, P. (1993). Q-learning. *Machine Learning, 8,* 279–292.

Weiss, S. M., & Kulikowski, C. A. (1991). *Computer systems that learn.* San Mateo, CA: Morgan Kaufmann.

CHAPTER 5

Connectionism and Neural Networks

Harry Barrow

I. INTRODUCTION

Connectionism is an approach to modeling perception and cognition that explicitly employs some of the mechanisms and styles of processing believed to occur in the brain. In particular, connectionist models usually take the form of so-called neural networks, which are composed of a large number of very simple components wired together. Neural network models were inspired by and resemble (to varying degrees) the anatomy and physiology of the nervous system. A key aspect of many neural network models is that they are able to learn and their behavior may improve with training or experience.

II. UNDERSTANDING AND MODELING COGNITION AND PERCEPTION

In investigating cognitive or perceptual abilities we may take a "black box" view and attempt to simulate the overt behavior of the biological system as closely as possible. It can be argued that if a model replicates behavior sufficiently well it must inevitably incorporate functional organization and internal representations similar to those of the biological system. Converse-

Artificial Intelligence

ly, we may take a "mechanistic" view and implement a model that simulates as accurately as possible the components and the structure of the biological system. In this case it can be argued that the model must inevitably behave the same way as the biological system.

Marr (1981) recognized the essentials underlying this dichotomy and identified three levels at which information processing tasks, including cognitive and perceptual ones, must be understood: computational theory, representation and algorithm, and hardware implementation. The *computational theory* level is concerned with identifying the goal of the process, its appropriateness, and the logic of its strategy. The *representation and algorithm* level is concerned with how the computational theory might be implemented, the representations of input and output, and the algorithm that transforms one into the other. The *hardware implementation* level is concerned with how the representation and algorithm can be realized physically.

Marr also advocated a methodology in which these three levels are dealt with in sequence. From everyday experience we can identify certain perceptual tasks, such as determining the three-dimensional shape of an object from a stereo pair of views. This leads to the specification of a computational problem to be addressed and identification of the constraints and processes involved. Various alternative algorithms and representations may then be proposed and detailed psychophysical experiments, such as experiments involving random dot stereograms, may be employed to evaluate and discriminate among the competing hypotheses. Finally, having identified a suitable algorithm, specific neural mechanisms may be proposed, and these, too, may be evaluated and filtered by appealing to detailed neuroanatomical or neurophysiological evidence. A model is thus arrived at that provides understanding consistently at all three levels.

This "top-down" methodology has provided some valuable insights into vision, but it has some unfortunate limitations. It was propounded partly to counteract a tendency in some quarters of the computer vision community to develop implementations in a "bottom-up" manner, which was significantly influenced by constraints on computer hardware. However, Marr's methodology confuses implementation of the model on a computer with implementation of the biological system. The *biological* implementation may indeed constrain the nature of the algorithms employed, and these in turn may influence the computational solutions to problems obtained. Biological systems may use techniques we do not yet understand and are unlikely discover if we proceed purely top down. Moreover, the top-down methodology possesses an Achilles's heel in the specification of the computational problem. It is all too easy to misconstrue human abilities. For example, our everyday experience of vision may lead us to believe that we see all parts of the visual field with equally good resolution (because we move our eyes to aim the high-resolution fovea at objects to which we are paying attention). We may thus specify and solve an inappropriate computational problem.

The top-down, behavior-oriented approach concentrates on problems, whereas the bottom-up, mechanism-oriented approach concentrates on solutions. During the past two decades of computer vision research we have learned much about the nature and complexity of visual perception. We are able to engineer computer systems to perform certain well-specified tasks, but we have not achieved the generality, flexibility, and robustness of natural vision. Consequently, there has been a considerable increase in research aimed at understanding biological implementation of visual systems, to find out why they are so much better than artificial ones.

More generally, the last seven years has seen a veritable explosion of research into connectionist and neural network approaches to modeling perception and cognition. Topics investigated include vision, audition, tactual and somatosensory data processing, natural language processing, mapping the environment, associative reasoning, planning actions, and controlling motor systems. Underpinning the implementation of models have been extensive theoretical investigations of computation in neural systems, including function approximation, properties of various network architectures, stability of feedback networks, and mechanisms of learning.

III. REFERENCE SOURCES

Many texts presently deal with neural networks and connectionism. An up-to-date introduction is Hertz, Krogh, and Palmer (1991). The original two-volume "PDP bible" is still a very valuable resource (Rumelhart, McClelland & the PDP Research Group, 1986),[1] as is the even earlier publication (Hinton & Anderson, 1981). There is also a flourishing journal literature. Leading journals include *Neural Computation, The Journal of Computational Neuroscience, Biological Cybernetics, Neural Networks, IEEE Transactions on Neural Networks, Connection Science, Network, Proceedings of the National Academy of Sciences.* Annual conferences include NIPS (Neural Information Processing Systems), ICNN (International Conference on Neural Networks), ICANN (International Conference on Artificial Neural Networks) and WCNN (World Congress on Neural Networks).

IV. BIOLOGICAL ORIGINS

The field of neural networks originated with attempts to understand how the nervous system works. The human nervous system is composed of approximately 10^{11}–10^{12} cells (*neurons*) specialized for the electrical trans-

---

[1] A new volume in this series is forthcoming.

mission of information (Kandel & Schwartz, 1981). They vary in their morphology, but a representative neuron is shown in Figure 1. It possesses a body, or *soma;* a treelike structure, its *dendrites,* which receive incoming information; and a thin, wirelike structure with branches at its end, the *axon,* which transmits and disseminates information. The soma is typically 20–70 microns in diameter (1 micron = 10^{-6} meters), and the axon may be less than a micron in diameter. Neurons may be densely packed in the brain, with as many as 90,000 or more per cubic millimeter. For comparison, a transistor or wire in an integrated circuit may be a few microns across. However, components in integrated circuits can be packed in only two dimensions rather than three.

The axon of a neuron may be extremely long. For example, peripheral neurons that connect sensory receptors or muscular effectors to the central nervous system may have axons a meter or more in length. To enable very rapid transmission of information over such distances mechanisms for electrical signaling have evolved. The outer membrane of a cell is an insulator, so any difference in concentration of ions inside and outside the cell causes a difference in electrical potential across the membrane. If ions are moved into or out of the neuron, a local change in *membrane potential* results, and this propagates rapidly throughout the cell. Cell membranes are not perfect insulators, however, and the change in potential is attenuated with distance.

To combat this attenuation neurons regenerate the potential change as it

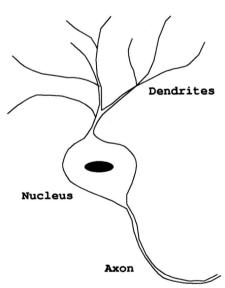

FIGURE 1   A simple neuron structure.

propagates along the axon, much as amplifiers are used for long-distance phone lines; and they signal "digitally" by means of impulses of fixed amplitude. The impulses, or *action potentials,* are about a millisecond in duration and travel at speeds of up to 130 meters per second.

The interior potential of a resting neuron is about -65 millivolts relative to the exterior of the cell. If the neuron is subjected to excitation, perhaps by means of a current injected into it via a fine electrode, the interior potential is raised to a new equilibrium value closer to 0. As the excitation is increased, the interior potential rises until at about -50 millivolts a sudden change occurs and the cell "fires." Channels in the membrane open and sodium ions flow into the cell, causing its potential to rise rapidly to about $+40$ millivolts. Other channels then open, allowing potassium ions to flow out, restoring the potential to about -75 millivolts. An action potential is thus generated. If the excitation is maintained, the membrane potential will again rise until it reaches the threshold value and another action potential is generated. A continuous stream of impulses is thus generated by excitation, and the *firing rate* increases with increasing excitation strength, up to a limit of several hundred impulses per second. The electrical activity of neurons was first accurately modeled mathematically by Hodgkin and Huxley (1952), and various computer models have been implemented subsequently.

A neuron may be inhibited instead of excited. For example, if the electrode current is reversed, the membrane potential is made more negative, taking it further from the threshold value, and action potentials are not generated.

A neuron does not simply transmit information; it may relay that information to other neurons. A branch of the axon of one neuron may make a connection, or *synapse,* with a branch of the dendrites of another. When an action potential travels down the axon and reaches the synapse, a small quantity of a *transmitter substance* is released. The transmitter rapidly diffuses across to receptor sites on the dendrite and causes associated channels to open in the membrane of the receiving neuron. Ions flow through the channels and the membrane potential changes appropriately. The effect may be excitatory or inhibitory, depending on the nature of the transmitter substance and the type of channel it opens. As a general rule, the synaptic connections a particular neuron makes onto others are either all excitatory or all inhibitory. This rule has become known as *Dale's law.*

The electrical characteristics of the neuron have the effect of causing it to integrate incoming excitation and inhibition over a time scale of a few milliseconds. If the net integrated input is excitatory then membrane potential will rise, and if it is sufficiently great, the neuron will fire repetitively. If the net input is inhibitory, of course, it will not.

An individual neuron in the brain may have a very large number of synaptic connections incident upon it. Pyramidal cells of the cortex may receive 10,000 synapses, while Purkinje cells of the cerebellum may receive 80,000. Again, for comparison, logic gates in a digital computer usually have only a few inputs, seldom more than eight. A single active synapse will not generally produce enough excitation to cause the receiving neuron to fire; spatiotemporal integration of perhaps hundreds of inputs is essential. Similarly, individual neurons may make large numbers of output connections. Pyramidal cell axons may form 6,000 output synapses. Clearly, there is an enormous fan-in and fan-out of information.

The delay in transmission from one neuron to another is typically 3–4 milliseconds. When we react to a stimulus in less than a second the processing between receptor input and muscle output cannot have involved more than a hundred or so neuronal stages. Digital computers, on the other hand, operate on a time scale on the order of microseconds, executing millions or billions of instructions to produce a similar response. Evidently, the breadth of the neural interconnections rather than their depth or speed gives rise to the remarkable perceptual and cognitive abilities of our brain.

Finally, biological neural networks are able to adapt their behavior in response to experience. We are well aware that even lower animals may learn. How this may be implemented has been demonstrated most clearly in experiments involving the hippocampus of the mammalian brain. When certain hippocampal cells are sufficiently stimulated to fire strongly it is found that the strengths of input connections that are simultaneously active are increased.

V. EARLY DEVELOPMENTS: LOGICAL MODELS

Early research aimed at understanding how biological neural networks function tackled a number of key issues and laid the foundations for much of today's research and applications. McCulloch and Pitts (1943) attempted to understand the behavior of networks of neurons in terms of logic. Because a neuron produces impulses of fixed amplitude they assumed outputs were binary: 1 signifying active output or 0 signifying inactive. They also assumed that all excitatory synaptic connections had the same fixed strength, although one neuron might make multiple connections to another, and that a single inhibitory input connection could veto output. In McCulloch and Pitts's model, neurons also possessed a threshold. If a neuron with threshold n has n or more active excitatory input connections, and no active inhibitory inputs, at time t, then at time $t + \delta t$ its output will be 1, where δt is (fixed) synaptic delay. Otherwise, the output at time $t + \delta t$ will be 0.

McCulloch and Pitts showed that their *threshold logic units* (TLUs) could compute logical functions. A unit receiving a single input connection from each of several other units and having a threshold of 1 computes the logical OR of its inputs, since its output will become 1 if any of its inputs are 1.

Similarly a unit receiving a single input connection from each of n units and having a threshold of n computes the logical AND of its inputs. A unit with a threshold of 0 will output 1 unless it has an active inhibitory input: it thus can compute the logical NOT of an input. Using units that implement the basic logical functions, a network may be constructed to implement any desired finite logical function. For example, since a conventional digital computer is built from components that perform basic logical functions, it could be constructed entirely from McCulloch and Pitts's threshold logic units. Thus, in principle, networks of TLUs can compute anything that a digital computer can.

VI. ADAPTIVE NETWORKS

The hypothesis that adaptation might occur in biological neural networks was postulated by Hebb (1949) long before direct evidence became available. Hebb attempted to bridge the gap between psychological and neuro-physiological phenomena. He suggested that neurons might organize themselves into "cell assemblies," groups of cells within which activity reverberated and that formed the basis of a distributed representation in the brain. The key to this self-organization was modification of connections between neurons. Indeed, Hebb introduced the term *connectionism* in describing his theory. He proposed that reverberatory activity carried memory temporarily until it was converted into a structural change of connections that made it permanent. As a basis for the structural change he hypothesized a basic mechanism:

> When an axon of cell A is near enough to excite a cell B and repeatedly or persistently takes part in firing it, some growth process or metabolic change takes place in one or both cells such that A's efficiency, as one of the cells firing B, is increased. (Hebb, 1949)

This qualitative statement is sometimes referred to as *Hebb's rule* and a model synapse that follows it as a *Hebbian synapse*. A particularly interesting characteristic of Hebb's rule is that it is purely local: the connection strength depends on the firing rates of only the presynaptic (A) and postsynaptic (B) cells and not on any others. Many self-organizing model neural networks have been implemented that rely upon various specific quantitative formulations of Hebb's rule.

VII. THE DARTMOUTH CONFERENCE

Work on neural networks has often been carried out within the general paradigm of artificial intelligence (AI). And this was so even in the earliest days of AI. In 1956, Marvin Minsky, John McCarthy, Nathanial Rochester, and Claude Shannon organized the first conference on intelligent behavior in machines, for which McCarthy coined the title *artificial intelligence* (Mc-Corduck, 1979). The other participants were Warren McCulloch, Tren-chard More, Arthur Samuel, Oliver Selfridge, Ray Solomonoff, Bernard Widrow, Allen Newell, and Herbert Simon. Minsky was a Harvard junior fellow in mathematics and neurology, whose Ph.D. research had focused on neural networks and who subsequently founded and directed the MIT AI Laboratory. McCarthy later founded the Stanford University AI Labora-tory. Rochester, of the IBM Corporation, had been experimenting with computer models of neural networks to investigate Hebb's ideas of cell assemblies and described his work at the conference (although the results were perhaps a little disappointing). Newell and Simon (1956) however, reported on their successes in developing the *Logic Theorist,* a symbolic theorem-proving program, and their "symbolic" approach to artificial in-telligence became the dominant one for over two decades.

VIII. PERCEPTRONS

Some of the most influential early work on neural networks was that of Rosenblatt (1958). Rosenblatt was a psychologist interested in three funda-mental questions.

- How is information about the physical world sensed or detected by the biological system?
- In what form is information stored or remembered?
- How does information contained in storage, or in memory, influence recognition and behavior?

He inclined to Hebb's "connectionist" view that information is stored in connections or associations. However, he eschewed McCulloch and Pitts's application of symbolic logic to the interpretation of neural behavior and preferred to use probability theory to address the inherent noise and ran-domness of biological systems.

Rosenblatt constructed various hardware devices which he called *per-ceptrons.* A diagram of the Mark I Perceptron is shown in Figure 2. Input to the Mark I was provided by a 20×20 array of photocells that produced trains of binary (0 or 1) impulses in response to image stimuli. The outputs of the photocells were connected to a collection of 512 *association units,* or A-units. Each photocell was connected to up to 40 A-units, chosen ran-domly. The A-units were threshold logic units that algebraically summed their (excitatory and inhibitory) inputs, compared them to a threshold, and gave a binary output (0 or 1). The A-units thus computed randomly chosen, but fixed, logical functions of their inputs. The outputs of the A-units were

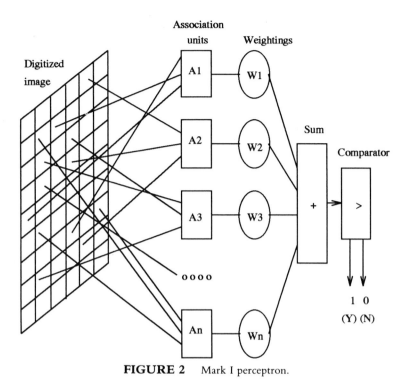

FIGURE 2   Mark I perceptron.

connected to the inputs of 8 *response units,* or R-units, through motor-driven potentiometers that could vary the strength of the connection. The R-units formed a weighted sum of their inputs and compared the sum to a threshold to determine a binary output (+1 or −1). In one of Rosenblatt's formulations, there were also mutual inhibitory connections among the R-units and inhibitory connections from each R-unit to the A-units that did *not* connect to its inputs. These connections were intended to implement a form of competition among the R-units so that only one of them was active at a time.

The crucial feature of the Mark I perceptron was that it was capable of "learning" by adapting the R-unit input connection strengths. It could be trained to produce a desired output (+1 or −1) for each input pattern. A variety of different learning algorithms was investigated. The most widely employed perceptron adaptation rule leaves weights unchanged when the output is correct, increments the weights of all active (1) inputs when the output is too low, and decrements the weights of all active inputs when the output is too high. Inactive (0) inputs do not affect the output, so their weights are left unchanged. Input patterns are selected and presented repeatedly, and the adaptation rule applied until the perceptron gives the desired response to all patterns. When solution weights are found, the algorithm makes no further changes.

The *perceptron convergence theorem* (Minsky & Papert, 1969) states that if there exists a set of weights such that the perceptron gives the desired responses to all input patterns, then the preceding adaptation rule will, after a finite number of steps, result in a set of weights that also give the desired responses. The set of solution weights is not, of course, unique.

It may not be possible for a perceptron to give desired responses to a set of patterns. Perhaps the simplest problem that *cannot* be learned by a perceptron R-unit is the XOR problem. For two inputs, x_1 and x_2, the desired output d is

x_1	x_2	d
0	0	0
0	1	1
1	0	1
1	1	0

The XOR problem cannot be learned because it is not linearly separable. The equation

$$\sum_{i=0}^{N} w_i x_i = 0$$

can be interpreted as the equation of a hyperplane in N-dimensional space, with variables x_i and parameters w_i. On one side of the plane the sum is greater than 0 and on the other side it is less than 0. The perceptron R-unit determines its output according to which side of the plane the input pattern lies on. The R-unit learns by moving the plane around to attempt to pro-

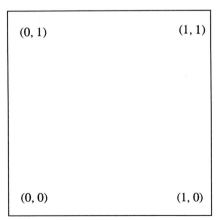

FIGURE 3   No line can be drawn separating (0, 0) and (1, 1) from (0, 1) and (1, 0).

duce the desired outputs. As can be seen from Figure 3, no position can be found for a line (a two-dimensional hyperplane) such that input patterns (0, 0) and (1, 1) lie on one side and (0, 1) and (1, 0) lie on the other. Nevertheless, the Mark I perceptron could learn to perform some interesting tasks, such as deciding whether a bar of light projected onto its retina was vertical or horizontal or discriminating among letters of the alphabet (Hecht-Nielsen, 1990). The promise of such early results led to research by hundreds of investigators worldwide, and the perceptron, or rather the R-unit, has been the key component in many subsequent artificial neural networks.

IX. ADALINES AND THE LMS ALGORITHM

The perceptron learning algorithm can be rather slow to converge because changes to the weights are made only when errors occur, but correcting an error may result in new errors for previously correctly handled patterns. Widrow and Hoff (1960) developed an adaptation rule for a perceptron like unit called an *adaptive linear neuron* (ADALINE). The ADALINE accepts binary (−1 or +1) inputs and computes a weighted sum that is then used to determine the output. The ADALINE is trained by presenting an input pattern and adjusting the weights and threshold so that the *sum,* rather than the binarized output, is brought closer to the value of the desired output. This is iterated over all patterns until desired results are obtained as closely as possible. Clearly, if the sums are close to the desired +1 or −1, or at least have the correct sign, the thresholded outputs will be correct. It can be shown that this training method, or algorithm, yields weight values that minimize the sum over patterns of the squares of the differences between the sum and corresponding desired output. It is therefore known as the least mean squared error, or LMS, algorithm (see Section XI).

The approach of adjusting the weights after each pattern is known as *on-line learning,* whereas the approach of presenting all the patterns and then adjusting the weights is known as *batch learning.* On-line learning tends to be more rapid in the early stages of adaptation, but adapting to the current pattern will undo some of the adaptation to previous patterns. Because of this effect, weights will not converge to fixed values, but will end up jumping around close to the optimum.

X. MINSKY AND PAPERT'S PERCEPTRONS

Despite the initial successes using perceptronlike devices to learn to discriminate simple patterns, considerable difficulty was experienced in scaling them up to deal with more complex problems. To understand their strengths and limitations, Minsky and Papert (1969) performed a thorough mathematical analysis of the capabilities of perceptrons. They considered a single adaptive R-unit with a set of A-units, each computing any logical function of its inputs, applied to a number of different tasks, and they derived some interesting results.

Minsky and Papert considered a generalization of the XOR problem, the *parity problem,* in which there are N inputs and the task of the perceptron is to decide whether the number of active inputs is odd or even. They found that to perform this task at least one A-unit must compute a function of all of the inputs. If the A-units each compute the AND of their inputs, then one A-unit is required for *every* subset of the retinal inputs.

They also considered the *connectedness problem:* the task for the perceptron is to decide whether the active inputs form a single connected region of the retina or multiple regions. Minsky and Papert found that this task could not be performed if the A-units each looked at only a local region of the retina: some of the A-units had to look at points distributed across the entire retina.

Some of the tasks discussed by Minsky and Papert, such as parity, could easily be performed by serial computation. They might also be performed reasonably economically by a system with multiple perceptrons wired together in layers. If we can define the desired output as a logical function of the inputs, then we can use R-units or TLUs to compute AND, OR, and NOT and wire them to implement the appropriate logical expression. If we have examples of only input–output behavior, the logical expression is unknown; it must be learned. However, effective learning algorithms for multilayer perceptrons were not known when Minsky and Papert performed their analysis. The theoretical difficulties they revealed and the practical difficulties encountered in scaling up perceptron systems to more ambitious tasks led to a diversion of effort away from neural networks and into symbolic serial computation.

XI. BACK PROPAGATION

As we noted, some problems (such as the XOR problem) cannot be solved by a single perceptron R-unit because they are not linearly separable. Such problems can be solved by a multilayer network, but there may be considerable difficulties in finding an appropriate network, particularly if units have binary outputs. However, Rumelhart, Hinton, and Williams (1986) developed an algorithm, known as *back propagation,* for training multilayer networks of continuous-valued units.

Each unit of the network first computes a weighted sum, s_i, of its inputs, x_j, and bias b_i

$$s_i = \sum_{j=1}^{N} w_{ij} x_j + b_i \tag{1}$$

We can eliminate special treatment of bias by assuming an additional input, x_0, which is kept constantly at 1, and an additional weight $w_{i0} = b_i$. Then,

$$s_i = \sum_{j=0}^{N} w_{ij} x_j \tag{2}$$

The corresponding unit output y_i is determined by a continuous differentiable function of s_i, σ_i:

$$y_i = \sigma_i(s_i) \tag{3}$$

Widely used output functions are the logistic function

$$y_i = \frac{1}{1 + e^{-s_i}} \tag{4}$$

which varies between 0 and 1, and the hyperbolic tangent

$$y_i = \tanh(s_i)$$

which varies between -1 and $+1$.

We shall consider a network with three layers of units: an input layer, a so-called hidden layer, and an output layer, as shown in Figure 4. Outputs of the first layer are the elements of the input pattern, x_i; those of the second layer are intermediate values, y_j; and those of the third layer are output values z_k. The numbers of units in the input and output layers are determined by the task; the number of units in the hidden layer may be chosen arbitrarily. The network is described by the equations

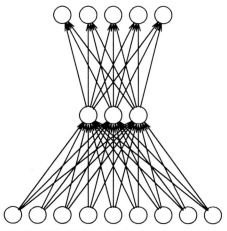

FIGURE 4   Feed-forward network.

$$y_j = \sigma_j^y \left(\sum_{i=0}^{I} w_{ji}^y x_i \right) \qquad 1 \le j \le J$$

$$z_k = \sigma_k^z \left(\sum_{j=0}^{J} w_{kj}^z y_j \right) \qquad 1 \le k \le K$$

where I, J, and K are the numbers of input, hidden, and output units, respectively; w_{ji}^y and w_{kj}^z are weights for the hidden and output units; and σ_j^y and σ_k^z are their output functions. We wish the network to produce a particular output pattern vector t_p in response to an input pattern vector x_p. We now define an error measure, E_p:

$$E_p = \sum_{k=1}^{K} (z_{pk} - t_{pk})^2$$

where z_{pk} is the response of output unit k to pattern p, and t_{pk} is the target output value.

We wish to determine the effect on the error measure of making a change to one of the weights. We differentiate E_p with respect to one of the weights, w (we do not yet specify which):

$$\frac{dE_p}{dw} = 2 \sum_{k=1}^{K} (z_{pk} - t_{pk}) \frac{dz_{pk}}{dw}$$

If w is one of the output layer weights, say, w_{kj}^z, then this reduces to

$$\frac{dE_p}{dw_{kj}^z} = 2(z_{pk} - t_{pk})\sigma_{pk}^{z\prime} y_{pj}$$

where $\sigma_{pk}^{z\prime}$ is the derivative of σ_k^z with input pattern p.

If w is one of the hidden layer weights, say w_{ji}^y, then

$$\frac{dE_p}{dw_{ji}^y} = 2 \sum_{k=1}^{K} (z_{pk} - t_{pk})\sigma_{pk}^{z\prime} w_{kj}^z \sigma_{pj}^{y\prime} x_{pi}$$

These derivatives can be made clearer if we let

$$\epsilon_{pk}^z = (z_{pk} - t_{pk}) \quad \delta_{pk}^z = \epsilon_{pk}^z \sigma_{pk}^{z\prime} \quad \epsilon_{pj}^y = \sum_{k=1}^{K} w_{kj}^z \delta_{pk}^z \quad \delta_{pj}^y = \epsilon_{pj}^y \sigma_{pj}^{y\prime} \qquad (5)$$

Hence,

$$\frac{dE_p}{dw_{kj}^z} = 2\delta_{pk}^z y_{pj} \qquad \frac{dE_p}{dw_{ji}^y} = 2\delta_{pj}^y x_{pi}$$

To reduce the error most rapidly we slide down the gradient of E_p in the direction of steepest slope. In vector notation,

$$\Delta w = -\eta \nabla E_p$$

In the case of our network this leads to the weight adaptation rules:

$$\Delta w_{kj}^z = -\eta \delta_{pk}^z y_j \qquad \Delta w_{ji}^y = -\eta \delta_{pj}^y x_i$$

Adaptation rules such as these are often referred to as *generalized delta rules*.

Note that the weight change is a product of a δ term associated with the destination of the connection and the signal associated with the source of the connection. From Equations (5) it is clear that the ϵ_{pk}^z are the actual errors measured at the network outputs. The corresponding δ_{pk}^z can be interpreted as the ϵ_{pk}^z propagated back through the output unit transfer functions. The ϵ_{pj}^y can also be interpreted as the δ_{pk}^z propagated back through the output connection weight matrix. Finally, the δ_{pj}^y are the ϵ_{pj}^y propagated back through the hidden unit transfer functions.

Clearly, the process can be applied to a feed-forward network with any number of layers. If we use superscript l to refer to layer l, and represent the outputs in layer l by y_j^l, with $y_i^0 = x_i$, then

$$\delta_{pk}^l = \epsilon_{pk}^l \sigma_{pk}^{l\prime} \qquad \epsilon_{pj}^{l-1} = \sum_{k=1}^{Kl} w_{kj}^l \delta_{pk}^l \qquad \Delta w_{kj}^l = -\eta \delta_{pk}^l y_j^{l-1}$$

It has been found, however, that learning becomes very slow with more than three or four layers.

The process of devising a multilayer network to perform a particular task, defined by a set of input–output pattern pairs (x_p, t_p) is now straight-forward:

1. Define the architecture of the network (number of hidden layers and number of units in each layer).
2. Set initial values for the weights (possibly random).
3. Choose a pattern pair (x_p, t_p), and set the network inputs to be x_p.
4. Calculate weighted sums and unit outputs, y, propagating values forward layer by layer.
5. Calculate the differences between actual and target network outputs.
6. Calculate the values of ϵ and δ, propagating values backward.
7. Calculate the Δw for weights in each layer.
8. Adapt the weights in each layer by adding the Δw to them.
9. Repeat steps 3–8 for all of the training pattern pairs.
10. Repeat steps 3–9 until task has been learned adequately.

This sequence is the *back-propagation* algorithm for feed-forward networks.

This algorithm implements on-line learning, with weight changes after each pattern presentation. Batch learning can be implemented by swapping steps 8 and 9; the Δw are computed (and summed) for all the training patterns and weights are adapted once after each pass through all the patterns. A pass through all the patterns is known as an *epoch*.

The simple steepest descent algorithm can be very slow to reach the optimum. Rumelhart and colleagues advocate the expedient of adding a *momentum term* to the calculation of weight increments:

$$\Delta w = -\eta \nabla E_p + \alpha \Delta w_{-1}$$

where Δw_{-1} is the previous Δw. This has the effect of increasing the learning rate when Δw is roughly constant, since if $\Delta w = \Delta w_{-1}$ then

$$\Delta w = -\frac{\eta}{1-\alpha} \nabla E_p$$

Clearly, we require $0 \leq \alpha < 1$: A suitable value is 0.9. The appropriate value for η is problem dependent, however: a steep error surface will generally require a smaller η than a shallow one.

XII. NETTALK

An early demonstration of the utility of neural networks and their training via back propagation was the NETtalk system (Sejnowski & Rosenberg, 1987). The task NETtalk performs is the translation of ordinary text into phonemes, or rather the articulatory features representing phonemes, which can drive a speech synthesizer. A commercial product, DECtalk, is a computer program that can perform this translation, using a dictionary for common words and a set of phonological rules. The task is not trivial because similarly spelled words, such as *gave* and *have,* may have different pronunciations.

NETtalk is based on a three-layer back-propagation neural network, as described in the previous section. The appropriate phoneme for a particular letter in the text depends on the local context, so the input to the network is a "window" of seven letters, the letter in question and the three on either side. To represent each letter a group of 29 input units is used, 26 corresponding to the letters of the alphabet and 3 to spaces and punctuation. The output of one unit in the group is set to 1, and those of the others are set to 0. In this way, the $7 \times 29 = 203$ input units encode the text in the window.

There are 26 output units, 23 representing articulatory features, such as point of articulation, voicing, and vowel height, and 3 representing stress and syllable boundaries. Various numbers of hidden units, from 15 to 160, were used in different experiments, and some experiments were conducted with a two-layer network, with 0 hidden units and inputs directly connected to outputs. The main results were reported for a network with 80 hidden units. Hidden and output units employed the logistic transfer function of Figure 5. Two different sets of training data were used, a phonetic transcription of informal continuous speech from a child, and a corpus of 20,012 words from a dictionary. In experiments involving the continuous speech, the text was moved past the seven-letter window, one letter at a time. In those involving the dictionary, words were moved past the window individually, in a random order. The back-propagation algorithm was used during learning (although errors were usually back propagated only when the output error was greater than 0.1). Error gradients were accumulated over several letters, and weights were updated only after each word. Momentum was used, with the learning rate $\eta = 2.0$, and momentum coefficient $\alpha = 0.9$. Training proceeded at about 2 letters per second on a VAX 780 FPA.

In evaluating performance, network output was considered to be a "perfect match" if each output was within 0.1 of its correct value. The network "best guess" was considered to be the phoneme vector that made the smallest angle with the actual output vector. With a corpus of 1024 words from the informal continuous speech, the score of phoneme best guesses increased rapidly at first and then more slowly, until after 50,000 words, 95% of best guesses were correct. Phoneme perfect matches rose more slowly and reached 55% after 50,000 words. Stress and syllable boundaries were learned much more rapidly, being almost perfect after only 5000 words.

With the 1000 most common English words from the dictionary, which

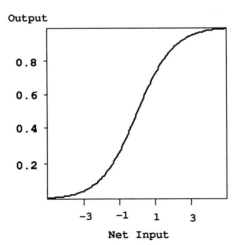

FIGURE 5   The logistic activation function.

included many of the most irregular words, comparable levels of performance were attained. With no hidden units, the best guess score saturated at about 82% correct, but with 120 hidden units the score was 98%. Testing the network on the full dictionary of 20,012 words gave a best guess score of only 77%, but after further training on the full dictionary this rose to 90%.

The performance of NETtalk is perhaps surprisingly good in view of the simplicity of the network architecture. There are only two stages of processing, and the outputs for each are just a nonlinear function of weighted sums of the inputs. The simple architecture is able to approximate both the dictionary lookup of special cases and the application of general rules performed by DECtalk. What is more, the performance was achieved without any lengthy analysis of the data to elucidate underlying principles and rules; all that was required was training by presentation of specific input and output vector pairs. The implications for understanding biological perception and cognition are that perhaps more can be accomplished by simple network architectures than might have been thought previously and that it is possible to construct interesting working models through a training process, rather than through a difficult, and perhaps flawed, analysis of the task domain.

It is sometimes argued that back propagation cannot possibly be a "biologically plausible" algorithm since no mechanism has been discovered resembling back propagation of errors in real neural networks. Even though that is true, it does miss a valuable point. If we are interested in modeling a particular component of a biological nervous system, we can set up a network architecture that is biologically plausible, and we can then use back propagation to optimize the network parameters and develop a particular target behavior. We can do this without needing to know how the real system organizes itself and adapts. We can then perform "neurophysiology" on the model and gain insights from the adapted values of its parameters. They may even tell us something about the real adaptation process. Back propagation is much more useful as a means of constructing models of adapted networks, rather than as a method of adaptation to be included in the model.

XIII. THE FUTURE

The space of connectionist systems has been only partially explored. In particular, no attention has been given to connectionist systems that support *unsupervised learning;* that is, learning in which the training data are not partitioned into inputs and outputs. Such systems discover regularities or patterns in the input data and typically make use of fully interconnected networks (every neuron connected to every other neuron) rather than the feed-forward style of architecture employed with back propagation. The work of Hopfield (1981, 1982, 1984) and Hopfield and Tank (1985) has been particularly influential in this area, as has that of Kohonen (1984) and Willshaw, Buneman, and Longuet-Higgins (1969). (See Meyer, this volume, pp. 336–338.)

Future research in connectionism will devise many new ways of doing connectionist computation. Interest may focus, for instance, on the possibilities of using more powerful versions of recurrent networks to provide better models of hierarchical structure (to which traditional AI is especially well suited). A closely related interest is in the ability of neural networks to construct new networks that function as models of (parts of) themselves, doing this on successive levels paralleling the increase in hierarchical complexity seen in psychological development. More generally, we can expect a continuation of research into the construction of "hybrid" computing systems, combining connectionism with some insights of classical AI. This may involve simulating classical systems on connectionist networks or combining the two techniques within a single model. In the latter case, each approach is used to effect what it does best, and new types of interface (allowing control to be passed appropriately from one side to the other) need to be designed. A further line of research is the use of biological neurons to grow predesigned networks, whose behavior can then be studied.

Alongside these examples of work on artificial systems, research will continue on actual nervous systems. Models of some simple neural mechanisms (such as the visuomotor responses of insects and amphibia) already exist, and others will be developed. Models of various aspects of human cerebral function will also be constructed. Some of these will address detailed intercellular (and even intracellular) mechanisms. Others will attempt to model communications between different parts of the brain, taking advantage where possible of evidence provided by noninvasive methods of brain scanning.

Much of this future work will be empirical, in the sense that novel types of network will be constructed and their (largely unpredictable) behavior observed. But a crucial aspect of connectionist research is the mathematical analysis and understanding of network properties. Ideally, researchers should be able to prove both the computational potential and the inherent limitations of the systems they use.

A further likely development, although exciting in itself, jeopardizes this research goal. Work has started on using genetic algorithms to evolve neural networks, as opposed to designing them. These networks can be used for any task, provided that some measure of fitness can be applied, either automatically or interactively. They are already being used, for example, to evolve sensorimotor controllers (i.e., simple "brains") for robots. But evolutionary programming, by definition, is largely random and uncontrolled. With increasing complexity, then, we can expect to see evolved neural networks whose empirically observed performance may be impressive but whose computational principles we do not fully understand. New types of retrospective analysis (based on experimental study) will be needed, since these evolutionary systems cannot be fully analyzed on first principles.

Much of this future work will require, or at least benefit greatly from, interdisciplinary cooperation, for it will combine abstract computational research and modeling with empirical observations in the real world— including field studies, laboratory experiments, and clinical observations. Mathematically sophisticated computer scientists, psychologists, ethologists, and neurophysiologists will need to learn to work together.

References

Hebb, D. (1949). *The organization of behavior.* New York: Wiley.

Hecht-Nielsen, R. (1990). *Neurocomputing.* Reading, MA: Addison-Wesley.

Hertz, J., Krogh, A., & Palmer, R. (1991). *Introduction to the theory of neural computation.* (Lecture Notes Vol. 1). Reading, MA: Addison-Wesley. Santa Fe Institute Studies in the Sciences of Complexity.

Hinton, G., & Anderson, J. (Eds.). (1981). *Parallel models of associative memory.* Hillsdale, NJ: Erlbaum.

Hodgkin, A., & Huxley, A. (1952). A quantitative description of membrane current and its application to conduction and excitation in nerve. *Journal of Physiology (London), 117,* 500–544.

Hopfield, J. (1981). Neurons with graded response have collective computational properties like those of two-state neurons. *Proceedings of the National Academy of Sciences of the U.S.A.,* 3088–3092.

Hopfield, J. (1982). Neural networks and physical systems with emergent collective computational abilities. *Proceedings of the National Academy of Sciences of the U.S.A., 79,* 2554–2558.

Hopfield, J. (1984). Neurons with graded response have collective computational properties like those of two-state neurons. *Proceedings of the National Academy of Sciences of the U.S.A., 81,* 3088–3092.

Hopfield, J., & Tank, D. (1985). Neural computation of decisions in optimization problems. *Biological Cybernetics, 52,* 141–152.

Kandel, E., & Schwartz, J. (1981). *Principles of neural science.* Amsterdam: Elsevier/North-Holland.

Kohonen, T. (1984). *Self-organization and associative memory.* Berlin: Springer-Verlag.

Marr, D. (1981). Artificial intelligence: A personal view. In J. Haugeland (Ed.), *Mind design* (pp. 129–142). Cambridge, MA: MIT Press.

McCorduck, P. (1979). *Machines who think: A personal inquiry into the history and prospects of artificial intelligence.* New York: Freeman.

McCulloch, W., & Pitts, W. (1943). A logical calculus of the ideas immanent in nervous activity. *Bulletin of Mathematical Biophysics, 5,* 115–133.

Minsky, M., & Papert, S. (1969). *Perceptrons.* Cambridge, MA: MIT Press.

Newell, A., & Simon, H. A. (1956). The logic theory machine. *IRE transactions on information theory.* September 1956.

Rosenblatt, F. (1958). The perceptron: A probabilistic model for information storage and organization in the brain. *Psychological Review, 65.*

Rumelhart, D., Hinton, G., & Williams, R. (1986). Learning representations by back-propagating errors. *Nature (London), 323,* 533–536.

Rumelhart, D., McClelland, J., & the PDP Research Group (Eds.). (1986). *Parallel distributed processing: Explorations in the microstructures of cognition* (Vols. 1 and 2. Cambridge, MA: MIT Press.

Sejnowski, T., & Rosenberg, C. (1987). Parallel networks that learn to pronounce English text. *Complex Systems, 1,* 145–168.

Widrow, B., & Hoff, M. (1960). Adaptive switching circuits. *1960 IRE WESCON Convention Record,* pp. 96–104.

Willshaw, D., Buneman, O., & Longuet-Higgins, H. (1969). Nonholographic associative memory. *Nature (London), 222,* 960–962.

CHAPTER 6

Expert Systems and Theories of Knowledge

John Fox

I. INTRODUCTION

A contemporary way of speaking about cognition is to describe it as the expression of an interaction between a fixed information processing "architecture" and an acquired body of "knowledge." Put simply, the ability to address challenges posed by one's environment is not governed solely by the power of our mental machinery, but also by how much we know about that environment.

The interests of researchers in these different aspects of cognition varies across cognitive science. Cognitive psychology, and kindred areas like neuropsychology and neurophysiology, have given priority to developing theories of the processes and structures corresponding to fixed information processing functions (the mechanisms underpinning memory, perception and so forth). In artificial intelligence (AI), however, more emphasis has been placed on formalizing the knowledge component. This is because the need to behave rationally (to act effectively to achieve one's goals) could be met by an indefinite number of different information-processing architectures, but no one type of architecture is best in all situations. Intelligent agents must augment whatever general-purpose capabilities they have with specific knowledge that reflects experience and adapts them appropriately to their particular circumstances.

Early AI research on the formalization of knowledge had primarily theoretical objectives. By 1975, however, there was an unexpected practical spin-off; computer programs had been developed that, to a degree, could emulate human cognitive skills such as medical diagnosis and decision making. Indeed a number of AI systems had been developed which solved, or appeared to solve, difficult but significant practical problems that are assumed to require high levels of human expertise in fields like medicine,

Artificial Intelligence

chemistry, geology and computer technology. E. A. Feigenbaum, one of the first to identify "knowledge-based systems" as a new and distinct technology, suggested in a famous and influential conjecture that solving problems at a high level depended less upon the sophistication of an agent's information processing architecture than upon its possession of appropriate specialist knowledge. Since it was claimed that the knowledge required to build practical problem solvers could be acquired from human experts such systems came to be called *expert systems*.

A worldwide effort to try to build practical expert systems followed. Expert systems for a wide range of tasks came to be constructed, including diagnosis, prediction, event monitoring, scheduling, planning, and designing.

By 1983 the "knowledge level" analysis of behavior was central to AI theory. In his presidential address to the American Association of Artificial Intelligence, one of the founders of AI, Allen Newell, suggested that the knowledge level represented a new level of description peculiar to cognitive science. Just as neurophysiological theories of cognition are described in terms of function, structure, and other concepts which are distinct from the concepts of chemistry and physics, the knowledge level has its own laws and appropriate formalisms that are disconnected from the architectural descriptions of mind.

The results of the international effort to build practical expert systems were mixed, but the interest in expert systems catalyzed a process that is of continuing importance to cognitive science—the development of formal and mathematical theories of knowledge. The purpose of this chapter is to provide a brief overview of expert systems technology and knowledge-based systems and some of the theoretical ideas about knowledge that are emerging.

Although the starting point for the discussion is technology, it touches on topics that are treated from a more psychological perspective in other chapters. These are, notably, representation of knowledge (Chapter 3), machine learning and connectionism (Chapters 1, 4, and 5), and problem solving and planning (Chapter 2). Other points of overlap are identified in the text.

II. KNOWLEDGE ENGINEERING—THE FIRST DECADE

A. The Nature of Expert Systems

Early expert systems were intended to help people without specialist knowledge of a field to make decisions as though they were expert in that field. For example, the MYCIN program, one of the first recognized expert systems, was intended to help physicians make diagnosis and treatment decisions in the area of bacterial infections (Shortliffe, 1976). PROSPEC-

TOR was designed to help geologists select drilling sites (Duda & Short-liffe, 1983), and the R1 system was designed to help computer engineers configure computer systems to meet customers' requirements (McDermott, 1982).

These expert systems were characterized in various ways. For some authors they were computer systems that could cope with tasks that require "expertise" if carried out by people and that emulate, at least in part, the cognitive processes implicated in such expertise. For other writers they merely represented a distinctive approach to information processing technology based on a collection of techniques known as "knowledge engineering." Although seemingly just a branch of technology, expert systems were held by both schools to be of interest to cognitive scientists, because they imply a model of certain kinds of human expertise or, at least, a set of formal tools for analyzing the knowledge content of cognitive skills.

The term *expert system* has been somewhat corrupted in recent years to include almost any kind of computer system that can help people solve problems at a high level. I have even seen a word-processing package referred to as an expert system. The account I give here attempts to reflect the historical and technical developments that led to the introduction of the term, rather than later and confusing revisions.

B. Making Knowledge Explicit

Expert systems were not the first technology designed to help decision makers. For a decade or more before their appearance statisticians and others had been developing mathematical techniques for medical diagnosis, educational assessment, personnel selection, staff allocation and many other problems. Expert systems were distinctive, however, because they emphasized qualitative, or "symbolic," methods rather than numerical ones. In order to illustrate the main differences between knowledge-based and earlier approaches I use examples from medical diagnosis and decision making.

Suppose a patient comes to a doctor with certain symptoms. The doctor's goal is to consider these symptoms and to decide the most likely diagnosis. A traditional mathematical method for making this decision with a computer is illustrated in Figure 1. The three boxes represent the essential components of the decision system. First, there are the symptoms and other information available about the patient—the case data. Second, there is a database of information about diseases, such as which diseases are associated with weight loss, which symptoms are more typical of young people than elderly people, and so on. This knowledge is typically represented by a set of numbers that indicate the overall likelihood of particular symptoms occurring with particular diseases. Third, the system incorporates some mathematical function which uses the contents of the database to calculate the

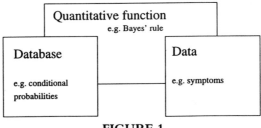

FIGURE 1

probability of each possible diagnosis, given a specific patient's symptoms. A number of methods have been developed for carrying out this sort of calculation, but they all fall within this general scheme.

Figure 2 is an analogous, schematic diagram of an expert system. Its form is superficially similar to Figure 1, but this is deceptive because the database or "knowledge base" of an expert system primarily encodes qualitative information about medicine rather than quantitative data.

Expert system designers aim to represent an expert's understanding of a subject rather than an abstract quantitative formalization of it. The meaning of the concepts of a specialist field or "domain" can be approximated in a form that computers can use by means of appropriate formal languages. For example, an important component of a knowledge base is often a body of facts that represents the way in which concepts are related to each other. Diseases cause symptoms, some symptoms are side-effects of treatments, particular diseases are specialized forms of more general categories, and so on. Figure 3 is a schematic representation of many of the things that may be found in the knowledge base of an expert system, shown as a "ladder" of increasing complexity.

I will now explain the steps involved. The most primitive element is the symbol. Now all computer programs manipulate symbols, but usually the symbols are merely strings of letters and numbers; "Mr. Jones," "measles," "age," and "55" have meaning for a human being who reads them, but no meaning to a computer. We are interested in formalizing the meaning of

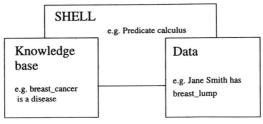

FIGURE 2

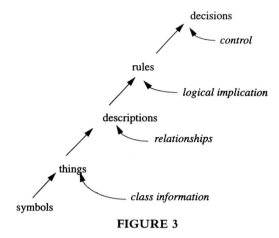

FIGURE 3

such ideas in a way that a computer can use. A first step is to say what classes of "things" are important in the domain, and use these to define other concepts. The following statements identify some specific medical concepts in terms of the basic categories of disease, treatment, and patient:

- Leukemia is a kind of disease.
- Chemotherapy is a kind of treatment.
- John Smith is a patient.

(Note that the apparent use of ordinary English in the examples should not be taken at face value. Some expert systems permit knowledge to be expressed directly in this sort of style but such languages are only superficially like English. I use this notation to make the material easier to read, but it should be borne in mind that it is really a formal language whose expressiveness is limited by comparison with true natural language. Also this "symbolic" approach to the representation of knowledge is not the only one and is controversial for many psychologists; the connectionist or subsymbolic approach assumes that knowledge is largely implicit in the organization of neural networks. Connectionism is discussed in Chapters 1, 4, and 5.)

The next step is to relate some "things" to other "things." As more and more relationships between symbols are established the contents of the knowledge base come more closely to approximate the human meaning of those symbols. In the following examples the main relationships are emphasized with italics:

- John Smith *suffers from* leukemia.
- Leukemia *is an abnormality of* blood.
- Anemia *is a side effect of* chemotherapy.

Symbolic descriptions are not by themselves sufficient for expert systems to reason, make decisions, or solve problems. We also need to be able to infer new facts, hypotheses, and the like from existing ones. This is typically done by means of *if…then…* rules, the third step in the ladder in Figure 3.

> If spleen is enlarged
> and asymmetrical enlargement of lymph nodes is confirmed
> then Hodgkin's disease is possible.

In the expert system field, knowledge of this kind is typically viewed as *heuristic*. It expresses rules of thumb, which are not guaranteed to be precise or correct, but nevertheless useful when, as in medicine, the field lacks a comprehensive body of theory and most practical knowledge is empirical. Given knowledge in this form we can use it to draw useful conclusions about the patient, such as inferences about possible diagnoses or treatments.

However, we cannot just put a large number of rules in a pot and stir, however useful they are individually. When we have many rules (some knowledge-based systems employ thousands) we need to control the reasoning process so that it operates coherently. For example, some rules should take priority over others. Consider these two rules:

> If anemia is present
> then iron supplement is required.   (1)

> If anemia is present
> and spleen is enlarged
> then investigation for Hodgkin's disease is desirable.   (2)

Rule 2 is more specialized than Rule 1; if the patient data satisfy Rule 2, then Rule 1 will also be satisfied. But Rule 2 refers to a situation where a significant disease may be present and an iron supplement might be quite inappropriate. A skillful decision maker does not apply such rules of thumb blindly, but selectively. An expert system must be similarly controlled.

The expert system shell (Figure 2) normally provides the necessary control. There are three main ways of controlling the use of knowledge when solving problems. In "forward chaining" the available data are examined and some of the rules that are satisfied are selected to derive conclusions (excluding more general rules in favor of more specific ones, for example). These conclusions are added to the fund of data, and this can lead to other rules being satisfied. The cycle may be repeated many times. In "backward chaining" the inference mechanism starts at the opposite end of the logical process. It identifies the conclusions it needs to establish and examines the rules to see which ones might prove these conclusions true (or false). If the conditions of the rules are satisfied by the available data it will deduce the conclusions, but if any of the conditions are not satisfied because data are missing then it tries to get that information (typically by asking the user). As in forward chaining, this may be repeated many times before the system obtains all the data necessary to establish whether the main conclusions are true or not. A third and potentially more flexible method of controlling decision making is to apply special knowledge called control knowledge. This explicitly encodes an understanding of the aims of, priorities, and constraints on the steps in the problem-solving process. (In other words it requires that the system has some ability to know what it is doing and why.) I will return to this technique in more detail in the next section.

Feigenbaum's conjecture can now be restated as follows: a knowledge base may be sufficiently comprehensive that it contains all the information that is required to make any decision—that is, all the information that is necessary to interpret data, identify relevant information, and control the decision-making process. The function of the shell is really only to make sure that items are retrieved when they are relevant to the decision or purpose at hand and that the appropriate inferences are made. Although many expert-system shells are more elaborate than my description and provide additional tools to make knowledge engineering practical, the power of these systems comes primarily from the quality and comprehensiveness of the knowledge base, not from the technical details of the architecture that uses it.

C. Semantic Networks, Frames and Objects

Collections of facts like "*a* causes *b*," "*b* is a kind of *c*," and "*d* can be used to treat *c*" have a close correspondence with semantic networks. The latter have long been used by psychologists as a semi-formal notation for representing knowledge, particularly for linguistic and other concepts. In expert systems and AI, however, techniques for knowledge representation have been developed much further. The introduction of rules is one obvious extension. Another is the introduction of "frame-based" and "object-oriented" representations. These provide a way of structuring large collections of interrelated facts and rules. They also capture an important set of intuitions about what we can infer in specific situations from general knowledge of the world.

In an object-oriented representation concepts are organized into hierarchies; objects that are higher in the structure normally represent "classes" or "generalizations" of concepts in the levels below them. For example, Figure 4 illustrates a simple generalization hierarchy, in which the most general class is that of a biological cell. This has two subclasses, animal and plant cells, which share a number of general properties. But the two sub-

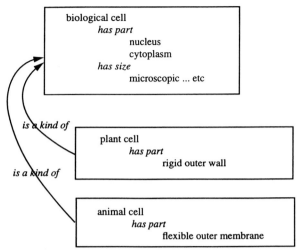

FIGURE 4   A simple generalization hierarchy.

classes are also different in important respects. For example the walls of plant cells are normally rigid, while those of animals are variable in structure and are typically flexible membranes.

This generalization hierarchy formalizes an obvious intuition about classes of object. The idea of classes pervades human thinking and appears to offer a powerful organizational principle around which to construct artificial reasoning systems. For example, we can apply techniques with which we can deduce, or at least guess, the properties of novel objects and concepts. If one encounters the concept of a t-lymphocyte, for example, and it is clear that a t-lymphocyte is an object in the more general class *blood cell* (actually it is a member of the class of white blood cell), then we can reasonably infer many of its properties from our general knowledge of blood cells. This kind of inference, or "property inheritance" as it is called, can be formalized using a rule-based formalism which permits "variables" to be included in rules. Variables can be used to write down inference rules that refer to classes of objects without being specific about details.

Consider the following rule, in which words that have a capital letter in the first position are logical variables.

If Object is *a kind of* Object-type,
and Object-type *has part* Part
then Object *has part* Part.

Given this rule, if we discover that a t-lymphocyte is a kind of blood cell, then, since we know that a blood cell is a kind of animal cell, it will probably have a flexible outer wall. Since it is a biological cell it should have

TABLE 1 Examples of "First-Generation" Expert Systems

MYCIN: decisions about diagnosis and treatment of bacterial infections
(Shortliffe, 1976)
CASNET: diagnosis of glaucoma (Kulikowski, 1977)
PROSPECTOR: identification of promising drilling sites (Duda
et al., 1977)
R1: configuring computer systems (McDermott, 1982)

---

a nucleus and a cytoplasm. We do not have to discover or be told these things explicitly, which contributes to the ability to reason flexibly. One caveat is that inheritance of properties is not always guaranteed to be correct because the conceptual hierarchies people have developed are frequently imperfect. Birds are animals that have the common property that they fly, except of course that penguins do not. Although inheritance does not guarantee correct conclusions the "informed guesswork" captured in inheritance rules is frequently very valuable.

D. Assessment of the First Generation of Expert Systems

The basic ideas of the first wave of expert systems are encapsulated by the ability to apply techniques like forward and backward chaining to a symbolic knowledge base in order to make inferences and decisions, together with associated techniques for knowledge representation, knowledge acquisition, and explanation of reasoning. Table 1 summarizes a few of the early expert systems that were developed during the 1970s, which employed the kind of rule- and frame-based knowledge representations outlined here. In the following decade or so this "first generation" of expert systems was found to have significant uses in certain industrial applications. Indeed, according to some authors, this amounted to a new industry (Feigenbaum & McCorduck, 1983). However, the limitations of simple systems also became apparent. In particular, the kinds of tasks they were capable of undertaking (notably decision tasks such as diagnosing faults in equipment) were rather limited. For more complex tasks such as planning and design, the knowledge representations were insufficiently sophisticated and inference techniques too inflexible.

III. SECOND-GENERATION EXPERT SYSTEMS—FROM DECISION MAKING TO EXPERTISE

In the next decade of expert-systems development, many attempts were made to overcome these limitations and to extend the functions and capabilities of the technology. Some authors identify "second generation" expert systems with the introduction of new problem-solving architectures (e.g., Rich & Knight, 1991), while others emphasize extended knowledge representation techniques (e.g., use of causal and other kinds of "deep" reasoning; Keravnou & Washbrook, 1989). Still others identify more advanced capabilities with the introduction of machine learning techniques (see Chapter 4 for a detailed discussion of machine learning), and an important recent development in the field has been "case-based reasoning," in which the computer system solves problems by relating them to examples from experience rather than reasoning logically from first principles (Liang & Turban, 1993). Many writers have emphasized the need for expert systems to give good explanations for their reasoning or to "critique" a user's own opinions on the problem, using natural language or other advanced user-interaction techniques (topics discussed in Chapter 8).

So many different experiments have been tried that it is hard to identify a clear pattern in the developments. I view the period as one in which knowledge engineers developed a deeper understanding of ways in which different kinds of knowledge can be used and exploited in systems designed to carry out different kinds of task (Chapter 10, on human–computer interaction, also discusses a task-centered view). However, it may be that the period should be viewed as little more than a transitional one, in which existing ideas about knowledge representation and use were consolidated and various new directions explored. The task-oriented view that I take in what follows should probably be seen as useful for a tutorial presentation but just one of many possible ones.

A. Task-Oriented Analysis of Knowledge

According to the Oxford Dictionary of Current English a *task* is simply "a piece of work to be done." A task may be trivial, like putting a question to a patient or asking a colleague to administer a drug. Or it may be complex, like formulating a patient care plan or designing a new treatment procedure.

Decision making, in the sense of making choices like medical diagnosis and therapy decisions, is only one kind of task that an expert system is capable of fulfilling. The range of tasks thought by Stefik et al. (1982) to be suitable for expert systems includes monitoring events, planning and scheduling actions, and designing artifacts or processes. A feature of the development of second generation expert systems has been a growing interest in understanding the nature of such tasks, and the construction of software capable of carrying them out.

Whatever their complexity, tasks can be modeled in terms of a small set of features that they all have in common. Consider the task of finding out how old a patient is (an information acquisition task), or administering a drug by injection (an action task). Both tasks can be viewed as having certain common features:

- A set of conditions under which the task is *needed*.
- A procedure to be followed to do the task (which may include simpler *subtasks*).
- Possible constraints on *when* the task may be carried out.
- Conditions that indicate when the task is *finished* (successfully or unsuccessfully).

The important feature of this kind of analysis is that it provides a framework for formalizing knowledge of the tasks that underlie complex behavior. For example, to plan a drug treatment we must decide on a drug, then how to administer it, and then the dosage. Industrial planning requires acquisition of components or raw materials before assembly and final inspection and so forth. The ability to formalize the steps involved in complex procedures, in turn, facilitates the construction of software that can emulate the behavior of skilled people carrying out comparable tasks. We can illustrate this by means of an expert system designed to schedule and control the administration of the steps in a medical treatment plan. The example I have chosen is taken, somewhat simplified, from a plan for giving radiotherapy to patients with a certain form of cancer. The general procedure in the therapy consists of a number of tasks carried out over time. The main tasks to be carried out are assessment of the patient prior to treatment, then radiotherapy (which involves a number of therapeutic sessions carried out over a number of days or weeks), and finally a task in which the patient's response to treatment is assessed in a follow-up phase. Figure 5 shows the state of the treatment schedule at three points in the therapy, two during the pre-treatment assessment and a third on the first day of therapy.

As soon as the treatment task has been started (it is identified in the figure as *in progress*) the scheduler identifies all the components of the treatment plan and introduces them as tasks that the system expects to carry out but that should not yet be initiated (they are *pending*). Now, recalling that capitalized words like Task and Subtask are variables that can be assigned any value, the following rule expresses this operation:

If Task is in_progress,
and Subtask is a subtask of Task
then Subtask is pending.

The values of the variables can be determined by comparing the conditions and action with each line in Figure 5, in which you will see that the three main tasks of the therapy, *pre_treatment_assessment, therapy,* and *follow_up,*

```
bronchial_cancer_treatment in_progress
point in treatment: start
        pre_treatment_assessment in_progress
                suitability_of_treatment in_progress
                        - age(Age) requested
                        pre_treatment_investigations pending
        radiotherapy pending
        follow_up pending


bronchial_cancer_treatment in_progress
point in treatment: start
        pre_treatment_assessment in_progress
                suitability_of_treatment completed
                pre_treatment_investigations in_progress
                        - chest_X_ray(Result)) requested
                        - full_blood_count(Result)) requested
        radiotherapy pending
        follow_up pending


bronchial_cancer_treatment in_progress
point in treatment: day(1), time(08.00)
        pre_treatment_assessment completed
                suitability_of_treatment completed
                pre_treatment_investigations completed
        radiotherapy in_progress
                radiotherapy(chart) in_progress
                monitoring in_progress
                        - therapy(day(1), treatment(1)) requested
        follow_up pending
```

FIGURE 5   Scheduling radiotherapy for bronchial cancer.

have been introduced. However, something else has happened; although radiotherapy and follow_up are pending, as described, pre_treatment assessment is in progress. The reason for this is that another rule which initiates selected tasks has been invoked:

If Task is pending,
and not(Task depends_on Previous_task,
    and not(Previous_task is done))
then Task is in_progress.

This rule uses control knowledge to work out dependencies between tasks. The gist of the rule is simply that a task should be initiated if and only if (a) it is pending and (b) it is not dependent on the completion of any other incomplete tasks. In this example the radiotherapy treatment should not be initiated before the *pre_treatment_assessment* has been completed, and *follow_up* should not be started until the treatment that we wish to follow up is complete.

The scheduling of tasks can be applied at any level (technically the scheduling process is "recursive"). In this example *pre_treatment_assessment* has two components of its own, and these are scheduled in the same way. The task *suitability_of_treatment* consists of a simple task to find out the patient's age and checking that the patient is not too young for the treatment; this component of the *pre_treatment_assessment* task is in progress while the remaining *pre_treatment_investigations* task is pending.

In the second panel of Figure 5 we have moved on in time; the *suitability _of_treatment* task is complete and the task *pre_treatment_investigations* is in_progress. In the third panel all the pretreatment tasks have been completed and the first session of radiotherapy has been initiated.

Although the rule formalism is very simple it is surprisingly powerful. The complete scheduler that was used to produce this example consists of eight rules. These can be used to control the execution of arbitrarily complex plans and are not restricted to medical applications.

A radiotherapy plan decomposes into simple tasks for obtaining information (patient's age, lab data, and so on) and for requesting standard procedures to be carried out (notably the radiotherapy treatment itself). The example involves limited decision making though, of course, most medical tasks involve a great deal of decision making throughout the disease-management process. In giving a drug, for example, the method of administration cannot be decided until the drug has been chosen, and in many cases the dosage can be settled only after it is decided whether to give the drug by mouth, injection, or another method.

There are many different kinds of decisions. In medicine, physicians have to make decisions about diagnosis (establish the disease someone is suffering from), treatment (e.g., what drug to give), investigation (e.g., what tests to do), and even decisions to "do something or do nothing." What is the common structure that distinguishes decisions from other kinds of tasks? Clearly, decisions imply alternative solutions to problems for which we must somehow weigh up the best alternative, such as the most likely diagnosis or most preferred treatment. In other words decision tasks are associated with

- Multiple solutions or "options."
- Strategies for arguing the pros and cons of decision options.
- Sources of data which are relevant to determining the pros and cons.

Decision making and scheduling are examples of "generic tasks," so called because they have a common structure. Many expert systems are now being built using software designed to represent and execute generic tasks.

Knowledge about tasks can be represented as an object generalization hierarchy analogous to the hierarchy of biological objects presented earlier. Here, however, the objects in the hierarchy are abstract tasks rather than concrete things like cells. However, they can inherit properties of more general classes of tasks in much the same way. All tasks may inherit a single set of scheduling rules for control; all decisions have the same general structure relating data and options, and so on.

To summarize, a major feature of recent expert-systems research is that it has led to a deeper understanding of a variety of issues to do with task organization, and the formalization of the knowledge necessary to construct complex behavior from elementary components. The various classes of tasks referred to in the introduction can be largely understood as the composition of simpler tasks, executed over time. Monitoring consists of continuous acquisition of information (e.g., patient data is continuously acquired from patients undergoing radiotherapy in order to decide whether there is some adverse reaction to the treatment), and, as we have seen, scheduling and plan execution can be carried out using knowledge of constraints on the order in which tasks must be done. Routine design processes (such as the design of a complex medical treatment, or a simple electronic or mechanical device) have much in common with planning but may have to take many other constraints into account apart from temporal constraints (e.g., constraints on cost, power consumption, ease of assembly, and so forth). Of course innovative, nonroutine design processes may not decompose so simply into somewhat standardized elementary tasks, although even here there are indications that the expertise involved in innovative design and other creative processes may be illuminated by an understanding of the generic tasks that underpin them.

B. Reasoning with Uncertainty

Uncertainty arises when we are ignorant of the true state of the world, of the consequences of our actions, or of unforeseen (and possibly unforeseeable) interactions between the two. The earliest expert systems, such as the medical expert systems MYCIN (Shortliffe, 1976) and INTERNIST (Pople, 1985) and the PROSPECTOR system for predicting the location of mineral deposits (Hart & Duda, 1977) all acknowledged the importance of uncertainty management. These systems set the pattern for many later applications. They viewed uncertainty as a quantitative concept, a "confidence factor." Instead of using rules like

> If patient has spots and a temperature
> then measles is possible,

we may annotate the rules to indicate our uncertainty,

If patient has spots and a temperature
then measles may be present (0.8).

Such numerical approaches are often appropriate for routine decisions that have to be taken repeatedly. In medicine, for example, patients presenting with acute abdominal pain routinely suffer from one of a small number of clinically distinct conditions, for which there is a finite set of relevant symptoms. Consequently, it is possible to establish a complete decision tree and associated probabilities, from which the most likely diagnosis or most preferred medical therapy can be determined.

The first generation of expert systems, however, were widely criticized for certain technical inadequacies, and the last few years have seen considerable success in developing better methods (for an excellent and comprehensive review, see Krause & Clark, 1993). Among the most developed techniques are those based on mathematical probability (Pearl, 1988; Lauritzen & Spiegelhalter, 1988). Other techniques have also reached a high degree of refinement, as in possibilistic reasoning (e.g., Dubois & Prade, 1988) and belief functions (e.g., Gordon & Shortliffe, 1986; Smets, 1990).

However, the appearance of expert systems triggered a debate about uncertainty management that is still very active. A continuing debate concerns the practical adequacy of quantitative methods for handling uncertainty. Human experts generally make do with vague or imprecise knowledge, such as some situation is "typically associated with" some other situation (cancer patients are typically elderly, for example). Indeed experts are frequently unwilling (and perhaps unable) to quantify such associations precisely, even though they are often capable of good decision making in difficult circumstances.

Interest is currently growing in the use of "semi-quantitative reasoning" methods for propagating increases and decreases in belief in situations where we know that some event is more likely in certain circumstances, but we do not know precisely how much more likely. Semi-quantitative reasoning appears to give a good account of much human decision making under uncertainty (Dawes, 1982), and such methods can certainly yield good practical results. For instance Barber, Fox and Bardha (1980), O'Neil and Glowinski (1990), and Chard (1991) show the effectiveness of semi-quantitative methods in a variety of medical diagnosis applications.

A very different approach that has been developed in AI is called *non-monotonic reasoning*. This attempts to capture a "commonsense" strategy for dealing with uncertainty in which we simply act as though one hypothesis or situation is true until we have some reason to change our minds, rather than attach degrees of certainty to the different alternatives. Suppose, for example, we are planning a business trip from Paris to Greece. We choose Air France flight AF97 from Paris to Athens, and then make a hotel reservation according to the scheduled arrival time in Athens. Nonmonotonic logic provides a sound framework for the following kind of reasoning: "AF97 is scheduled to arrive at time t and there is no reason to believe that it will not arrive at that time so I will assume that it will arrive in Athens at t."

This kind of reasoning will usually yield reliable conclusions, but mistaken commitments are not irrevocable. In many situations mistaken beliefs are not costly, and if actions are taken on the basis of an incorrect assumption the consequences of such actions can frequently be corrected later. There is, of course, a modest, and theoretically measurable, probability of strikes, fog or cancellation but it would be difficult to find out this probability and not help much with planning. It suffices to know that airline timetables are generally reliable, and in the event of a problem, the hotel will probably still have rooms. If not there are always other hotels or, at worst, an uncomfortable night at Athens airport.

Krause and Clark (1993) discuss a wide range of quantitative, semi-quantitative and qualitative methods for handling uncertainty in AI and expert systems.

C. Assessment and Critique

Notwithstanding these developments, the current status of expert systems technology is ambiguous. In *The Rise of the Expert Company,* Feigenbaum and McCorduck (1988) reviewed the state of the field and concluded that the predicted emergence of a new industry based on knowledge-based technology is taking place and that the development and deployment of expert systems is growing into an economically significant activity. This is supported by some independent reviews. An assessment in 1992 by management consultants Touche Rosse concluded that a substantial number of companies in Europe had adopted expert-systems technology and continued to be optimistic about their wide use. *Expert Systems with Applications,* perhaps the leading journal that reports on research and development in this field, and the proceedings of major international conferences on applied AI document a wide range of practical applications, a selection of which is given in Table 2.

Against such positive analyses one must also set the fact that assessments of the industrial importance of expert systems have tended to be revised down over the last decade, and industrial and commercial interest has probably fallen somewhat. Perhaps one should not place too much significance on such observations, however, since expectations about new technologies are frequently exaggerated in their early years. In due course the euphoria dissipates as the real value, and limitations, of the technology become better

TABLE 2   Example Expert System Applications (1980–Present)

Prediction and forcasting
Scheduling railway crew assignment
Other scheduling applications
Power system planning
Railway route planning
Financial accounting
Planning and Design in Manufacturing
Computer aided design
Equipment configuration
Crisis management

appreciated. Perhaps the safest assessment of expert systems is (1) they are being successfully applied in a range of situations that call for relatively simple decision making, scheduling, planning, and similar tasks, while (2) the wider discipline of knowledge engineering remains somewhat experimental and immature.

IV. THE THIRD DECADE—SYSTEMATIC ENGINEERING OF KNOWLEDGE

Although first- and second-generation technologies have found a limited niche, the limitations of the underlying engineering discipline are increasingly appreciated. This awareness is reflected in the principal themes of current research and development in knowledge-based systems. As with the parent discipline of AI itself there are both technological and theoretical themes. In this section I describe both of these directions; for completeness, however, I will concentrate on certain theoretical problems and advances that probably have as much relevance for cognitive science as for technology.

As in so much of this discussion, clinical medicine can illuminate many of the limitations of current knowledge-based systems. While the applications of expert systems in commerce and industry have made clear progress, their penetration into clinical use remains extremely limited. Why? It is often said of course that doctors are conservative and unwilling to accept new ideas. This is debatable, but even if true the serious consequences of adopting unproven technologies in life-threatening situations would obviously justify a high degree of caution. Certainly, the special sensitivities that surround medical decision making have played an important part in delaying the adoption of expert systems, since one of their weaknesses has been the relatively *ad hoc* nature of their development. The idea of constructing knowledge bases from "rules of thumb" is hardly likely to inspire confidence in doctors or patients. In short, a manager in industry may be willing to experiment with some new box of tricks in the hope that it will improve a company's competitiveness, but in medicine it is unsurprising if we continue to place our trust in professional human judgement rather than a technology that is still rather poorly understood.

The lack of a strong underlying discipline for knowledge engineering compares unfavorably with many other branches of engineering. For example, systematic design and development techniques have been generally adopted by the software industry; development of small-scale computer programs by individuals has given way to design of systems consisting of hundreds or thousands of components developed by large teams. For this to be practical it was necessary to provide many aids and tools; better software design techniques, standard components and automated testing have improved the quality and reliability of software. The use of systematic methods for managing large development projects has also improved the quality of software and ease of development and has reduced delivery times. Most recently, academic research in computer science has led to the development of formal mathematical techniques for designing and verifying computer software. These methods are particularly important for safety-critical applications in industry, aerospace, medicine, and so forth, because they can help to ensure that the computer program is sound and correct.

The earliest expert systems were small-scale and emerged from academic cognitive science labs, not from the software industry. Consequently, the first two generations of systems were not much influenced by industrial experience. Under the twin pressures of industrialization of expert systems and the desire to build more complex and reliable applications this is beginning to change. Among the more prominent developments in this direction are the introduction of advanced development methodologies that are appropriate for expert systems and techniques for establishing the consistency and adequacy of knowledge bases. Particularly interesting from the point of view of the current account are attempts to develop standard or "generic" components for the tasks that are typically carried out by expert systems, such as diagnosis, planning, and design tasks (Chandrasekaran, 1988).

Most recently we are beginning to see the development of appropriate formalisms for specifying and analyzing knowledge-based systems. Van Harmelen and Balder (1992) summarize the advantages of using formal languages for describing the structure and/or behavior of software systems as

- removal of ambiguity about what the knowledge represents,
- facilitation of communication and discussion about how expert systems work,
- ability to analyze properties of the design "on paper."

Van Harmelen and Balder remark that "if 'knowledge engineering' wants to live up to its name and is to become a proper engineering activity, a similar development of the field towards a formal treatment of the models it is concerned with must take place." Formal specification languages are intended to enable knowledge engineers to produce a mathematical model of the knowledge base they wish to build before committing themselves to coding it. As well as providing an unambiguous statement of the program's intended behavior, the specification may be subject to mathematical proofs and analysis of its properties, helping to avoid potentially disastrous errors.

A. Ontological Engineering

Some writers claim that expert systems emulate the problem solving and decision making capabilities of human experts. However, such a claim is not really credible. Many of the characteristics of expert-system architectures are primarily motivated by engineering requirements, not by any desire to model human information processing. Furthermore, it is clear that current expert systems have fundamental limitations on their ability to capture the meaning of the concepts they are dealing with. As we have seen, it is not difficult to formulate our intuitive knowledge in rules like

> If anemia is present
> and spleen is enlarged
> then investigation for Hodgkin's disease is required.

To the unguarded reader, it appears as though the machine "understands" concepts like anemia, spleen, Hodgkin's disease, present/absent, enlargement, investigation, requirements, and so forth. This is a long way from reality. Indeed, we might rewrite the knowledge base so that we substitute symbols like "a" for "anemia," "." for "is," and so forth. This might yield a version of the rule like

> If a . b
> and c . d
> then g(i) . r.

If the symbols are substituted consistently throughout the knowledge base and there are appropriate conventions for applying the rules, then the behavior of the new expert system will be equivalent to the old one. That is, as certain critics of AI have emphasized, current expert systems generally reason syntactically not semantically. Much of the meaning that you, a human reader, assign to words like "disease" is not available to the expert system. Although, as I have emphasized, the tradition of knowledge-based systems is precisely to introduce explicit semantic information into a knowledge base, this does not typically go very far. In the vast majority of knowledge bases that have been constructed to date, most of the symbols used receive no semantic analysis. Even where some effort is made to represent the meaning of a concept explicitly, the complexity and richness of our intuitive understanding of the concept is not emulated. For example, we may wish to use the term "Hodgkin's disease" in our knowledge base, and define a formal object to represent the concept, such as

> Hodgkin's disease
> > *is a kind of* disease
> > *causes* enlargement of lymph nodes and spleen
> > *has subtypes* I, II, III, and IV.

But the designer may not include more general information, such as the features of the general class "disease," which are common to Hodgkin's and other diseases and seem obvious to us: diseases are all abnormalities; they result from some sort of pathological process; they affect people (possibly in different ways); it is usually important to treat them, but the treatment should not be worse than the disease, and so on. The reason that knowledge engineers do not normally carry out this sort of conceptual analysis is that it is a difficult task with no obvious limits. Consequently, knowledge engineers restrict development of knowledge bases to a relatively shallow analysis of a limited number of technical concepts, the minimum that seem to be needed for the narrow band of expertise of interest.

There are practical and theoretical consequences of limiting the analysis in this way. The practical implications are that expert systems are, as it is generally accepted, "brittle." That is to say, they give satisfactory advice for a range of routine problems but, when faced with a situation that is somewhat novel, unusual, or just not anticipated by their designers, they commit howlers. Lenat and Guha (1990) give the example of a medical diagnosis program that is told about a follow-up visit by a patient on whose case it had worked the previous week. The program asks for the patient's blood pressure and temperature again—and then asks for the patient's birthdate and gender this week—it has no commonsense understanding that gender and birthdate do not change over time. This kind of brittleness is not characteristic of human thinking. Naturally, people frequently lack detailed knowledge of some situation, but their performance is not normally so brittle just because some small specialized fragment of knowledge is not available to them.

Lenat and Guha argue that brittleness is telling us something fundamental, not just about current limitations on expert systems but also about our understanding of knowledge and its role in intelligent behavior. The root cause of the brittleness problem, they believe, is that the semantic content of the knowledge bases is so impoverished that expert systems cannot use their knowledge flexibly. They observe that when people are faced with a problem that they have not seen before, they do not blindly use what they know but can adopt a number of adaptive strategies. These strategies include (1) recalling a similar problem situation and adjusting the solution that was found then so that it is appropriate for the current situation; (2) considering analogies with situations that are superficially very different but have similar structure and using the analogy to suggest a solution in the new situation (see also Chapter 4 and Chapter 9, IIIB for discussions of analogical reasoning), and (3) falling back on general knowledge of how the world is organized and operates in order to create a novel solution that is tailored to the situation at hand.

One strand of current expert systems research, on "case-based reasoning," is developing techniques based on strategy 1 and is producing quite promising results (Liang & Turban, 1993). Lenat and Guha's own approach is much more radical. They believe that an expert system that could solve new and difficult problems from general principles and by means of analogies as well as simple generalizations from experience must have a deep understanding of the nature of the world and the general principles by which it operates. Lenat and Guha are leading a large project to develop a general-purpose knowledge base that embodies a deep understanding of our "commonsense understanding" of the world. The Cyc project is attempting to build a single intelligent agent whose knowledge base provides an explicit representation of the basic ontology of the abstract yet fundamental concepts that we all possess—such as the concepts of object, material, space and time, events and processes.

The fundamental idea behind the organization of the Cyc knowledge base is that relatively specialized concepts, such as diseases, are defined in terms of more general ideas. Technically, they can be viewed as objects in a very complex generalization hierarchy. A disease is an abnormal *state,* but also a *process* and an *event* that occurs in time; it will therefore inherit the attributes of all three of these general ideas. A person may suffer from a peptic ulcer (an abnormal state) at a certain period of her life (an event) during which the condition may develop progressively (through some process).

The Cyc group expect that the Cyc knowledge base may include tens of millions of entities. Relatively little of the core ontology is likely to be technical knowledge (like the knowledge required to diagnose Hodgkin's disease, or the information needed to plan a medical treatment), but the Cyc knowledge base could become a vital component of other technical expert systems. Lenat and Guha believe that a body of commonsense knowledge could be a standard component in many specialized expert systems that, when their technical knowledge fails, could fall back on Cyc's general knowledge to augment their specialist problem solving and decision making. The Cyc group's analysis, and the ontological framework they are developing, are largely based on informal intuitions about how the designers themselves understand everyday concepts. Partly as a consequence, the group hopes that Cyc will also have a basis for understanding something about itself as well as the world. It should have explicit beliefs and purposes and be able to reflect upon them in order to explain and, if necessary, question its own behavior.

Cyc is a ten-year project, which represents not just an attempt to overcome some of the principal weaknesses of expert systems technology but also a desire to understand the nature of knowledge itself. "The Cyc project is outrageously ambitious; it is actually doing what AI has been theorizing about for three decades" (Lenat and Guha, 1990). The project reported early results in 1994. If it succeeds then it will have much to say of importance to cognitive scientists about how we, as well as machines, may understand the world.

B. Developing Formal Theories of Knowledge

The Cyc group are not alone in recognizing that even the best AI systems are inflexible by comparison with human beings, nor in identifying the need to come to grips with the idea of common sense. As Davis (1990) puts it, sooner or later "all parts of AI—vision, natural language, robotics, planning, learning, expert systems—must . . . make use of commonsense knowledge and commonsense reasoning techniques" (1990, p. 21). Davis, however, represents a community that believes that an intuitive style of ontological engineering, such as that of Lenat and Guha, is vulnerable to serious errors. Davis observes that (a) commonsense inferences tend to use a great variety of partial and incomplete knowledge, and representations for partial knowledge whose meaning is left at all open to intuitive understanding are very liable to be ambiguous or unclear in important respects; and (b) the very familiarity of commonsense concepts and their close connection to basic natural language forms renders them liable to ambiguity.

These kinds of concerns encourage many researchers to advocate a more rigorous, formal approach to the representation of knowledge. They are particularly concerned with providing systematic notations that permit us to capture ontological concepts in such a way that the properties of the concepts are expressed mathematically, and hence their properties—what they can and cannot express in principle—can be properly analyzed. A particularly natural class of tools for this kind of formalization is the class of systems called mathematical logics.

Historically, the development of logic was particularly motivated by the desire to be able to discriminate valid from invalid arguments by means of some objective method. Classical propositional logic and, later, the predicate calculus, were developed as the principal tools. Developments in AI have produced a significant new emphasis in the study of logic. Rather than merely providing a standard for judging whether particular forms of reasoning are justified, logic can now be used to construct theories that formalize particular intuitions or conjectures about the world. Logic facilitates experiments on the practical value of these theories by means of programs and artificial "agents" that embody the theories. Such theories often take the form of new logics, specialized for representing and reasoning with particular classes of concepts.

Among the countless logics which have been developed for the needs of rational agents are logics of

• *Belief:* How may we validly reason about hypotheses? (cf. reasoning under uncertainty; see above), and how may an agent reason about its own "mental" state (e.g., the justifications for its beliefs), consider counterfactuals (what if . . . ?) or examine the plausibility or reliability of its own knowledge?

• *Goals and intentions:* This work addresses questions such as how can we formalize the concept of an intention to achieve some condition? How are goals and plans adopted, maintained, achieved, modified or abandoned?

• *Actions and plans:* What are the general conditions that must be satisfied for an agent to carry out some operation that changes the world? How may the possible side-effects of some action (consequences of the action which were not the motivating intentions) be efficiently anticipated?

• *Time, events, and situations:* We traditionally model time in terms of a continuous time line. However, it is often more natural to reason about events than the passing of time. Classical ideas are formalized in *temporal logics,* which define commonsense concepts like "before" and "after," "during," and so forth, while the *event calculus* provides a logic for talking about "occurrences" and the "changes" that are produced by events.

• *Space and structure:* Classical geometry provides a powerful tool for reasoning about continuous space, but it is frequently more natural for an agent to reason about discrete objects, regions, and their interrelationships. For example, we may know that two objects are both "in" a box, or whether an object is "out of reach," but it is not necessary to know the precise geometric positions of those objects. Spatial logics provide a consistent set of primitive concepts with which complex spatial relationships can be represented.

• *Objects, forces, and the like:* Engineers and scientists take it for granted that traditional theories of physics provide the proper way of thinking about force, energy, mass, and so forth. However, the plumber and builder, and perhaps their future robot counterparts, need more flexible ways of reasoning about the physical world than numerical functions. The builder wants to reason about whether it is possible to get a large piece of equipment into a room, while the plumber wants to identify the source of a fluid loss. For such purposes intuitive concepts of rigidity and solidity, liquidities and flows, and appropriate rules of inference are more practical than those of traditional physics.

The development of logics alternative to classical propositional and predicate logics is not new, nor to be credited entirely to AI (e.g., see Haack, 1978). However, the development of logics which are specialized for reasoning with commonsense concepts has been motivated by the needs of AI and expert systems (see also the discussion of logic-based approaches to knowledge representation in Chapter 3). The study of commonsense knowledge is developing rapidly and, while many issues remain to be addressed, it is likely to make significant contributions to both advanced technology and cognitive science.

V. CONCLUSIONS

The key idea introduced in expert systems is that of making the knowledge that underlies expertise *explicit*. AI tries to capture the meaning of technical and everyday concepts in a way that can be used by a computer for decision making, problem solving, and so forth. Most of the early work on expert systems concentrated on systems for specialist, technical applications, and to this extent expert systems have found a significant industrial niche in such areas as equipment fault diagnosis and other kinds of simple decision making. The classical techniques of rule-based reasoning, semantic networks, frames, and the like, continue to be used in more advanced systems. However, they have been progressively refined and developed to yield more sophisticated applications. An important area of development has been in *generic* techniques for such tasks as monitoring, scheduling, and planning.

Practical experience with expert systems, however, has also underlined the limitations of current knowledge-engineering techniques. Human understanding is complex and subtle, particularly our commonsense understanding of the world. However, in this author's judgement, there are now indications of significant progress in this area. Advances in mathematical logic are providing powerful formal tools for understanding ontological concepts. These developments are exciting, not just from the point of view of the technological possibilities that they herald, but also because they point to a future for cognitive science in which a comprehensive understanding of the machinery of mind may be complemented by deep insights into the nature of knowledge and our intuitive understanding of the world.

References

Chandrasekaran, B. (1988). Generic tasks as building blocks for knowledge based systems: The diagnosis and routine task examples. *Knowledge Engineering Review, 3*(3), 183–210.

Chard, T. (1991). Qualitative probability versus quantitative probability: A study using computer simulation. *Medical Decision Making, 11,* 38–41.

Davis, E. (1990). *Representations of commonsense knowledge.* San Mateo, CA: Morgan Kaufmann.

Dawes, R. M. (1982). The robust beauty of improper linear models in decision making. In D. Kahneman, P. Slovic, and A. Tversky (Eds.), *Judgement under uncertainty: Heuristics and biases* (pp. 391–407). Cambridge, U.K.: Cambridge University Press.

Dubois, D., & Prade, G. (1988). *Possibility theory—An approach to computerised processing of uncertainty.* New York: Plenum.

Duda, R. O., & Shortliffe, E. H. (1983). Expert systems research. *Science, 220,* 261–268.

Feigenbaum, E. A., & McCorduck, P. (1983). *The fifth generation.* New York: Addison-Wesley.

Feigenbaum, E. A., McCorduck, P., & Nii, J. P. (1988). *The rise of the expert company.* New York: MacMillan.

Fox, J., Barber, D. C., & Bardhan, K. D. (1980). Alternatives to Bayes: A quantitative comparison with rule-based diagnosis. *Methods of Information in Medicine, 19*(4), 210–215.

Gordon, J., & Shortliffe, E. H. (1986). The Dempster-Shafer theory of evidence. In B. G. Buchanan and E. H. Shortliffe (Eds.), *Rule-based expert systems: The MYCIN experiments of the Stanford Heuristic Programming Project* (pp. 272–294). Reading, MA: Addison-Wesley.

Haack, S. (1978). *Philosophy of Logics.* Cambridge: Cambridge University Press.

Hart, S. & Duda, R. O. (1977). Report 155. Menlo Park, CA: SRI International.

Keravnou, E. T., Washbrook, J. (1989). What is a deep expert system? An analysis of the architectural requirements of second-generation expert systems. *Knowledge Engineering Review, 4*(3), 205–234.

Krause, P. J., & Clark, D. A. (1993). *Representing uncertain knowledge: An AI approach.* Oxford: Intellect Press.

Lauritzen, S. L., & Spiegelhalter, D. J. (1988). Local computations on graphical structures and their applications to expert systems. *Journal of Royal Statistical Society, B, 50,* 157–224.

Lenat, D. B., & Guha, R. V. (1990). *Building large knowledge-based systems, Representation and Inference in the Cyc project.* Reading, MA: Addison-Wesley.

Liang, T-P., & Turban, E. (Eds.) (1993). *Expert Systems with Applications, 6*(1). Special issue on case-based reasoning and its applications.

McDermott, J. (1982). R1: A rule-based configurer of computer systems. *Artificial Intelligence, 19,* 39–88.

O'Neil, M., & Glowinski, A. J. (1990). Evaluating and validating very large knowledge-based systems. *Medical Informatics, 15,* 237–251.

Pearl, J. (1988). *Probabilistic reasoning in intelligent systems: Networks of plausible inference.* San Mateo, CA: Morgan Kaufmann.

Rich, E., & Knight, K. (1991). *Artificial Intelligence* (2nd edition). New York: McGraw-Hill.

Shortliffe, E. H. (1976). *Computer based medical consultations: MYCIN.* New York: Elsevier.

Smets, P. (1990). The transferable belief model and other interpretations of the Dempster-Shafer model (pp. 101–114). *Proceedings of the Sixth Conference on Uncertainty in AI,* Boston, pp. 101–114.

Stefik, M., Aikens, J., Balzar, R., Benoit, J., Birnbaum, L., Hayes-Roth, F., Sacerdoti, E. (1982). The architecture of expert systems. In F. Hayes-Roth, D. Waterman, & D. B. Lenat (Eds.), *Building expert systems* (Chap. 3). Reading, MA: Addison-Wesley.

Van Harmelen, F., & Balder, J. (1992). (ML)²: A formal language for KADS models of expertise. *Knowledge Acquisition, 4,* 127–161.

CHAPTER 7

Machine Vision

David C. Hogg

I. INTRODUCTION

Machine vision has come a long way since its beginnings in the late 1950s and early 1960s. The pace of discovery and innovation has continued to the present day, although there is still a long way to go in understanding how best to construct intelligent systems incorporating vision. This chapter reviews the state of the art in the field and looks at some of the promising recent developments.

A. Aims of Machine Vision

The broad aims of machine vision have been to segment the world into objects, to classify these objects into categories, and to describe their geometric structure.

A hypothetical general purpose vision system in the mid 1990s looks something like the following. The input consists of two TV cameras mounted on a movable head. This gives the capability of binocular stereo and also allows the gaze of the system to change by moving the head and swivelling the cameras. The entire head is mounted on a mobile platform, allowing exploration of the world by moving around within it.

Artificial Intelligence

Output from the cameras is fed directly into an onboard computer that performs the analysis of the video stream from both cameras. Often, special purpose hardware is attached to the computer to perform computationally intensive image processing operations rapidly. The computer itself may have several processors, giving faster response and more flexibility for designers and programmers.

This characterization of a typical vision system is, of course, an oversimplification. There are many different kinds of vision system, each adapted to a particular application area. In remote sensing, the cameras are suspended on satellites revolving around the earth or traveling through the solar system. In medicine, images can come from a wide variety of machines, each providing different and complementary information on the human body. Some of these machines (e.g., CT and MR scanners) even produce three-dimensional (3D) images, very unlike the kinds of image available to the human vision system. In surveillance applications, visual input is often provided by TV cameras mounted in fixed locations, perhaps throughout a building complex or inside a shopping mall.

With all of this diversity, one thing is becoming clear: it is essential not to lose sight of the *purpose* of vision within the context of an overall system (Sloman, 1989). Only through this understanding can we ensure vision research is addressing the right problems.

By way of illustration, consider the standard robotics task of grasping objects using a mechanical gripper guided by visual input. In practice, this problem is tackled by dividing the control system into two parts: a vision module and a gripper-control module. One might reasonably argue (and many have) that the job of the vision module is to produce an initial three-dimensional description of the scene on which the gripper-control module bases its actions. Picking up an object becomes a two stage process: *looking* followed by *grasping*. By adopting this characterization, the generation of 3D descriptions from images can be viewed as a standalone problem, and we can forget about the original robotics task, at least until the two parts are plugged together.

Although this approach has practical advantages, not the least of which is that the field of machine vision gains a set of canonical problems to work on, it severely restricts the design space by partitioning the problem into two parts and poses individual problems that may have no robust solution. In the robotics example, it turns out, better results can be obtained using vision throughout the grasping action in a feedback loop, linking perception of the decreasing separation between gripper and object to generate control signals.

In the subsumption architecture of Brooks (1986) and some neural network control mechanisms (see Chapter 5), this link would be implemented as a *behavioral* loop, involving no explicit and detailed geometric description of the world. Alternatively, it can be implemented using an *evolving* description of the spatiotemporal interaction between gripper and object, constructed and maintained by monitoring the video sequence throughout the activity. This description mirrors what is going on "outside" but in a way that is accessible to task specific programs inside the computer. As the world changes, the description changes in lock step.

The robotics task domain and others have motivated an accelerating trend in machine vision, away from the analysis of single images toward dealing with temporal sequences of images. In this context, Alomoinos, Weiss, and Bandyopadhyay (1987) and later Ballard (1991) initiated exploration of an *active* role for vision in monitoring changes in the world and guiding continuous action. This includes enabling the vision module to alter the position of its sensors, perhaps to keep track of an object or to disambiguate a scene using parallax.

A task-oriented approach can also motivate integration of different paradigms. For example, Torras (1993) suggests using symbolic reasoning to plan a global strategy for grasping an object and a neural network to perform the feedback control of the grasping action itself. Of course, symbolic processing may be implemented as a neural network, but such processing does not invalidate the more abstract symbolic specification, particularly when this provides a design space facilitating experimentation with alternative solutions.

The lesson then is to take a task-oriented approach in the study of vision to avoid posing unnecessary and possibly ill-conditioned research problems.

An extreme position is adopted in recent evolutionary approaches to visually guided robotics. Using a genetic algorithm (Holland, 1992) to search a space of possible control architectures for a visually guided vehicle, Cliff, Harvey, and Husbands (1993) embody task specifications directly in the fitness function driving the evolutionary process. This produces control systems that are (nearly) optimal with respect to the task specification and from within the chosen space of possible architectures.

B. A Hierarchy of Models

Machine vision makes sense of images through using models of the world to "fit" the stream of intensity measurements from which the images are composed. These models operate at all levels of specificity (Figure 1). At one extreme are models of the general physical properties of objects, such as

Model hierarchy

| General physical properties | Generic objects | Particular objects |

FIGURE 1   Machine vision is based on a hierarchy of models.

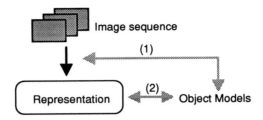

FIGURE 2   Object models are invoked (1) to mediate construction of geometric representation or (2) after geometric representation is complete.

the spatial (and temporal) connectedness of their constituent material, the inertia of a moving body, and the homogeneity of surface reflectance properties and material constitution.

At the opposite extreme are models of the geometric shape of particular objects or classes of object with fixed structure, such as the computer on my desk or a specific make and model of automobile. Somewhere along the spectrum between these two extremes are models characterizing the geometric shape of generic objects, like person, house, and vehicle.

Section IV explores the use of general properties of objects in constructing descriptions of the world. Section V is concerned with the use of models for particular objects and generic objects. Study of the latter is called *model-based* vision when the models themselves are represented explicitly.

An enduring issue in machine vision is over when to use object models in the constructive process (Figure 2). One view has it that the first aim should be to construct a geometric representation, without naming objects, using only the most general knowledge about the world at the left of the spectrum in Figure 1. Classification of objects takes place only after the "anonymous" description is complete and uses all of the information then available. The implication is that there is sufficient information in the general properties of objects to make sense of the world without resorting to object specific information.

The opposite view is that object models should be invoked at the start, to assist in the construction of a scene description.

The right answer probably lies somewhere between these two extremes. On the one hand, a general purpose vision system must be able to deal with unfamiliar objects when it first sees them, using only general object properties. Equally, however, processing time may be saved and noisy and ambiguous data analyzed through using all information to hand, including models for particular objects. The use of general object properties also provides a mechanism for learning object models from examples.

An appealing way of restating this is to say that vision should use all available models in making sense of images as quickly and reliably as possible, focusing on general object properties to deal with unfamiliar objects and acquire new models from examples.

C. Computational Models of Biological Vision Systems

As with most areas of artificial intelligence, research on machine vision is carried out both to provide a technology with a host of current and potential applications and to help our understanding of the way in which biological systems work. The influence of machine vision in the study of natural vision systems is perhaps most in evidence in providing computational models for findings in neurobiology and psychophysics, notably in the work of Marr (1982), who proposed plausible explanations for multiple spatial frequency channels found in human vision (Campbell & Robson, 1968), and oriented receptive fields discovered by Hubel and Wiesel (1968). However, it is also relevant in the study of higher level visual processes, such as those addressed in the mental rotation experiments of Shepard and Metzler (1971).

II. IMAGE FORMATION

A. Projection

In the human visual system and standard TV cameras, images are formed by the projection of light through a lens onto a sensitive surface. The most widely used abstraction of this process in machine vision is the *pinhole camera,* in which rays of light passing through a single point (the pinhole) fall onto a flat light sensitive surface known as the *image plane* (see Figure 3).

The geometry of the pinhole camera is *perspective projection,* in which the projected size of an object is inversely proportional to its *depth;* that is, its distance from the camera in the direction perpendicular to the image plane.

There are several commonly used approximations to full perspective. These either simplify the mathematics or give better numerical results when perspective effects are small (e.g., for distant objects). A particularly useful approximation is *weak perspective,* in which points are projected as if they are

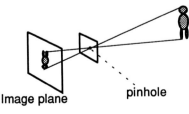

Image plane   pinhole

FIGURE 3   The pinhole camera.

at constant depth. In principle, this depth is allowed to vary *between* objects of interest, so that expansion and dilation with changing depth are correctly modeled.

The weak perspective approximation is sufficiently good over any 3D spatial region that is small in relation to its depth from the camera. Thus, it works well for the projection of a house observed in the distance, but is unsuitable for the projection of rows of houses observed from the sidewalk.

B. Digital Images

Although the image plane is notionally infinite, TV cameras detect light falling onto a bounded area that is normally rectangular. A digitizing device turns the video signal into numbers (called *gray levels*), representing the light intensity at many tiny receptive fields on the image plane. The dominant spatial organization of receptors is as a rectangular tessellation with each tile representing a receptive field and referred to as a *pixel* (for "picture element"). Figure 4(b) is an enlargement of part of the digital image in Figure 4(a), showing detail of the stonework above the doorway. Individual pixels are clearly visible, although it is hard to make out what is depicted with only 32 × 24 pixels.

Typically, gray levels range from 0 (low intensity) to 255 (high intensity), allowing storage as a single byte (8 bits) of computer memory. However, many commercial vision systems work perfectly well using binary gray levels, distinguishing just two bands of intensity.

Pixel resolutions employed vary widely and generally depend on the task requirements and computational resources available. The full content of a typical TV picture, which has an aspect ratio of 4:3, can be captured using arrays of around 640 × 480 square pixels. However, much smaller arrays are common.

Color images require three intensity measurements at each pixel, one for each of the three primary color bands. Finally, for full motion video, successive snapshots of the scene must be acquired at regular intervals. For standard TV cameras, images are acquired 25 or 30 times a second.

The total data rate is therefore over 220 million bits per second (i.e., 3 × 8 × 640 × 480 × 30). A pair of cameras giving binocular stereo doubles this rate. Real-time video processing, therefore, requires enormous computing power, and in practice, therefore, experiments with TV image sequences are performed at a more leisurely pace using prestored data. Real-time vision in the mid-1990s requires either highly parallel and expensive computers or subsampling of the data stream (e.g., to 3 images per second, at 160 × 120 pixel resolution).

The arrangement of receptors in human vision as a central fovea with lower resolution surround has inspired various alternatives to the rectangu-

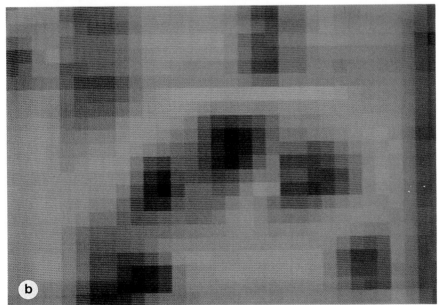

FIGURE 4 (a) Digital image of 640 × 471 pixels, (b) detail from stonework above the doorway.

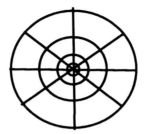

FIGURE 5   Log-polar tessellation of the image.

lar tessellation. For example, the "log-polar" tessellation (see Figure 5) gives a logarithmic fall-off in resolution away from a central foveal region (Tistarelli & Sandini, 1993; Weiman & Chaikin, 1979; Young, 1989). There are good computational reasons for preferring this arrangement, especially within the context of active vision.

Assuming a standard rectangular tessellation of part of the image plane, a natural way to address individual pixels is by their column and row address, x and y, respectively. To relate the observable intensity values to the outside world, the size, shape, and position of the pixel array within the image plane, referred to as the *intrinsic* parameters of the camera, must be known.

C. Steerable Cameras

When animals look at their surroundings, they rarely remain still for very long with a fixed gaze. Instead, they are constantly active—moving around, turning their heads, and rotating their eyes to extract needed information about the world. There are good reasons for this activity, and similarly there are good reasons for actively moving cameras in machine vision.

For example, visual guidance of autonomous vehicles is generally best achieved by mounting a camera on the vehicle rather than using a fixed vantage point, which limits the range of the vehicle and provides only a distant view of its immediate surroundings. Similarly, the geometric shape of an object can be deduced by making deliberate movements of a camera mounted on a steerable gantry (e.g., Blake, Zisserman, & Cipolla, 1992). A similar setup can also be used to find the boundaries of objects through locating discontinuities in the optical flow field.

However, these examples mirror only part of the mobility and agility of animate visual sensors. For example, the mobility of the human head and shoulders can be resembled more closely by mounting a pair of steerable cameras on a swivel platform. Such a setup, known as a *steerable stereo head,* has many uses. Using cameras with high-resolution foveal regions (e.g., a log-polar tessellation), the head can be adjusted to make objects of interest

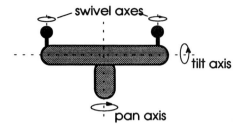

FIGURE 6   Schematic of a steerable camera head.

project onto these regions. Similarly, when an object of interest is moving, the head can be continually adjusted to keep the object in view and minimize motion blur.

In a representative setup (Murray et al., 1992), a pair of cameras are mounted on a common platform that is free to pan and tilt. Each camera is also free to swivel independently to allow for vergence movements, as shown in Figure 6. The apparatus thus has a total of four degrees of freedom.

The physiology of the human occulomotor system provides strong hints on how to control the electric motors that power a steerable stereo head, and for many purposes this control naturally partitions into three familiar subsystems associated with very different kinds of head movement:

- *Saccadic movement,* in which both cameras steer rapidly to point toward a target object.
- *Pursuit,* in which both cameras follow a target moving along a smooth trajectory.
- *Vergence,* in which both cameras turn to point directly at a target object.

Effective controllers for each of these subsystems have been demonstrated (e.g., Brown, 1990). However, it is by no means obvious how they should work together to control complex actions involving all three kinds of movement.

III. FEATURE DETECTION

The aim of the first layer of processing in machine vision is to extract from the enormous quantity of raw image data, salient features that have a plausible geometric interpretation in terms of the shape and structure of the objects in the scene, including markings on the surfaces of objects. This is the basis of Marr's *raw primal sketch* (Marr, 1982), in which images are represented by simple intensity features such as blobs, straight edges, and bars.

To illustrate the kinds of processing involved, this section is devoted to the detection of edge features. Other important "low-level" topics such as the characterization of texture (see Ballard & Brown, 1982; Pratt, 1978; Sonka, Hlavac, & Boyle, 1993) are beyond the scope of this chapter.

There are strong analogies between the early stages of visual processing in machines and natural vision systems. Perhaps the most compelling similarity is between the receptive field models of ganglion and cortical cells, obtained by single cell recording (Hubel & Wiesel, 1968) and *edge detection* schemes used in machine vision, the aims of which are to locate localized changes in image intensity, since these often represent depth discontinuities in the scene.

Much (but by no means all) of the information about the objects in a scene appears to be carried by regions of abrupt intensity changes in images. It therefore seems reasonable, as a first step, to focus attention on just these areas, thereby reducing significantly the quantity of data to be processed.

Perhaps the simplest edge detection schemes are based on the intensity gradient vector at each pixel in the image:

$$\text{gradient}(x, y) = \begin{bmatrix} g_x(x, y) \\ g_y(x, y) \end{bmatrix}$$

where $g_x(x, y)$ and $g_y(x, y)$ are the horizontal and vertical derivatives of the intensity image $g(x, y)$. An estimate of the horizontal derivative at pixel (x, y) is simply the difference between its gray level and that of the adjacent pixel to the left:

$$g_x(x, y) = g(x, y) - g(x - 1, y)$$

Similarly, an estimate of the vertical derivative is the difference in gray level between the pixel and the adjacent pixel on the row above.

The magnitude of the gradient vector $[\sqrt{(g_x^2 + g_y^2)}]$ and its direction give the slope and direction of steepest ascent of the local intensity "surface" at each point in the image. In the simplest schemes, fragments of an edge (known as *edgels,* for edge elements) are defined at those pixels for which the gradient magnitude exceeds a predetermined threshold (Figure 7). The collection of edgels is the basis for further processing.

Each edgel may be succinctly represented by an assertion of its properties, as for example,

edgel(<x>, <y>, <direction>, <magnitude>)

A problem with the simple edge detection scheme just outlined is that edge cross-sections typically extend over many pixels, particularly for larger scale structures in an image. The result is a band of edgels several pixels wide extending along the edge, when ideally we would like a string of edgels just one pixel thick.

FIGURE 7   Edge detection of the image in Figure 4(a): (a) gradient magnitude, (b) edgels.

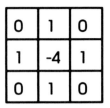

FIGURE 8   Laplacian mask.

One solution is to select only those edgels where the slope is at its peak value; that is, where the second spatial derivative across the edge passes through 0 (i.e., a zero-crossing).

A way of implementing this general approach is to look for zero-crossings of the Laplacian of the image:

$$\nabla^2 g(x,\ y) = g_{xx}(x,\ y) + g_{yy}(x,\ y)$$

where $g_{xx}(x,\ y)$ and $g_{yy}(x,\ y)$ are the second derivatives in the horizontal and vertical directions.

An estimate of the second derivative of intensity in the horizontal direction is given by subtracting estimates of the first derivative at adjacent pixels in the same row; similarly for the second derivative in the vertical direction. The overall computation of the Laplacian is neatly expressed using the 3 × 3 *mask* in Figure 8.

To compute the Laplacian at a pixel $(x,\ y)$, the mask is superimposed on the 3 × 3 subimage centered on the pixel and the values in the mask are multiplied by the gray levels immediately beneath it. The required estimate is the sum of these products.

Unfortunately, the Laplacian is most responsive to very fine-scale detail in an image, tending to obscure the larger scale edge structure. This problem can be overcome by blurring the image first to remove unwanted detail. Indeed, edges at different spatial scales may be detected through blurring the image by varying amounts.

A computational way of blurring the image is to replace the gray level at each pixel with the average of the gray levels in a local neighborhood. The size of the neighborhood determines the extent of blurring and therefore depends on the scale of edges sought.

This process is strongly reminiscent of the spatial frequency channels known to exist in natural vision systems (Campbell & Robson, 1968). Marr (1982) proposed using a Gaussian-shaped weighted average to blur the image, since this ensures an optimal balance between the need to average over local neighborhoods in the image and the need to remove detail up to a given resolution in terms of spatial frequency. This is implemented using convolution by the Gaussian mask plotted in Figure 9(a).

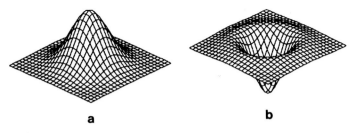

a   **b**

FIGURE 9   (a) Gaussian mask, (b) Laplacian of Gaussian mask.

The result of convolving the image in Figure 4(a) with a Gaussian mask is shown in Figure 10(a). Convolving this output with the Laplacian mask gives the result shown in Figure 10(b). In this picture, negative values are shown dark and positive values are light. Notice that light and dark bands of positive and negative values border either side of the positions of edges. Figure 10(c) traces the curves between negative and positive regions (i.e., the zero-crossings)—these are the required edges.

Preprocessing the image by convolution with a Gaussian mask followed by convolution with a Laplacian mask can be combined into a single convolution with a Laplacian-of-Gaussian mask (written $\nabla^2 G$; (Figure 9(b)). A similarly shaped mask is obtained by subtracting a pair of Gaussians of suitable sizes (called the *difference of Gaussians* mask or *DoG* for short).

IV. BUILDING DESCRIPTIONS USING GENERAL PROPERTIES OF OBJECTS

This section examines the detection of objects and estimation of their geometric shape, using only general object properties. Detection is taken to include not only finding individual objects as they appear but also tracking these objects over time.

In general, the position and orientation of an object, known as its *pose,* is expressed with respect to the camera or other structures within the scene. This pose is completely determined by six parameters: three to position the object along the three perpendicular axes in space, and three to specify the orientation relative to these axes. For some applications, the number of degrees of freedom may be reduced by constraints on the allowable motion of an object (see, for example, Worrall, Sullivan, & Baker, 1993).

Often, objects are observed from only a small number of fixed directions (or *aspects*). In these circumstances, it is convenient to treat the object observed from each direction as a *separate* object, removing two degrees of freedom from the object's pose with respect to the camera. Each new object remains free to rotate about an axis perpendicular to the image plane and to move about in space—a total of four degrees of freedom. If, in addition, the

FIGURE 10   (a) Image convolved with a Gaussian, (b) Laplacian of (a), (c) zero-crossings.

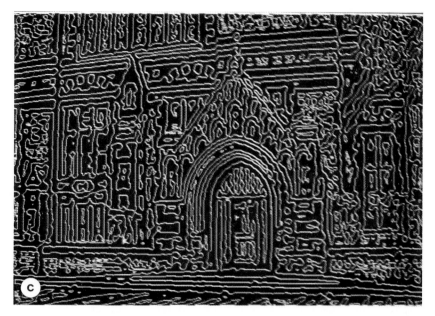

FIGURE 10   (*Continued*)

weak perspective camera model is used (Section II. A), movement in depth may then be modeled by uniform scaling in the image plane.

The result is that it is more convenient to think of the object as being embedded in the image plane, where it is free to translate, rotate, and scale, than to deal with the full generality of 3D. This is the justification for so-called 2D vision (as opposed to 3D vision)—a significant proportion of all work in the field. For simplicity, we also refer to the restricted notion of position and orientation in the image plane as the *pose* of an object.

In the early days of machine vision, from the 1950s to the early 1970s, the emphasis was on 2D vision, with some notable exceptions (e.g., Clowes, 1971; Huffman, 1971; Roberts, 1965). The next 20 years saw a shift in emphasis towards work on 3D vision (e.g., Brooks, 1981; Marr, 1982). Today, both approaches remain important.

Within the context of 2D vision, the detection of objects is normally expressed as a problem of *image segmentation;* that is, partitioning the image into parts corresponding to different objects. A vast published literature exists on this topic, reflecting its importance in the field. A brief introduction to the area is given in Section IV. A.

A binocular video stream contains many kinds of information on the depth, orientation, and motion of visible surfaces with respect to the cameras. This makes possible generation of a full 3D representation of the world without invoking specific object models. Section IV.B focuses on the use of binocular and motion stereo to acquire pointwise depth information and the integration of this information into descriptions of the visible surfaces.

A. Image Segmentation

Segmentation aims to partition images into objects, or more precisely, to detect and represent the 2D spatial extent of each object's projection in the image. Two very simple schemes have been widely applied in many areas: thresholding and differencing. Both techniques are described briefly later, along with active contours, a more recent idea based on the simulation of an "elasticlike" loop, deforming over the image and coming to rest around the boundary of the desired object.

1. Thresholding

The visible surface of an object is typically divided into a small number of areas where the reflectance properties are relatively homogeneous. Furthermore, if the inclination of different parts of the surface varies little with respect to the camera (or if such variations make little difference because of special surface properties), the projected light intensity will remain relatively constant across the projection of each homogeneous area.

Using controlled lighting conditions and restricted scene domains, it is often possible to segment objects of interest by simply defining all pixels with gray levels above (or beneath) a fixed threshold value to be part of an object. The separate connected regions of such pixels are taken as the required objects. To illustrate, this process does a pretty good job of segmenting out individual parts of the stonework for the image in Figure 11, using a carefully chosen threshold value.

Gray level and texture homogeneity form the basis for many segmentation algorithms going beyond simple thresholding (Sonka et al., 1993).

2. Differencing

When sequences of images are available, subtraction of successive image pairs on a pixel-by-pixel basis can reveal approximations to the projections of moving objects through simply thresholding the absolute value of the difference and placing the results into an identical pixel array. When an object moves, the gray values in those pixels under its projection change and therefore show up in the thresholded difference image. Clustering *change pixels* not only isolates (nonoverlapping) moving objects within a single video frame but also enables the object to be tracked through several frames by establishing correspondences between successive clusters based on continuity of motion and size.

FIGURE 11 Thresholding image in Figure 4(a).

Although susceptible to changing lighting conditions (e.g., from clouds moving in front of the sun), the differencing method has been used for many years within video motion detection systems for surveillance applications.

3. Active Contours

In the mid–1980s, Kass, Witkin, and Terzopoulos (1987) introduced a novel way for detecting object boundaries in images, through simulating the motion of an elastic string (called a *snake* or *active contour*) with assumed physical properties discouraging bending and stretching. The snake moves from an initial position under the action of forces induced by a potential energy field shaped by intensity gradients in the image. The boundaries of objects lie along the bottom of potential energy wells into which the snake (ideally) slides and eventually comes to rest. The idea is that the physical properties of the snake encourage it to adopt 2D shapes that are plausible within the domain of object boundaries to be detected.

Figure 12 illustrates the use of a snake to detect metacarpal bones in X-ray images of the human hand. Figure 12(a) shows the initial state of a snake surrounding one of the bones in an X-ray image of part of the hand. This image is blurred (by convolution with a Gaussian) and the magnitude

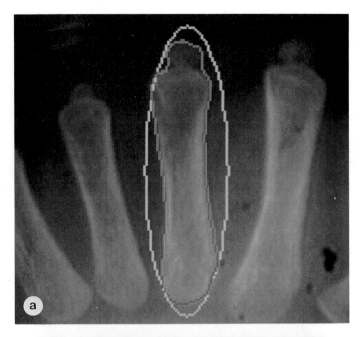

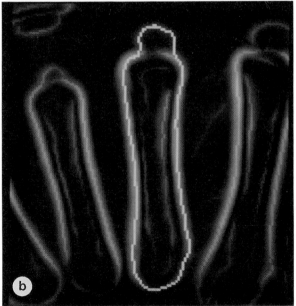

FIGURE 12   Detecting the boundary of a metacarpal bone in an X-ray image: (a) initial state of the snake superimposed over original image, (b) magnitude of the gradient of blurred image, with final resting state superimposed, (c) the potential energy landscape.

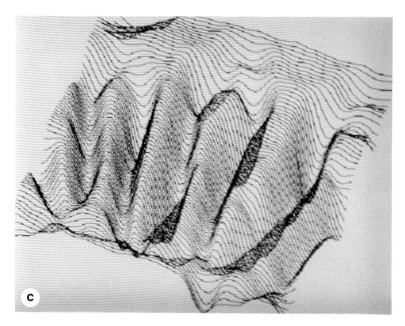

FIGURE 12   (*Continued*)

of the gradient computed (output shown in Figure 12(b)). The result is inverted to produce a potential energy field in which movement of the snake is simulated. The energy field is illustrated in Figure 12(c) as a 3D landscape in which the potential wells are visible as deep valleys. The final resting state (i.e., equilibrium) into which the snake is attracted is shown superimposed on Figure 12(b).

Active contours were the inspiration for *active surfaces,* able to mold around surfaces in space. For example, they have been used to reconstruct the surfaces of rotationally symmetric objects through simulating the motion of an elastic tube with a predisposition to rotational symmetry. As with the snake model, the tube moves within an energy field shaped by the intensity gradients in the image (Terzopoulos, Witkin, & Kass, 1988).

B. Stereo Vision

The estimation of three-dimensional structure from two overlapping views of a scene has been extensively studied in machine vision and a high level of interest continues to the present day, especially within the context of steerable camera heads (Section II.C).

Overlapping views arise when two cameras are used (resulting in *binocular stereo*) and when image sequences are obtained from a moving camera

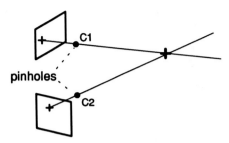

FIGURE 13   A point in the scene projects to points on each image plane.

(resulting in *motion stereo*). Although the two situations have much in common, there are significant differences and so they are examined separately.

The final part of this section looks at putting the information gained from stereo together in the construction of 3D shape descriptions for visible surfaces.

1. Binocular Stereo

The geometry of binocular stereo is illustrated in Figure 13. No constraints need be placed on the relative orientation and displacement of the two cameras. However, in practice, the hardware setup may limit the degrees of freedom. For example, the cameras are commonly assumed to be positioned side by side and parallel to one another.

The general approach proceeds in two stages (Marr, 1982). First, a one-to-one correspondence is established between points in the two images that are believed to be projected from the same visible points in the scene. This is known as the *correspondence problem*. Second, the 3D position of each scene point is computed as the intersection of rays from the corresponding image points through the camera pinholes as shown. The difference in position between corresponding points in the two images is known as the *disparity*. The relative disparities relate directly to the relative depths.

For a given scene point, the projected points in a pair of images may fall anywhere, depending on the intrinsic parameters, position, and orientation of the cameras. Finding the pairwise correspondences is therefore a hard problem, but fortunately one that has a solution through the operation of constraints on individual pairings and on the relationship between sets of pairings.

One of the most powerful of these is the so-called epipolar constraint, deriving from the epipolar geometry of a pair of cameras and illustrated in Figure 14. For diagrammatic simplicity, the pinholes are drawn behind the image planes. This is a common convention, and although physically impossible, the geometry works out just the same.

Suppose we are looking at a point P in space. This point, together with

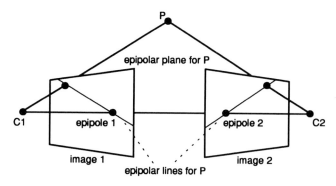

FIGURE 14   The epipolar geometry of a pair of cameras.

the pinholes, C_1 and C_2, defines a plane, known as the *epipolar plane* for P. As P moves around in space, the associated epipolar plane rotates about the line through C_1 and C_2.

Any given epipolar plane slices through each of the image planes along a pair of lines known as the *epipolar lines*. Clearly any point in the epipolar plane projects into each image somewhere along these epipolar lines. Now, any given point p_1 in image 1 fixes the epipolar plane (together with C_1 and C_2) and thereby determines the epipolar line in image 2, along which p_2 must lie. This reduces the search space for p_2 from the whole image to a single (epipolar) line.

The axis through C_1 and C_2 intersects the image planes at two fixed points, known as the *epipoles,* through which all epipolar lines must pass. In the special case of a pair of parallel cameras, the epipoles are "points at infinity" and the epipolar lines are parallel to one another.

Construction of epipolar planes and lines requires some knowledge of the intrinsic parameters of the two cameras, and their relative position and orientation. The necessary information may be contained within a single 3 × 3 matrix **Q,** known as the *essential* or *fundamental* matrix (Longuet-Higgins, 1981). This matrix can be used to generate epipolar lines in one image directly from points in the other, as required. Although **Q** is completely determined by the intrinsic parameters of the two cameras and their relative position and orientation, considerable effort has been expended in finding ways to compute **Q** automatically from observables in each image, and in particular from correspondences between points (Longuet-Higgins, 1981).

A second constraint on the position of corresponding points is to limit the magnitude of the allowed disparity (this is related to Panum's fusion area). Operation of this constraint requires vergence of the cameras to point directly at the object of interest to maintain disparities at or close to 0.

A common approach to the correspondence problem involves seeking pairings only between a relatively small number of point features extracted from each image. This greatly reduces the number of possible pairings, but of course delivers only a sparse correspondence. Typically, the features are edgels (see Section III). Under the epipolar constraint, edgels lying along an epipolar line in one image must match to those lying along the corresponding epipolar line in the other. Several constraints combine to discover the actual pairings.

First, the ordering of corresponding points should be the same along the two lines. Initially this looks like a recipe for a perfect match, but missing point features and exceptional events causing reordering complicate the situation.

Second, figural information about the local edge from which an edgel derives may be used to disambiguate a match. Also the sense (i.e., light to dark or dark to light) and other features of an edgel provide powerful clues as to likely pairings (Marr, 1982).

The *disparity gradient* across the image plane (i.e., the rate of change of disparity) should be small except at depth discontinuities and may also be limited by an upper bound. This provides a powerful constraint on possible sets of pairings and leads naturally to iterative schemes for discovering mutually consistent sets of pairings (Marr & Poggio, 1976; Pollard, Mayhew, & Frisby, 1985).

A further method for reducing the scope for ambiguity is through a multiresolution approach (Marr & Poggio, 1979) in which correspondences are first assigned between feature points detected at a coarse scale. This provides a coarse disparity map that is used to restrict the possible matches between feature points at a finer resolution. The process repeats until pairings are established between feature points at the finest resolution.

As an alternative to feature-based solutions to the correspondence problem, a dense pointwise correspondence is obtained by comparing gray-level windows surrounding each point in one image with identical windows surrounding potential matching points in the other. The best matches deliver the required point correspondences (e.g., Nishihara, 1984).

The preceding discussion related entirely to the correspondence problem. Once solved, the geometric calculation of where each point is in space is straightforward if the intrinsic parameters of both cameras and the relative position and orientation of the cameras are known. Remarkably, it is also possible to estimate the positions of observed points from two views without this information (Faugeras, 1992; Hartley, Gupta, & Chang, 1992; Koenderink & Van Doorn, 1991).

Assuming weak perspective, point positions are recovered with respect to a coordinate system constructed from four of the matched points. Let the four points be **P, Q, R, S** (Figure 15). The origin is assigned to **P** and the basis vectors are $\overrightarrow{PQ}$, $\overrightarrow{PR}$, $\overrightarrow{PS}$. A similar reconstruction, involving five points, is also possible for full perspective.

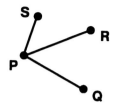

FIGURE 15   Constructing a 3D coordinate system from four points.

However, without knowledge of the intrinsic parameters, the positions of the four (or five) points are unknown with respect to the camera. Hence, all positions are discovered only with respect to the constructed coordinate system. Furthermore, since the constructed basis vectors need not be perpendicular to one another nor of equal length, the relative distances between points cannot be computed. On the other hand, the ordering of points along straight lines is maintained.

An open question is whether or not the lack of metrical information in the recovered point positions matters for the range of tasks in which vision is used.

2. Motion Stereo

Motion of a camera relative to objects in the world provides a rich source of information about the shapes of those objects and about the motion of the camera itself (Ullman, 1979b). Understanding the ability of the human visual system to extract this information from the constantly changing array of light intensities falling on the retinas provides one of the most challenging problems for studies of perception (Gibson, 1966).

In many ways, the recovery of 3D structure from a temporal sequence of images acquired from a moving camera is equivalent to the recovery of structure from two or more static cameras, since each static view mimics one of the views on the trajectory of the moving camera. However, in practice, there are several significant differences.

First, it is relatively easy to acquire more than two images from a moving camera, whereas configurations of three or more static cameras, although possible and sometimes desirable, are rarely used in practice. Ullman (1979a) showed that the image plane positions of just four noncoplanar points in three views were sufficient to recover the 3D positions of those points, assuming orthogonal projection.

Frequently, nothing is known about the trajectory of a moving camera, whereas in binocular stereo there is normally good information about the relative position and orientation of the two cameras. Sometimes trajectory information is available from nonvisual sources (e.g., gyroscopic dead reckoning, feedback from drive motors). Consequently, the epipolar constraint

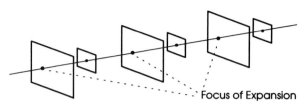

FIGURE 16 For a camera undergoing translation only, the focus of expansion is coincident with the epipoles between any pair of images.

on point correspondences between images is not immediately applicable until sufficient information can be inferred to compute epipolar lines. In practice, the absence of the epipolar constraint is overcome by focusing on a relatively small number of identifiable point features, such as intensity corners (Harris & Stephens, 1988), and comparing frames separated by small time intervals to minimize the distance traveled by features between frames.

Finally, much of the work on the recovery of shape from motion has dealt with estimates of the instantaneous optical flow field and its derivatives rather than with two or more discrete snapshots (Longuet-Higgins & Prazdny, 1980), although in practice the flow field is itself derived from the latter and implicitly encodes the point correspondences.

The motion of a camera can be decomposed into two components: translation and rotation about the center of projection. The latter induces no shape information about the scene since the projections of points move under rotation irrespective of their distances from the camera. All of the information about shape is induced by the translational component of camera motion.

For a camera undergoing only translation, it is well known that all points in the scene appear to move along lines diverging from a single point, the *focus of expansion*. Figure 16 demonstrates that the epipoles for any pair of snapshots taken along the motion trajectory are coincident with this point.

3. Shape Reconstruction

Stereo processing provides estimates of the 3D positions of visible surface points. This is adequate in itself for certain tasks and also sufficient for recognizing objects when the points correspond to identifiable landmarks on the surface (e.g., using geometric hashing; Section V.B.6). In general, however, a richer surface (or volume) based *shape* description is required. Unfortunately, the problem of generating such a description is under constrained—we need to make plausible guesses at the surface, given only the 3D points.

But first there is the question of the form of representation to be used for shape descriptions.

a. Choosing a Shape Representation

The choice of criteria for the evaluation of a representational scheme for shape is task dependent. For the task of recognizing objects, Marr (1982, pp. 296–298) identified the following criteria:

- *Accessibility.* Are shape descriptions readily derivable from images?
- *Scope.* How large is the class of describable shapes?
- *Uniqueness.* Do all shapes have a canonical description? In other words, is the description for a given shape always the same no matter how the shape is presented to the viewer? This is important in recognizing objects by comparing descriptions of visible objects with stored descriptions.
- *Stability.* Do small variations in a shape cause correspondingly small variations in its description?
- *Sensitivity.* Are small differences in shape captured by the representational scheme?

Nonrecognition tasks demand other (possibly overlapping) sets of criteria. For example, shape sensitivity may be important for controlling the fingers of a robot gripper, yet unimportant for navigating a mobile robot through a cluttered environment, for which a relatively coarse shape description may suffice (e.g., minimally enclosing vertical cylinders; see Figure 17).

Many kinds of shape representation have been proposed for use in machine vision. Common among these are representations based on compositions of shape primitives, such as spheres, cylinders, and cubes. Biederman (1987) has proposed a large set of shape primitives (*geons*), from which many everyday objects can be approximated through composition. Pentland (1981) proposed using generalizations of quadric surfaces, called *superquadrics,* as shape primitives.

Two different kinds of shape representation are described here: the triangular mesh and the depth map. Both are particularly well suited to reconstruction from 3D points acquired through stereo processing. In Section V, several other kinds of shape representation are introduced.

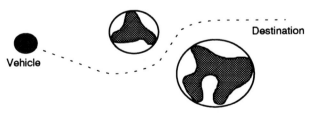

FIGURE 17 Path planning using minimally enclosing vertical cylinders to represent obstacles.

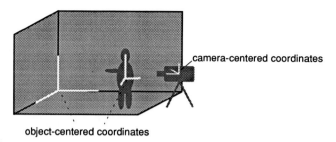

camera-centered coordinates

object-centered coordinates

FIGURE 18   Two kinds of coordinate systems.

Surveys on the representation of shape are contained in Besl (1988), Koenderink (1990), Marshall (1989), and Hogg (1993).

b. Coordinate Systems

In general, shape descriptions involve specifications of point sets in the plane or in space, requiring a coordinate system in which to denote these points. Two principal kinds of 3D coordinate system arise in machine vision: camera-centered and object-centered (Figure 18).

A *camera-centered* (or *viewer-centered*) coordinate system is rooted to the camera and arises naturally as the frame of reference for preliminary shape descriptions derived from images (e.g., using binocular stereo). Unfortunately, as a basis for representing the shapes of objects, it scores badly on uniqueness, since the descriptions produced are not invariant to rigid motion with respect to the camera (i.e., to changes in viewpoint).

In contrast, an *object-centered* coordinate system is intrinsic to the object itself; it does not depend on the viewer or the surrounding environment. Shape descriptions expressed using object-centered coordinates are invariant to all rigid motions of the object.

In general, there may be an embedded hierarchy of object-centered coordinate systems corresponding to the embedded structures within a scene. In particular, it is often convenient to assign a coordinate system to the global environment (e.g., fixed on the ground plane) to provide a camera-independent means for specifying the position and orientation of objects contained in the scene. Such a *world-centered* coordinate system would, for example, be appropriate for planning the path of a mobile robot, for which the shape of the robot is of interest only insofar as it relates to the overall shape of the environment.

c. Triangular Meshes

Triangulation between points is an easy way of filling in the gaps for visible parts of a surface, yielding a patchwork or mesh of triangular faces with the given 3D points at the vertices (Charnley & Blissett, 1989; Figure 19(a)).

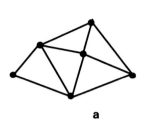 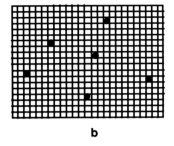

a   b

FIGURE 19   (a) Triangulation of landmark points, (b) sparse depth map.

Creases running between vertices are normally illusory, although they may correspond to real surface features.

Triangulation has been used very successfully for generating terrain models of planetary surfaces from spot heights (i.e., 3D landmarks) inferred from multiple aerial views.

d. Depth Maps

A common aim of reconstruction is the generation of a viewer-centered *depth map* (i.e., a digital surface model) in which surface depths, from a chosen viewpoint, are recorded over a rectangular grid of sample points and stored in the cells of a 2D array. Stereo vision, typically, provides depth data at sample points scattered sparsely across the depth map (Figure 19(b)). The aim of reconstruction is to assign entries to all cells of the depth map so that the discrete surface passes through, or close to, the sparse depth data.

Unfortunately, the problem as stated has no unique solution and additional assumptions are needed to obtain a plausible solution. The most common assumption is that the surface is smooth (as opposed to jagged or discontinuous). Stating that an object has smooth surfaces is a strong constraint but gives only partial information about the detailed shape of the object. Nevertheless, if the domain in which we are working is made up of smooth objects about which nothing further is known, this information should be exploited in reconstruction.

One way of handling the degree of smoothness explicitly, as well as the presence of errors in data points, has been to formulate an optimization problem in which the best surface is that which maximizes a cost function, balancing smoothness against faithfulness to the sparse depth data (Blake & Zisserman, 1987; Terzopoulos, 1983).

Suppose the surface we seek is $Z(x, y)$, where x, y are the coordinates of cells in the depth map (Figure 20). The sparse depth data are $Z_0(x_i, y_i)$, $1 \leq i \leq n$. The cost function operating on a proposed surface Z is defined by

$$\text{cost}(Z) = \alpha \left\{ \sum_{i=1}^{n} \left[Z_0(x_i, y_i) - Z(x_i, y_i) \right]^2 \right\} + \beta \text{ smoothness } (Z)$$

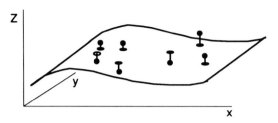

FIGURE 20   Approximating sparse depth data with a smooth surface.

The first term measures deviation of the surface from the data and the second term measures the smoothness of the surface. The weights α, β determine the relative importance of these two components of the cost function. Measures of smoothness typically include first or second derivatives of Z, summed across the depth map.

Solving this optimization problem amounts to finding a least squares approximation to the data points with an additional (*regularization*) term introducing a bias toward smooth surfaces. In principle, terms could be added to the cost function, measuring the extent to which the surface satisfies other generic properties, such as symmetry.

A problem with the blanket smoothness term is that it tends to obliterate genuine discontinuities in depth occurring around the edges of objects. One way of overcoming this is to allow "breaks" in the surface between cells of the depth map across which no smoothness penalty is incurred, but with a small fixed cost to prevent breaks occurring unnecessarily (Blake & Zisserman, 1987).

V. USING OBJECT MODELS

Section IV focused on the use of general models based on general physical principles. The current section reviews the use of object specific models in machine vision. Such models may be invoked at different times in visual processing. *Feature space* methods are intended to be used to classify already detected objects, either in the image or in 3D. *Model-based object recognition* approaches, on the other hand, are used to form new object hypotheses from among collections of primitive image features or surface fragments.

A. Feature Space Methods

The use of feature spaces is one of the earliest approaches to object classification. Although it has traditionally been applied within the context of 2D vision, there is no reason in principle for it not to be applied to the classification of objects detected in 3D.

The idea is that detected objects (e.g., using image thresholding) are represented in terms of a small number of numerical measurements characteristic of the target object categories. Each set of measurements forms an *n*-tuple (called a *feature vector*) that can be thought of as a single point within an *n*-dimensional *feature space,* spanning all possible categories. Typical measurements are the perimeter length and area of segmented blobs and non-spatial measurements such as the mean gray level inside a blob.

The idea is that instances from the same category should form clusters within the feature space, so that unknown entities can be classified by identifying the cluster into which they fall. An easy way to implement this is through representing each cluster by an exemplar feature vector and assigning unknown entities to the cluster with the nearest exemplar. Alternatively, each cluster may be represented by a number of exemplars (Dasarathy, 1991).

The *k-means* algorithm (MacQueen, 1967) is perhaps the best known method for extracting exemplars automatically from instances of the different kinds of object sought (i.e., from training data). The idea is to start out with *k* exemplars placed randomly in the feature space. Each member of the training set is allocated to its "nearest" exemplar. Next the mean of each cluster so formed updates the associated exemplar, and the process is repeated until there is little or no movement of exemplars. *K*-means is similar in operation to unsupervised neural network learning algorithms (e.g., Kohonen, 1989).

B. "Model-Based" Methods

Model-based approaches are characterized by the use of detailed models of the geometric shapes of objects to be recognized (Besl & Jain, 1985). These models may be two-dimensional when pose is effectively restricted to transformations within the image plane or fully three-dimensional otherwise. The aim is to index appropriate models and to find the correct poses for the current scene (referred to as *pose estimation*).

The predominant strategy in model-based object recognition is divided into two stages: (1) hypothesis generation and (2) verification (e.g., Roberts, 1965). In *hypothesis generation,* a number of promising objects and poses worthy of further investigation are singled out as plausible hypotheses. In the *verification* stage, each of these hypotheses is examined more closely to eliminate those that are false. This involves seeking confirming evidence in the image for all parts of the chosen object at the hypothetical pose.

This two-stage strategy works well, since objects and poses are accepted only once they have been through a rigorous verification stage, which, although expensive, is used sparingly by focusing on promising hypotheses. Of course, it is important that all true hypotheses should be identified in the first stage, otherwise they will be missed altogether.

In most available methods (excepting pose sampling and local optimization; see later), hypothesis generation involves matching subsets of features of the model (e.g., edges, vertices, planar faces, shape primitives) to 2D and 3D features extracted from one or more images of the scene. For example, a straight edge on a polygonal model could be matched with a straight intensity edge extracted from a single image or with a 3D surface edge deduced from a stereo pair of images.

Although it is clearly important to be able to recognize different objects in a scene, most methods are concerned with pose estimation for only a single given object. Relatively little work in machine vision has focused on *indexing* a database of models, except by trying each one in turn (but see, for example, Fisher, 1989).

A continuing debate in machine vision exists over whether recognition is best carried out by relating stored models to 3D shape descriptions extracted from images or to 2D image structures directly. On the one hand, relating object models to 3D descriptions appears to be easier, since elements of each are expressed in the same underlying spatial dimension. On the other hand, 3D reconstruction (e.g., by binocular stereo) is error prone, especially for distant objects, and may not be reliable enough for recognition. Furthermore recognition is postponed while 3D reconstruction is carried out. Examples of both approaches can be found in the current literature and will be addressed.

1. Pose Sampling

Pose sampling is perhaps the simplest pose estimation method. The space of all possible poses is densely sampled and each sample (hypothesis) submitted for verification. The sampling density is such that any true pose will be sufficiently close to one of the samples that verification will succeed on that hypothesis. This method is infeasible when pose is unconstrained in 3D, since the number of samples required is prohibitive. It is viable only when pose is severely restricted and therefore has limited applicability.

2. Local Optimization

Local optimization involves treating the verification procedure as an objective function to be maximized over a local region of "pose space." Here it is supposed that verification returns a numerical plausibility value rather than a yes–no answer. Generally, the optimal pose is found by hill climbing from an initial pose, which should be sufficiently nearby to avoid becoming stuck at nonoptimal local maxima.

Both pose sampling and local optimization work well when objects are being tracked from frame to frame, since the space of possible poses is then severely constrained by what is physically possible in a short time step from the previous (known) pose (e.g., Hogg, 1983; Worrall et al., 1993).

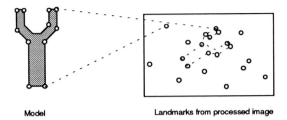

Model   Landmarks from processed image

FIGURE 21   Two pairings of model landmarks with image landmarks.

3. Alignment

Alignment methods (Huttenlocher & Ullman, 1990) generate candidate poses from small sets of pairings between image features and model features. Each set is minimal in that it is just sufficient to determine a unique pose (or a finite number of poses), which is then verified. The idea is to generate all possible minimal sets of pairings or preferably to focus on plausible minimal sets by using additional knowledge about the features (e.g., the number of lines terminating at a vertex). To illustrate, consider the 2D pose estimation problem requiring the discovery of an object's position, orientation, and size in the image plane.

Models are represented as sets of landmark points (e.g., corners in edge contours) expressed in an object-centered coordinate system. Although sparse, this representation of shape can be good enough for recognizing objects, particularly when the points are in motion. The moving light displays of Johansson (1964) give compelling evidence of this. For the current method, the objects are recognized from a single snapshot.

The image is preprocessed to find all possible landmarks, some of which should be derived from the target object, but many of which may come from the background (Figure 21).

Candidate poses derive from all possible combinations of two distinct pairings of model points with image points (Figure 22). Each combination

FIGURE 22   Two pairings of landmarks are sufficient to estimate a pose.

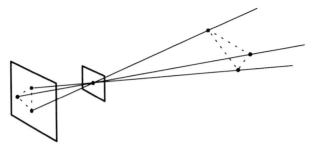

FIGURE 23   One of a finite number of poses determined from a triplet of points.

uniquely determines the pose for which corresponding points are superimposed on one another.

Correct poses are those for which all or most of the remaining object points are superimposed on image points—this is established in the verification stage.

In 3D, triplets of pairings between image points and model points determine finite numbers of poses (Linnainmaa, Harwood, & Davis, 1988). This can be visualized as follows (Figure 23). Assuming all intrinsic parameters of the camera are known, each image point of a triplet defines a line passing through the pinhole and out into space. Points on the model are constrained to lie along the line defined by their corresponding image point. With just one line, the model is free to rotate but can translate only along the line. With two lines, the model still retains two degrees of freedom; but with three lines, the model is either fixed in one of a small number of poses (no more than four) or there is no legal pose.

4. Pose Clustering and the Hough Transform

Pose clustering is similar to the alignment approach except that only the most frequently occurring poses are verified (Ballard, 1981; Linnainmaa et al., 1988). Since a correct pose should be voted for many times by different sets of correctly paired features, these poses should receive greater numbers of votes than incorrect poses. Unfortunately, in practice, things are not quite this straightforward, since correct sets of pairings will generally produce poses that are similar to one another but not identical, due to a variety of sources of error (e.g., small deviations in the shape of an object from that idealized in the model). The way to cope with this is to look for clusters of poses (hence the name). This could be achieved in several ways; for example, using the k-means procedure outlined in Section V.A.

In practice, a simple voting scheme is implemented. The pose space is divided into cells by partitioning each axis of variation into equal intervals and taking the product set. Associated with each cell is a voting bin ini-

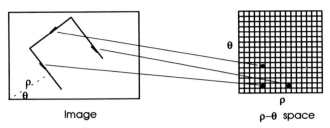

FIGURE 24   Mapping from edgels into ρ–θ space.

tialized to 0. These are conveniently represented by an *n*-dimensional array. Next, as each feature pairing is produced, a vote is cast for the cell containing the implied pose (i.e., the corresponding array cell is incremented by 1). When all votes have been cast, those bins containing more than a given number are readily identified—these are the pose clusters sought. Finally, a pose at the center of each cluster is sent forward for verification.

Pose clustering methods have been widely studied and are better known as generalizations of the Hough transform (Ballard, 1981), originally proposed for the detection of straight edges in images (Hough, 1962). Any straight edge in the image plane can be represented using two parameters (Figure 24): the perpendicular distance ρ of the edge from the origin and the angle θ between the perpendicular line through the origin and the positive *x*-axis.

Thus, the "pose" space of an edge is two-dimensional and the voting bins are held in a 2D array. Each edgel detected in the image has a position and a direction. A vote is cast in the bin associated with the single edge passing through this edgel at the required orientation (Figure 24). Every edgel detected in the image is used to cast votes in this way. The Hough transform is an efficient way to detect straight edges and copes well with breaks in edges caused by sensor errors and occlusion.

Extending the Hough transform to deal with the pose of an object in 3D is not straightforward, since the six-dimensional array required to accumulate votes is prohibitively large. One solution is to estimate a subset of the pose parameters first and then use that information to estimate the remainder; for example, the three orientation parameters followed by the three position parameters.

5. Interpretation Tree Search

Alignment and clustering methods generate pose hypotheses directly from minimal sets of pairings between model features and image features. The elimination of incorrect hypotheses is performed by direct verification with an optional clustering step.

By contrast, interpretation tree search methods (Grimson, 1990; Grimson & Lozano-Perez, 1984) set out to assign model features to all sensed features in all feasible combinations. Each assignment is called an *interpretation,* and the method involves performing a tree search to generate all of the combinations of interpretations as required—hence the name *interpretation tree search.*

The method has been used to estimate 3D pose from 3D sensed features, which may be derived from visual or nonvisual sensors (e.g., pressure sensors on the tips of a robot gripper, laser range finders, stereo vision), and for estimation of 2D pose from 2D image features. Estimation of a 3D pose from 2D image features is also possible through considering broadly different views independently (Goad, 1986).

In the following, we consider the estimation of 3D pose from 3D sensed features. This uses a 3D geometric model composed of planar faces, represented by lists of vertices expressed in a model-centered coordinate system (Figure 25(a)).

The sensed features are small planar patches believed to be on the surface of the target object. Each patch is represented by its 3D position **P** and an estimate of the direction perpendicular to the surface **N** (a 3D unit vector), expressed in camera coordinates (Figure 25(b)).

The method has two steps. In the first, a set of plausible complete interpretations for all sensed patches is generated. In the second, each complete interpretation is tested to see if a 3D pose could have given rise to the pairings of model faces with sensed patches (Figure 26). Normally only one such pose is found (there may be more for symmetric objects).

Plausible complete interpretations are produced by performing a methodical depth-first search through the interpretation tree (Figure 27). Each level of the tree corresponds to a different sensed patch, and each branch

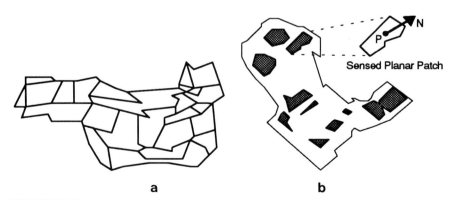

a   b

FIGURE 25   (a) 3D model composed of planar faces, in model-centered coordinates, (b) sensed patches, consisting of position and normal vector, in camera-centered coordinates.

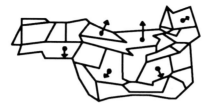

FIGURE 26   Correct pose transforms each sensed patch onto a model face.

corresponds to a different model face. Thus, any route from the root to a leaf of the tree is a complete interpretation of the sensed patches.

As described, the method would be infeasible, since the number of possible interpretations for even a moderately complex model is vast. The trick is to avoid generating all interpretations by applying a small set of fast geometric checks on the consistency of partial interpretations as they arise in the tree search. In this way, the tree is pruned beneath any partial interpretations found to be inconsistent.

Whenever a new node is added to the tree (i.e., a new pairing between a sensed patch and a model face) it is checked for pairwise consistency with each of the nodes on the way back to the root of the tree (Figure 28). In other words, a series of binary constraints are applied to weed out poor partial interpretations.

As described, the constraints operate between pairs of patch-face assignments. A typical constraint could be on the angle between the normals to the patches ($\mathbf{N}$ and $\mathbf{M}$ in Figure 29). Allowing for some error in the estimation of patch normals, this angle should be approximately the same as the actual angle between the two paired model faces. Upper and lower bounds on the acceptable range of angles are computed from the model in a once-only precompilation stage. Two other possible constraints involve the di-

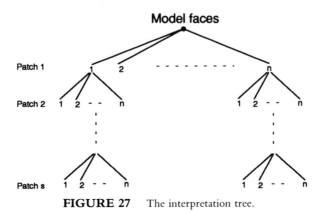

FIGURE 27   The interpretation tree.

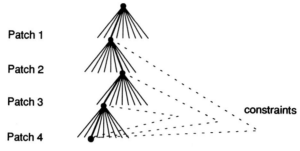

Patch 1

Patch 2

Patch 3

Patch 4

constraints

FIGURE 28   Backward checking of binary constraints.

rection vector **D** from one patch to the other. The first checks the angle between **N** and **D,** and the second between **M** and **D.**

In themselves, the binary constraints do not guarantee that plausible interpretations are globally consistent, in the sense that there may be no object pose for which the sensed patches are jointly mapped onto their assigned model faces. Consequently, all interpretations generated are subject to a final verification stage to identify the one or more globally consistent interpretations that determine the pose of the object.

6. Geometric Hashing

The geometric hashing paradigm (Wolfson & Lamdan, 1992) is a collection of recognition methods that achieve fast and robust recognition through precompilation of geometric information in a once-only off-line process prior to recognition. Moreover, model indexing and pose estimation are handled together in a unified procedure.

To illustrate the approach, we consider a method for the recognition of flat objects free to move in 3D. This depends crucially on the construction of Cartesian coordinate systems based on subsets of any three noncollinear landmark points on the object.

Consider three landmark points **P, Q, R** (Figure 30). The origin is assigned to **P,** and the basis vectors are $\vec{\mathbf{PQ}}$ and $\vec{\mathbf{PR}}.$ Thus, grid lines of the Cartesian coordinate system run parallel to $\vec{\mathbf{PQ}}$ and $\vec{\mathbf{PR}},$ spaced in propor-

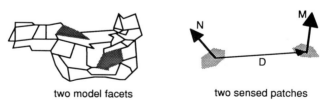

two model facets

two sensed patches

FIGURE 29   Constraints operate between pairs of patch-face assignments.

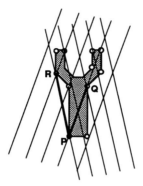

FIGURE 30   A Cartesian coordinate system constructed from three points.

tion to the length of these vectors. In general, the Cartesian grid will not be rectangular. For expository purposes, this coordinate system will be referred as a *three-point basis*.

A property of the three-point basis is that the coordinates of points remain the same under any rotation, translation, scaling, and skewing of points in the plane (including the basis points themselves; see Figure 31).

It is no coincidence that two of the transformed spanners shown in Figure 31 convey a sense of depth, since the weak perspective image of a flat object is related by precisely the same set of transformations.

As a consequence, the coordinates of an object point in a constructed three-point basis are identical with those of the projected point in the corresponding three-point basis constructed in the image.

In the precompilation phase, three-point bases are constructed from all ordered subsets of three landmark points in the model. For each basis, the coordinates of all other landmark points in the model are computed. These are entered into a table alongside the name of the model and the three landmarks forming the current basis (Table 1).

FIGURE 31   Coordinates in constructed basis are invariant to affine transformations of points.

TABLE 1 Model and Basis Points
Indexed by Coordinates

Coordinates	Model name, 3-point basis
(3, 4)	Spanner, $\mathbf{P}_{S_1}$, $\mathbf{P}_{S_2}$, $\mathbf{P}_{S_3}$
(7, 8)	Spanner, $\mathbf{P}_{S_4}$, $\mathbf{P}_{S_5}$, $\mathbf{P}_{S_6}$
(4, 9)	Ratchet, $\mathbf{P}_{R_1}$, $\mathbf{P}_{R_2}$, $\mathbf{P}_{R_3}$
(3, 4)	Hammer, $\mathbf{P}_{H_1}$, $\mathbf{P}_{H_2}$, $\mathbf{P}_{H_3}$

To recognize an object, the image is preprocessed to detect possible landmark points. Three arbitrary landmark points believed to lie on the object are chosen, and a three-point basis constructed from these points (Figure 32). The coordinates in this basis of all other landmarks points are generated and used to index the table, where we hope to find the name of the object and the original basis. Those table entries accessed most frequently are selected for verification. From a three-point basis constructed in the image and a corresponding basis on the model, we can determine the transformation between the two. This is sufficient to enable rigorous verification.

The geometric hashing paradigm can also be used to recognize objects from sets of non-coplanar visible points, although this is much trickier since there is no invariant basis for images of these points under projection (see Wolfson & Lamdan, 1992).

Geometric hashing depends on the derivation of invariants to weak perspective from landmark points on an object. More generally, invariants to full perspective also exist and may be used in recognizing planar objects (Mundy & Zisserman, 1992; Rothwell, Zisserman, Forsyth, & Mundy, 1992). For example, the cross-ratio of four collinear points (Figure 33) is the same in any full perspective projection of those points and can therefore be used to characterize the configuration from any viewpoint.

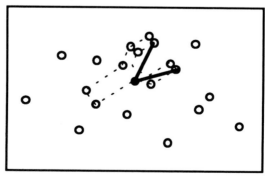

FIGURE 32 Coordinates of points in a basis chosen from preprocessed image.

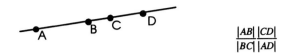

$$\frac{|AB|\ |CD|}{|BC|\ |AD|}$$

FIGURE 33   The cross-ratio of four collinear points.

C. Dealing with Generic Objects and Nonrigid Objects

So far we have looked at indexing and pose estimation for particular objects with fixed shape and size. This is fine for recognizing machined components in an industrial context or particular buildings, but is inadequate for classifying previously unseen objects as instances of generic objects or for dealing with nonrigid objects. For example, a system monitoring traffic scenes needs to be able to identify vehicles whether or not they are familiar models—this requires some kind of built-in shape characterization for the class vehicle.

The second reason for wanting to use generic object models is to provide for inheritance in the specification of shapes, so that shared characteristics (e.g., of individual faces) need not be repeated.

A straightforward way for representing object classes is by the introduction of parameters into object models for fixed shapes. These might vary the dimensions of a component part, alter the relative positions of parts or even switch parts in and out of the shape description. Together, the collection of parameters defines a *shape space* made up of all possible combinations of parameter substitutions. Each point in this space represents a possible shape. The problem now is to find ways to characterize those regions of the shape space corresponding to particular classes of shape and to find ways of recognizing instances of a generic object from images.

1. ACRONYM

Permissible substitutions for parameters may be succinctly expressed as inequality constraints. For example, the dimensions of a vehicle could be related by

$$2 < \frac{Height}{Length} < 3$$

to prevent it from getting too short and fat or long and thin.

In ACRONYM, Brooks (1981) proposed a mechanism for defining class hierarchies by associating sets of inequality constraints with the nodes of a tree structure. Each node represents the class of objects satisfying all inequality constraints assigned to itself and to all of its ancestors in the tree on the way back to the root node. Thus, the root of the tree represents the most

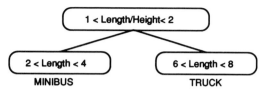

FIGURE 34   Constraint tree representing the feasible dimensions of two kinds of vehicle.

general object class and the leaves are the most specialized, since they each inherit all constraints on the nodes leading back to the root. To illustrate, the class hierarchy shown in Figure 34 defines *truck* as being constrained by the inequalities

$$1 < \frac{Length}{Height} < 2 \quad \text{and} \quad 6 < Length < 8$$

Instances of a modeled object are recognized in ACRONYM by matching features in the image with parts of the model, in such a way that all inequality constraints are satisfied.

2. Point Distribution Models

Variations in the shapes of many natural forms (e.g., hands, faces) do not lend themselves to characterization by the addition of small numbers of variable parameters into shape descriptions. What seems to be required is variation in almost every component of the shape with global control over the feasible configurations.

Point distribution models (Cootes, Taylor, Cooper, & Graham, 1992) provide one way of achieving this for classes consisting of geometrically similar shapes. An individual shape in 2D is represented by a fixed number of sample points around its boundary. Thus, the silhouette of a person walking could be represented as in Figure 35(a).

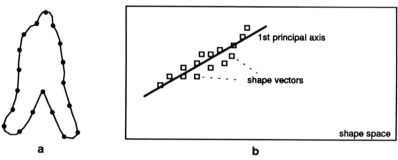

a   **b**

FIGURE 35   (a) Discrete point boundary representation, (b) cluster of shape vectors with a principal axis.

Assuming n sample points around the boundary, each shape is succinctly represented by placing the x, y sample point coordinates end to end into a vector containing $2n$ components:

$$(x_1, y_1, x_2, y_2, \ldots, x_n, y_n)$$

The *shape vector* for the silhouette in Figure 35(a) has 38 components (i.e., 2 × 19). The set of all possible shape vectors of length $2n$ define a *shape space* spanning all possible discrete boundary representations with n points.

We suppose a *training set* of typical instances of a target shape class is available. By selecting a fixed number of corresponding sample points from each shape, a set of shape vectors is obtained, forming a cluster within the shape space. Figure 35(b) shows a cluster of training shape vectors within a (trivial) 2D shape space.

Several ways of characterizing this cluster suggest themselves, inspired by work on pattern recognition and neural networks. Cootes et al. (1992) use a principal component analysis centered on the cluster to find its principal axes of variation. In other words, they find an ordered set of perpendicular axes passing through the center of the cluster, such that most variation in the distribution of the cluster is along the first axis. Removing this axis of variation, the greatest residual variation is along the second axis, and so on to the $2n$th axis.

The principal axes provide an alternative parameterization for the shape space. Remarkably, many classes of shape can be approximated to within acceptable error tolerance by coordinates along the first few principal axes only. These axes therefore provide a succinct parameterization for the shape class represented by the original training set. For example, the principal axis shown in Figure 35(b) captures most of the variation within the cluster.

To illustrate using a real example, Figure 36 shows shape instances along the principal axis of variation computed from the projected silhouettes of people, detected automatically from video sequences (Baumberg & Hogg, 1994). The most noticeable feature of the variation is the characteristic appearance and disappearance of the gap between the legs.

Instances of a point distribution model may be recognized through a procedure similar to active snakes (Section IV.A.3), in which an initial shape (represented by a shape vector) is adjusted to slide the boundary down into a potential energy well shaped by intensity gradients in the image (Cootes & Taylor, 1992).

Nonrigid objects can be recognized in a similar fashion, through the introduction of variable parameters to allow deformation and articulation. The class of shapes into which a nonrigid object can be deformed is thereby treated in the same way as a generic object class. Thus, for example, a walking person can be tracked using pose sampling augmented by "posture" sampling to deal with articulation of the body (Hogg, 1983). Equally,

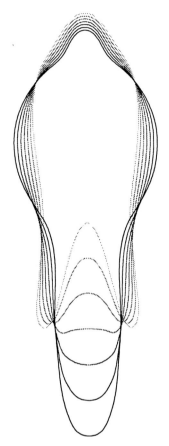

FIGURE 36 The principal axis of variation computed from the silhouettes of people walking.

a 2D point distribution model may be used to track a nonrigid object such as a person in much the same way as it would be used to recognize instances of a generic shape class.

VI. CONCLUSION

Machine vision is a rapidly evolving field with many different kinds of approach and a wide variety of uses. There is a good deal of shared understanding on the aims of vision, particularly given the broad range of tasks for which it is currently being used.

At the time this chapter is being written, there are several promising trends and exciting directions for future research. To select just two examples, recent developments on the representation of shape and stereo vision should have a significant impact in the next few years.

An important challenge for the field is to develop new ways of learning more of what is currently handcrafted into vision systems. Only in this way will truly general purpose machine vision become possible.

Acknowledgments

Thanks to Nick Efford for providing the images in Figure 12 and to Alex Le Bek for reading and commenting on draft versions.

References

Aloimonos, J., Weiss, I., & Bandyopadhyay, A. (1987). Active vision. *Proceedings of the IEEE First International Conference on Computer Vision*, pp. 35–54.

Ballard, D. H. (1981). Generalizing the Hough transform to detect arbitrary shapes. *Pattern Recognition, 13*(2), 111–122.

Ballard, D. H. (1991). Animate vision. *Artificial Intelligence, 48*, 57–86.

Ballard, D. H., & Brown, C. M. (1982). *Computer vision.* Englewood Cliffs, NJ: Prentice-Hall.

Baumberg, A., & Hogg, D. C. (1994). Learning flexible models from image sequences. In J-O. Eklundh (Eds.), *Computer Vision—ECCV '94* Vol. 1 (pp. 299–308). Berlin: Springer-Verlag.

Besl, P. J. (1988). Geometric modelling and computer vision. *Proceedings of the IEEE, 76*(8), 936–958.

Besl, P. J., & Jain, R. C. (1985). 3D object recognition. *ACM Computing Surveys, 17*(1), 75–154.

Biederman, I. (1987). Recognition-by-components: A theory of human image understanding. *Psychological Review, 94*, 115–147.

Blake, A., & Zisserman, A. (1987). *Visual reconstruction.* Cambridge, MA: MIT Press.

Blake, A., Zisserman, A., & Cipolla, R. (1992). Visual exploration of free-space. In A. Blake & A. Yuille (Eds.), *Active vision* (pp. 175–187). Cambridge, MA: MIT Press.

Brooks, R. A. (1981). Symbolic reasoning among 3-D models and 2-D images. *Artificial Intelligence, 17*, 285–348.

Brooks, R. A. (1986). A robust layered control system for a mobile robot. *IEEE Journal of Robotics and Automation, 2*, 14–22.

Brown, C. M. (1990). Prediction and cooperation in gaze control. *Biological Cybernetics, 63*, 61–70.

Campbell, F. W. C., & Robson, J. (1968). Application of Fourier to the visibility of gratings. *Journal of Physiology (London), 197*, 551–566.

Charnley, D., & Blissett, R. (1989). Surface reconstruction from outdoor image sequences. *Image and Vision Computing, 7*(1).

Cliff, D., Harvey, I., & Husbands, P. (1993). Explorations in Evolutionary Robotics. *Adaptive Behaviour, 2*(1), 73–110.

Clowes, M. B. (1971). On seeing things. *Artificial Intelligence, 2*(1), 79–116.

Cootes, T. F., & Taylor, C. J. (1992). Active shape models—'smart' snakes. In D. C. Hogg & R. D. Boyle (Eds.), *British machine vision conference 1992* (pp. 266–275). London: Springer-Verlag.

Cootes, T. F., Taylor, C. J., Cooper, D. H., & Graham, J. (1992). Training models of shape from sets of examples. In D. C. Hogg & R. D. Boyle (Eds.). *British machine vision conference 1992* (pp. 9–18). London: Springer-Verlag.

Dasarathy, B. V. (Ed.). (1991). *Nearest neighbor pattern classification techniques.* Los Alamitos, California: IEEE Computer Society Press.

Faugeras, O. D. (1992). What can be seen in three dimensions with an uncalibrated stereo rig. In G. Sandini (Ed.), *Computer vision—ECCV'92* (pp. 563–578). Berlin: Springer-Verlag.

Faugeras, O. D. (1993). *Three-dimensional computer vision.* Cambridge, MA: MIT Press.

Fisher, R. B. (1989). *From surfaces to objects: Computer vision and three-dimensional scene analysis.* Chichester: Wiley.

Gibson, J. J. (1966). *The senses considered as perceptual systems.* Boston: Houghton Mifflin.

Goad, C. (1986). Fast 3D model-based vision. In A. P. Pentland (Ed.), *From pixels to predicates* (pp. 371–391). Norwood, NJ: Ablex.

Grimson, W. E. L. (1990). *Object recognition by computer: The role of geometric constraints.* Cambridge, MA: MIT Press.

Grimson, W. E. L., & Lozano-Perez, T. (1984). Model-based recognition and localization from sparse range or tactile data. *International Journal of Robotics Research 3*(3), 3–35.

Harris, C. G., & Stephens, M. J. (1988). A combined corner and edge detector. *Proceedings of the Fourth Alvey Vision Conference,* pp. 147–152.

Hartley, R., Gupta, R., & Chang, T. (1992). Stereo from uncalibrated cameras. *Proceedings of the IEEE Conference on Computer Vision and Pattern Recognition 1992.* Champaign, Illinois, June.

Hogg, D. C. (1983). Model-based vision: A program to see a walking person. *Image and Vision Computing Journal, 1,* 5–20.

Hogg, D. C. (1993). Shape in machine vision. *Image and Vision Computing Journal, 11*(6), 309–316.

Holland, J. H. (1992). *Adaptation in natural and artificial systems* (2nd ed.). Cambridge, MA: MIT Press.

Hough, P. V. C. (1962). *Method and means for recognizing complex patterns.* U.S. Patent 3,069,654.

Hubel, D. H., & Wiesel, T. N. (1968). Receptive fields and functional architecture of monkey striate cortex. *Journal of Physiology (London), 195,* 215–243.

Huffman, D. A. (1971). Impossible objects as nonsense sentences. *Machine Intelligence, 6,* 295–323.

Huttenlocher, D. P., & Ullman, S. (1990). Recognizing solid objects by alignment with an image. *International Journal of Computational Vision, 5*(2), 195–212.

Johansson, G. (1964). Perception of motion and changing form. *Scandinavian Journal of Psychology, 5,* 181–208.

Kass, M., Witkin, A., & Terzopoulos, D. (1987). Snakes: Active contour models. *International Journal of Computational Vision, 1,* 321–331.

Koenderink, J. J. (1990). *Solid shape.* Cambridge, MA: MIT Press.

Koenderink, J. J., & Van Doorn, A. J. (1991). Affine structure from motion. *Journal of the Optical Society of America, 8*(2), 377–385.

Kohonen, T. (1989). *Self-organisation and associative memory* (3rd ed.). Berlin: Springer-Verlag.

Linnainmaa, A., Harwood, D., & Davis, L. S. (1988). Pose determination of a three-dimensional object using triangle pairs. *IEEE Transactions on Pattern Analysis and Machine Intelligence, PAMI-10*(5), 634–647.

Longuet-Higgins, H. C. (1981). A computer algorithm for reconstructing a scene from two projections. *Nature (London), 293,* 133–135.

Longuet-Higgins, H. C., & Prazdny, K. (1980). The interpretation of a moving retinal image. *Proceedings of the Royal Society of London, Series B, 208,* 385–397.

MacQueen, J. (1967). Some methods for classification and analysis of multivariate observations. In L. M. LeCam & J. Neyman (Eds.), *Proceedings of the Fifth Berkely Symposium on Mathematics, Statistics, and Probability* (pp. 281–297).

Marr, D. (1982). *Vision.* San Francisco: Freeman.

Marr, D., & Poggio, T. (1976). A cooperative computation of stereo disparity. *Science, 194,* 283–287.

Marr, D., & Poggio, T. (1979). A theory of human stereopsis. *Proceedings of the Royal Society of London, Series B, 204,* 301–328.

Marshall, S. (1989). Review of shape coding techniques. *Image and Vision Computing Journal,* 7(4), 281–294.

Mundy, J. L., & Zisserman, A. (1992). Towards a new framework for vision. In J. L. Mundy & A. Zisserman (Eds.), *Geometric invariance in computer vision* (pp. 1–39). Cambridge, MA: MIT Press.

Murray, D. W., Du, F., McLauchlan, P. F., Reid, I. D., Sharkey, P. M., & Brady, M. (1992). Design of stereo heads. In A. Blake & A. Yuille (Eds.), *Active vision* (pp. 155–172). Cambridge, MA: MIT Press.

Nishihara, H. K. (1984). Practical real-time imaging stereo matcher. *Optical Engineering, 23*(5), 536–545.

Pentland, A. P. (1981). Perceptual organisation and the representation of natural form. *Artificial Intelligence, 28*(3), 293–331.

Pollard, S. B., Mayhew, J. E. W., & Frisby, J. P. (1985). PMF: A stereo correspondence algorithm using a disparity gradient limit. *Perception, 14,* 449–470.

Pratt, W. (1978). *Digital image processing.* New York: Wiley.

Roberts, L. G. (1965). Machine perception of three-dimensional solids. In J. T. Tippett et al. (Eds.), *Optical and electro-optical information processing* (pp. 159–197). Cambridge, MA: MIT Press.

Rothwell, C. A., Zisserman, A., Forsyth, D. A., & Mundy, J. L. (1992). Fast recognition using algebraic invariants. In J. L. Mundy & A. Zisserman (Eds.), *Geometric invariance in computer vision* (pp. 398–407). Cambridge, MA: MIT Press.

Shepard, R. N., & Metzler, J. (1971). Mental rotation of three-dimensional objects. *Science, 171,* 701–703.

Sloman, A. (1989). On designing a visual system: Towards a Gibsonian computational model of vision. *Journal of Experimental and Theoretical AI, 1*(4), 289–337.

Sonka, M., Hlavac, V., & Boyle, R. (1993). *Image processing, analysis and machine vision.* London: Chapman & Hall.

Terzopoulos, D. (1983). Multilevel computational processes for visual surface reconstruction. *Computer Vision, Graphics and Image Processing, 24*(1), 52–96.

Terzopoulos, D., Witkin, A., & Kass, M. (1988). Constraints on deformable models: Recovering 3D shape and non rigid motion. *Artificial Intelligence, 36,* 91–123.

Tistarelli, M., & Sandini, G. (1993). On the advantages of polar and log-polar mapping for direct estimation of time to impact from optical flow. *IEEE Transactions on Pattern Analysis and Machine Intelligence, PAMI-15*(4), 401–410.

Torras, C. (1993). From geometric motion planning to neural motor control in robotics. *AI Communications, 6*(1), 3–17.

Ullman, S. (1979a). The interpretation of structure from motion. *Proceedings of the Royal Society of London, Series B, 203,* 405–426.

Ullman, S. (1979b). *The interpretation of visual motion.* Cambridge, MA: MIT Press.

Weiman, C. F. R., & Chaikin, G. (1979). Logarithmic spiral grids for image processing and display. *Computer Graphics and Image Processing, 11,* 197–226.

Wolfson, H. J., & Lamdan, Y. (1992). Transformation invariant indexing. In J. L. Mundy & A. Zisserman (Eds.), *Geometric invariance in computer vision* (pp. 335–353). Cambridge, MA: MIT Press.

Worrall, A. D., Sullivan, G. D., & Baker, K. D. (1993). Advances in model-based traffic vision. In J. Illingworth (Ed.), *British machine vision conference 1993* (Vol. 2, pp. 559–568). BMVA Press.

Young, D. (1989). Logarithmic sampling of images for computer vision. In *Proceedings of the Seventh Conference of the Society for the Study of Artificial Intelligence and the Simulation of Behaviour AISB* (pp. 145–150). London: Pitman.

CHAPTER 8

Natural Language Processing

Mark Steedman

I. INTRODUCTION

A. Scope of the Study

The subject of natural language processing can be considered in both broad and narrow senses. In the broad sense, it covers processing issues at all levels of natural language understanding, including speech recognition, syntactic and semantic analysis of sentences, reference to the discourse context (including anaphora, inference of referents, and more extended relations of discourse coherence and narrative structure), conversational inference and implicature, and discourse planning and generation. In the narrower sense, it covers the syntactic and semantic processing of *sentences* to deliver semantic objects suitable for referring, inferring, and the like. Of course, the results of inference and reference may under some circumstances play a part in processing in the narrow sense. But the processes that are characteristic of these other modules are not the primary concern.

This chapter is confined mainly to the narrower interpretation of the topic, although it will become apparent that it is impossible to entirely separate it from the broader context. The reader interested in the more global problem is directed to the readings mentioned in the section on Further Reading.

Artificial Intelligence

B. The Anatomy of a Processor

All language processors can be viewed as comprising three elements. The first is a grammar, which defines the legal ways in which constituents may combine, both syntactically and semantically, to yield other constituents. The syntactic class to which the grammar belongs also determines a characteristic automaton, the minimal abstract computer capable of discriminating the sentences of the language in question from random strings of words, and assigning structural descriptions to sentences appropriate to their semantics.

The second component of a processor is a nondeterministic algorithm that uses the rules of the grammar to deliver such structural descriptions for a given sentence. Such an algorithm schema determines, for example, whether the rules are used "top down" or predictively, or "bottom up," or some mixture of the two, and whether the words of the sentence are examined in order from first to last or in some less obvious order. However, as the term *nondeterministic* suggests, this component does not itself determine what happens when more than one rule can apply in a given state of the processor.

This last responsibility devolves to the third component, the oracle, or mechanism for resolving such local processing ambiguities. The oracle decides *which* action should be taken at points in the analysis where the nondeterministic algorithm allows more than one.

Such nondeterminism can arise from two distinct sources. The first source is lexical syntactic ambiguity, as in the case of the English word *bear,* which can be either noun, noun phrase, or verb. The second source is structural syntactic ambiguity, which arises when there is more than one way to combine the same lexical categories to yield a legal sentence. For example, a parser for English that has dealt with the words *put the book on the table . . .* is likely to be in a state in which the verb *put,* the noun phrase *the book,* and the prepositional phrase *on the table* could be combined to yield a complete verb phrase, but where the noun phrase and the prepositional phrase could also be combined to yield a noun phrase *the book on the table.* If the sentence ends at that point, as in sentence 1a, then this "local" parsing ambiguity is resolved in favor of the former analysis. However, if the sentence continues as in 1b, then the latter analysis, in which *on the table* modifies the noun phrase rather than the verb phrase, is available, and in fact preferred. (Another analysis is possible, so this sentence is also said to be syntactically "globally" ambiguous.)

1. a. Put the book on the table.
   b. Put the book on the table in your pocket.

C. The Relevance of Computation

Computer science provides a rich source of models for theories of all three modules of the human processor, drawing not only on the manner in which similar modules are treated in constructing compilers and interpreters for artificial programming languages, but also work within the artificial intelligence paradigm. This work provides both theories and working examples of the way in which syntactic processing, semantic processing, and referential processing can be interleaved and may in very restricted senses interact during processing. This has been made possible by the development of computational systems for knowledge representation and inference within AI that have provided notations for the contextual and domain-specific knowledge involved in linguistic comprehension.

The contribution of AI knowledge representations is at least as important as that of compiler theory, for we should be clear at the outset that in many ways programming languages are strikingly unlike their natural counterparts. Programming languages typically have tiny grammars by comparison with human languages. Compilers typically cope with very complex expressions, and are required to be "complete"; that is, to guarantee a correct analysis for any legal expression of the language. Human processors, on the other hand, deal with expressions that are structurally rather simple. There is also every indication that the human parser is in syntactic terms very far from complete. The most obvious evidence for incompleteness is the well-known apparent nonparsability of "center-embedded" sentences such as 2a, in comparison with their "right-embedded" relatives like 2b:

2. a. The rat the cat the dog bit chased escaped.
   b. This is the dog that bit the cat that chased the rat that escaped.

The difficulty of a sentence has widely been supposed to arise from some limitation in the size of working memory—say from a bound on the size of the push-down stack that is characteristic of context-free grammars and whose use is crucial in the case of center-embedding. Interestingly, this very old suggestion has never been really successfully formalized, and recent work by Gibson (1994) suggests that the catastrophic effect in 2a is due to center embedding *within subjects,* rather than center-embedding alone. Niv (1993) cites the increased acceptability of examples like "a book that some Italian I've never heard of wrote will be published next week" (which he attributes to B. Frank) to suggest that the effect stems from an interaction of subjecthood and other discourse factors related to definiteness.

Even more striking evidence of incompleteness arises from certain well-known "garden-path" sentences first noted by Bever (1970). Example 3a includes a lexical ambiguity that leads the processor so seriously astray that naive subjects are typically unable to identify any analysis for a sentence with which they would otherwise have no trouble, as shown by the syntactically identical 3b:

3. a. The horse raced past the barn fell.
   b. The horse driven past the barn fell.

II. COMPUTATIONAL THEORIES OF PROCESSING

A. The Grammar

1. Competence and Performance

The grammar that we have identified as a component of the processor is a module of the "performance" system, rather than of "competence," in the linguist's sense of those terms. When we contemplate the human processor as a whole, we should be aware that this performance grammar is conceptually distinct from the competence grammar that the linguist provides. In fact there is no logical necessity for the structures that the processor builds to have anything to do with the structures implicated by the competence grammar; that is, the structures required by the semantics (and the linguist). As Berwick and Weinberg (1984, esp. pp. 78–82) have noted, the processor can, in principle, parse according to a grammar that is quite different from the one most directly related to the semantics, provided that there exists a computable homomorphism mapping the structures of this "covering grammar" on the structures of the competence grammar. If the homomorphism is simple, so that the computational costs of parsing according to the covering grammar plus the costs of computing the mapping are less than the costs of parsing according to the competence grammar, then there may be a significant practical advantage in this strategem. For this reason, it is quite common for compilers and interpreters to parse according to a weakly equivalent covering grammar, mapping to the "real" grammar as defined by the reference manual via a homomorphism under concatenation on a string representing the derivation under the covering grammar. This strategem has sometimes been used in programming language compilers, when a parsing algorithm desirable for reasons of efficiency demands grammars in a normal form not adhered to by the grammar in the reference manual. Such a tactic has also been used in at least one early artificial parser for natural languages, in which it was necessary to use a top–down algorithm. As we shall see later, such algorithms are ill-suited to the left-recursive rules that commonly occur in natural grammars.

Nevertheless, considerations of parsimony in the theory of language evolution and language development might also lead us to expect that, as a matter of fact, a close relation will turn out to hold between the competence grammar and the structures dealt with by the psychological processor and that it will in fact incorporate the competence grammar in a modular fashion. One frequently invoked argument depends on the speed of language development in children. This speed in turn suggests that learning proceeds via the piecemeal addition, substitution, and modification of individual rules and categories of competence grammar. However, the addition of, or change to, such a rule will not in general correspond to a similarly modular change in a covering grammar. Instead, the entire ensemble of competence rules will typically have to be recompiled into a new covering grammar. Even if we assume that the transformation of one grammar into another is determined by a language-independent algorithm and can be computed each time at negligible cost, we have still sacrificed parsimony in the theory and increased the burden of explanation on the theory of evolution. In particular, it is quite unclear why the development of either of the principal components of the theory in isolation should confer any selective advantage. The competence grammar is by assumption unprocessable, and the covering grammar is by assumption uninterpretable. It looks as though they can evolve only as a unified system, together with the translation process. The evolution of such a system is likely to be much harder to explain than that of a more directly competence-based system.

Indeed the first thing we would have to explain is why a covering grammar was necessary in the first place. The reference grammars of programming languages and the competence grammars of natural languages have syntaxes ill-suited to parsing with our favorite algorithms because they are constrained from outside by our own requirements. It is we who find Greibach normal form tedious and find grammars with left-recursive rules congenial, forcing the use of covering grammars by some artificial processors. It is quite unclear what comparable external force could have the effect of making natural grammars similarly ill-matched to the *natural* sentence processor. The natural processor could certainly require grammars to be in some normal form. However, provided that the normal form is a class of grammars of the same automata-theoretic power that the semantics of the language requires (and therefore of the same power as the competence grammar), we would expect that normal form to simply be a characteristic of the grammars we observe. In other words, we would view it as a (processing-based) constraint on the form of the competence grammars that actually exist.

For similar reasons, we should expect that the syntactic categories and rules of the competence grammar will stand in the closest possible relationship to the categories and rules of a compositional semantics, in which the interpretation of complex expressions is determined wholly by the interpretation of their component parts and where the assembly of semantic interpretations can be carried out in lock-step with syntactic derivation.

Since the sole purpose of syntax is to identify semantic interpretation, anything else seems to pointlessly complicate the problems of evolution and acquisition.

Therefore, in the remainder of the chapter, we shall adopt the assumption that the grammar used by or implicit in the human sentence processor is the competence grammar itself, a position that Kaplan and Bresnan (Bresnan, Ed., 1982) have named the *strong competence hypothesis*. To adopt this position is not to assume that linguists will have had the foresight to provide their grammars in the form in which we need them to make predictions on the basis of this hypothesis or even that any of the (disturbingly numerous) alternative formulations are entirely correct. However, the fact that our access to the underlying semantic representations is very limited indeed, and that there are so many possible parsers for each grammar, both mean that the linguists' methods for studying competence grammar remain an essential aid. Indeed, in the history of the formal theory of natural grammar, linguists and computationalists have been like climbers roped together on a mountainside, each in turn helping the other toward the summit.

2. Computational Theories of Grammar

a. The Context-free Core

To talk about this collaboration we need a notation. We will start with a computational notation for grammars called *definite clause grammars* (DCG). This notation is convenient both because it is so close to phrase structure (PS) grammar and because it is directly compatible with a useful computational device called *unification,* which we can use to build derivations or even interpretations very simply indeed. A DCG for a fragment of English might begin with rules that we can write as follows:

$$
\begin{aligned}
4. \qquad S : vp\ np1 &\rightarrow N P_{agr} : np1 \quad V P_{agr} : vp \\
V P_{agr} : iv &\rightarrow V_{INTR,agr} : iv \\
V P_{agr} : tv\ np2 &\rightarrow V_{TRAN,agr} : tv \quad N P : np2 \\
N P_{SING} : pn\ e_1 &\rightarrow P N_{SING} : pn \\
N P_{agr} : (q\ e_2)(n\ e_2) &\rightarrow DET_{agr} : q \quad N_{agr} : n
\end{aligned}
$$

In this notation, the familiar PS rules such as $S \rightarrow NP\ VP$ are expanded as in the first rule to include interpretations. Thus, an expression of the form S: $vp\ np1$ denotes a grammatical category of syntactic type S (a sentence) and semantic interpretation $vp\ np1$, in which the variable vp is a predicate that is applied to an argument $np1$. Whenever possible, we shall abbreviate such categories as $S,$ and so forth. In the first rule, both vp and $np1$ also occur as the interpretations of two subconstituents of type NP and VP. Subscripts on symbols like V_{INTR} and V_{TRAN} are a convenient notation for categories that we want to think of as bundles of feature–value pairs, like $\pm transitive$. Features with lower case, as in NP_{agr}, are to be read as variables, or feature–value pairs with unbound values. Corresponding unsubscripted categories like NP are to be read as categories whose value on its features is irrelevant to the application of the rule.

We pass over the details of the actual semantic types of variables like iv, tv, pn, and q, except to note we are assuming that they range over higher order types of the kind familiar from the work of Montague (1974), so that the latter two are varieties of what are called *generalized quantifiers,* binding the variables e_n that range over entities in the model or database, and that the former two are even higher types. The important thing to note about this semantics is that it is completely integrated into the syntactic rules and that interpretations can therefore be assembled simultaneously with syntactic analysis.

Rules written as in 4 leave the string order of subconsituents on the right of a rule, such as NP and VP in the first rule, implicit under an obvious convention in the linear order of those symbols on the page. An alternative notation, which makes linear order explicit but which is in other respects very similar to DCG grammars, is that of augmented transition network grammars (ATNs; Woods, 1970), which we can think of as replacing groups of one or more DCG rules by a finite automaton, where each automaton can "call" the others recursively. The earlier DCG rules might be written as in Figure 1, although the notation used here differs considerably from Woods's own. (The original ATN grammars packed as many PS rules as possible into each network, and so produced "flatter" grammars than this example suggests. In effect they used a covering grammar to make life easy for the algorithm.)

Like the PS rules that they resemble, the rules in either notation can be applied top down ("To find a sentence meaning $S : vp\ np1$, find a noun phrase meaning $np1$ to the left of a verb phrase meaning vp") or bottom up ("If you find a noun phrase meaning $np1$ to the left of a verb phrase meaning vp, make them into a sentence meaning $S : vp\ np1$"). However, it is important to remember that both DCGs and ATNs are *grammars* not parsers and can be fitted up with any algorithm/oracle combination we like.

Whichever notation we use and however the algorithm applies the rules, a mechanism called *unification* can be used to ensure that the S resulting from a successful analysis of a given string is associated with the appropriate interpretation. (Again, the notation is not standard. The original ATN grammars associated explicit "register-changing" rules with transition networks to achieve the same effect of information passing.)

Informally, unification can be regarded as merging or amalgamating terms that are "compatible" and as failing to amalgamate incompatible ones via an algorithm that "instantiates" variables by substituting expressions for

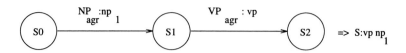

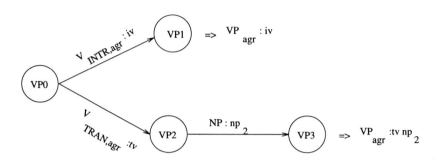

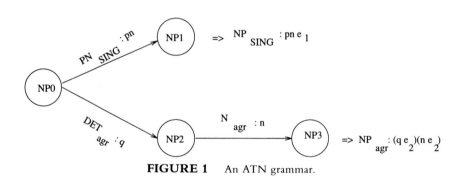

FIGURE 1   An ATN grammar.

them in one or another of the terms. More technically, the result of unifying two compatible terms is the most general term that is an instance of both the original terms. For example, the following pairs of terms unify to yield the results shown. (Note that the unification of two variables is a "new" variable, distinct from either, and that uppercase identifies constants, while lowercase identifies variables.)

5. x A $\Rightarrow A$

    $F(GA)$ x $\Rightarrow F(GA)$

    Fx $F(G\gamma)$ $\Rightarrow F(Gz)$

    $(FA)x$ $(F\gamma)y$ $\Rightarrow (FA)A$

The following pairs of terms do not unify:

6. A B $\Rightarrow$ fail
    Fx $G\gamma$ $\Rightarrow$ fail
    $(FA)B$ $(F\gamma)\gamma$ $\Rightarrow$ fail

For example, suppose the lexicon tells us that the word *Harry* bears the category $NP : HARRY\ e_1$, and suppose that *walks* has the category $VP : WALKS$. (The variable e_1 ranges over individuals in the discourse model, which we can think of as a database of facts.) If we find the word *Harry* to the left of the word *walks,* it follows that we can unify this sequence of categories with the right-hand side of the first rule in 4. This has the effect of replacing the variable vp by $WALKS$ and the variable $np1$ by $HARRY\ e_1$ throughout the rule. The resulting S is therefore associated with the expression $WALKS\ (HARRY\ e_1)$. The derivation, in which the unification does the work of a compositional semantics, can be represented by the usual sort of tree diagram as in Figure 2. In fact, there is a little more to it than this: the variable or undefined value agr on the syntactic categories NP_{agr} and VP_{agr} in the rule also got bound to the value $3SING$ by the unification. Had the subject and verb borne different values on the agreement feature, as in the following illegal string, the unification, and hence the whole derivation, would have failed.

7. *Harry walk

Thus we have the rudiments of an account of linguistic agreement. Of course, it is not a very *good* account. In a more complete fragment of English we would want to further unpack the feature *agr* and its values like $3SING$ into a bundle made up of a number of features like *num* (number) and *per* (person). Linguists would probably point out that some phenomena of agreement appear to be most parsimoniously described in terms of *disjunction* of feature–value pairs, which may suggest we need a more refined representation altogether. However, these refinements are of less interest for

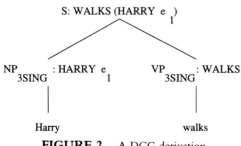

FIGURE 2   A DCG derivation.

present purposes than the observation that we have here the beginnings of a very simple account of a phenomenon that in the early days of generative grammar was thought to require "*Aspects*-style" transformations (Chomsky, 1965), a potentially very powerful class of rule indeed.

The interpretation delivered by the preceding derivation is closely related to the derivation tree itself. The observation generalizes to other derivations that are permitted. This generalization suggests that what we have so far developed is merely a computationally convenient form of context-free grammar, "slaved" via unification to a device that builds interpretation structures as derivation proceeds, an idea that seems to originate with Kuno in the 1960s. This is a helpful way to think about the processor, but some caution is in order. We have so far been quite vague about the unification mechanism and in particular about the types of values that features may bear. In particular, if we allow the values to be lists, then we shall change the automata-theoretic power of the grammar (which may, of course, be what we want). Completely unrestricted feature systems can also threaten the tractability of the parsing problem (cf. Barton, Berwick, & Ristad, 1987).

With this notation in place, we can begin to look at more complex constructions. It is convenient to collect these into three classes. The "bounded" constructions, which include many phenomena that were originally thought to require transformations, are those that relate argument positions *within a single tensed clause*. These constructions are to be contrasted with "unbounded" constructions, such as relativization, which can relate elements of sentences across one or more tensed clause boundaries. The unbounded constructions can be divided into "well-behaved" constructions, like relativization itself, and "less well-behaved" constructions, notably including coordination. The computational implications of this last class are a topic in their own right and will be touched on only very briefly. The first two classes have received most attention, both from linguists and from computational linguists.

b. Bounded Constructions

All languages of the world appear to include devices, usually morphologically marked, that affect the mapping between semantic predicate argument relations and linear order or the surface case of the corresponding expressions in the sentence. An example in English is afforded by the contrast between active and passive morphology, which produces clauses in which the semantic object is respectively realized as accusative or sentence final and nominative or sentence initial:

8. a. I like Ike.
   b. Ike is liked.

Others relate the same surface argument expression to more than one semantic argument role and sometimes to arguments of different verbs stand-

ing in a semantically subordinating relation, as in morphological reflexiviza-
tion or various raising or control constructions, as in the following English
example:

9. I persuaded Ike to leave.

The languages of the world show very striking similarities in the range and
type of such constructions that they offer. To capture and explain these
regularities is a major goal of contemporary linguistic research.

All of these constructions share an important distinguishing property
called *boundedness*. That is to say, the semantic arguments whose relations to
surface grammar these constructions determine must either be involved in
the same proposition (as in the case of the passive and morphological reflex-
ivization) or in a proposition and an *immediately* subordinate complement
proposition (as in the last example).

The bounded and structure-preserving properties of these constructions
immediately suggest that they should be handled *in the context-free base
component of the grammar,* as proposed in the ATN framework by Woods
(1970). Many modern theories of syntax make a related assumption, which
goes by the name of the *base generation hypothesis* (cf. Brame, 1978). In the
DCG notation we can capture the idea as follows. (As usual, the interpretation here is highly simplified, and all the real work is being done by the
translation *ocv* of the object control verb. A linguist would foresee a problem for the binding theory in this particular representation, which we pass
over here in the interests of brevity.)

10. $VP : ocv \ (vp \ \gamma) \ \gamma \rightarrow V_{oc} : ocv \ NP : \gamma \ VP_{to-inf} : vp$

Another very natural way to interpret base generation is to capture the
bounded constructions *in the lexicon;* that is, in the subcategorization frames
for object control verbs and the like. This is the tactic that is adopted in
generalized phrase-structure grammar (GPSG; Gazdar, Klein, Pullum, &
Sag, 1985) categorial grammar (CG; Oehrle, Bach, & Wheeler, 1988),
lexical–functional grammar (LFG; Bresnan, 1982), certain versions of tree-
adjoining grammar (TAG; Joshi, Vijay-Shanker, & Weir, 1991; Joshi &
Schabes, 1992), and head-driven phrase-structure grammar (HPSG; Pollard
& Sag, 1994).

A DCG grammar expanded in this way continues to be closely related to
Woods's ATN analysis of the bounded constructions, with unification again
doing the work of "register modification." That both the ATN and the
DCG work exclusively at the level of argument structure or the interpretations of immediate constituents goes a long way toward explaining the
bounded character of these constructions. This benefit of the computational
approaches has become standard and is implicit in nearly all linguistic theories of the constructions, including GPSG, HPSG, LFG, lexicalized TAGs,
and certain versions of government-binding theory (GB; Chomsky, 1981).

For this reason, we shall have little more to say about the bounded constructions here, except to note that this is one place where computational linguistics has directly influenced mainstream linguistics and psycholinguistics (see Bresnan, 1978, for further discussion of the relation between linguistic accounts and the ATN.)

c. Unbounded Constructions

The languages of the world show similar consistency in respect to another family of constructions. These are known as *unbounded* because they involve dependencies at the level of the interpretation or argument structure between expressions that may be separated by unboundedly many intervening elements. Examples in English are relativization, *wh*-question formation, topicalization, and arguably, right node raising, exemplified in 11:

11. a. People that . . . I like.
    b. People, . . . I like!
    c. I like, and . . . you merely tolerate, people who own cats.

For each of these expressions, an infinite number of further well-formed expressions of the same type can be generated by recursively inserting instances of the string "O'Grady says that . . ." in place of ". . ." It follows that the verb *like* can be unboundedly distant from the head noun *people* of its semantic object argument. Even though there are a number of patterns of relativization across languages, including cases where the relative pronoun is either *in situ* with the verb or is omitted entirely, in all languages such constructions involve an unbounded dependency. (Some of these other possibilities are actually exhibited in restricted forms in English, in pronoun-free relatives and multiple *wh*-questions.)

These constructions seem quite different from those that we encountered in the last section. We cannot build the predicate-argument structures needed for semantic interpretation merely by identifying elements in translations of immediate constituents in a traditional context-free (CF) rule, since in general the elements related by the dependency cannot be elements belonging to a single CF rule.

All approaches to the unbounded dependency exhibited by constructions like the relative take the form of a context-free core, augmented by some extra apparatus for handling the unbounded dependencies themselves. Many of the interesting contrasts between the theories concern the automata-theoretic power that such extensions implicate. Although we have no very clear information concerning an upper bound on the power of human grammar, mechanisms of lesser power than a universal Turing machine clearly have considerable theoretical interest, if only to show where they break down.

Linguistic and computational theories of this "weakly non–context-free" kind have fallen broadly into two categories. The first type can be characterized as using the context-free base to determine an argument structure for an entire complex sentence, then using additional apparatus to establish long-range dependencies in one fell swoop. An example is *Aspects*-style transformational grammar (Chomsky, 1965), which introduced tree-to-tree rules including variables to transform arbitrarily deeply embedded trees with *wh*-items in situ into trees with those items fronted. The other type of mechanism established long-range dependencies by "trickling" pointers or indices down a path through the derivation tree connecting the two dependent elements.

Aspects-style rules themselves were quickly identified as implicating full Turing machine power (Peters & Ritchie, 1973). They also failed to explain a number of asymmetries in extractability of different arguments. A striking example of this is the "fixed subject constraint," according to which, in English and many other SVO languages, subjects cannot unboundedly extract, unlike other arguments, as illustrated in the following example. (Subjects of bare complements, as in *a man who(m) I think likes Ike* are exceptional in this respect.)

12. a.   A man who(m) I think that Ike likes.
    b. *A man who(m) I think that likes Ike.

For both of these reasons, considerable interest centered around certain computational versions of the swoop mechanism that appeared to be potentially more constrained. Following early work by Thorne and Bobrow, the idea was most elegantly formulated by Woods (1970) for the ATN.

Woods's ATN allowed certain kinds of register-changing *side effects* to be associated with state transitions. Most of Woods's register-changing operations have up till now been subsumed under the unification mechanism. However, to handle long-range dependency, we shall associate such actions with a number of transitions that we shall add to the *NP* and *VP* nets in Figure 1. These actions will transfer special terms or markers into and out of a special globally accessible register or store, called *HOLD*, extending the grammar as in Figure 3. The actions concerning the HOLD register are enclosed in braces. They allow the grammar to achieve the same effect as a swoop transformational rule. To derive a relative clause, you simply use the ordinary rules of context-free grammar, except that whenever you encounter a relative pronoun, you make it one end of a potentially unbounded *NP* dependency, expressed as a note in the HOLD register, and whenever a verb needs an *NP* argument, it has the option of satisfying the need for that argument and making it the other end of an unbounded dependency by retrieving an *NP* from HOLD. A further check that the index has indeed been removed from HOLD is included on exit from the complex *NP*, in order to prevent accepting examples like *A man that I like Ike.

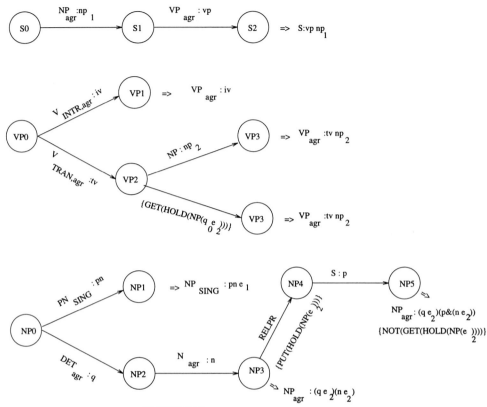

FIGURE 3   The ATN HOLD mechanism.

Part of the attraction of the ATN HOLD mechanism is that it offers a way to think about constraints on long-range dependencies. For example, because we do not include the option of the subject being obtained from the HOLD register, we capture the fixed subject condition illustrated in 12. (A linguist would notice, however, that nothing in the present theory explains why this constraint appears to conspire with other aspects of word order, cross-linguistically. Nor have we revealed how bare complement subject extraction is allowed.)

Furthermore, that sentences like 13a involve more than one dependency and that those dependencies nest, as revealed by 13b, can be explained as arising from limitations on the HOLD store; perhaps it is a push-down stack, as suggested by Woods (1973):

13. a. Which violin$_1$ is this sonata$_2$ easy to play$_2$ on$_1$.
    b. *Which sonata$_1$ is this violin$_2$ easy to play$_1$ on$_2$.

The importance of this latter observation is considerable. When one sees a stack, one immediately thinks of a characteristic automaton, such as the push-down automaton (PDA) characteristic of context-free grammars. Since a push-down store is already implicit in the context-free rules and adding a further stack to mediate long-range dependencies would, in principle, jump us up to full Turing machine power, the intriguing possibility is that the stack involved in long-range dependencies is in some sense the *same* stack involved in context-free rules, as proposed by Ades and Steedman (1982, p. 522) and further specified in the work of Joshi et al. discussed later.

Of course, to claim this much is not the same as claiming that natural languages are context free. We know from work by Aho (1969) that a "nested stack" automaton, equipped with a single stack whose contents may themselves be stacks, is of greater than context-free power (but of lesser power than context-sensitive grammars). However, it does suggest that we should try to account for unbounded dependencies in much the same way we accounted for bounded ones, by putting as much of the work as possible into the base rules themselves. This insight can be seen as underlying the second group of mechanisms for unbounded dependencies, in which a similar kind of pointer or index is "trickled" down the sentence during derivation, as opposed to being established in one fell swoop.

Within mainstream linguistics, this kind of explanation can be seen as surfacing in proposals by Bresnan and Chomsky, which resulted in the "comp-to-comp movement" account of unbounded dependencies including relativization. According to this theory, unbounded dependencies were the sum of a series of local dependencies between argument positions and the complementizer position in individual clauses. Thus transformational "movement" was restricted to bounded movement.

Since we have seen that bounded dependencies can be captured within generalized PS rules, clearly, it is a comparatively short step to grammars that eliminate movement entirely and bring unbounded dependencies under the base generation hypothesis. The proposal takes an extreme form in the generalized phrase structure grammars (GPSG) of Gazdar, Klein, Pullum, and Sag (19850. The GPSG treatment can be included in our DCG rules by associating a feature–value pair SLASH, equivalent to a local HOLD register. In the original version of the theory, the value of this feature was simply a pointer identifying a unique long-range dependency, and the theory was therefore weakly context-free. The original base set of rules for each category such as *S* are included again with an empty slash feature. It is convenient to write such categories simply as *S, NP, VP,* and so on and to write the corresponding categories in which the SLASH pointer is of type *NP* as *S/NP, NP/NP, VP/NP,* and so forth. For every old style rule defining "nonslash" categories, one or more rules may specify how an *S/NP* with nonempty SLASH feature passes that feature to its offspring. For example, we might introduce the following additional rules, among others. (In the original version of the theory, such extra rules were induced via "meta-rules.")

14. $S : vp\ np_1/NP : x\ \rightarrow\ NP_{agr} : np_1\quad VP_{agr} : vp/NP : x$
 $VP_{agr} : tv\ np_2/NP : x\ \rightarrow\ V_{TRAN,agr} : tv\quad NP : np_2/NP : x$
 $NP_{agr} : (q\ e_2)(p\&(n\ e_2))\ \rightarrow\ DET_{agr} : q\qquad N_{agr} : n\qquad RELPRO\quad S : p/NP : q_0 e_2$

The category NP/NP corresponds to the linguists' notion of a trace or empty NP. We have again slyly captured the constraint on extracting subjects by not including a rule of the form $S/NP \rightarrow NP/NP\ VP$. The multiple unbounded dependencies exhibited in sentences 13 could be handled within this type of GPSG by a combination of the techniques we have seen for bounded and unbounded dependencies. However, the multiple intersecting unbounded dependencies that occur in Scandinavian languages and the arbitrarily many verb-argument dependencies that can intercalate in Germanic infinitival complements provide evidence that natural languages cannot be contained within the class of CF languages (see Gazdar, 1988, for discussion). A number of other grammar formalisms with a computational orientation were developed in response to such observations, including tree-adjoining grammars (Joshi et al., 1991) and combinatory categorial grammars (CCG; Ades & Steedman, 1982), and Gazdar's proposal to permit SLASH features to be stacks (Gazdar, 1988; Pollard & Sag, 1994). Joshi et al. (1991) showed that a number of these grammars were weakly equivalent to indexed grammars and, under certain limiting assumptions, to *linear* indexed grammars in which only a single stack-valued feature is involved.

d. Less Well-Behaved Constructions

Before leaving the topic of grammar, it should be remarked that a number of constructions remain that are much less well-behaved with respect to both linguistic and computational theories of the kind we have discussed so far. Coordination, parentheticalization, and intonational phrasing all appear to operate on a very wide range of fragments that bear very little resemblance to traditional constituents, while remaining subject to very strong and apparently syntactic constraints. The seriousness of the problems examples like the following present for both the theory of competence grammar and the possibilities of efficient processing are an enduring problem that should not be underestimated:

15. a. I will buy, and may read, your latest novel.
    b. Give Dead-eye Dick a sugar stick, and Mexican Pete, a bun.
    c. Harry likes Adlai, and Mike, Ike.

The lack of truly explanatory coverage of such examples suggests that there may be more to say about the computational nature of the competence grammar than we have been able to consider here. (I address this question elsewhere; see Further Reading.)

B. The Algorithm

1. Natural and Unnatural Algorithms

The parsing algorithms that have been developed to compile and interpret programming languages come in a bewildering variety, each distinguished from the others on a number of parameters. The parameters determine the order in which the space of parser states is searched, the manner in which the rules of the grammar are applied (top down, bottom up, or a mixture of the two), and the use of various auxiliary "tables" or "charts" to increase efficiency.

The extent to which we can distinguish these devices empirically as models of the human parser is very limited, partly because of residual uncertainties about the nature of the competence grammar itself, but mostly because of their considerable dependency upon the third module of the processor, the oracle. We have already noted that these algorithms have been developed for languages very unlike our own, with no global ambiguity and very limited nondeterminism, so this result is perhaps not surprising. Nevertheless, these algorithms remain an important source for models of the human algorithm, and it is important to understand the consequences of variation along each of these dimensions.

The appeal of the strong competence hypothesis lies in the observation that it is evolutionarily and developmentally simpler to keep to a minimum the apparatus that the parser demands over and above the competence grammar itself. A parsing algorithm that requires a great deal of "extra" apparatus—particularly when that apparatus is language specific—therefore tends to be less plausible as a candidate. However, the algorithm must, given a natural competence grammar and the assistance of an oracle, be capable of parsing efficiently. An algorithm for which natural grammars appear to induce inefficiency, or for which we find it hard to identify an effective oracle, will also appear implausible. We shall find that at first glance all the algorithms score rather badly for psychological plausibility on one or another of these criteria.

All of the algorithms that are discussed in this section were in the first instance defined for context-free grammars and the associated push-down automaton, since that is the effective level of the grammar for most programming languages. Indeed, the desire to exploit these algorithms, and therefore to keep to a minimum the additional apparatus required to deal with the apparently non-context-free properties of natural languages, was a major impulse behind the development of the computational alternatives to grammatical transformations discussed in the earlier section on competence grammar. (The "weakly non-context-free" grammars discussed at the end of that section have a characteristic automaton called an *extended push-down automaton*. The classic algorithms discussed here, such as Earley's, generalize fairly directly to this automaton.)

2. Parsing as Search

We can view the workings of the nondeterministic algorithm as a search problem, in which the task is to find all paths through a maze to the exit(s) corresponding to successful parser terminations. The choice points in the maze, where more than one path can be taken, correspond to states of the parser in which the grammar allows more than one continuation; and the transitions between parser states correspond to actions such as reading another word or applying a rule of grammar.

The complexity of a parsing algorithm—that is, the relation that the number of computational operations and the amount of working memory required bear to the length of the sentence under analysis—depends on the characteristics of this search space. The maze may be built on a chain of "islands," so that all paths pass through certain "bridges" or "bottlenecks" corresponding to the same state, so that all overall paths share the same analysis or analyses on each island. If so, the algorithm may be able to "share" these analyses. If the paths through the maze never cross then this saving will be impossible. Some paths through the maze are dead ends. Some paths are endless, leading neither to success nor to a dead end. These the parser should try to avoid.

If paths never cross, the search space can be viewed as a tree. There are two basic methods of searching trees. If the tree has b branches at each branching point, we will refer to b as the *branching factor*. (More realistically, since the degree of nondeterminism at a branch point may vary, we should think of the branching factor b as the *average* number of branches that do not immediately succeed or fail.)

One way to search the tree is to work "breadth first," starting at the root, looking at the first branches to see if they lead to success states or are dead ends, and otherwise iterating over all the successor states. This search clearly has exponential costs in terms of both the number of alternatives that must be examined (and hence time) and the memory we need to keep track of the b^n alternative states on the "frontier" of the search.

Another way is to work "depth first," choosing one branch from the root (say, the leftmost or the "best" under some criterion) and then choosing from its successors by the same criterion. Whenever you reach a success or failure point, you back up to the last choice point, and take the *next* leftmost (or best, or whatever) alternative. This regime also takes exponential time in the depth of the search (although its memory requirements are only order n, because it needs to keep only the n states on the path back to the root).

Clearly, the greater is the nondeterminism induced by the grammar, the more complex the maze and the larger the number of wrong alternatives leading to blind alleys.

We have already noted that a huge degree of nondeterminism appears to be characteristic of all natural languages. A lower bound estimate of what we are up against can be obtained by observing that the branching factor b must be at least as great as the average lexical ambiguity, and the depth n of the search tree must be at least as great as the number of words in the sentence. (This lower bound is over-optimistic, since it takes no account of structural ambiguity.) It follows that an exhaustive search is likely to be unacceptably costly in computational terms. Nor should we expect parallelization of our search algorithm to solve this problem. For any fixed n, we can, in principle, make the search linear in n by providing b^n processors. But this number is also exponential in n and impracticably large for the range involved here.

As with all arguments from worst-case complexity, caution is in order here. The effective branching factor b may be smaller than we think, say, because the search space has islands in the sense mentioned earlier. Moreover, n is quite small for natural sentences—on the order of 24 for written text in the *Wall Street Journal* (sd. 11). We shall see that, within such bounds, an exponential algorithm may perform better than a polynomial one. Nevertheless, even before we start to consider particular algorithms in detail, it is likely that we shall find ourselves in the same position as large search problems like chess playing; that is, of having to adopt heuristic search strategies to narrow the effective branching factor. In the case of sentence processing, the heuristics must identify with high reliability the alternative at each point that will in fact lead to an analysis. Although some less favored alternatives may be stored for later use in case of failure, we may be forced to adopt a "best-first" version of the depth-first search. Such methods are likely to be incomplete; that is, there may well be sentences that are allowed by the grammar but for which our algorithms will fail to deliver analyses. Ambiguous sentences may have alternative analyses that our algorithms will fail to detect.

This will come as no surprise. We have already noted that human processors are rarely aware of global ambiguities. We have also seen in the case of subject center-embedded sentences like 2 and garden path sentences like 3 that both the psychological algorithm and the psychological oracle are incomplete. The significance of this observation for the nondeterministic algorithm is that individual algorithms differ in where computational costs show up and in what particular problems they leave for the oracle to solve.

3. Left-to-Right Processing

A further dimension of variation for the algorithm concerns the order in which the words in the string are examined. In nearly all cases they are examined in order of utterance from first to last, usually referred to as *left to right*, though this term chauvinistically assumes European orthography. This regime has an obvious intuitive appeal, but it is worth noting that, regardless of other details, one wants the parser to examine the most informative items earliest to limit uncertainty, and it seems to be an empirical fact about English and other languages that leftmost boundaries are much less ambiguously marked than right.

There is one exception to the standard left-to-right regime in modern natural language processors. Under a similar rationale of starting with unambiguous information, in tasks involving text derived via speech processing or other sources of noise and error, it is sometimes expedient to begin anywhere that yields a comparatively unambiguous analysis. This regime is known as *island-driven* parsing.

4. Simple Bottom Up versus Simple Top Down

a. Simple Bottom Up

The simplest bottom-up nondeterministic algorithm is often referred to as the *shift–reduce* algorithm, because it is defined in terms of two processes: shifting, or pushing a category onto the stack of the push-down automaton; and reducing, or combining categories on top of the stack according to a grammatical rule. Confusingly, the term *bottom up* is sometimes used to refer to what is discussed later as the "left-corner" algorithm, and the term *shift–reduce* is sometimes used to refer to a particular kind of deterministic shift–reduce algorithm discussed later as the $LR(k)$ algorithm.

One version of this algorithm can be defined in terms of the stack of the PDA (which initially is empty) and a buffer (which initially contains the words of the sentence in order), as follows:

16. While the buffer and the stack are nonempty, *either*
    a. If the topmost items on the stack match the right-hand side of a production rule, remove them from the stack, *reduce* them according to the rule, and place the result on top of the stack, *or*
    b. remove the next word from the buffer and *shift* its grammatical category to the top of the stack.

Any empirical predictions from such a minimal algorithm must wait for the discussion of possible oracles that will determine which of these actions is preferred when both are possible, but we can make the following general remarks.

First, we should note that the nondeterminism of this algorithm is of three distinct kinds, which we can refer to as SHIFT/SHIFT conflicts (which arise when a lexical item has more than one grammatical category), SHIFT/REDUCE conflicts, and REDUCE/REDUCE conflicts (when more than one rule can apply).

Second, the simple bottom–up parser is entirely nonpredictive. This threatens efficiency, for a reason that will become obvious from considering the following sentence:

17. The men walk.

Any grammar of English must reflect the fact that *men* can (like most common nouns) be an *NP* as well as a noun. This fact introduces a SHIFT/SHIFT conflict when the word *men* is encountered, so that unless the oracle rules otherwise, the parser is likely to build the useless sentence *Men walk,* even though no possible continuation of the words *the men walk* could require an S at this point. Since the *VP* may be arbitrarily complex, this redundant analysis is likely to proliferate, threatening the usual exponential consequences. Of course, the oracle may indeed be smart enough to prevent this, and the chart-based techniques discussed later can also be applied, but it is a generic problem with the algorithm. Nevertheless, purely as a nondeterministic algorithm, it retains the appeal of requiring the absolute minimum of extra apparatus, in addition to the grammar and the corresponding automaton.

b. Simple Top Down

The simple top-down or "recursive descent" algorithm is entirely predictive. Starting with the start symbol *S,* the algorithm nondeterministically picks a rule that expands that symbol, say rule 1 of the fragment 4, $S \rightarrow NP$ *VP.* For each nonterminal symbol in the expansion, the algorithm recursively calls itself on that symbol. To exploit the standard left-to-right order of processing discussed in Section 2, it is usual to carry out this recursion "leftmost first"—in this case, to process the *NP* before the *VP.* For each terminal or preterminal symbol, a lexical item of the right category must be present at the appropriate point in the string. The algorithm uses the stack of the PDA to keep track of the recursion.

This process is conveniently described in terms of a dot notation, which captures the notion of a partially parsed expansion. Therefore, when we first call the algorithm recursively to parse the *NP* in the preceding expansion, we stack the following "dotted rule," so that when the algorithm returns from parsing the *NP,* it knows that it must parse the *VP:*

18. $S \rightarrow NP . VP$

When it returns successfully from a recursion, it removes this symbol from the top of the stack and checks whether the dot is at the right-hand end. If it is, the constituent is complete, and it returns. If it is not, the algorithm moves the dot on past the next symbol, replaces the dotted rule on top of the stack, and recurses. That is, in this case the algorithm stacks the following dotted rule and goes off to look for a *VP:*

19. *S → NP VP.*

The left-to-right version of this algorithm can be informally stated as follows:

20. To parse a category of type *C,*
    a. Look at the category *W* of the next word in the string. If *W =* *C,* exit.
    b. Choose a rule that expands *C* and recursively parse the elements of the expansion in order from leftmost to rightmost, using a dotted rule and the stack to keep track.

This is the nondetermistic algorithm that was used in early implementations of ATN parsers.

The top-down algorithm minimizes the wasteful construction of spurious constituents that can never take part in any derivation. For example, under the standard leftmost-first regime, since the rules of the grammar of English never predict *S* immediately succeeding a determiner, the algorithm never builds the spurious *S Men walk* in sentence 17.

However, there are also countervailing disadvantages to the algorithm. Precisely because it is predictive, the search space that it must find its way through is effectively the entire space permitted by the grammar, including states corresponding to analyses for which there is no support whatever in the string itself. Of course, this search space is narrowed considerably once the first words of the sentence have been accounted for. But it makes life more difficult for the oracle, and in the absence of the chart-based techniques discussed later, the recursive descent parser is exponential in the worst case.

c. Mixed Bottom-Up Top-Down Algorithms

Because of the respective disadvantages of pure top-down and bottom-up algorithms, considerable attention has focused on a group of algorithms that attempt to combine the advantages of the two.

The simplest left-to-right version of the idea is the "left-corner" algorithm, which can be thought of as starting bottom up, with a word or a constituent that is actually present in the sentence, and then using those rules of which that constituent is the leftmost daughter to recursively left-corner parse further constituents to the right. The algorithm can be informally stated as follows:

21. To parse a category of type C,
    a. Look at the category W of the next word in the string.
    b. If $W = C$, exit.
    c. Choose a rule that expands any category N such that the leftmost element of the expansion is W.
    d. Recursively parse the remaining elements of the expansion in order from leftmost to rightmost, using a stacked dotted rule to keep track.
    e. Assign the category N to W and go to step b.

This elegant algorithm combines the "data-driven" advantage of the bottom-up algorithm with the "predictive" virtues of the recursive-descent algorithm.

d. Chart Parsing

All three nondeterministic algorithms described in the previous section are, in the absence of an effective oracle, technically computationally intractable. That is to say, if all we do to make them deterministic is to equip them with a "backtracking" memory for all choice points and an apparatus for falling back to these choice points to try other alternatives, then all of them have worst case exponential costs.

Like all worst case computational complexity results, this one should be treated with some caution. Whether the worst case is encountered in practice depends on a number of factors, including the particular grammar involved. In particular, the left-corner algorithm can perform better than the nonexponential Cocke–Kasami–Younger algorithm considered later for quite practically useful grammar fragments (Slocum, 1981).

Nevertheless, it is important to know that the complexity of the search problem can be greatly reduced, because of an important property of the parsing search space that has not been discussed here so far.

Natural language sentences are typically made up of a number of "islands," corresponding to substrings whose analysis or analyses are independent of those on the neighboring islands and of the sentence as a whole. To take an example from Marcus (1980), a processor who has encountered only the words *Have the students who missed the exam* . . . cannot know whether the word *have* is an auxilliary, as in the interrogative 22a, or a main verb, as in the imperative 22b:

22. a. Have the students who missed the exam taken the makeup?
    b. Have the students who missed the exam take the makeup!

It can resolve this question only when the next word, *take* or *taken*, is processed.

A predictive algorithm that happens to have chosen the wrong rule for expansion in analyzing one or the other sentence up to this point should be able to take advantage of the work that it has done in parsing the NP *the students who missed the exam,* since its analysis is identical in both cases. But blind backtracking back to the state where the wrong choice was made will lose this information. Similar arguments apply, mutatis mutandis, to a blindly backtracking shift–reduce parser.

To take advantage of this characteristic of the search space, we must record that a noun phrase has been found spanning words 2–7 of the sentence, together with the analysis. Any other analysis requiring a noun phrase starting at position 2 can then simply use the result of the earlier analysis.

The data structure in which this information is stored is called a *chart*. All of the preceding exponential algorithms can be made to parse context-free grammars in worst-case time n^3 by the use of a chart. Many of the most efficient techniques known for computational natural language systems are of this kind, including the Cocke–Kasami–Younger (CKY) algorithm (which is bottom up) and Earley's (1970) algorithm (which is a refinement of the left-corner technique). The latter algorithm gains particular efficiency by the use of an "active" chart, in which not only complete constituents are stored, but also *incomplete* constituents, corresponding to the "dotted rules" used in the predictive algorithms.

5. Deterministic Parsing

Costs that go up in proportion to n^3, the cube of the sentence length n, can still be impracticably expensive, especially if the worst case is also the average case, as it can be in practice for the CKY algorithm, and if n can get large, as it does in compiling programming languages, so there is some interest in briefly considering a further class of algorithm that can have computational costs *linear* in n for a subset of grammars. So far we have considered only general-purpose nondeterministic algorithms. But we can, in principle, consider more grammar-specific algorithms, which tell us more about the action(s) that should be taken in particular states. If the grammar allows us to make this machine so specific that it is entirely deterministic, then we shall have eliminated the oracle entirely. Of course, by definition, we cannot do this for a truly nondeterministic grammar. But if the apparent nondeterminism in the grammar happens to be resolvable by looking ahead at a bounded number of immediately adjacent symbols in the string, then such a deterministic algorithm exists. One particular variety of deterministic parser of this kind is called the *LR(k)* parser (Aho and Johnson, 1974), because it does a left-to-right scan, delivers a rightmost derivation, and uses a *k* symbol to look ahead. Since it is convenient to express the control for this algorithm as a matrix indexed by (1) the state, (2) the topmost element on the push-down stack, and (3) the remaining input, such controls are refered to as *LR tables*. Such tables can be quite complicated, so there is intense interest among computer scientists in known techniques for constructing such deterministic algorithms automatically from the original grammar. In fact, such techniques provide the basis for one of the most widely used methods for automatically generating compilers, and as a result many programming languages are in the class $LR(1)$; that is, all nondeterminism can be resolved by a one-symbol look ahead.

We know that natural languages are not $LR(k)$ languages from examples like example 22, as Marcus (1980) pointed out. That is, after the word *have* in the example, there is a nondeterminism between an analysis according to which it is an auxiliary followed by a subject, *the students . . .* , and one where it is a main verb followed by an object. This nondeterminism is resolved by the word *take* or *taken*. But because of the embedding property of English, the noun phrase may be indefinitely large—*the students, the students who missed the exam, the students who missed the exam that I set in the morning,* and so on. Therefore no bound is placed on the size k of the look ahead that this construction would require.

Nevertheless, we shall see that human performance in resolving natural lexical ambiguity does look as if it might depend on examining a strictly bounded number of neighboring symbols. The techniques for automatically building LR tables also deliver coherent (albeit nondeterministic) results for non-LR grammars, which has led to a number of generalizations of the technique. It is therefore interesting to ask whether some modification of the idea can be applied to natural languages.

Marcus (1980) describes an LR-like parser with three distinctive characteristics. First, he allowed looking ahead for up to three items; that is, $k = 3$. Second, to handle the nondeterminism just discussed, which manifestly does not cause human processors any noticeable difficulty, he allowed the look-ahead window to include NPs (but no other constituent types), as well as words. Third, he assumed that the equivalent of the LR table was inexact. The residual nondeterminism was then to be resolved by default. (However, certain other residual sources of nondeterminism—in particular, noun–noun compounding—were to be resolved by other more semantic mechanisms, discussed later.) Marcus then claimed that, although English itself remained a nondeterministic language, the *parser* was complete only with respect to the deterministic fragment thus defined. (This technique also has been used in LR-based compilers.) On occasion, the defaults would engender the classical garden path effects.

These moves restore the oracle to a position of importance and in some sense compromise the original attraction of the LR algorithm. Nevertheless, deterministic parsing remains an attractive idea for practical applications, particularly where large volume is at a premium and the work of the oracle can be deferred by building "underspecified" syntactic derivations, as in the approach known as *D-theoretic* parsing (Marcus, Hindle, & Fleck, 1983; Weinberg, 1994).

6. Summary: The Psychological Algorithm

Where among this maze of parameters is the psychological algorithm situated? Is it top down, or bottom up, or a mixture of the two? Does it use a chart, or an *LR* table, or not?

Evolutionary considerations prejudice us against any theory of parsing that requires large amounts of extra apparatus, in addition to the grammar and the corresponding automaton, for reasons similar to those that led us to reject the possibility of parsing by covering grammar. To that extent, the bottom–up algorithm continues to exercise a considerable appeal. However, it passes on a considerable burden to the oracle.

By contrast, the predictive algorithms such as left-corner, which ask less of the oracle, import extra mechanisms such as dotted rules to control the predictive search. This may not be too bad: such mechanisms are likely to be quite generally needed for a variety of hierarchically organized behavior such as planned actions and even for such lowly motor tasks as getting objects out of boxes and reaching around obstacles.

Among the predictive algorithms, the simple top-down recursive-descent algorithm has a strike against it that makes it perhaps the least psychologically plausible of all. Grammars that include left-recursive rules of the form $A \rightarrow AB$ introduce a danger of infinite recursion in the leftmost-first version of the algorithm, as the parser predicts an A, which predicts an A, which predicts . . . (Nor can we get around this with some other parsing regime, such as rightmost-first, since *some* kind of recursion will cause similar versions for *all* recursive descent regimes.) Guarding against this possibility complicates the algorithm and its operations in ways that seriously stretch psychological credibility.

For similar reasons, the *LR* parser, which also complicates the algorithm by introducing a language-specific *LR* table, seems to be implausible in evolutionary and developmental terms, since, like a covering grammar, it needs to be recomputed every time a modification is made to the grammar. When we come to discuss the oracle, we shall see that the consequences of lexical nondeterminism can be minimized in other ways, so that the structural nondeterminism that causes *LR* tables for natural languages to be inexact is the major problem for the oracle.

The psychological relevance of the chart is also questionable. That naive subjects and everyday language users are so rarely aware of syntactic ambiguity, together with the existence of garden path sentences, makes it unlikely that human language processors have access to such a powerful memory device and suggests that they depend on an oracle that usually gets it right the first time. Most of the psychological theories discussed here make this assumption.

Unfortunately, until we know more about that oracle, just about the only further conclusion we can state with any confidence is that the grammar itself does seem to favor algorithms that go from left-to-right, because of the tendency to mark left boundaries. (This is probably a major reason why simple left-corner parsing works as well as it does.) This conclusion hardly comes as a surprise. In other respects, natural grammars look surprisingly *un*helpfully designed for *all* these algorithms. For example, for all left-to-right algorithms, processing right-branching structures causes the stack to grow, but left-branching structures keep the stack small. (In the case of bottom-up algorithms, the items on the stack are unattached constituents. In the case of top-down algorithms, they are dotted rules or the equivalent.) In view of the earlier observation that limitations on center embedding seem likely to arise from stack limitations, one might therefore have expected natural grammars to minimize this burden by favoring left-branching constructions. In fact, however, right branching appears to be widespread among the languages of the world, according to the usual linguistic analyses. We shall return to this curious fact later.

C. The Oracle

1. Stochastic Techniques

One of the most important and useful techniques for reducing nondeterminism, at least at the level of the lexicon, is also one of the oldest, with origins in information theory that predate artificial intelligence and even generative grammar itself.

It has been known since the work of Shannon and Weaver in the early 1950s that natural language text can be modeled to a close approximation by stochastic finite-state Markov processes. Of course, this tells us nothing about the grammar that in part determines the stochastic behavior, as Chomsky (1957, p. 17) influentially pointed out. However, it follows that the part of speech corresponding to any given word in a sentence is in principle highly predictable solely on the basis of the parts of speech of the two or three preceding words, solely on the basis of the stochastic model, and without benefit of higher level analysis.

This observation does not in itself solve the problem, for the finite automata in question are large, and the sheer volume of distributional information that they depend on is gigantic. For this reason, stochastic and probablistic techniques played very little part in the early development of the computational natural language processing techniques discussed previously.

However, it was always likely that such techniques would eventually prove useful in drastically reducing lexical ambiguity (cf. Chomsky, 1957, p. 17, Note 4). Two developments at the start of the 1980s allowed this possibility to be realized. The first was that computing machinery became fast enough, big enough in terms of memory, and cheap enough to actually try what had become at the time a rather unfashionable approach. The second crucial development was the invention of some quite new algorithms for constructing such "hidden" Markov models automatically, via re-estimation procedures, on the basis of exposure to fairly large amounts of text annotated by hand with part-of-speech tags (Jelinek, 1976; Merialdo, 1994). The assembly of such text corpora was also crucial to this development. With the use of such techniques, it is possible to disambiguate part of speech with a reliability of around 97% for text where all words are known (Brill, 1994).

These figures should be kept in perspective. They mean that roughly every other sentence will include a word for which the preferred part of speech is incorrect. It should also not be forgotten that choosing a part of speech on the basis of basic or unigram frequency alone yields around 93% correct disambiguation. However, the efficiency of all of the algorithms considered previously can be greatly increased by using part-of-speech disambiguation as a component of the oracle in an "n-best" parser architecture, whereby the parser considers only a small number of alternative part-of-speech categories for ambiguous words, in the order of their likelihood according to the model down to some threshold. For example, it is likely that such a model would make the simple bottom-up algorithm more efficient by excluding the possibility of the word *men* being a noun phrase rather than a noun in the earlier example 17, *The men walk,* thereby avoiding the creation of a redundant *S men walk.* That is, it is likely that SHIFT/SHIFT conflicts can be largely eliminated for the shift–reduce algorithm by this method.

Once the Markov model is trained, it is computationally extremely cheap, because it is a finite state device. It is therefore likely that such stochastic oracles and the n-best architecture will be standard in large-coverage natural language processing programs in future. It will be interesting in this period to see how a number of proposals to generalize the techniques will fare, including proposals to disambiguate word senses as well as parts of speech and a number of computationally less resource-intensive rule-based training methods. There are also a number of interesting proposals to embed such mechanisms in neural networks and other "connectionist" devices, whose computational implications go beyond the scope of the present chapter. Although there have been related proposals for stochastic context-free grammars, it seems much less likely that these techniques will cope with the other variety of syntactic nondeterminism, arising from structural ambiguity in examples like sentence 1, *Put the book on the table in your pocket,* and that some of the other techniques discussed later will be needed as well.

The psychological relevance of stochastic lexical disambiguation is less clear. On the one hand, there is plenty of evidence that humans and other animals are sensitive to statistical regularities across extended periods. It seems somewhat less likely that they can compute higher order statistics of the kind required to train hidden Markov models. However, some of the rule-based alternatives may be more psychologically plausible. Nevertheless, it should be borne in mind that the high redundancy of real text these techniques exploit is in actual fact a by-product of the grammar and the content of the text. The possibility remains open that it is at these higher levels that humans filter out nondeterminism.

2. Strategy-Based Techniques

One important group of proposals for the psychological oracle come from the psychologists themselves. They have been enthusiastically taken up by computational linguists attempting to increase efficiency for natural language parsers. These proposals originate in work by Fodor, Bever, and Garrett (1974), who suggested that the garden path effect of sentences like 3, *The horse raced past the barn fell,* arose from the use by the parser of the "canonical sentoid strategy," which essentially said that if the parser ever encountered an NP followed by what could be a tensed verb, then it should act on the assumption that both elements are the subject and tensed verb of a "sentoid" or underlying tensed clause. The claim was that this strategy, which resolves the lexical nondeterminism of the word *raced,* is usually beneficial but in this case commits the processor to a blind alley.

The canonical sentoid strategy was only one of a number of such heuristics that supposedly guided the parser through the search space. To a modern eye, rules like this look uncomfortably as if they duplicate the rules of the grammar itself—such as rule 1 of the ATN 1—and in fact later strategy-based approaches all attempt to separate the heuristic and grammatical components via the assumption of more "surfacey" theories of grammar, including the ATN, rather than the framework of the standard theory assumed by Fodor et al.

One important early modification of the strategy idea was presented by Kimball (1973), who proposed seven very general principles of "surface structure parsing." Kimball was primarily a linguist and influential in the development of the base generation hypothesis concerning the competence grammar. He was, therefore, in a position to make a much cleaner separation between the grammar, the algorithm, and the oracle than Fodor et al. had been.

Many of Kimball's principles are properly regarded as properties of grammar or the algorithm, rather than the oracle. But two of them seemed to capture a large number of phenomena concerning the resolution of structural ambiguity and had the attraction of really looking like properties of a *parser* rather than misplaced rules of grammar. In fact, Kimball offered a number of conjectures as to *why* the parser might have these properties, in terms of comparative structural complexity, time to completion, and so on. Close relatives of these two principles turn up in a number of proposals that are often called *two-factor* theories of the oracle. Kimball called them *Right Association* and *Closure,* but it will be convenient to refer to the latter as *Minimal Attachment,* the name of a more specific but related principle in Lyn Frazier's theory, for these two principles reached their most refined form in her work (Frazier, 1978; Frazier and Fodor, 1978).

The detailed formulation of these principles need not concern us here, since our principal concern is with their computational interpretation. It will suffice to say that the first principle, Right Association, captures the preference for the following form in sentences where the VP modifier *last Tuesday* is predicated of Nixon's death rather than Bill's announcement:

23. Bill said Nixon died last Tuesday.

Minimal Attachment, on the other hand, captures the preference for the following form where the modifier *for Susan* modifies carrying the package rather than the package:

24. Tom carried the package for Susan.

It is this principle that captures the error we make in Bever's garden path sentences (although both Kimball and Frazier need further apparatus to explain why recovery is impossible). That is to say, in the following fragment of the sentence 3, exactly the same factors favor the attachment of the *VP raced past the barn* to the *NP* as subject, rather than as a past-participial modifier attached to the *NP* itself.

Following Frazier's work, which initiated a considerable body of experimental research supporting the reality of these effects, a number of computational accounts attempted to capture them in terms of simple properties of parsers. Among these, Wanner (1980) showed that right association could be captured in the ATN in terms of a global ordering of transition types equivalent to rule ordering in a more conventional grammar. Perhaps the most elegant computational account was provided by Pereira (1985), who showed that right association was equivalent in a shift–reduce parser to resolving all SHIFT/REDUCE conflicts in favor of shifting, and resolving all REDUCE/REDUCE conflicts in favor of the reduction that removes most nodes from the stack. (Pereira's parser was in fact an *LR*(1) parser with a not fully deterministic *LR* table, which these two heuristics were used to render fully deterministic.)

However, at the very time these elegant computational accounts were being put forward, the very basis of the effects that they were to explain was being called into question by certain other experimental approaches with close links to computational models.

3. Lexical Preferences

First, it was immediately noticeable that effects like minimal attachment were sensitive to the particular lexical items involved. Thus, minimal attachment makes the right prediction in 25a, but in 25b, it makes the wrong prediction:

> 25. a. The woman positioned the dress on the rack.
>   b. The woman wanted the dress on the rack.

One effect of the move to base generation by Bresnan and others had been to emphasize lexicalism in the theory of grammar and include more information concerning subcategorization or function-argument relations into the lexical entries for verbs. This proposal, originally motivated by purely linguistic considerations, suggested a natural way to capture the phenomenon in the performance theory, via differential ordering of the lexical entries determining the various subcategorization possibilities for different verbs in LFG (Ford et al., 1982). Such an ordering of lexical entries might also be produced dynamically, as a result of an n-gram based lexical disambiguator of the kind described earlier, with the lexical categories taking the part of the part-of-speech tags. (This approach is currently being pursued in n-best parsers for other varieties of lexicalist grammars, including TAG and CCG.)

The lexicalist account of attachment preferences contributes a major piece to solution of the puzzle and has been further refined by Pritchett (1992), Trueswell, Tanenhaus, and Garnsey (1994), and Gibson (1994). However, it was also clear that similar effects inconsistent with minimal attachment could be found for the *same* verb in combination with different arguments, suggesting that something more was involved.

4. Incremental Semantic Filtering

In his first identification of the garden path sentences, Bever noted that the effect was sensitive to content. Therefore, whereas 26a is a standard garden path, in 26b the effect is greatly reduced:

> 26. a. The doctor sent for the patient arrived.
>   b. The flowers sent for the patient arrived.

The observation suggests that human processors can take into account the relative plausibility of doctors versus flowers as agents of the action of sending for something or someone. In fact, it suggests that they can take account of this plausibility information early on in the course of processing, *even before the spurious clause is complete.* (Otherwise, we would have no explanation for the persistence of the garden path effect in case 26a.) This and a number of other experimental phenomena led Marslen-Wilson, Tyler, and Seidenberg (1978) to argue that the primary source of disambiguating information drawn upon by the oracle was semantic.

This argument for semantically "interactive" parsing aroused surprisingly strong opposition among psychologists at the time. The reason had much to do with doubt and confusion concerning the computational feasibility of the proposal. This is surprising, for there was already available a very vivid existence proof of something like the necessary mechanism, embodied in the well-known natural language understanding program of Winograd (1972), which interpreted questions and commands in a simple simulated world of toy blocks on a table, using a dynamically changing discourse model.

Winograd proposed not only that the parser should pay attention to semantic requirements such as animacy that verbs like *send for* imposed on their subjects, but also that attachment ambiguities of the kind found in his domain in instructions like the following should be resolved simply by adopting whichever analysis successfully referred to an entity in the world:

27. Put the block in the box on the table.

The program resolved this ambiguity on the basis of whether, in the discourse model, a block was unique by virtue of being the only block or a recently mentioned block, plus a box could be similarly unique by virtue of being on the table, or whether instead a block was unique by virtue of being in a unique box plus a unique table. Thus Winograd's proposal was that the oracle worked by semantically "filtering" the alternatives proposed by the parser.

This definition of semantically interactive parsing is often called *weak* interaction, because it assumes that the grammar and the algorithm propose well-formed analyses entirely autonomously and that the oracle merely disposes among the alternatives, killing off or interrupting those analyses that are either semantically incoherent (flowers being unqualified to send for things) or referentially unsuccessful (there being no block in the box).

Part of the resistance to Marslen-Wilson et al.'s proposal arose from a confusion of the weakly interactive or filtering processor with an alternative proposal for "strong" interaction, according to which an autonomously produced interpretation could supposedly manipulate the syntactic component itself, activating or suppressing rules and thereby determining in advance which analysis was built. The sense in which it is possible to build semantic analyses independent of syntax, and the question of what this bought the processor if it still had to build the syntactic analysis to check its predictions, were never very clearly resolved, and it is not clear whether any truly strongly interactive processor was ever built. Such a model was strenuously (and in the view of the present author, correctly) opposed by Fodor (1983) on the grounds that it violated the modularity criterion—in effect, that it really did not qualify as an explanation at all. However, Fodor himself pointed out that the weak or filtering interaction was entirely modular (1983, see pp. 78 and 135).

Crain and Steedman (1985) argued that some version of the weakly interactive oracle proposed by Winograd could account not only for attachment preferences, but also for the phenomenon of garden pathing, or unrecoverably incorrect attachment preferences. They made the following further assumptions about the processor.

First, they argued, from minimal pairs like example 26, that filtering had to occur very early in the analysis, well before the end of the clause. It followed that semantic interpretations had to be constructed in parallel with syntactic analysis, much as the earlier DCG notation suggests, and that partial interpretations, corresponding to syntactically incomplete fragments such as *the flowers sent for* . . . must be available.

Second, they argued that, unlike syntactic well-formedness, semantic and referential anomaly was *relative* rather than all or none. It followed that, unlike structural strategy-based parsers, the weakly interactive processor had to produce all partial analyses at a choice point, complete with partial interpretations, and then reject or interrupt all but the best before continuing the "best-first" search.

Third, they claimed that, when sentences are processed in isolation and out of context, as in the typical psycholinguistic experiment of the day, the oracle chooses that analysis whose (semantic and referential) pragmatic presuppositions were easiest to "accommodate" or add to the discourse model. In the case of garden path examples like *The horse raced past the barn fell,* they argued that the single presupposition that there was a unique horse was easier to accommodate than the presupposition that there were many horses, one of which was distinguished by the property that a hitherto unknown agent caused it to race somewhere. They presented experimental evidence that attachment preferences were under the control of referential context, by prefacing minimal pairs of locally attachment-ambiguous target sentences by contexts that either established two women respectively with and without a distinguishing property or one woman with that property:

28. For contexts,
    a. A psychologist was counseling two women. He was worried about one of them, but not about the other.
    b. A psychologist was counseling a man and a woman. He was worried about one of them, but not about the other.

For targets,

   c. The psychologist told the woman that he was having trouble with *her husband.*

   d. The psychologist told the woman that he was having trouble with *to visit him again.*

Both target sentences have a local ambiguity at the word *that*, which is only resolved when the italicized words are encountered. Minimal attachment would predict that the second target would always cause a garden path. In fact, however, this garden path effect is eliminated when the sentence is preceded by the first context, which satisfied the presupposition of the relative clause analysis. And a garden path effect is induced in the first target when it is preceded by the same context, because by the same token it fails to support the presupposition that there is a unique woman. These authors also show that certain predictions follow concerning the effect of definiteness on garden paths in the null context. The experiments were repeated and extended with improved materials by Altmann and Steedman (1988).

Disagreement continues on the question of what *other* mechanisms may also be involved in the oracle. Perhaps the most interesting questions for the computer scientists to ask the psychologists is whether the low-level stochastic mechanisms play a psychological role that has proven effective in practical applications, and whether structure-based strategies play a residual role or human processors work exclusively at the level of semantics to achieve the same filtering effect. However, agreement is now fairly general that the weak interaction plays an important role.

III. CONCLUSION

Many open questions remain concerning the exact computational nature of all three modules of the psychological processor. The explanatory coverage of the theory of competence grammar remains incomplete. The choice among the various available algorithms depends on the further identification of the oracle and to some extent on further questions concerning the computational architecture itself. The range of resources that the oracle itself draws on remains an open question for further research.

Nevertheless, the results and notations of computer science make it possible to see that everything we know experimentally about the psychological sentence processor is compatible with the expectation it will eventually be seen to be an extremely simple, explanatory, and modular device in both computational and evolutionary terms. The working models that computational linguistics offers provide a proof of concept for systems involving extremely surfacey grammars, in which syntactic composition and semantic composition are very closely related indeed and in which such grammars can be used directly by algorithms that may require very little more than the minimal automaton characteristic of the class of grammars in question and the simplest language-independent algorithm, working under the guidance of an oracle that exploits to the full the weak interaction that such semantically transparent grammars allow.

A number of puzzles remain. One is that the predominantly right-branching structure evinced by natural languages according to most theories of grammar still appears to maximize the working memory requirements for left-to-right parsers. Another is that the same predominance of right branching seems to require some extra apparatus for the weakly interactive oracle to work. Right-branching grammars like the one introduced in example 4 are immediately compatible with incremental interpretation of *constituents*. However, we have seen that interpretations for left prefixes like *The flowers sent for . . . ,* which are not constituents under such grammars, appear nevertheless to be available to the parser. Even though interpretations for nonconstituents can be built under any grammar, doing so requires extra structures not available from the grammar and thus compromises the strictest interpretation of the strong competence hypothesis. (I address this question elsewhere; see Further Reading.) It is likely that computational linguistics will continue to play an important part in research toward a resolution of these further problems.

IV. FURTHER READING

I have assumed familiarity with the basic ideas of generative grammar. Most introductory texts on linguistics, psycholinguistics, and computational linguistics cover this material. I have also assumed a nodding acquaintance with formal language theory, in particular the Chomsky hierarchy. This and much other useful material is covered by Partee, ter Meulen, and Wall (1990). The standard reference on the subject, Harrison (1978), is more technical. Allen (1987) is an excellent introductory text to the broader field of computational linguistics, and the indispensible collection edited by Grosz, Sparck-Jones, and Webber (1986) gathers a number of key research papers in this broader area, including several of those cited previously. Pereira and Grosz (1993) bring together some more recent papers. The best gentle introduction to the computer scientist's view of algorithmics in general is Harel's (1987).

A trustworthy guide to the characteristics of a number of alternative parsing regimes is Kay (1980), from whom I have borrowed the general trimodular view of the processor, generalizing his notion of an "agenda" to the notion of the oracle presented in the text. The grammars, algorithms, and oracles described in the text are all very readily implementable in the programming language Prolog, and the elegant text by Pereira and Shieber (1987) provides all the help that is needed. The most complete accessible account of the ATN, including many important features not discussed here, is Woods (1973). Stochastic techniques are reviewed by Merialdo (1994). The question of the automata theoretic power required for Natural Languages is helpfully discussed by Gazdar (1988) and Joshi et al. (1991). The important collection edited by Dowty, Kartunnen, and Zwicky (1985) brings together a number of computational and psycholinguistic papers, including several discussed previously. Hirst (1987) provides a readable survey of computational work on interactive parsing. Perrault and Grosz (1988) survey the variety of knowledge sources that can be brought to bear on the analysis of discourse. I have not attempted to survey the huge and rapidly changing experimental psycholinguistic literature on this topic here.

This chapter is a companion to my "Computational Aspects of the Theory of Grammar (1995)," in which the question of the nature of the competence grammar itself and its relation to the problem of incremental semantic interpretation and weakly interactive parsing under a very strict reading of the strong competence hypothesis are investigated in greater depth. Both papers are intended to be read independently, and as a consequence certain sections concerning notation and the theory of natural language grammar are common to both.

Acknowledgments

Thanks to Stephen Isard, Michael Niv, and Mike White for reading and commenting upon the draft. The work was supported in part by NSF grant nos. IRI90-18513, IRI91-17110, and CISE IIP,CDA 88-22719, DARPA grant no. N00014-90-J-1863, and ARO grant no. DAAL03-89-C0031.

References

Ades, A., & Steedman, M. (1982). On the order of words. *Linguistics & Philosophy, 4,* 517–558.
Aho, A. (1969). Nested-stack automata. *Journal of the Association for Computing Machinery, 16,* 383–406.
Aho, A., & Johnson, S. (1974). LR parsing. *Computing Surveys, 6,* 99–124.
Allen, J. (1987). *Natural language understanding.* Menlo Park, CA: Benjamin-Cummings.
Altmann, G., & Steedman, M. (1988). Interaction with context during human sentence processing. *Cognition, 30,* 191–238.
Barton, G. E., Berwick, R., & Ristad, E. (1987). *Computational complexity and natural language.* Cambridge, MA: MIT Press.
Berwick, R., & Weinberg, A. (1984). *The grammatical basis of linguistic performance.* Cambridge, MA: MIT Press.
Bever, T. (1970). The cognitive basis for linguistic structures. In T. Hayes (Ed.) *Cognition and Development of Language* (pp. 279–352). New York: Wiley.
Brame, M. (1978). *Base generated syntax.* Seattle, WA: Noit Amrofer.
Bresnan, J. (1978). A realistic transformational grammar. In M. Halle, J. Bresnan, & G. Miller (Eds.), *Linguistic structure and psychological reality* (pp. 1–59). Cambridge, MA: MIT Press.
Bresnan, J. (Ed.). (1982). *The mental representation of grammatical relations.* Cambridge, MA: MIT Press.
Brill, E. (1995). A report of recent progress in transformation-based error driven learning. In

Proceedings of the ARPA Human Language Technology Workshop, Plainsboro, NJ, March 1994 (pp. 727–796). Palo Alto, CA: Morgan Kaufmann.

Chomsky, N. (1957). *Syntactic structures.* The Hague: Mouton.

Chomsky, N. (1965). *Aspects of the theory of syntax.* Cambridge, MA: MIT Press.

Chomsky, N. (1981). *Lectures on government and binding.* Dordrecht: Foris.

Crain, S., & Steedman, M. (1985). On not being led up the garden path: The use of context by the psychological parser. In D. Dowty, L. Kartunnen, & A. Zwicky (Eds.), *Natural language parsing: Psychological, computational and theoretical perspectives* (pp. 320–358). Cambridge, UK: Cambridge University Press.

Dowty, D., Kartunnen, L., & Zwicky, A. (Eds.). (1985). *Natural language parsing: Psychological, computational and theoretical perspectives,* ACL Studies in Natural Language Processing. Cambridge, UK: Cambridge University Press.

Earley, J. (1970). An efficient context-free parsing algorithm. *Communications of the ACM, 13,* 94–102.

Fodor, J. A. (1983). *The modularity of mind.* Cambridge, MA: MIT Press.

Fodor, J. A., Bever, T., & Garrett, M. (1974). *The psychology of language.* New York: McGraw-Hill.

Ford, M., Bresnan, J., & Kaplan, R. (1982). A competence-based theory of syntactic closure. In J. Bresnan (Ed.), *The mental representation of grammatical relations* (pp. 727–796). Cambridge, MA: MIT Press.

Frazier, L. (1978). *On comprehending sentences.* Ph.D. dissertation, Amherst, MA: University of Massachussetts.

Frazier, L., & Fodor, J. D. (1978). The sausage machine: A new two-stage parsing model. *Cognition, 6,* 291–325.

Gazdar, G. (1988). Applicability of indexed grammars to natural languages. In U. Reyle & C. Rohrer (Eds.), *Natural language parsing and linguistic theories* (pp. 69–94). Dordrecht: Reidel.

Gazdar, G., Klein, E., Pullum, G., & Sag, I. (1985). *Generalised phrase structure grammar.* Oxford: Blackwell.

Gibson, E. (1994). *Memory limitations and linguistic processing breakdown.* Cambridge, MA: MIT Press.

Grosz, B., Sparck-Jones, K., & Webber, B. (1986). *Readings in natural language processing.* Palo Alto, CA: Morgan-Kaufmann.

Harel, D. (1987). *Algorithmics: The spirit of computing.* Reading, MA: Addison-Wesley.

Harrison, M. (1978). *Introduction to formal language theory.* Reading, MA: Addison-Wesley.

Hirst, G. (1987). *Semantic interpretation and resolution of ambiguity.* Cambridge: Cambridge University Press.

Jelinek, F. (1976). Continuous speed recognition by statistical methods, *Proceedings of IEEE, 64,* 532–556.

Joshi, A., Vijay-Shanker, K., & Weir, D. (1991). The convergence of mildly context-sensitive formalisms. In P. Sells, S. Shieber, & T. Wasow (Eds.), *Processing of linguistic structure* (pp. 31–81). Cambridge, MA: MIT Press.

Joshi, A., & Schabes, Y. (1992). Tree adjoining grammars and lexicalized grammars. In M. Nivat & M. Podelski (Eds.), *Definability and recognizability of sets of trees.* Princeton, NJ: Elsevier.

Kay, M. (1980). *Algorithm schemata and data structures in syntactic processing,* CSL-80-12. Xerox PARC. (Reprinted in Grosz et al., 1986)

Kimball, J. (1973). Seven principles of surface structure parsing in natural language. *Cognition, 2,* 15–47.

Marcus, M. (1980). *A theory of syntactic recognition for natural language.* Cambridge, MA: MIT Press.

Marcus, M., Hindle, D., & Fleck, M. (1983). D-theory: Talking about talking about trees. In

Proceedings of the 21st annual meeting of the Association for Computational Linguistics, Cambridge, MA, 1983, pp. 129–136.

Marslen-Wilson, W., Tyler, L., & Seidenberg, M. (1978). The semantic control of sentence segmentation. In W. J. M. Levelt & G. Flores d'Arcais (Eds.), *Studies in the perception of language*. New York: Wiley.

Merialdo, B. (1994). Tagging English text with a probabilistic model, *Computational Linguistics 20*, 155–171.

Montague, R. (1974). *Formal philosophy: Papers of Richard Montague*, (R. H. Thomason, Ed.). New Haven, CT: Yale University Press.

Niv, M. (1993). Resolution of syntactic ambiguity: The case of new subjects. In *Proceedings of the 15th annual meeting of the Cognitive Science Society, Boulder, CO, 1993*.

Oehrle, R., Bach, E., & Wheeler, D. (Eds.). (1988). *Categorial grammars and natural language structures*. Dordrecht: Reidel.

Partee, B., ter Meulen, A., & Wall, R. (1990). *Mathematical methods in linguistics*. Dordrecht: Kluwer.

Pereira, F. (1985). A new characterisation of attachment preferences. In D. Dowty, L. Kartunnen, & A. Zwicky (Eds.), *Natural language parsing: Psychological, computational and theoretical perspectives* (pp. 307–319). Cambridge, UK: Cambridge University Press.

Pereira, F., & Grosz, B. (1993). *Special volume on natural language processing: Artificial Intelligence, 63* (1–2), 1–532.

Pereira, F., & Shieber, S. (1987). *Prolog and natural language understanding*. Chicago: CSLI/University of Chicago Press.

Perrault, R., & Grosz, B. (1988). Natural language interfaces. In H. Shrobe (Ed.), *Exploring artificial intelligence* (pp. 133–172). San Mateo, CA: Morgan-Kaufmann.

Peters, S., & Ritchie, R. (1973). On the generative power of transformational grammars. *Information Science, 6*, 49–83.

Pollard, C., & Sag, I. (1994). *Head-driven phrase structure grammar*. Chicago: CSLI/University of Chicago Press.

Pritchett, B. (1992). *Grammatical competence and parsing performance*. Chicago: University of Chicago Press.

Slocum, J. (1981). A practical comparison of parsing strategies. In *Proceedings of the Nineteenth annual meeting of the Association for Computational Linguistics, Stanford, CA, 1981*, pp. 1–6.

Steedman, M. (1995). Computational aspects of the theory of grammar. In L. Gleitman & M. Liberman (Eds.), *Invitation to cognitive science I: Language*. Cambridge, MA: MIT Press.

Trueswell, J. C., Tanenhaus, M. K., & Garnsey, S. M. (1994). Semantic influences on parsing: Use of thematic role information in syntactic ambiguity resolution. *Journal of Memory & Language*. 285–318.

Wanner, E. (1980). The ATN and the Sausage Machine: Which one is baloney? *Cognition, 8*, 209–225.

Weinberg, A. (1994). Parameters in the theory of sentence processing. *Journal of Psycholinguistic Research, 22*, 339–364.

Winograd, T. (1972). *Understanding natural language*. Edinburgh: Edinburgh University Press.

Woods, W. (1970). Transition network grammars for natural language analysis. *Communications of the ACM, 3*, 591–606. (Reprinted in Grosz et al., 1986)

Woods, W. (1973). An experimental parsing system for transition network grammars. In R. Rustin (Ed.), *Natural language processing*, (Courant Computer Science Symposium 8, pp. 111–154). New York: Algorithmics Press.

CHAPTER 9

Creativity

Margaret A. Boden

I. THE DEFINITION OF CREATIVITY

A. Psychological Studies of Creativity

Psychological studies of creativity are legion (Boden, 1994; Eysenck, 1995; Finke, Ward, & Smith, 1992; Gardner, 1993; Ochse, 1990; Perkins, 1981; Sternberg, 1988, Sternberg & Davidson, 1994; Weber & Perkins, 1992). Many focus on whether, and how, creativity can be measured. Others ask how scientific and artistic creativity differ, what sort of personality profile is involved, what neurophysiological factors favor creativity, or what is contributed by upbringing, family position, and psychodynamics. But few ask just how creative ideas are generated. Often, this question is answered by default, creative ideas being assumed to arise from (unspecified) processes of association or analogy. How these processes actually function is not explained.

By contrast, AI models of creativity cannot escape the question of how creative ideas can arise. Candidate processes must be precisely specified, if the models are to work at all. Whether these processes are psychologically realistic is, of course, another question.

Before considering any computational models, a methodological warning is needed. Creativity is not a natural kind, such that a single scientific

Artificial Intelligence
Copyright © 1996 by Academic Press, Inc. All rights of reproduction in any form reserved.

theory could explain every case. There are three reasons for this. First, positive evaluation is essential (see Section IB). Evaluative criteria can be included in AI models. But *whether they are valuable* is not a scientific question. Second, the psychological processes concerned are very varied. We can hope only for an account of their general types and a more detailed understanding of a few examples. Third, creative ideas often involve chance or individual idiosyncrasies. No psychological theory could explain every such instance. (Creative ideas are not random, however; they must fit within certain cognitive constraints; see Section II.)

A philosophical warning is needed, too. Psychologists want to know whether AI models can illuminate human creativity. They are not, qua psychologists, interested in the philosophical question whether any computer could "really" be creative. This question will not be considered here (but see Boden, 1990, Chap. 11; Chapter 1, this volume).

B. Defining Creativity

Over 60 definitions of *creativity* appear in the psychological literature (Taylor, 1988). In addition to the ambiguities regarding *product, process,* or *person,* the definition is problematic for four reasons.

The first problem is that positive evaluation is essential to the concept. An idea counted as "creative" must be interesting. But what is interesting depends, largely, on the domain. Moreover, this judgment often rests on social and historical factors. What counts as a scientific "discovery" is decided by (sometimes lengthy) negotiation among the relevant peer groups (Schaffer, 1994). Similar negotiations occur in the arts. No purely psychological (ahistorical) theory could explain these evaluations.

The second problem concerns the question whether the originator must recognize the value of an idea for it (and them) to be called *creative.* If so, then someone who has a good idea but rejects it as uninteresting is not creative. This definition, in emphasizing evaluation, is preferable to one allowing evaluative "blindness" on the originator's part. But both senses occur in the literature.

The third difficulty is the tension between psychological (P) and historical (H) senses. An idea is P-creative if it is creative with respect to *the mind of the person concerned,* even if others have had that idea already. An idea is H-creative if it is P-creative *and* no other person has had the idea before. H-creativity is more glamorous, but P-creativity is more fundamental.

The fourth problem is that the familiar operational definition fits only *some* cases. Many psychologists define *creativity* as the novel combination of familiar ideas. This does not distinguish P-novelty from H-novelty nor mention evaluation (although judges may evaluate responses implicitly). Most important, it focuses on only *improbabilities,* on ideas (combinations) that are merely *statistically* surprising. However, we often encounter a deeper form of originality. Here, the novel ideas—relative to the pre-existing knowledge of the rules defining the specific domain or conceptual space concerned—could not have occurred before. The surprise concerns the occurrence of *impossibilities,* not improbabilities. (This apparent paradox underlies the paradoxical flavor of many discussions of creativity.)

We therefore need two definitions of creativity (both requiring that the novel idea be interesting). *Improbabilist* creativity concerns novel and improbable combinations of familiar ideas; it is discussed in Section III. *Impossibilist* (or exploratory–transformational) creativity concerns novel ideas that, relative to the pre-existing conventions of the domain, the person could not have had before. Section II considers the type of theory appropriate to impossibilist creativity.

II. IMPOSSIBILIST CREATIVITY

A. Mapping Conceptual Spaces

Apparently "impossible" ideas can be generated if the previously existing conceptual constraints are transformed. Impossibilist creativity therefore involves the mapping, exploration, and transformation of conceptual spaces (Boden, 1990). Conceptual spaces are styles of thinking in the sciences and arts. They are defined by generative rules, or stylistic conventions, for generating ideas—some of which may be new, but all of which lie within the potential of the relevant (untransformed) conceptual space. These conventions are "positive constraints," specifying not what is forbidden but what is desired.

An idea can be "possible" or "impossible" only with respect to a specific conceptual space. It is possible if the rules for generating new structures allow for it; impossible if they do not. The more clearly we can map the conceptual space, the better we can identify a given idea as creative, in this way or that.

This is the first point where AI models can help. Musicologists, literary critics, and historians of art and science map conceptual spaces. Their descriptions are often subtle and illuminating, but their standards of rigor are low. An AI model can help to show the precise generative potential of the space concerned (as defined within the model) and suggest detailed questions not thought of by the humanist scholar.

Some AI models that are *not* models of creativity are therefore relevant. For instance, Longuet-Higgins (1987, 1994) provides maps of various conceptual spaces (expressive, harmonic, and metrical) involved in tonal music.

Longuet-Higgins gives programmed rules for interpreting marks of expression in a piano score (including legato, staccato, piano, forte, sforzando, crescendo, rallentando, and rubato), thereby modeling, in part, the conceptual space of expressive sensibility. Working with two Chopin piano compositions, he has discovered some counterintuitive facts. For example, a crescendo is not uniform, but exponential: a uniform crescendo does not sound like a crescendo but like someone turning the volume-knob on a radio. Moreover, acceptable decisions as to where to begin and end the crescendo require that the composition be "parsed" by the performer. Where sforzandi are concerned, the mind is highly sensitive: a centisecond differentiates acceptable from clumsy performance. But our appreciation of piano and forte is surprisingly insensitive, for (with respect to these compositions) only five absolute levels of loudness are needed for acceptable performance. How far these rules suit other music is an interesting question. (For a program that learns to play "unmarked" scores expressively, see Widmer, 1994.)

Maps of conceptual spaces are internal representations of the creator's own thinking skills. They may be many leveled and are not necessarily conscious. They articulate the structure of the spaces concerned, indicating pathways, boundaries, and potential "tunnels" into closely related spaces.

Psychological evidence supports this view. Children's skills are at first utterly inflexible. Later, imaginative flexibility results from "representational redescriptions" (RRs) of (fluent) lower level skills (Karmiloff-Smith, 1992). These RRs provide many-leveled maps of the mind, which are used by the subject to do things they *could not* do before (Boden, 1990, Chap. 4). Children (and adults) need RRs of their lower level drawing skills in order to draw nonexistent objects: a one-armed man or seven-legged dog. Lacking such cognitive resources, a 4-year-old simply *cannot* draw a one-armed man. But 10-year-olds can explore their own man-drawing skill by using strategies such as distorting, repeating, omitting, or mixing parts.

The development of RRs is a mapping exercise, whereby people develop explicit mental representations of knowledge already possessed implicitly. In computational terms, knowledge embedded in procedures becomes available, after redescription, as part of the system's data structures.

Few AI models of creativity contain reflexive descriptions of their own procedures or ways of varying them. Accordingly, most AI models are limited to exploring their conceptual spaces rather than transforming them (see Sections IV and V).

B. Exploring Conceptual Spaces

Creativity, when it is not merely novel combination, involves more or less daring explorations of conceptual space. At the limit, when the space is not just explored but transformed, ideas arise that were previously impossible.

Consider post-Renaissance Western music. This is based on the generative system of tonal harmony. Each composition has a "home key," from which it starts, in which it must finish, and from which—at first—it did not stray. Traveling along the path of the home key alone soon became boring. Modulations between keys then appeared. At first, only a few were tolerated, and these only between keys very closely related in harmonic space. With time, the modulations became more daring (distant) and more frequent. By the late nineteenth century, there might be many distant modulations within a single bar.

Eventually, the notion of the home key was undermined. With so many, and so daring, modulations, a "home key" could be identified not from the body of the piece but only from its beginning and end. Inevitably, someone (Schoenberg) suggested that the home-key convention be dropped, since it no longer constrained (shaped) the composition as a whole.

Within a given conceptual space, many thoughts (structures) are possible, some of which are never thought. Exploration locates (some of) these and finds their neighbors and pathways. It even produces valued novelties, which we regard as creative because we had not realized that the space held such a potential. For instance, Mozart's music, in general, exploits the possibilities already inherent in contemporary musical genres. This sort of space exploration may involve slight changes to relatively superficial dimensions of the space or the addition of new (also superficial) dimensions. But it involves no fundamental transformations of it. (Mozart could be a less adventurous composer than Haydn, even though he is widely regarded as the greater.)

The criteria of identity of a given conceptual space are not always clear. If a domain's rules for dealing with a conceptual space include mechanisms for changing some of its rules, one may argue over whether the space is "closed" over all the rules, and all their mutations. Accordingly, one may regard this modulation example as the continuing exploration of the same musical space. Or one may prefer to think of it as a continual *extension* of the space, by minimal changes ("tweakings" rather than "transformations") to the rules of composition. In either case, the creativity involved is less fundamental, less surprising, than that involved in creative transformation.

C. Transforming Conceptual Spaces

Transformation involves heuristics lying outside the domain rules. A heuristic may be especially relevant to certain sorts of mental "landscape", and it may be domain general or domain specific.

One example of transformation is Schoenberg's creation of atonal music, which involved ignoring the "home-key" constraint. In atonal music, all 12 notes of the chromatic scale (not just 7) have an equal "right" to be used. Similar examples from other domains could be mentioned, for *dropping a constraint* is a general heuristic for transforming conceptual spaces. For instance, non-Euclidean geometry results from dropping Euclid's fifth axiom, according to which parallel lines meet at infinity.

Another very general way of transforming conceptual spaces is to *consider the negative;* that is, to negate a constraint.

One instance concerns Kekulé's discovery of the benzene ring. He described visualizing atoms "in long rows, sometimes more closely fitted together; all twining and twisting in snakelike motion. But look! What was that? One of the snakes had seized hold of its own tail . . ." This vision was the origin of his hunch that the benzene molecule might be a ring—not a string—of atoms.

We can understand how he could pass from strings to rings, as plausible chemical structures, if we assume three things (each supported by independent evidence): that snakes and molecules were already associated in his thinking, that the topological distinction between open and closed curves was also present, and that the "consider the negative" heuristic was available.

A string molecule is an open curve. The negative of an open curve is a closed curve. Moreover, a snake biting its tail is *a closed curve that one had expected to be an open one.* For that reason, it is surprising, even arresting ("But look! What was that?"). Finally, the change from open to closed curves is a topological change, and Kekulé knew that a change in atomic neighbor relations will have some chemical significance. So his hunch that this tail-biting snake molecule might solve his problem is understandable.

A third common way of transforming a conceptual space is to *vary the variable.* Chemists after Kekulé, knowing that carbon is one of about 90 elements, asked whether ring molecules might contain nitrogen or phosphorus atoms. And many examples exist of people substituting numerals, where the space is partly described in numerical terms. Thus Kekulé's successors asked whether there might be less than six atoms in a ring molecule; and Hindus asked whether Kali might have six arms, not two.

We shall see in Section VI that some AI models of creativity can modify their own rules to transform the conceptual spaces they inhabit. These systems model impossibilist creativity, generating structures they could not have generated before.

III. IMPROBABILIST CREATIVITY

A. AI Models of Association

We saw in Section I.B that some creative ideas are (valuable) novel combinations of familiar ideas. Much poetic imagery falls into this class (Boden, 1990, Chap. 6). In science, too, novel combinations may be fruitful. Such creative associations are often taken for granted, the question of *how* they happen being ignored. However, AI work in connectionism (neural networks) suggests ways in which they might come about.

Among the questions that can now be given preliminary answers in computational terms are the following: how can ideas from very different sources be spontaneously thought of together? how can two ideas be merged to produce a new structure, which shows the influence of both ancestor ideas without being a mere "cut-and-paste" combination? how can the mind be "primed," so that one will more easily notice serendipitous ideas? why may someone notice—and remember—something fairly uninteresting, if it occurs in an interesting context? how can a brief phrase conjure up an entire melody from memory? and how can we accept two ideas as similar ("love" and "prove" as rhyming, for instance) in respect of a feature not identical in both?

The features of connectionist AI models that suggest answers to these questions are their powers of pattern completion, graceful degradation, sensitization, multiple constraint satisfaction, and "best-fit" equilibration. The computational processes underlying these features were described in Chapter 5. Here, the important point is that the unconscious, "insightful," associative aspects of creativity can be explained—in outline, at least—by AI methods.

B. AI Models of Analogy

1. Fixed-Structure Analogy

Analogy is a special case of association, grounded in structural similarity. It is common in both arts and science. Sometimes the analogy is merely noted, but often it is explored further, being used for systematic rhetorical comparison or creative problem solving. This involves comparisons between specific structural features and decisions about which features are most relevant. There are many AI models of analogy, both symbolic and connectionist (Chapter 4, Section VI). Computational models of metaphor are also relevant (Way, 1991).

For the "structure-mapping" theory (Gentner, 1989), mere similarity of features is not enough. There must be a similarity of structure, allowing objects and relations in one idea to be systematically mapped onto their equivalents in the other, and shared relational structure outweighs differences in observable properties. Semantic relations are more important than formal ones and higher order semantic relations (between relations) are preferred over lower order ones (between objects). In the analogy between the atom and the solar system, the nucleus is mapped onto sun and electrons onto planets, and the central body's attraction for the outer bodies is noted. But irrelevant properties (absolute size, temperature, color) are ignored.

Gentner locates her original theory on Marr's "computational" level. But an AI model (on the "algorithmic" level) now exists: the SME, or structure-mapping engine (Falkenhainer, Forbus, & Gentner, 1989). Given structured representations of concepts, SME constructs various global matches and evaluates them. The matches can suggest "candidate inferences," wherein a predicate applying to one concept is hypothetically applied to the other. This is crucial for gaining new knowledge in analogical problem solving. (Harvey postulated invisible capillaries linking arteries and veins, because a closed hydraulic system has connected channels.)

For Gentner, analogy differs from thinking about goals and plans (although the "external" pragmatic context can influence analogies). Otherwise, we could not explain analogies that are irrelevant to, or even contradict, the thinker's current goals. She criticizes computational models in which analogy depends on pragmatics, such as the PI (processes of induction) system (Holyoak & Thagard, 1989a, 1989b, 1994; Thagard, 1992).

PI is a (localist) connectionist system. It is an inductive problem solver, using multiple constraint satisfaction. Its analogy modules—ARCS for generating analogies, ACME for interpreting them—consider structure only as relevant to the current pragmatic context. It allows access to a huge semantic network, whose units are linked by features like *super/subordinate, part, synonym,* and *antonym* (others can be added at will). There are three general constraints on analogy: pragmatic centrality, semantic similarity, and structural consistency—the first taking precedence.

PI prefers mappings it takes to be important because it has been specifically informed of a correspondence between two items or because some element is so central to its parent structure that *some* mapping for it must be found. For example, ACME was asked to interpret Socrates' analogy between *philosopher* and *midwife.* The item *baby* is so central to the concept of *midwife* that ACME must find a match for it—even though that match (Socrates' pupil's new idea) is semantically very dissimilar, being nonhuman and nonanimate.

Likewise, pragmatics constrains the generation of analogies. Given a concept, ARCS finds a large set of semantically similar ideas and uses multiple constraint satisfaction to identify the nearest ones. It then assesses these by its three general criteria, with pragmatics being heavily weighted. Having found "the best" solution, it deletes all other candidates. The examples cited by ARCS's programmers include outline plots of Aesop and Shakespeare, and the problem of how to use X rays to destroy a tumor without damaging the surrounding tissues.

2. Flexible Analogy

Often, several different analogies might be drawn between two concepts. Much creativity involves seeing just what features, among a host of possibilities, are relevant in context. Often, too, seeing an analogy changes our perception of things. (To describe the heart as a pump is to see its movement in a new way, with contraction—not expansion—being perceived as the active moment.)

Most computer models do not address these matters. Scientific discovery programs use concepts and principles of inference provided by the programmer and model conscious reasoning rather than analogical insights (see Section V.B). Similarly, most analogy programs (like those of Section III.B.1) work by mapping similarities between concepts carefully structured by the programmer, who already knows the relevant aspects. (The pragmatics dimension of ARCS/ACME allows for context, but the programmer has to specify this also.) Moreover, in these AI systems, the two concepts involved remain unchanged by the analogy.

The "Copycat" model is different (M. Mitchell, 1993). It treats seeing a new analogy as much the same as perceiving something in a new way. Copycat can generate many different analogies, favoring contextually appropriate ones. It does not rely on ready-made, fixed representations, but constructs its own in a context-sensitive way: new analogies and new perceptions develop together. A part-built description that seems to be mapping well onto the nascent analogy is maintained and developed further. One that seems to be heading for a dead end is abandoned, and an alternative is begun that exploits different aspects.

Copycat's task domain is alphabetic letter strings, such as *ppqqrrss*, which it can liken to *mmnnoopp, tttuuuvvvwww*, and *abcd*. Its self-constructed "perceptual" representations describe strings by descriptors like *leftmost, rightmost, middle, same, group, alphabetic successor*, and *alphabetic predecessor*. It is a parallel-processing system, descriptors competing simultaneously to build the overall description. The analogy-mapping functions used at any given time depend on the representation already built up. Looking for *successors* or for *repetitions*, for instance, will be differentially encouraged according to context. So the letters *mm* in the string *ffmmtt* will be perceived as a sameness pair, whereas in the string *abcefgklmmno* they will be perceived as parts of two different successor triples: *klm* and *mno*.

The system generates pairs of letter strings that it regards as analogous to the input pair. Usually, it produces several analogies, each justified by a different set of abstract descriptions. This is as it should be, for analogy is not an all-or-nothing matter.

Even in this highly idealized domain, interesting problems arise. For instance, Copycat may be told that *abc* changes into *abd* and asked to decide what *xyz* changes into. Its initial description of the input pair is couched in terms of alphabetic successors. But this has to be destroyed when it comes across *z*, which has no successor. Different descriptors then compete to represent the input strings, and the final output depends partly on which are chosen.

On different occasions, Copycat comes up with the answers *xyd*, *xyzz*, *xyy,* and others. However, its deepest insight occurs when it notices that it is dealing with the *first* letter of the alphabet at one end of the string and with the *last* letter at the other end. This opens up a new way of mapping the strings onto each other; namely, with *a* mapping onto *z,* and simultaneously *left* onto *right.* As a consequence of this conceptual reversal, *successor* and *predecessor* also swap roles and so the idea of "replacing the rightmost letter by its successor," which applied to the initial string, is transformed into "replace the leftmost letter by its predecessor." As a result of all this, we get the surprising and elegant answer, *wyz.* (This example has something "impossibilist" about it, in that the initial description—via two "consider the negative" transformations—gives rise to a fundamentally different one.)

Copycat shows why P-creativity may be easier after someone else's H-creativity. If certain descriptors are marked beforehand as relevant, Copycat will probably use them. Similarly, a schoolchild (or an AI program described in Section V.B) may quickly understand, perhaps even P-discover, an analogy that the H-creator took months to grasp. The particular analogy is P-new, but its general type is familiar. For example, if the notion that linear equations capture many physical properties is established in the child's mind (or the AI model's heuristics), this mapping can be used in dealing with new evidence.

Similarly, Copycat shows how a system may be "blind" to features it is capable of seeing. In cases of "functional fixedness," people think only of familiar uses of a tool, failing to see that it could also be used in other ways. Likewise, the effective availability to Copycat of various "thinkable" analogies depends on which aspects (if any) have been preferentially marked.

This section has discussed AI models of analogy as such. Other AI models of creativity may include analogy as one feature of a wider system (see Section VI.A).

C. AI Models of Induction

Induction, like association and analogy, is crucial to artistic and scientific creativity. In the arts, it familiarizes people with a certain aesthetic style (conceptual space), which is necessary for creative flexibility in that style (see Section II.A). In science, induction may discover unknown regularities in nature.

Various classical AI methods for modeling induction are described in Chapter 4, Sections II, VII, and VIII. Inductive AI programs specifically intended as models of scientific discovery are described in Section V.C of this chapter.

Also relevant is explanation-based learning or case-based reasoning: a way of generalizing from novel experiences on the basis of prior knowledge

(Chapter 4, Section VI). Some AI workers have described creativity primarily in terms of explanation-based learning. For example, *scripts* (see Chapter 3) plus general *explanation patterns* suggest new questions, when anomalies "remind" the system of previously encountered events (Schank & Childers, 1988). This approach assimilates induction to analogy: when an existing explanation pattern is tweaked to cover anomalies, we move from "pure" induction toward analogy.

Induction is studied in nonclassical AI, too. Evolutionary programming is widely applied to inductive problems (see Section VI.A). Connectionist models learn patterns (Chapter 5). And PI ("processes of induction") is a connectionist model of inductive problem solving (Section III.B.1).

IV. AI MODELS OF THE ARTS

A. Music

1. Symbolic Approaches

Various hierarchical "grammars" map different kinds of music (Balaban, Ebcioglu, & Laske, 1992; Schwanauer & Levitt, 1991). For instance, Longuet-Higgins's (1987) computational maps of tonal harmony underlie a computer model of jazz composition (Johnson-Laird, 1991).

The generation of basic chord sequence requires a powerful computational grammar (and, for all but simple cases, cannot be done on the fly by human musicians). But *improvisation* is done in real time, so must use processes making minimal demands on short-term memory. Accordingly, this computer model relies on surprisingly simple heuristics for improvisation, referring to previous notes only minimally.

Consider melody, for example. Even if every note is from the same scale, the overall contour of the intervals must be melodic. For this to be achieved in real time (with limited short-term memory), the constraints on the choice of the next note must be simple. Johnson-Laird's melody grammar has four instructions: first note, repeat of previous note, and small/large interval. He also defines simple rules regarding harmony, meter, tempo, and chord playing (random choices decide between alternative possibilities).

Johnson-Laird's work explores musical space rather than transforms it. The program (like many human musicians) sticks to a particular musical style, having no rules capable of transforming lower level rules. In common with most other "creative" programs, it uses random choices whenever the stylistic constraints allow for several possibilities (human musicians who make explicitly random choices do so only against the relevant stylistic background (Jones, 1991). It produces unpredictable jazz, but never music that it *could not* have produced before.

The same applies to Cope's (1991) EMI (experiments in musical intelligence), which composes in the styles of Mozart, Stravinsky, Joplin, and others. EMI possesses powerful musical grammars expressed as ATNs (see Chapter 8). It also uses lists of "signatures": melodic, harmonic, metric, and ornamental motifs characteristic of individual composers. Using general rules to vary and intertwine these, it often composes a musical phrase nearly identical to a signature that has *not* been provided. This suggests a systematicity in individual composing styles.

A similar system has been designed for jazz improvisation, though it can also be applied to other types of music (Hodgson, in preparation; Waugh, 1992). Given a particular melody, harmony, and rhythm by the user, it improvises by exploring (making random choices on) many dimensions of musical space simultaneously. Among the musical structures it improvises are fragments of (the harmonically relevant) ascending or descending scales, "call" and "reply" over two or more bars, chromatic runs between adjacent melody notes or substitute notes drawn from the same scale, and new cut-and-paste versions of stored melodic and rhythmic patterns.

If left to wander through the space by itself, the program often originates interesting musical ideas, which jazz professionals can exploit in their own performance. Alternatively, the human user can make the program concentrate on one (or more) dimension at a time and explore it (or them) in a very simple way. It can, therefore, help jazz novices, who can focus on the dimension currently causing them difficulty. (A later version of this program generates jazz in the style of Charlie Parker, and sounds as though Parker himself was playing.)

Both this model and EMI can be used, interactively, for teaching and aiding composition. The human user decides on (or handcrafts) the exploratory steps and provides the evaluations—following up some steps but not others. The interactive GA systems described in Section VIB2 make their own exploratory/transformational moves, evaluation again being done by the human user. They, too, can be used for artistic purposes, but because their transformations are random, they cannot be used for systematic teaching.

2. Connectionist Models of Music

Connectionist models of music contain no heuristics defining deep musical grammar. Rather, they learn to recognize surface features, and generate compositions of the same type. They can learn non-Western styles, for which the programmer may have no musical grammar. But, lacking good maps of their musical space, their compositional power is limited.

WOLFGANG (Riecken, 1992) is based on a connectionist theory of memory, using activation spreading, distributed problem solving (by domain experts in melody, harmony, and so on), and a blackboard memory. It learns to recognize regularities in its musical input, tries to compose in the relevant style, and is "reinforced" by its human teacher.

Given a few notes as a "seed", it composes *exposition, development,* and (cut-and-paste) *recapitulation.* A 10-point scale determines its degree of stylistic conservatism, and it avoids self-repetition by keeping a file of its own compositions. As well as learning patterns of meter, dynamics, and harmony, WOLFGANG learns their "emotive" combinations (categorized as happy, sad, meditative, and angry) and—within any given style—can compose in four ways accordingly. The K-line architecture gives it flexibility, but (like many connectionist systems) its detailed processing is often opaque.

A similar system is described in (Kohonen, Laine, Tiits, & Torkkola, 1991). Its initial musical ignorance enables it to learn to compose in indefinitely many styles. It learns a style progressively, by being exposed to examples (using a connectionist pattern-recognition technique). Kohonen et al. suggest that its surface grammars might be combined with (symbolic) deeper ones. The resulting compositions would be richer, but the more detailed mapping of musical space would then exclude alternative styles.

A special issue of the journal *Connection Science,* focuses on connectionist models of musical creativity (P. M. Todd, 1994).

B. Visual Arts

1. Line Drawing

Cohen's program AARON (McCorduck, 1991) generates pleasing line drawings. They are individually unpredictable (because of random choices) but all lie within the preassigned genre.

One version of AARON draws acrobats. The program's "body grammar" specifies human anatomy (head, trunk, arms, legs) and how the body parts appear from different points of view or in different bodily attitudes. But it does so only in a very limited way. AARON can draw acrobats with only one arm visible (because of occlusion) but cannot draw one-armed acrobats. The relevant conceptual space does not allow for the possibility of one-armed people: they are unimaginable.

If AARON could "drop" one of the limbs, as a geometer may drop an axiom, it could draw one-armed figures. (To maintain the realism of AARON's style, complementary changes would be needed in the bodily balance rules.) A superficially similar, but more powerful, transformation might be made if the numeral 2 were used to denote the number of arms. For 2, being a variable, might be replaced by 1 or even 7. A tweaking-transformational heuristic might look for numerals and substitute varying values. (Kekulé's successors did this in asking whether any ring-molecules could have five atoms.) A program that (today) drew one-armed acrobats for the first time by employing a "vary-the-variable" heuristic *could* (tomorrow) draw seven-legged acrobats as well. A program that merely "dropped the left arm" *could not.*

AARON's powers of evaluation are limited and not self-corrective. Some evaluative criteria (about aesthetic balance, for instance) are built into its generative processes, and it may consider what it has already done in deciding what to do next. But AARON cannot reflect on its own productions nor adjust them to make them better.

2. Alphabetic Font Design

The Letter Spirit project (Hofstadter & McGraw, 1993) aims to model the perception and self-critical creation of alphabetic style. (As yet, only the perception has been implemented.) Letter Spirit's task is to design a 26-letter alphabet, given 1 or 2 sample letters. Each letter is composed of straight lines drawn on a 3-by-7 grid (with diagonals, 56 line quanta are available). Using this grid, humans have designed 1500 versions of the letter *a* and over 600 complete gridfonts.

Every *a* must be recognizable as an *a,* every *b* as a *b,* and so on. And within any given graphic style, the *z* must be designed in the same spirit as the *a* and all other letters. So analogies must exist at two levels: between the *a* in this font and all conceivable *a*s and between all 26 letters in this particular font. If these two analogical requirements conflict, some compromise must be found. (An *i* that does not look much like an *i* may be acceptable, if it fits within a 26-letter font.)

Ideas like those in Copycat (Section III.B.3) are used in Letter Spirit, but this system will be even more complex. Top-down and bottom-up influences will be dynamically combined, and the program's global behavior will emerge from lower level, competitive, parallel processes. At the bottom level are micro-agents, or "codelets," concerned with tiny details. As processing proceeds, patterns of codelet activity develop that can conveniently be thought of as larger scale agents.

Four large-scale agents are envisaged, to guide the processing: Imaginer (to explore the abstract concepts behind letter forms), Drafter (to produce letter forms as actual graphics on the grid), Examiner (to categorize letter forms as letters), and Adjudicator (to perceive the stylistic aspects of letter forms and build a description of the style). Through interaction between these agents, the evolving style can be evaluated and adjusted incrementally.

Given that the Examiner has categorized a letter as an *a* (not a simple matter), the Adjudicator has to decide what are the stylistic constraints on this *a* and whether the style is an acceptable one. Then, when another letter has been categorized as a *g,* the Adjudicator has to look for stylistic consistency between those two letters and so on. Interaction between the Adjudicator and the Imaginer may suggest stylistic modifications, to be realized by the Drafter and interpreted by the Examiner . . . and so the highly interactive, highly dynamic, process continues.

Despite not being fully implemented, Letter Spirit merits discussion here: it promises an unusual degree of exploratory freedom, abstract understanding (of letters), and evaluative self-adaptation. A completed Letter Spirit could reasonably be said to be making (and justifying) its own decisions.

3. Architecture

Generative shape grammars describing (for example) Palladian villas (Stiny & Mitchell, 1978) or Frank Lloyd Wright's prairie houses (Koning & Eizenberg, 1981) have been available for some time. These can identify some of the dimensions of the relevant architectural space, showing which are relatively fundamental. In a prairie house, the addition of a balcony is stylistically superficial, for it is a decision on which nothing else (except the appearance and ornamentation of the balcony) depends. By contrast, the "addition" of a fireplace results in overall structural change, because many design decisions follow and depend on the (early) decision about the fireplace.

Other architectural grammars, and some functioning design programs, are described in W. J. Mitchell (1990). A recent program focused on Palladian villas designs both plans and facades and takes into account proportions and dimensions as well as abstract shapes (Hersey & Freedman, 1992). The authors are aware that their program could be used to design new buildings in the Palladian style. Their primary interest in writing it, however, was not practical but theoretical. As they put it, "knowing what Palladio would and would not do deepens our understanding of what he actually did do" (p. 10). It would be hard to find a clearer statement of the use of computer modeling for the scholarly and aesthetic purposes of the humanities.

(Further self-transforming models of visual arts are discussed in Section VI.)

C. Verbal Texts

Several story-writing programs have been based on scripts and related knowledge representations (Chapter 3). A number of story writers are reviewed, together with a helpful discussion of the narrative problems involved, in Ryan (1991).

TALE-SPIN (Meehan, 1981) generated simple problem-solving plots involving two or three characters, similar to Aesop's (simpler) fables. However, only preprogrammed problems could be considered (and many tales were "misspun," due to the program's lack of common sense).

MINSTREL (Turner, 1992) is a more powerful version of TALE-SPIN.

It adds case-based reasoning (Sections III.C in this chapter, and Chapter 4, Section V) and TRAM heuristics (transform–recall–adapt methods), enabling it to solve novel problems similar to familiar ones. Cumulative small transformations can generate significantly novel cases. MINSTREL distinguishes the author's goals from the characters' goals, so it can solve meta-problems about the story as well as problems posed within it.

For example, it may have the (storytelling) goal of describing a situation in which a knight kills himself. Initially, it knows nothing about suicide. But its starting knowledge includes two story scenes, Knight Fight ("a knight fights a troll with his sword, killing the troll and accidentally injuring himself") and Princess and Potion ("a lady of the court drank a potion to make herself ill"). MINSTREL transforms and adapts these scenes to create three suicides: the knight deliberately loses a fight with a dragon, or drinks poison, or falls on his sword.

MINSTREL's stories are more complex than TALE-SPIN's, although structurally limited by human standards. However, it has only about 30 authorial plans and 10 story scenes to work with, whereas people learn many different "cases" and storytelling techniques. Humans' (highly complex) recall and transformation may involve cognitive processes comparable to those modeled in MINSTREL.

V. AI MODELS OF SCIENCE

A. Meta-DENDRAL

DENDRAL (Lindsay, Buchanan, Feigenbaum, & Lederberg, 1993) was an early expert system and has been very influential in AI. It embodies inductive principles modeled on human thinking and nonhuman methods such as exhaustive search. Its conceptual space concerns the behavior of certain chemical compounds when disintegrating inside a mass spectrometer. Because molecules break at "weak" points, chemists can discover the structure of an unknown molecule by identifying the fragments. DENDRAL's task is to aid the chemist, and it is provided with rules about how the relevant molecules usually break.

Meta-DENDRAL (a module added later) is able to induce further constraints on the decomposition of the molecules and add them to the list of rules. Meta-DENDRAL searches for unfamiliar patterns in the spectrographs of known compounds and suggests chemically plausible explanations for them. For instance, if it discovers that molecules of certain types break at certain points, it looks for a smaller structure located near the broken bonds; if it finds one, it suggests that other molecules containing the same submolecular structure may also break there. It has H-created some useful new rules for analyzing several families of molecules, and parts of it are routinely used by computational chemists.

However, the reasoning used by meta-DENDRAL is of a relatively simple kind. Many other expert systems, including some based on neural networks, have identified unknown patterns in scientific (and financial) data. Meta-DENDRAL modeled the extension of highly sophisticated chemical knowledge, not its origination.

B. The BACON Family

Computational models of inductive reasoning in general (Section III.C) are relevant to scientific discovery. But BACON, GLAUBER, STAHL, and DALTON (Langley, Simon, Bradshaw, & Zytkow, 1987) were developed with an eye to the history of science, as well as psychology. Their P-creative activities are modeled on H-creative episodes recorded in the notebooks of human scientists.

BACON induces quantitative laws from empirical data. Its data are measurements of various properties at different times. It looks for simple mathematical functions defining invariant relations between numerical data sets. For instance, it seeks direct or inverse proportionalities between measurements or between their products or ratios. It can define higher level theoretical terms, using the slope or intercept of a linear graph relating the data sets. It can construct new units of measurement, by taking one object as the standard. And it can use mathematical symmetry to help find invariant patterns in the data. It can cope with noisy data, finding a best-fit function (within predefined limits). BACON has P-created many physical laws, including Archimedes's principle, Kepler's third law, Boyle's law, Ohm's law, and Black's law.

GLAUBER discovers qualitative laws, summarizing the data by classifying things according to (nonmeasurable) observable properties. Thus, it discovers relations between acids, alkalis, and bases (all identified in qualitative terms). STAHL analyzes chemical compounds into their elements. Relying on the data categories presented to it, it has modeled aspects of the historical progression from phlogiston theory to oxygen theory. Many of its heuristics were culled from the notebooks of the scientists concerned. DALTON reasons about atoms and molecular structure. Using early atomic theory, it generates plausible molecular structures for a given set of components (it could be extended to cover other componential theories, such as particle physics or Mendelian genetics).

These four programs have rediscovered many scientific laws. However, their P-creativity is shallow. They are highly data driven, their discoveries lying close to the evidence. They cannot identify relevance for themselves (see Section III.B.2) but are "primed" with appropriate expectations. (BACON expected to find linear relationships and rediscovered Archimedes's principle only after being told that things can be immersed in known volumes of liquid and the resulting volume measured.) They cannot model spontaneous associations or analogies, only deliberate reasoning. Some can suggest experiments, to test hypotheses they have P-created, but they have no sense of the practices involved. They can learn, constructing P-novel concepts used to make further P-discoveries. But their discoveries are exploratory rather than transformational: they cannot fundamentally alter their own conceptual spaces.

C. An Integrated Discovery System

The programmers of the BACON family planned to integrate the programs, using output from one as input to the next. Ideally, processes (such as quantitative reasoning) originally included in only one system would be available to all. An integrated discovery system (IDS) is now being developed (Shrager & Langley, 1990, Chap. 4). It can P-create hierarchical taxonomies, qualitative laws, and quantitative laws. It draws heavily on the BACON family and also on AI studies of qualitative physics and knowledge representation (Chapter 3).

IDS is a novel computational framework, combining various forms of reasoning within one system. Qualitative states are organized in taxonomies, representing class inclusion and "history" (observed successions of qualitative states). Numerical laws and quantitative data, too, can be represented (in context) in these taxonomies. IDS reasons more efficiently than the BACON family. For example, a complex process of qualitative reasoning in GLAUBER is replaced by a simple process of finding the closest common ancestor of two nodes in the hierarchy; similarly, IDS has rediscovered most of the laws found by BACON, but more economically.

IDS is being extended, to represent intrinsic properties (such as specific heat), which the latest version of BACON could deal with. It is being extended, also, to design experiments (Shrager & Langley, 1990, Chaps. 8–10). The programmers plan to add the origination of new measuring instruments, which could then be assumed in designing more sophisticated experiments. Other work in progress includes systematic testing of IDS's power and limitations, in both historically realistic and artificial domains.

D. Scientific Revolutions

The PI system (Section III.B.1) has been applied to scientific discovery (Thagard, 1992). This computational work focuses on the evaluation of scientific hypotheses.

PI's (connectionist) ECHO module assesses the "explanatory coherence" of a theory. This covers both internal self-consistency and coherence with the evidence. A given hypothesis coheres with propositions that explain it or are explained by it, which cooperate with it in explaining other propositions or which occur in analogous explanations. Evidence is acceptable unless it is inconsistent with a coherent set of hypotheses.

Several scientific advances have been modeled by this system, including the wave theory of sound, the phlogiston–oxygen controversy, and plate tectonics. Thagard challenges the claim that scientific revolutions involve "Gestalt switching" between incommensurable theories. ECHO can compare the explanatory coherence of competing theories. The historical development of the theories of phlogiston and oxygen has been modeled, showing when—and why—it became reasonable to accept the new conceptual framework.

VI. SELF-TRANSFORMING PROGRAMS

A. AM and EURISKO

Some AI-models of creativity can transform their own conceptual spaces, to some extent. Lenat's (1983) AM and EURISKO are examples.

The Automatic Mathematician (AM) generates and explores mathematical ideas. It does not prove theorems or do sums but generates "interesting" ideas (including expressions that might be provable theorems).

AM starts with 100 primitive concepts of set theory—such as *set, list, equality,* and *ordered pair*—but not including any arithmetical concepts. It also has about 300 heuristics that can examine, combine, and transform its concepts. For example, some can compare, generalize, specialize, or find examples of concepts. One generates the inverse of a function (compare "consider the negative"). Some ask which operations can be performed on a given concept or which can result in it. Yet others search for potential theorems involving the concept. Newly constructed concepts are fed back into the pool.

Evaluation is modeled by heuristics saying what is mathematically "interesting." In effect, AM has hunches: its heuristics suggest which new structures it should concentrate on. For example, AM finds it interesting whenever the union of two sets has a simply expressible property that is not possessed by either of them (a set-theoretic version of the widely held notion that *emergent* properties are interesting). Conversely, AM finds it interesting if a property is *conserved* when sets are combined. AM finds it interesting, also, whenever it notices that a single operation (for instance, multiplication) has been defined in several different ways.

AM's value judgments are often wrong. Nevertheless, it has constructed some powerful mathematical notions, including prime numbers, square roots, Goldbach's conjecture, and an H-novel theorem concerning maximally divisible numbers (which Lenat had never heard of). In short, AM appears to be significantly P-creative and slightly H-creative, too.

However, AM has been criticized (Haase, 1986; Lenat & Seely-Brown, 1984; Ritchie & Hanna, 1984; Rowe & Partridge, 1993). Critics have argued that some heuristics were included to make possible certain discoveries, such as prime numbers; that the use of LISP provided AM with mathematical relevance "for free," since any syntactic change in a LISP expression is likely to result in a mathematically meaningful string; that the program's exploration was too often guided by the human user; that AM had fixed criteria of interest, being unable to adapt its values; and that Lenat's verbal descriptions of the program did not correspond clearly with the code. The precise extent of AM's creativity, then, is unclear.

EURISKO has heuristics for changing heuristics. It can transform not only its stock of concepts but also its own processing style. (Lenat had to design a way of representing heuristics such that syntactic changes would normally result in heuristically meaningful expressions.)

For example, one heuristic asks whether a rule has ever led to any interesting result. If it has not (but has been used several times), it will be used less often in future. If it has occasionally been helpful, though usually worthless, it may be specialized in one of several different ways. (Because it is sometimes useful and sometimes not, the specializing heuristic can be applied to itself.) Other heuristics generalize rules or create new rules by analogy with old ones. There are various methods for constructing generalizations or analogies: EURISKO monitors their success and favors the most useful.

Using domain-specific heuristics to complement these general ones, EURISKO has generated H-novel ideas in genetic engineering and very large-scale integration design. One has been patented (so was not "obvious to a person skilled in the art"): a three-dimensional computer-chip enabling one unit to carry out two logical functions (NOT-AND and OR) simultaneously.

B. Genetic Algorithms

1. Automatic Evaluation

Many self-transforming programs use genetic algorithms, or GAs (see Chapter 11). Most GA systems model inductive problem solving rather than creativity more broadly conceived (but see Section VI.B.2).

GA systems have two main features. They all use rule-changing algorithms (mutation and crossover) modeled on biological genetics. Mutation makes a random change in a single rule. Crossover mixes two rules, so that (for instance) the left-hand portion of one is combined with the right-hand portion of the other; the break points may be chosen randomly or may reflect the system's sense of which rule parts are the most useful. Most GA systems also include algorithms for identifying the relatively successful rules, and rule parts, and increasing the probability that they will be selected for "breeding" in future generations. Together, these algorithms generate a new system, better adapted to the task.

For example, an early GA program developed a set of rules to regulate the transmission of gas through a pipeline (Holland, Holyoak, Nesbitt, & Thagard, 1986). Its data were hourly measurements of inflow, outflow, inlet pressure, outlet pressure, rate of pressure change, season, time, date, and temperature. It altered the inlet pressure to allow for variations in demand and inferred the existence of accidental leaks in the pipeline (adjusting the inflow accordingly).

Although the pipeline program discovered the rules for itself, the potentially relevant data types were given in its original list of concepts. How far that compromises its creativity is a matter of judgment. No system can work from a tabula rasa. The primitive codelets used by Letter Spirit (Section IV.B.2) are provided by the programmer, but they are so far removed from the higher level emergent processes that this hardly seems to matter. The structures (rules) adaptively developed by GA systems are also distinct from the system's primitives and may or may not clearly be constructed out of them.

2. Interactive Evaluation

If a GA system is to do its own evaluating, its data and selectional criteria must be clearly defined (as in the pipeline program). It is more difficult to apply GAs to art, where many evaluative criteria are not only controversial but also imprecise—or even unknown. One way around this problem is to construct GA systems to effect the mutations but to rely on people to do the evaluating.

Interactive GA systems for visual art have been designed by Sims (1991) and Latham (S. Todd & Latham, 1992). Sims's aim is to provide an interactive graphics environment, in which human and computer cooperate in generating otherwise unimaginable images. Latham's is to produce his own art works, but he, too, uses the computer to produce images he could not have produced unaided.

In both cases, the (random) self-transformations are carried out by the system. But, at each generation, the human decides which individual images will be used for breeding the next set of offspring images. The choice is normally made on aesthetic grounds (but curiosity can play a part, too).

In a typical run of Sims's GA system, the first image is generated at random. Then the program makes 19 independent mutations in the image-generating rule and displays 20 images: the first, plus its 19 offspring. The human now chooses one image to be mutated or two to be "mated" (through crossover). The result is another 20 images. The process can be repeated indefinitely.

Sims's program can transform the image-generating code in many ways. It starts with 20 basic LISP functions. Some can alter parameters in pre-existing functions: they can divide or multiply numbers, transform vectors, or define sines or cosines. Some can combine two functions or nest one function inside another (so many-leveled hierarchies can arise). Some are simple image-generating functions, defining (for example) two vertical stripes. Others can process a pre-existing image, for instance, making lines more or less distinct.

The human user selects the seed images for breeding but cannot tell the program how those images should be used: one cannot ask the system to deepen the purple color or to make certain curves more curly. If evaluative rules were added to the program, it could make aesthetic choices (but not necessarily recommendations) for itself.

With no evaluative algorithm, randomness enters at many points. The first image-generating function is selected at random. Whenever a chosen function has parts missing, the program assigns them by chance. If it decides (randomly) to *add* something to a numerical parameter inside a pre-existing image-generating function and the "something" has not been specified, it adds a random amount. Or it may *combine* the pre-existing function with some other randomly chosen function.

Many of Sims's computer-generated images are highly attractive, even beautiful. Moreover, they often cause a deep surprise. The change(s) between parent and offspring are sometimes amazing. One cannot say how the two images are related. The one appears to be a radical transformation of the other—or even something entirely different. In short, random changes here seem to underlie creativity of the impossibilist sort.

Latham's interactive GA program is much more predictable. Its mutation operators can change only the parameters within the image-generating code not the body of the function. Consequently, Latham's program never comes up with radical novelties. All the offspring in a given generation are obviously siblings and obviously closely related to their parents—indeed, to their great-great-grandparents. So Latham's system is less exciting than Sims's. But it is arguably even more relevant to artistic creativity.

The interesting comparison is not between the aesthetic appeal of a Latham image and a Sims image. Aesthetics is largely a matter of taste. The point is that Latham, as a professional artist, has a sense of what forms he hopes to achieve and specific (largely tacit) aesthetic criteria for evaluating intermediate steps. His image generation is guided by artistic discipline. Random changes at the margins are exploratory and may provide some useful ideas, but fundamental transformations—especially, random ones—

would be counterproductive. (If they were allowed, Latham would want to pick one and then explore its possibilities in a disciplined way.)

This fits the definition of impossibilist creativity in Section I. B: creativity works within constraints, which define the conceptual spaces with respect to which creativity is identified. Only after a space has been fairly thoroughly explored will the artist want to transform it in deeply surprising ways. A convincing computer artist would therefore need not only randomizing operators but also heuristics for constraining its transformations and selections in an aesthetically acceptable fashion. And, to be true to human creativity, the evaluative rules should evolve also.

VII. CONCLUSION

Creativity is not a separate "faculty," but an aspect of general intelligence—which involves many kinds of thought process. Computer models of creativity therefore draw on diverse types of AI. Further progress will depend on AI research in many areas, including the integration of currently distinct types of processing.

It requires, also, the definition of additional conceptual spaces and heuristics for exploring and transforming them. This work will need input from scholars of the (artistic and scientific) domains concerned. Computational psychology must also assess these models for their psychological reality. The study of creativity is inescapably interdisciplinary.

References

Balaban, M., Ebcioglu, K., & Laske, O. (Eds.). (1992). *Understanding music with AI: Perspectives on music cognition.* Cambridge, MA: AAAI Press/MIT Press.

Boden, M. A. (1990). *The creative mind: Myths and mechanisms.* London: Weidenfeld & Nicolson. (Expanded ed., London: Abacus, 1991)

Boden, M. A. (Ed.). (1994). *Dimensions of creativity.* Cambridge, MA: MIT Press.

Cope, D. (1991). *Computers and musical style.* Oxford: Oxford University Press.

Eysenck, H. J. (1995). *Genius: The natural history of creativity.* Cambridge, UK: Cambridge University Press.

Falkenhainer, B., Forbus, K. D., & Gentner, D. (1989). The structure-mapping engine: Algorithm and examples. *AI Journal, 41,* 1–63.

Finke, R. A., Ward, T. B., & Smith, S. M. (1992). *Creative cognition: Theory, research, and applications.* Cambridge, MA: MIT Press.

Gardner, H. (1993). *Creating minds: An anatomy of creativity seen through the lives of Freud, Einstein, Picasso, Stravinsky, Eliot, Graham, and Gandhi.* New York: Basic Books.

Gentner, D. (1989). The mechanisms of analogical learning. In S. Vosniadou & A. Ortony (Eds.), *Similarity and analogical reasoning* (pp. 199–241). Cambridge, UK: Cambridge University Press.

Haase, K. W. (1986). Discovery systems. *Proceedings of the European Conference on AI, 1,* 546–555.

Hersey, G., & Freedman, R. (1992). *Possible Palladian villas (plus a few instructively impossible ones)*. Cambridge, MA: MIT Press.

Hodgson, P. (in preparation). *Modelling cognition in creative musical improvisation*. Doctoral thesis, University of Sussex.

Hofstadter, D. R., & McGraw, G. (1993). *Letter spirit: An emergent model of the perception and creation of alphabetic style* (CRCC Tech. Rep. No. 68. Bloomington: Indiana University, Department of Computer Science.

Holland, J. H., Holyoak, K. J., Nisbett, R. E., & Thagard, P. R. (1986). *Induction: Processes of inference, learning, and discovery*. Cambridge, MA: MIT Press.

Holyoak, K. J., & Thagard, P. R. (1989a). Analogical mapping by constraint satisfaction. *Cognitive Science, 13*, 295–356.

Holyoak, K. J., & Thagard, P. R. (1989b). A computational model of analogical problem solving. In S. Vosniadou & A. Ortony (Eds.), *Similarity and analogical reasoning* (pp. 242–266). Cambridge, UK: Cambridge University Press.

Holyoak, K. J., & Thagard, P. R. (1994). *Mental leaps: Analogy in creative thought*. Cambridge, MA: MIT Press.

Johnson-Laird, P. N. (1991). Jazz improvisation: A theory at the computational level. In P. Howell, R. West, & I. Cross (Eds.), *Representing musical structure* (pp. 291–326). London: Academic Press.

Jones, K. (1991, December 14). Dicing with Mozart. *New Scientist*, pp. 26–29.

Karmiloff-Smith, A. (1992). *Beyond modularity: A developmental perspective on cognitive science*. Cambridge, MA: MIT Press.

Kohonen, T., Laine, P., Tiits, K., & Torkkola, K. (1991). A nonheuristic automatic composing method. In P. M. Todd & D. G. Loy (Eds.), *Music and connectionism* (pp. 229–242). Cambridge, MA: MIT Press.

Koning, H., & Eizenberg, J. (1981). The language of the prairie: Frank Lloyd Wright's prairie houses. *Environment and Planning B, 8*, 295–323.

Langley, P., Simon, H. A., Bradshaw, G. L., & Zytkow, J. M. (1987). *Scientific discovery: Computational explorations of the creative process*. Cambridge, MA: MIT Press.

Lenat, D. B. (1983). The role of heuristics in learning by discovery: Three case studies. In R. S. Michalski, J. G. Carbonell, & T. M. Mitchell (Eds.), *Machine learning: An artificial intelligence approach* (pp. 243–306). Palo Alto, CA: Tioga.

Lenat, D. B., & Seely-Brown, J. (1984). Why AM and EURISKO appear to work. *AI Journal, 23*, 269–294.

Lindsay, R., Buchanan, B. G., Feigenbaum, E. A., & Lederberg, J. (1993). DENDRAL: A case study of the first expert system for scientific hypothesis formation. *Artificial Intelligence, 61*, 209–262.

Longuet-Higgins, H. C. (1987). *Mental processes: Studies in cognitive science*. Cambridge, MA: MIT Press.

Longuet-Higgins, H. C. (1994). Artificial intelligence and musical cognition [Special issue on Artificial intelligence and the mind: New breakthroughs or dead ends? (M. A. Boden, A. Bundy, & R. M. Needham, Eds.)] *Philosophical Transactions of the Royal Society of London, Series A, 349*, 103–113.

McCorduck, P. (1991). *Aaron's code*. San Francisco: Freeman.

Meehan, J. (1981). TALE-SPIN. In R. C. Schank & C. J. Riesbeck (Eds.), *Inside computer understanding: Five programs plus miniatures* (pp. 197–226). Hillsdale, NJ: Erlbaum.

Mitchell, M. (1993). *Analogy-making as perception*. Cambridge, MA: MIT Press.

Mitchell, W. J. (1990). *The logic of architecture: Design, computation, and cognition*. Cambridge, MA: MIT Press.

Ochse, R. (1990). *Before the gates of excellence: The determination of creative genius*. Cambridge, UK: Cambridge University Press.

Perkins, D. N. (1981). *The mind's best work*. Cambridge, MA: Harvard University Press.

Riecken, D. (1992). WOLFGANG—A system using emoting potentials to manage musical design. In M. Balaban, K. Ebcioglu, & O. Laske (Eds.), *Understanding music with AI: perspectives on music cognition* (pp. 206–236). Cambridge, MA: AAAI Press/MIT Press.

Ritchie, G. D., & Hanna, F. K. (1984). AM: A case study in AI methodology. *AI Journal, 23*, 249–263.

Rowe, J., & Partridge, D. (1993). Creativity: A survey of AI approaches. *Artificial Intelligence Review, 7*, 43–70.

Ryan, M.-L. (1991). *Possible worlds, artificial intelligence, and narrative theory*. Bloomington: Indiana University Press.

Schaffer, S. (1994). Making up discovery. In M. A. Boden (Ed.), *Dimensions of creativity* (pp. 13–52). Cambridge, MA: MIT Press.

Schank, R. C., & Childers, P. (1988). *The creative attitude: Learning to ask and answer the right questions*. New York: Macmillan.

Schwanauer, S., & Levitt, D. (Eds.). (1991). *Machine models of music*. Cambridge, MA: MIT Press.

Shrager, J., & Langley, P. (Eds.). (1990). *Computational models of discovery and theory formation*. San Mateo, CA: Morgan Kaufmann.

Sims, K. (1991 July). Artificial evolution for computer graphics. *Computer Graphics, 25*(4), 319–328.

Sternberg, R. J. (Ed.). (1988). *The nature of creativity: Contemporary psychological perspectives*. Cambridge, UK: Cambridge University Press.

Sternberg, R. J. & Davidson, J. E. (Eds.). (1994). *The nature of insight*. Cambridge, MA: MIT Press.

Stiny, G., & Mitchell, W. J. (1978). The Palladian grammar. *Environment and Planning B, 5*, 5–18.

Taylor, C. W. (1988). Various approaches to and definitions of creativity. In R. J. Sternberg (Ed.), *The nature of creativity: Contemporary psychological perspectives* (pp. 99–121). Cambridge, UK: Cambridge University Press.

Thagard, P. R. (1992). *Conceptual revolutions*. Princeton, NJ: Princeton University Press.

Todd, P. M. (Ed.) (1994). [Special issue on connectionism and musical creativity.] *Connection Science, 6*(2,3).

Todd, S., & Latham, W. (1992). *Evolutionary art and computers*. London: Academic Press.

Turner, S. (1992). *MINSTREL: A model of story-telling and creativity* (Tech. Note UCLA-AI-17-92). Los Angeles: University of California, AI Laboratory.

Waugh, I. (1992, September). Improviser. *Music Technology*, pp. 70–73.

Way, E. C. (1991). *Knowledge representation and metaphor*. Dordrecht: Kluwer.

Weber, R. J., & Perkins, D. N. (Eds.). (1992). *Inventive minds: Creativity in technology*. Oxford: Oxford University Press.

Widmer, G. (1994). The synergy of music theory and AI: Learning multi-level expressive interpretation. *Proceedings of the American Association for Artificial Intelligence*, AI Seattle, WA.

CHAPTER 10

Human–Computer Interaction

Mike Sharples

I. INTERACTING WITH COMPUTERS

Human–computer interaction (HCI) is the study of the ways people interact with and through computers. It grew out of work on human factors (the U.S. term) or ergonomics (the European term) with the intellectual aim of analyzing tasks that people perform with computers and the practical concerns of designing more usable and reliable computer systems. As computers have infiltrated homes and businesses, the scope of HCI has broadened to include the cognitive, social, and organizational aspects of computer use. HCI can provide techniques to model people's interactions with computers, guidelines for software design, methods to compare the usability of computer systems, and ways to study the effect of introducing new technology into organizations.

The chapter covers the background to HCI, interaction with computers, computer-mediated communication, the psychology of computer use, models of human–computer interaction, computer system design and evaluation, and the social and organizational aspects of computer use.

Artificial Intelligence

A. Pioneers of HCI

HCI has been influenced greatly by a few visionaries who imagined new ways of working with computers. They should not be seen as isolated prophets. Their work was well known to later researchers and has had a strong influence on present-day methods of interaction with computers. Baecker and Buxton (1987) provide a valuable historical survey of HCI.

1. Vannevar Bush and the MEMEX

In 1945, Vannevar Bush, a scientific advisor to the United States government, had an article published in the *Atlantic Monthly* which argued that a successful peacetime research effort would depend on people having ready access to appropriate information. He proposed a future device called the MEMEX, which would extend the human memory by presenting and associating diverse pieces of information. An operator would call up text or images stored on microfilm and choose to follow trails of association to other related information or would add new trails to indicate a train of thought or a cluster of ideas. The MEMEX was never implemented, but the ideas—of using a machine to augment the intellect, of direct manipulation of information, and of trails of association—laid the foundations of multimedia computing.

2. Ivan Sutherland and Sketchpad

By the early 1960s, experimental time-sharing computers were being built that allowed a computer to work on several jobs simultaneously. Computer time could be switched automatically between users, allowing people to work at the computer screen in bursts of activity and solve problems by *interacting* with the computer rather than presenting it with pre-prepared programs. Early work on military computer systems had shown that it was possible to display and manipulate images on a computer console, and researchers began to explore the possibilities of graphical interaction between humans and computers.

Ivan Sutherland, a researcher at the MIT Lincoln Laboratory, implemented a drawing system named *Sketchpad* that demonstrated the power of pictorial interaction and introduced techniques, such as applying constraints to objects, still being developed for contemporary graphics packages.

3. Doug Engelbart and Augment

Doug Engelbart, as a graduate student at the University of California in the 1950s, advocated the computer as an "augmentation device," offering people new ways to study problems, experiment with ideas and hunches, and test possible solutions. Instead of being designed to solve a single problem, computer programs could be constructed as toolkits, with parts that could be reused and extended. The synergy that comes from combining these tools into an integrated "workshop" makes each tool considerably more valuable than if it were used alone, and the combined effort of people working together on the computer augments the abilities of individuals into computer-assisted communities.

With colleagues at Stanford Research Institute in the 1960s, Engelbart developed NLS (oNLine System, later called NLS/Augment), which assisted people in working together on tasks such as planning, analysis, and problem solving (Engelbart & English, 1988). It provided many novel facilities, such as active links between pieces of information, user-controlled windows, filters that displayed files with a specified content, the ability to send electronic mail, and shared-screen conferencing.

4. Alan Kay and the Dynabook

In the 1970s, Alan Kay wrote about an imagined self-contained knowledge manipulator in a portable package the size and shape of an ordinary notebook. It would be able to store and display text, drawings, music, and animations; and the owner would be able to design documents, compose music, create pictures, and communicate directly with other people through sound and image. Alan Kay named this notebook computer *The Dynabook* and in 1972 suggested that "The Dynabook is now within reach of current technology." As a member of the Xerox Palo Alto Research Center, Alan Kay was uniquely placed to realize his vision.

For 10 years he and colleagues developed a series of personal computers (which they called *interim Dynabooks*) and a computer language called *Smalltalk* to support the construction and manipulation of dynamic objects. In April 1981, Xerox announced the 8010 Star Information system, a personal computer designed for office use. Although the Star was a desktop machine rather than a portable package, it realized much of the Dynabook vision. The Star was the first commercial computer to be designed around a *graphical user interface,* which offered a consistent analogy to the top of an office desk with surrounding furniture and equipment. The objects on the simulated desktop were represented by pictorial *icons* indicating "in" and "out" baskets for electronic mail, file drawers, folders, and other electronic metaphors for objects in an office. Operations on the Star were carried out by *direct manipulation* of objects. For example, to file a document the user would move an icon representing the document over a picture of a file drawer.

The novel aspects of HCI found in the Star computer, such as the desktop metaphor, "windows," icons, and "pull down menus," were brought to the mass market in the Apple Macintosh computer. As well as providing a consistent "look and feel" to its range of computers, Apple set down guidelines for designers of Macintosh software which ensured that the Apple's investment in interface design and human–computer interaction would be reflected in software produced by other companies. By the mid-1980s, companies such as Apple, Microsoft, and Aldus were developing software for small business and home use that allowed people with no knowledge of computing and little training in use of the software to perform complex and highly interactive tasks such as producing spreadsheets and designing page layouts. The commitment of these companies to good practice in human–computer interaction, and their subsequent commercial success, has meant that research in HCI has an increasingly strong influence on commercial practice.

B. Interfaces

The interface to a computer is the combination of devices (such as a keyboard, mouse, light pen, screen display, and loudspeaker) that enable a user to interact with the computer. A main aim of interface design is to produce interfaces that hide the complexity of the computer, giving a user the impression of working directly on a productive task such as writing a document or creating an illustration. One way to do this is by presenting the interface as a *metaphor* for some more familiar system, such as a typewriter or set of illustrator's tools.

The advantage of an interface metaphor is that it provides a short-cut to learning a complex system, by offering concepts and operations that fit with the user's existing experience (such as "cutting" and "pasting" objects on the screen). Although metaphors play a central part in interface design, they can lead to faulty reasoning, when the interface does not match the familiar system. For example, in most interfaces cutting and pasting an object does not exactly match the physical process. When a screen object is cut, it "disappears" until the paste operation is performed. Metaphors can also be restrictive, tying the interface to concepts and operations that occur in the noncomputer world, rather than exploiting the possibilities of computer technology.

C. Interaction Devices

As computers are adapted for diverse tasks, from control of industrial processes to art and design, they are being fitted with *interaction devices* that enable objects on the screen to be created, selected, oriented, tracked, and moved. New input devices include trackballs, DataGloves, eyetrackers, digitizing tablets, and thumb wheels. The keyboard is still the main method of providing data to a computer, but the design of keyboards is changing to address concerns about fatigue and "repetitive strain injury." Some new keyboards include wrist supports and can split down the center, so that each half can be swung outward to keep the hand in a comfortable position.

Direct pointing devices such as a light pen, stylus, or finger on touch-screen can be moved directly to a point on the screen and can perform all the main interaction tasks, but writing on an upright screen can cause severe fatigue. A screen mounted at 30 to 45 degrees from the horizontal is more convenient both for pen input and for reading. Indirect pointing devices such as a mouse or trackball overcome the problem of writing on a vertical screen, but require hand–eye coordination and take up additional desk space. Coordination is not a major problem, however, and a child can learn to use a mouse in a matter of minutes.

There is much debate about the merits of different pointing devices, and factors affecting their use include the time required to select a near or distant target on the screen, ability to carry out fine movement for handwriting or drawing, muscular strain, and durability. Shneiderman (1992) proposes a touchscreen for durability in public-access applications, a mouse or trackball for accurate pointing, and a keyboard cursor when there are a small number of targets. Joysticks offer a firm grip and easy movement but are slow and inaccurate in guiding a cursor to a fixed destination.

A major limitation of all the devices just described is that they are in-tended for moving around a two-dimensional space on the computer screen. With the advent of three-dimensional simulations, shown on a computer screen or through helmet-mounted displays, there is a need for input devices with six degrees of movement (movement through three-dimensional space plus forward and sideways tilt and rotation). Such de-vices include the DataGlove (which fits over the hand and can register its position and gestures), the Polhemus tracker (a wand whose position and orientation in space is transmitted to the computer), and the spaceball (a small ball, mounted on a base, which can be twisted and pushed).

D. Communicating with a Computer

An influential account of human–computer communication is Norman's *execution-evaluation cycle* (Norman, 1986). The user of a system starts with a goal to perform some activity, forms an intention, and then specifies and performs some action. As the system responds, the user perceives the state of the system, interprets that state, and evaluates it with respect to the goals and intentions. This leads the user to set further goals and continue the interaction. The user's goals are expressed in psychological terms (such as "check the spelling of this word") but the system presents its current state in physical terms (such as a list of possible word corrections). The goals and the system state differ in form and content, creating "gulfs" that need to be bridged to ensure successful communication.

The *gulf of execution* represents the gap between a user's intentions and the means by which they can be carried out on the computer. The user specifies an appropriate sequence of actions and then carries them out (for example, by selecting an item from a menu) in a form that the computer can interpret. The *gulf of evaluation* is the gap between the computer's presentation of its current state and the user's expectation. To bridge that gap, a user must compare the state of the system, as presented on the computer screen or other output devices, with the original goals and intentions. If the computer does not appear to have satisfied the goal then the user must reformulate it (and possibly first attempt to undo the action that led to the wrong response).

A system designer can narrow the gulfs of execution and evaluation by such means as providing an interaction language that matches the user's intentions (for instance, by providing a spell checker, which can be applied to selected pieces of text and operated by a memorable and easily accessible physical act), by supplying interaction devices that allow a user to translate intentions into actions, and by presenting the system in a form that can be easily interpreted in terms of psychological goals. As an example of poor mapping in everyday objects, Norman describes a room with a panel of light switches where there is no simple relationship between the position of the switches and the position of the lights, so that it is necessary to discover by trial and error which switch controls which light.

For an interface controlling a power plant, a chemical installation, or an airplane, the difficulties and dangers can be considerably greater. Michie and Johnston (1984) argue that complex systems need a "human window" that, in an emergency, can give the human operator an intelligible précis of the situation. However, the term *window* is highly misleading; a monitoring computer is not a sheet of glass but one complex system interpreting another complex system to the human user. Adding a program that summarizes the data may give an appearance of clarity but cause human controllers to lose contact with the real world and, at worst, treat a crisis as a computer game.

E. Styles of Communication

The cycle of activity and response creates a dialogue between the human user and the computer that has some similarity with human-to-human conversation. Successful communication depends on establishing a shared representation and holding a dialogue to carry out a task.

1. Command Line Interaction

The earliest interactive computers communicated via commands typed at a console and responded with printed output. Command line interaction is still found on powerful environments such as the UNIX operating system, because it gives the user direct access to computer operations. These can be strung together into "scripts" to carry out multiple tasks, with the output from one operation being used as input to the next. The penalty for this flexibility and power is that the computer offers little assistance as a conversational partner. The user must remember the commands and the syntax required to combine them into scripts. Command line interaction may be suitable for experienced "power users" of a general-purpose computing environment, but in many tasks, such as drawing, issuing commands to the computer is tedious and unintuitive.

2. Menus and WIMP Interfaces

Menus pack together commands into a list from which one or more can be selected. Styles of menu include pull down (where selecting a header word causes a menu to appear below it), pop up (where the menu appears beside an item selected on the screen), walking (where selecting a menu item can cause a submenu to appear beside it), and pie (where the menu radiates out from a central point). Menus overcome some of the learning and memory problems of command line interfaces but do not offer the power of combining commands into programlike scripts.

Menus form a part of WIMP (*windows, icons, menus, pointers*) interfaces. A WIMP screen displays a number of overlapping, bounded windows and a pointing device such as a mouse moves a cursor to one of the windows. Menus allow commands to be directed to the selected window and icons can represent commands or objects (such as "closed" windows) in pictorial form. Other screen elements, such as "buttons," "palettes," and "dialogue boxes" allow the user to communicate in a variety of modes.

3. Natural Language

Some tasks, such as dictating a memo, would clearly be made easier by speaking to the computer and having the spoken word translated directly into text. Speech input may also be valuable for public-access systems, such as timetable enquiries or tourist information, where there is limited, information-seeking communication. Early natural language interfaces were limited to single word input and had to be trained to recognize the speaker's voice and intonation. More recent systems can recognize continuous, slowly spoken speech and require less or no training. Natural language offers new forms of interacting with machines, such as by telephone conversation, but the apparent ease of spoken conversation hides the difficulty of conducting a useful dialogue. A computer program is designed to perform a restricted task, such as giving tourist information, and cannot behave like a human conversational partner. Either the user must adapt to the limited linguistic capabilities of the computer (by guessing what language forms the computer might recognize and rephrasing commands until they are accepted) or the computer must direct the dialogue (leaving the user to give limited responses such as yes, no, or numerals).

4. Pen Input

Software for the automatic recognition of handwriting has encouraged the development of pen interfaces, which allow informal communication with the computer through writing, sketching, and gesturing. Software to recognize cursive (joined-up) handwriting is still slow and unreliable but good enough to provide an interface to *personal digital assistants,* or PDAs, which combine the facilities of a diary or personal organizer with communication by fax or electronic mail. A form displayed on the screen can be filled out by writing responses with a stylus that are then converted into digits or words. A handdrawn diagram can be tidied by converting roughly drawn shapes into exact straight lines, circles, and boxes. A gesture, such as moving the stylus back and forth over an object, can be interpreted as a command, such as "delete this object." Pen input is slower than typing for simple text input, but it opens possibilities for "informal interaction" with the computer through sketches and gestures.

5. Direct Manipulation

The term *direct manipulation* describes the alteration—by pressing, dragging, and reshaping—of objects displayed on a screen or in a simulated "visual world." Instead of commanding the computer to perform an action, the user performs the action directly on the simulated object. *Virtual reality,* in which the user is placed in a simulated world presented on a screen or through helmets with miniature displays for each eye, is an extreme form of direct manipulation, where the objects in the simulation can be manipulated as if they were in the real world. But direct manipulation is not restricted to everyday objects. The same interaction techniques can be used to operate on diagrams, charts, and documents. Direct manipulation can provide the user with a rapid response to actions and can lessen the gulf of execution and evaluation by allowing the system state to be changed directly, rather than obliquely through commands.

Direct manipulation allows many tasks to be performed quickly and naturally, but it lacks the expressiveness and combinatorial power of language. Even the restricted syntax of command line interfaces allows new expressions to be constructed by combining primitive commands, and natural language offers the subtlety of referring to classes of objects, indicating conditionality ("if the diagram does not fit the screen then show me the center portion"), and indirect reference ("are there any objects that have the following properties . . . ?").

New methods of communication can combine the immediacy of direct manipulation and the expressiveness of natural language. These include *programming by example,* where the user performs a sequence of operations and the machine records them as a generalized procedure, and direct communication with *agents,* which perform complex, general tasks (such as arranging a meeting, or searching multiple databases) on behalf of the user.

F. Communicating Through the Computer

As computers became linked through *local area networks,* providing communication between machines in a building or locality, and *wide area networks,* such as the Internet, which connects computers throughout the world, it became possible to use the computer as a communication device between people. *Asynchronous* connection, such as by electronic mail, is still the main method of communicating between computer users, but techniques for compressing data and high-bandwidth data lines now allow direct, *synchronous,* communication from computer to computer by voice and moving image. The styles of communication range from *videophones* to *awareness* systems (where windows on the screen give an impression of activities in other offices or buildings).

The computer acts as a *mediator* of person-to-person communication. It may be designed to be unobtrusive, as in a *video tunnel* with a camera directly behind the computer screen, so that users can converse and hold eye contact as if face to face, or it may offer a *shared medium,* such as a space on the screen where two or more users can draw and write. The study of *computer-supported cooperative work* is concerned with the design and use of computers to facilitate shared working.

II. THE PSYCHOLOGY OF COMPUTER USE

Most interactive computer systems are designed to engage the mind, so cognitive psychology has the potential to assist in their design and evaluation. Surprisingly few psychological theories, however, make predictions about human–computer interaction or can be used directly to guide design. The findings of cognitive psychology have generally been used either as broad (and often inaccurate) guidelines, such as "show seven plus or minus two items on the screen," or as general frameworks. For example, work on mental models leads to the design of systems based on deliberate metaphor (such as the desktop metaphor of the Apple Macintosh interface).

Landauer, in an influential paper, "Relations between Cognitive Psychology and Computer System Design" (1987), suggests four principal ways in which cognitive psychology can interact with computer system invention and design:

1. We may apply existing knowledge and theory directly to design problems.
2. We may apply psychological ideas and theories to the creation of new models, analyses, and engineering tools.
3. We may apply methods of empirical research and data analysis to the evaluation of designs, design alternatives, and design principles.
4. We can use problems encountered in design to inform and guide our research into the fundamentals of mental life.

A. Applying Psychology to Design

A computer system that interacts with a human user should take account of the properties and limitations of the human mind and body. The nature of the human mind has been studied by successive generations of psychologists, and some results of this work are directly applicable to system design.

1. Memory

Findings from research on human memory that could influence computer system design include recency and primacy effects, chunking, and the associativity of semantic memory.

Information in short-term memory decays rapidly. If items are presented in serial order, those items toward the end of the series will be remembered well for a short period of time (the *recency* effect); items at the start of the series will be remembered well for a longer period of time (the *primacy* effect); and items in the middle of the list will be less well recalled after a short or longer delay. This suggests that list presentations, such as pull-down screen menus, should be organized so that less important items are placed in the middle of the list or, if all items are important, then the user should be given assistance in recall and selection.

Miller's (1956) work suggests that human retention of short-term information is limited to around seven *meaningful chunks*. Thus, if information on a computer screen can be grouped into meaningful chunks, then it is likely to be more memorable than as disparate items. As a simple example, presenting the time as 19:55:32 is likely to be more memorable than as 195532. Considerable work has been done on how to present computer commands in ways that are meaningful and well-structured. Suggested guidelines (from Shneiderman, 1992) include the following: choose names for commands that are meaningful and distinctive, group the commands into easily understood categories, present the commands in a consistent format such as action–object (e.g., "delete word"), support consistent rules of abbreviation (preferably truncation to one letter), offer frequent users the ability to create "macros" that group a series of commands, limit the number of commands and the ways of accomplishing a task.

The final guideline seems counterintuitive, and certainly limiting the commands and functions too far could impede use, but *interference effects* can occur when there are alternative ways to perform tasks. For example, in Microsoft Word a selected piece of text can be turned to italic by (among other ways) selecting "italic" from the "format" menu, pressing the COMMAND–*i* keys, or pressing COMMAND–shift–*i*. Some of these methods work with other word processors; some do not or they invoke other commands. Ensuring consistency of appearance and operation within a program and across related programs is a major aim of interface design. Manufacturers such as Apple, IBM, and Sun Microsystems provide detailed *interface guidelines* to developers of software for their products, to ensure a consistent *look and feel* and to set standards for command names and methods of interaction.

Long-term memory appears to be organized around concepts sharing similar properties and related by association. This *associativity* can be mirrored in the computer through *hypermedia* systems that present information as texts or images, with explicit links to associated items. Thus, a hypermedia guide to an art gallery might display a painting on the screen and provide buttons allowing the user to display other paintings by the same artist, or in the same style, or on display in the same room. The computer can also offer aids to learning or invention by providing *external representations* of associative memory, allowing learner, writer, or designer to set down ideas as visual notes on the screen and to associate them by drawing labeled links.

2. Perception and Attention

A computer assaults the senses and demands a high level of attention. Unlike a book, it has an active light-emitting display; unlike a television, it requires the user to sit close to the screen and interact with it. Helmet-mounted virtual-reality displays have been claimed to cause fatigue and disorientation after 10 minutes of use. The ability of the computer to abuse the senses means that special care should be given to designing interfaces that complement human perception. *Visual acuity* is the ability to distinguish fine detail. Acuity increases with brightness so, in general, a bright screen will be more readable than a dark one, and dark characters on a white background will be more readable than light characters on a dark background. But high luminance displays are perceived to flicker, and since flicker is more noticeable in peripheral vision, a larger screen will appear to flicker more.

The choice of color for displays is fraught with difficulty. When color displays first appeared, programmers splattered primary colours on the screen, hoping to make them more attractive, but generally causing confusion and headache. Different colors are perceived as having different depths (for example, red appears to stand out, whereas blue recedes) and strong differences in visual depth can be fatiguing and distracting. Blue lines on a black background, or yellow lines on a white background, are hard to distinguish. Eight percent of the European male population is colorblind and cannot distinguish red from green. In general, color should be used sparingly, and for a purpose, such as to distinguish items in a list or to indicate important information.

Maguire (1990) collated the following guidelines for the use of color in displays:

1. A neutral color helps set off a full color.
2. Colors near in hue (on the hue circle) form pleasing combinations and will lend a predominant tone.
3. Complementary colors (opposite on the hue circle) contrast and give a warm–cool effect.
4. Colors that are 120° apart on the hue circle are easy to distinguish but often appear garish.
5. Color edging enhances polygons.
6. Common denominations of colors should be used where possible. For example, red: danger or stop, yellow: caution or slow, green: OK or go.

Sound has been little used in interfaces, other than to provide warnings. However, experiments on *auditory icons* (which simulate everyday sounds in computer simulations of, for example, industrial processes) and on *earcons* (which use structured combinations of notes to represent actions and objects), suggest that sounds can be effective in complementing visual presentations and in monitoring of off-screen processes. Dix, Finlay, Abowd, and Beale (1993) provide a good overview of multisensory systems.

3. Motor Skills and Selection

Studies of reaction time have some application to computer design, particularly in computer interfaces to machinery, but most interaction with computers is premeditated (the user forms an intention and then specifies and performs an action), so considerations of speed and accuracy are generally more important. Fitts' law (1954) is a good predictor of the time to move a given distance to a target of a specified size; it takes longer to point to more distant and smaller targets. This suggests that, in general, targets on the screen such as buttons should be large and close to the user's start point.

Landauer (1987) combines Fitts' law with Hick's law to predict the time a user takes to find an item in a hierarchical menu (a menu with two or more levels). Hick's law states that the mean response time in simple decision tasks is a linear function of the transmitted information. This suggests that menus with more items per level will require a longer time to select an item; and Fitts' law suggests that more alternatives will require targets that are smaller and harder to select. But the total search time is equal to the mean time per step, multiplied by the number of steps down the menu hierarchy. A menu with many items at each level but fewer levels will have a longer choice time, but fewer steps. By combining the equations, Landauer showed that search time will be minimized by using menus with as few levels and as many items as are feasible within the constraints of space and display. Studies of menu-selection tasks broadly support the finding, and this is one of the few direct applications of experimental psychology to interface design.

4. Skill Acquisition

An experienced user of a computer system will not perform the same actions and require the same assistance as a novice. Computer use is an acquired skill, and studies of skill acquisition suggest that a learner progresses from learning facts and applying general procedures, to acquiring directly applicable and more specific procedures, and finally to automatic execution of tasks. A expert in a skill such as chess does not consider many alternatives and make explicit plans, to the extent that a novice might, but instead relies on a meaningful pattern of pieces to prompt a good move.

The implications for human–computer interaction are that novice computer users should be offered help in learning the basic objects and actions of the system, through tutorials and context-specific help. The Macintosh interface, for example, offers *balloon help,* whereby "balloons" offering simple advice pop up over objects on the screen. As they gain expertise, users need practice and assistance in forming a *command set* of the most useful commands (which will depend on the user's needs and abilities). Experienced *power users* can be offered ways to reduce time and effort by, for example, invoking commands directly from the keyboard rather than using a mouse and menu.

B. Using Psychology to Create New Models

The earliest use of computers was to solve specific problems, in mathematics, engineering, ballistics, logic. Accordingly, the research psychology of problem-solving was applied and adapted to the study of computer use. Newell and Simon's (1972) "information processing psychology" both described human problem solving in information-processing terms and was applied to the study of problem solving with computers. It led directly to the development of cognitive models of problem solving, from high-level descriptions of the writing process (Flower & Hayes, 1980) to a keystroke-level model of interaction (Card, Moran, & Newell, 1983). These models have been used to predict the behavior of users solving problems with computers and to inform the design of more effective and comprehensive computer systems.

More recently, it has been recognized that people use computers for tasks that do not easily fit the problem-solving mold, such as design, exploration, and communication. New models are being developed that draw on studies of human creativity, exploration, and social interaction. The modeling of human–computer interaction is discussed in Section III.

C. Applying Psychology to Evaluation

The computer is a piece of equipment, and many of the experimental psychology techniques for evaluating human interaction with equipment are applicable to human–computer interaction. For example, Reece (1993) has carried out an elegant investigation, using standard experimental methods, to compare the relative merits of pen and paper, a computer word processor, and a simulated speech-driven word processor. Shneiderman (1992, p. 18) indicates five measurable human factors that are central to evaluation: time to learn, speed of performance, rate of errors by users, retention over time, subjective satisfaction.

Where the computer differs from everyday equipment is in its flexibility of function and appearance, resulting in a large space of possible system designs and presentations. Much of the work in human–computer evaluation is not concerned with testing clear hypotheses and comparing fixed products, but with assessing the quality of early designs. New techniques have been devised to evaluate prototypes and design possibilities rather than finished systems. These include *Wizard of Oz* evaluation (where a human pretends to be the computer, for example, by mimicking a speech-understanding system) and *design space analysis* (for organizing and comparing alternative designs). Section V covers the topic of system evaluation in more detail.

D. Applying Studies of Human–Computer Interaction to Psychology

The versatility of the computer makes it a valuable device for studying the psychology of learning and problem solving. As well as providing a tool for problem solving and a medium for communication, it can automatically record data and analyze patterns of interactions.

The study of children as programmers has provided insight into children's development of problem-solving skills, such as the use of physical devices like the Logo "turtle" to catalyze understanding (Papert, 1980).

Investigations of programming as a skill have revealed differences between the problem-solving behavior of novices and experts (Jeffries, Turner, Polson, & Atwood, 1981). Both novices and experts tend to start from a general problem goal and refine it into subgoals and down to lines of program code. But novices tend to expand one part of the problem down to its lowest level before starting on the next part, whereas experts generally consider the entire problem before developing it to a deeper level.

Computer games have formed the basis of studies of motivation (Malone, 1981) and collaboration and conflict (Hewitt, Gilbert, Jirotka, & Wilbur, 1990).

As people have begun to use computers as an everyday tool to augment their intellect, to extend their memory, and to distribute cognition among a group of coworkers, this has led to the study of computer-augmented and computer-mediated cognition.

III. MODELING HUMAN–COMPUTER INTERACTION

Models of human–computer interaction serve much the same purposes as architectural, scientific, or engineering models. They can be used to predict behavior, assist in design, and evaluate competing theories and designs. Where they differ is in the importance given to modeling human cognition. Understanding the psychology of the computer user is important in creating systems that solve interesting problems, respond in appropriate ways, and are engaging and easy to use.

There has been much confusion in the literature about the types, names, and purposes of models of HCI. Young (1983) attempted to sort out the mess by suggesting two types of models—models of the user and models of the computer—that may be held by different entities: designers, researchers, computer systems, and users. Thus, a researcher may develop a model of a user to understand the psychology of computer use or a computer may hold a rudimentary model of its user to offer individualized help or guidance. The models with most significance to HCI are the designer's model of the computer, the designer's model of the user, and the user's model of the computer.

A. The Designer's Model of the Computer

A software designer has direct control over the form and function of the software but not of the people who use it, so designers' models of the computer tend to be more detailed and formal than their models of its users. Software descriptions can be divided broadly into *syntactic models,* concerned with the structure of the dialogue between user and machine, and *semantic models,* which describe what the user's actions do. The simplest syntactic models describe the desired states of the computer system and transitions

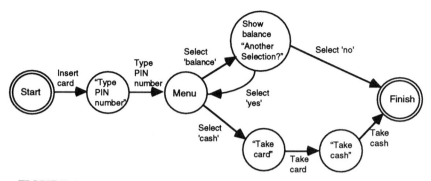

FIGURE 1   A state transition diagram for a simplified automated teller machine.

between them. They can be represented as *state transition diagrams,* with each state shown as a circle and each transition as a labeled, arrowed line. The transitions correspond to actions performed by the user, such as selecting from a menu or pressing a key. Figure 1 shows a state transition diagram for a simplified bank automated teller machine.

A state transition network is easy to create and understand, but for a large system it can become complex and tangled. A *hierarchical state transition network* deals with complexity by showing subsystems as "boxes" in the diagram, where each box can be described as a separate diagram. Another problem is that the diagrams do not show events and dialogues that can occur concurrently or that interrupt each other, such as might appear in a computer-aided design package with concurrently active windows, menus, palettes, and forms. Harel's (1988) *state charts* provide a way of showing complex, concurrent systems as diagrams.

An alternative way of representing the syntax of computer systems is as formal grammars or rules. The *BNF* notation is typically used to describe the structure of programming languages, but has been applied to HCI. Condition–action rules, or *production rules,* of the form

IF (condition) THEN (action)

can specify events which change the system state or cause program actions. For example, the rule

Insert card → <display "Type PIN number"> Wait-for-PIN

indicates that the event of inserting a card causes the ATM to display the message "Type PIN number" and puts it into a state of waiting for a PIN number to be typed. Production rules are better than state transition networks at describing concurrent events but less appropriate for specifying sequences of events.

Semantic models of interaction with the computer specify not just the transitions between states of the computer system but also what functions are invoked at each transition. The most straightforward way is to add functional descriptions to syntactic representations such as state transition diagrams or production rules. These could be specified in a notation of formal semantics or simply as calls to programming language procedures. More sophisticated formalisms such as Z (Spivey, 1988) provide a complete formal notation to describe the semantics of programs. They were developed to reason about the behavior of programs but have been adapted for producing precise specifications of interactive software. Producing a formal description of an interactive system can be difficult and time consuming, and it may not tell what a designer most wants to know, such as "will the program be easy and intuitive to use?"

B. The Designer's Model of the User

The ideal user, as far as the software designer is concerned, is someone who behaves in a predictable manner, forming clear goals and then carrying them out in a series of steps that can be programmed as basic operations for the computer. In practice, no user behaves in this way. Real users are unpredictable, have conflicting goals (or may not even be able to express their needs in terms of clear goals), change their minds, make mistakes, and may end up muddled and maddened. Not surprisingly, it is easier to model an ideal user than a real one. An idealized model can help the designer to produce software that performs well with competent users, but too little attention has been given in HCI to individual differences in software use.

The most influential approach to modeling the user is Card et al.'s (1983) GOMS (goals, operators, methods, and selection rules) method. GOMS characterizes a user of a computer system as an information processor, with interacting perceptual, motor, and cognitive subsystems. It assumes that the user acts rationally by forming *goals* that define some state to be achieved. A goal can be achieved by one or more alternative *methods,* where a method is a sequence of elementary perceptual, motor, or cognitive *operations* (such as "Move cursor over word," "Double click mouse button," "Press delete key"). *Selection rules* choose between alternative methods to accomplish a goal. Using the GOMS formalism, a high-level goal, such as "edit manuscript" can be broken down into a sequence of methods and operators, where each operation can be provided by an elemental computer procedure.

GOMS can make some broad predictions of human behavior. The depth of the subgoals gives an indication of the load on a user's short term memory, and the length of the sequence of operations provides a rough measure of the time taken to carry out a method.

Card, Moran, and Newell (1980) demonstrated the power of GOMS by using it to predict the time expert users will take to execute tasks on a computer. They proposed that, at the level of individual motor actions, the time taken to execute a computer task can be described as the sum of the times taken in keystroking, pointing (e.g., with a mouse), homing (on a target), drawing, thinking (by the user), and responding (by the system). They encoded methods, such as editing text with keyboard and mouse-operated editors, in the GOMS notation and produced estimates of individual operations by means such as Fitts' law. This enabled them to predict the times taken to carry out tasks such as replacing a five-letter word with another five-letter word. Comparing their predictions with the performance of human users, they found that the time required for experts to perform a unit task can be predicted to within 20%.

Kieras and Polson (1985) clarified and enriched the GOMS model by providing two parallel descriptions, of the user and the computer. The user's knowledge is expressed as condition–action rules where the condition can match goals, information in the user's memory, or information provided by the computer. If a pattern matches successfully, the action part of the rule is performed, to alter the representation of the user's memory or carry out some operation on the computer. For example, a simple rule for moving the cursor to a given line might be (from Dix et al., 1993, p. 199):

```
(MOVE-UP
IF      (AND   (TEST-GOAL move-up
               (TEST-CURSOR-BELOW  %LINE)  )
THEN (        (DO-KEYSTROKE 'K')  )   )
```

This means that if the user has the goal of "move-up" and the current position of the cursor is below the desired line on the screen, then the user should perform the operation of pressing key *k* (which in the particular text editor moves the cursor up a line). This rule would "fire" repeatedly so long as the condition is satisfied; that is, until the cursor is at the desired line. To describe the states and operations of the computer, Kieras and Poulson use a form of state transition network. Combining a model of the user with one of the computer system enables the method to describe mappings and mismatches between a user's goals and the provisions of the computer.

GOMS and its associates offer fine-grain accounts of a user's interaction with the computer. But, particularly in the early stages of design, a system designer may be attempting to understand the task and choose between alternative designs. In that case the designer needs a more general model of problem solving and user behavior which can help to ensure that the software is comprehensive and suited to a broad range of users.

Distributed cognition (Hutchins, 1990) provides an account of interactions beyond the individual. A *functional system* is the collection of human participants, computer systems, and other objects used in the work practice. Functional systems that have been studied include air traffic control, computer programming teams, and civil engineering practices. The aim of the distributed cognition approach is to analyze how the different components of the functional system are coordinated. This involves studying how information is propagated through the system and how work is maintained by the participants adjusting their activities in synchronization with each other.

C. The User's Model of the Computer

People spontaneously employ *mental models* to assist their understanding of complex systems. Mental models are simplifications, often in terms of a metaphor, such as a word processor as a "computer typewriter." They frame our understanding of the world and enable people to operate and make predictions about new technology, by relating it to prior experience.

The term *system image* (Norman, 1986) describes the user's conception of a computer system, which may be in terms of a metaphor or a set of functions. If the user is given a system image before interacting with the system, then the image will determine how the user conceives and begins to operate the equipment. Designers can draw on mental models by designing software to fit a metaphor. Thus, electronic mail has deliberate similarities to the postal system, with "mail boxes," "addresses," and "postmasters." A system image need not represent the way the system is actually constructed, but a well-chosen system image should enable the user to interact with the computer in a way that meets with expectations. It allows the user to make reliable predictions about the system's behavior and be satisfied that the system is not going to carry out unexpected actions.

So long as the computer works according to the system image then the user is led to treat it as a familiar object. But, if the system image ever fails, then the user is left stranded, without the depth of knowledge needed to repair the problem. For example, if a computer network fails to deliver an electronic mail message, then the message is usually returned to the sender with a detailed diagnosis of the error. The diagnostic information is given in terms of gateway computers and message handling programs, far from the image of electronic mail as a postal system. Studies of breakdowns in human–computer interaction, and of the user's subsequent attempts at repair, can be valuable in revealing people's (sometimes surprising) mental models of technology (Sharples, 1993).

IV. SYSTEM DEVELOPMENT

The conventional approach to developing a computer system is to split the process into a number of discrete stages, leading up to the finished working product. Definitions of the stages vary, but they usually include the following:

Requirements analysis, which describes the purpose of the system along with the main tasks it has to perform.

System design or *functional specification,* which specifies how the tasks are to be performed, and breaks the system into components that need to be either programmed or adapted from existing software.

Detailed design, where each component of the system is described in sufficient detail that a programmer can code it.

Implementation, which must be done in a suitable programming language.

Integration and testing, which is done to the different pieces of program.

Maintenance of the system, by correcting errors and updating the software to cope with changes in hardware and requirements.

This staged or *waterfall* (or cascade) approach was introduced to assist the development of large corporate systems such as payroll packages, which typically have tight specifications, large teams of programmers, and very little interactivity. A major industry has grown around the waterfall method of software development, with structured design methods such as JSD (Jackson structured design) and SSADM (structured systems analysis and design methodology) promoting a strict discipline of design and testing. The basic principles, of ensuring that the software meets requirements and that it should be well integrated and tested, apply equally to payroll packages and painting programs. But the main difference is that the operation of highly interactive systems cannot be fully specified in advance of implementation. Any reasonably complex interactive program will be used in ways unforeseen by its designers. For example, spreadsheet programs were originally introduced to ease the job of repetitious calculation. But since their introduction, users have adopted spreadsheets for forecasting, visual presentation of information, database management, producing timetables, and many other purposes.

User-centered design is a general term for a design process that considers the needs of users in the design of interactive systems. User-centered design relies on understanding the users and their interaction with technology. Designers must respond sympathetically to the, often conflicting, demands of users while maintaining the integrity of the system. Not surprisingly, attempts have been made to reconcile the two approaches to design, by adapting the waterfall model to the design of interactive systems.

A. Adaptations of the Conventional Software Development Method

Usability engineering provides information to guide software development by specifying *usability metrics* that the finished system should satisfy. *Usability metrics* are normally quantitative measures in the areas of *learnability* (the time and effort needed for learning to use the system), *throughput* (the number of tasks accomplished in a given time and the errors made), *flexibility* (the extent to which users can adapt the system to new ways of working as they become more experienced in its use), and *attitude* (the attitude of the users toward the system). The measures, such as "time taken to install the system," can be specified in advance as part of the system design to provide guidelines for the programmers.

Usability metrics are only one type of guideline. Other, more qualitative guidelines specify general attributes of the system, such as the colors to be used or the appearance of objects on the screen. They can be very specific, for example indicating the phrases to be used in error messages. At their best, guidelines reflect good design practice, match what is known about the needs of the users, and give the software a consistent "look and feel." The major software manufacturers issue books of guidelines to their software developers, such as Apple's *Human Interface Guidelines* (Apple Computer Inc., 1987).

User interface design environments automate or assist the work of designing user interfaces by providing a kit of "interface parts" such as buttons, menus, and forms, each with appropriate functionality, which can be fitted together into a complete user interface. Each of the components adheres to interface guidelines, so a design environment can provide a short-cut to design and an assurance of basic quality.

B. Departures from the Conventional Software Development Method

The departures from the conventional method of software development can be classed under the general heading of *user-centered design,* since they give high priority to the needs of the eventual users. They do this either by analyzing the tasks that typical users will perform or by involving actual users in the design process. The second approach is the more radical because it requires an empirical "trial and error" process, with designers testing out early prototypes of the software on users and making repeated revisions to the plans. In terms of the waterfall model of software design, the later stages of the design process provide information to the designer that may result in revisions of the earlier stages and a series of evolving prototype systems. In some cases, such as the development of systems for casual use in a public area, such as a tourist information center, users may be recruited as part of the design team, offering advice and criticizing mockups and prototypes.

Task analysis is the study of what people do when they carry out tasks. It differs from user models such as GOMS in that the emphasis is on observable behavior, rather what might be happening in the user's mind. Task analysis has a long history in the study of work behavior. Its more modern variants, such as *TAKD* (task analysis for knowledge description; Diaper,

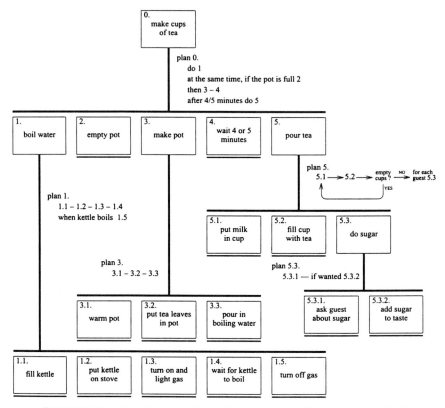

FIGURE 2   Task hierarchy for making cups of tea (from Dix et al., 1993)

1989), combine a behavioral description with an analysis of the knowledge people require to perform the task. The start of a task analysis is usually to break down an observed task into a hierarchy of subtasks, accompanied by plans that describe in what order and under what conditions the subtasks are performed. Figure 2 shows a task hierarchy for making cups of tea (from Dix et al., 1993). The analysis may then go on to produce taxonomies of the objects and actions involved in the task, accounts of the goals of a person engaged in the task and plans for accomplishing a goal.

To carry out a task analysis requires detailed observation and recording of people engaged in appropriate activities. A video recording can reveal the structure and sequence of activities, but other methods are needed to infer a user's goals and plans. One general and useful technique is *protocol analysis.* A person is asked to talk about his or her intentions and plans at the same time as performing the task. These *concurrent verbal protocols* are recorded and matched against the activities to give an understanding of not only *what* activity is being performed, but also *why* it is being carried out, for what purpose and to achieve what goal.

Task analysis can show the structure and sequence of a task, such as composing a document or designing a building, that could be supported by a computer. It can also be carried out for people working with computers, to measure usability or to study problems and breakdowns in performance. The weakness of task analysis is that it can be time consuming to prepare, and although it may reveal the structure of the task, it may not be much help in deciding how to design a system that supports and augments that task.

Rapid prototyping is one of a number of methods that involve eventual users in the early stages of design. One or more mockups or prototypes are constructed that exemplify some aspects of the system, such as alternative interfaces or different presentations of the data. The prototypes may be quite simple. They could be in the form of sketches of an interface, "storyboards" or "slideshows" to show a sequence of actions. These prototypes are shown to users, for comment, as part of systematic surveys and comparisons, or to raise users' understanding and enable them to contribute to further design. Rapid prototyping environments, such as HyperCard, allow screen displays to be constructed rapidly using screen drawing tools. They can then be given limited functions, such as allowing objects on the screen to become buttons that, when pressed, cause a move to another screen display. The original rapid prototyping tools required the mockups to be thrown away once they had been tested. But more recent development environments offer more powerful programming languages, allowing the mockups and early prototypes to be developed into full systems.

Rapid prototyping is one method employed in the *iterative* approach to software development. This maintains that, unlike conventional software development, the design of interactive systems is not primarily concerned with specifying the functions and input–output behavior of the computer, but with fitting the computer into the plans and interleaved activities of a human user. Not only are the plans and actions of users of paramount importance to the software designer, they are inherently ill-defined. The art of iterative system design is to *anticipate* the many ways in which the system might be used and *adapt* the system to suit the users' needs as they become identified.

V. EVALUATION

Evaluation of HCI is concerned with making judgments and measurements of the usability and potential usability of interactive computer systems. An evaluation can be carried out at any point in the software life cycle: to choose between competing requirements, to decide what features and functions should be included in a proposed system, to validate the system with respect to the requirements, to verify that the system meets the specifications to compare different implementations, or to provide metrics such as learnability, ease of use, or speed of operation. The type of evaluation can range from formal measures of usability (for example, to ensure that the system meets industry standards) to offering the system for informal comment.

The Open University Guide to Usability (The Open University, 1990) classifies evaluation methods into five categories:

• *Analytic evaluation* uses semi-formal methods, such as task analysis, to predict the performance of expert users of a system. It allows designers to predict the performance of users in terms of the physical activities and cognitive operations they must carry out to perform a given task. It can be applied early in the development process, reducing the need for iterative prototyping. But it should be used with care, since it is intended to model the performance of an ideal user carrying out tasks without error.

• *Expert evaluation* calls on people who are experienced in interface design or human factors to make judgments about the usability of the system and to suggest improvements. This can range from demonstrating the system to colleagues for informal comment to presenting a set of design issues that need to be resolved.

• *Observational evaluation* involves collecting data on how users interact with a prototype of a finished system. It may be a controlled study, carried out in a usability laboratory, or a naturalistic study, with the system set up in the workplace of a potential user. The data can come from direct observation and field notes, video recordings, automatic logging of the user's interactions, or analysis of verbal protocols.

• *Survey evaluation* asks users to give their opinions of a system that they have used, through a structured interview or questionnaire.

• *Experimental evaluation* requires the investigator to form hypotheses about the interaction, which are then tested using the methods of experimental psychology. Thus, one might compare the time taken to perform a given task, such as editing a document, using two different interfaces.

The different approaches to evaluation reflect the differing paradigms of psychology and come laden with prejudice and anecdotal evidence about the "best" way to develop and assess interactive software.

A team from Hewlett-Packard laboratories (Jeffries, Miller, Wharton, & Uyeda, 1991) performed a careful comparison of four methods of user interface evaluation: heuristic evaluation, software guidelines, cognitive walkthroughs, and usability testing. Heuristic evaluation is similar to "expert evaluation," where specialists in user interfaces study the interface in depth and look for properties that they know, from experience, will lead to usability problems. The use of published guidelines is not strictly a method of evaluation, but it does provide specific recommendations about interface design that can help to identify problems. A cognitive walkthrough is a type of analytic evaluation, where the developers of an interface carry out a series of tasks that a typical user might perform. They compare the actions of the interface with the users' goals and knowledge and record discrepancies between the users' expectations and the steps required by the interface. Usability testing begins by analyzing the users' needs and setting usability criteria for the system. Experimental evaluation is then used to test whether the system meets the criteria.

The comparison of the different techniques found that heuristic evaluation produced the best results. Heuristic evaluation uncovered the most problems with the interface (50% of the known problems compared with around 14% for each of the other methods) and at the least cost in terms of time. The method does, however, depend on finding several people with the knowledge and experience necessary to apply the technique.

The main divergence in approach to evaluation is between laboratory studies, carried out in a *usability laboratory* under carefully controlled conditions, and *situated studies* of people interacting with computer systems in their normal working environment.

The main advantage of usability engineering is that it sets explicit measures of usability (such as the time taken to perform a task, the number of errors, the number of commands used, and the ratio of successful completions to failures), which can be used to judge the value of the system once it is finished. The concomitant problem is that the measures may not capture the real qualities and failings of the system and may divert the designer into fixing minor defects rather than considering alternative solutions. For example, usability measures applied to the design of a word processor may help in rearranging items on a menu (for some word processors this is equivalent to rearranging deck-chairs on the Titanic), but they do not address the deeper issues of "how do people write?" and "what computer tools can best support the writing process?"

Situated studies can call on the techniques of ethnography and social psychology to provide a rich picture of the ways in which technology mediates the activity of individuals and groups. They can reveal breakdowns in understanding or communication caused by system failure or human misconception, and they can suggest new areas of concern to a system developer (such as the importance of tactile feedback). But the amount of data collected from such studies can be overwhelming, and there may be no guarantee that a detailed investigation of one working environment can be applied to the technology set in a different situation.

The best conclusion is that usability measures and situated studies can inform system design, but there is no substitute for the heuristic knowledge and experience of experts in HCI.

VI. BEYOND HUMAN–COMPUTER INTERACTION

The phrase *human–computer interaction* invokes an image of a person sitting alone at a console, communing with a computer program. That image fits only one aspect of computer use and is becoming increasingly inappropriate. Lawrence Tesler (1991), in one of a perceptive series of articles on computer networks in *Scientific American,* describes four paradigms of computing—batch, time sharing, desktop, and network—associated with the four decades from the 1960s to 1990s (see Table 1).

The 1990s is seeing the emergence of fully mobile computers, in communication by wireless networks. They can integrate communication services (such as fax and electronic mail), personal organizers (such as diaries and meeting schedulers), and work tools (such as document processors and expert systems). Instead of interacting with a computer, a person will work with many tools and applications, situated on a number of computers

TABLE 1   The Four Paradigms of Computing[a]

	BATCH	TIME-SHARING	DESKTOP	NETWORK
DECADE	1960s	1970s	1980s	1990s
TECHNOLOGY	MEDIUM-SCALE INTEGRATION	LARGE-SCALE INTEGRATION	VERY LARGE SCALE	ULTRA LARGE SCALE
LOCATION	COMPUTER ROOM	TERMINAL ROOM	DESKTOP	MOBILE
USERS	EXPERTS	SPECIALISTS	INDIVIDUALS	GROUPS
USER STATUS	SUBSERVIENCE	DEPENDENCE	INDEPENDENCE	FREEDOM
DATA	ALPHA-NUMERIC	TEXT, VECTOR	FONTS, GRAPHICS	SCRIPT, VOICE
OBJECTIVE	CALCULATE	ACCESS	PRESENT	COMMUNICATE
USER ACTIVITY	PUNCH & TRY (SUBMIT)	REMEMBER & TYPE (INTERACT)	SEE & POINT (DRIVE)	ASK & TELL (DELEGATE)
OPERATION	PROCESS	EDIT	LAYOUT	ORCHESTRATE
INTER-CONNECT	PERIPHERALS	TERMINALS	DESKTOPS	PALMTOPS
APPLICATIONS	CUSTOM	STANDARD	GENERIC	COMPONENTS
LANGUAGES	COBOL, FORTRAN	PL/1, BASIC	PASCAL, C	OBJECT ORIENTED

[a] From "Networked computing in the 1990s," by L. G. Tesler. Copyright © 1991 by Scientific American, Inc. All rights reserved.

throughout the network, and will communicate through the computers to other people.

A. Computer-Supported Cooperative Work

Computer-supported cooperative work (CSCW) is the term used to describe a group of people working together, with the aid of computers, on a common task. It can range from a group of people in a meeting room using laptop computers to contribute to a shared "electronic whiteboard" to a conference conducted over electronic mail. CSCW allows people in physically dispersed organizations to work together, and a study by Sproull and Kiesler (1991) showed that using a network induced the participants to talk more frankly and more equally. People who were reluctant to contribute to a face-to-face meeting reported feeling more lively and confident when expressing themselves in a computer conference.

However, computer-mediated communication is less rich than face-to-face discussion. It lacks the visual cues that signal, for example, impatience, annoyance, and dissent. Partly as a consequence, people in a computer conference took longer to reach a consensus than an equivalent face-to-face group, and they tended to express more extreme opinions. On a wider scale, communication by computer can alter patterns of work and the exercise of power within an organization. The free sharing of information and frank exchange of views that typifies network discussion may threaten established management and information channels within an organization. Worldwide networks such as the Internet allow an "information anarchy" across political boundaries.

The Internet already links together several million users on more than 300,000 computers in around 30 countries. An Internet user can send mail to any other user, connect to remote machines, and share work across the network. The World Wide Web gives a global hypertext network to each Internet user, so that a single set of options might offer satellite weather maps, catalogues from major academic libraries in the United States, and a program to search for the e-mail address of any user of the Internet. Clicking one of these options will automatically connect to the relevant computer and run software to display a map, show a library catalogue index, or return an e-mail address.

The information carried on Internet and the services it provides are not managed by a central agency, but are contributed by individual sites and users. Access to such a wealth and diversity of information can be seen as overwhelming (there are thousands of "newsgroups" on the Internet, each contributing a hundred or more messages a day), threatening (people throughout the world can exchange politically and socially inflammatory messages), or liberating (computer networks cut across established boundaries of power and influence). New social and technical challenges include finding ways to allow colleagues who have never met face to face to work together productively, developing "information rejection" methods to filter out unwanted information, and providing mechanisms to manage the electronic pathways, to stop them being choked by an exponential growth in communication or by deliberate sabotage using computer viruses. The phenomenal growth of the Internet offers new possibilities of global information exchange and brings new problems, of information overload, breaking of copyright, and lack of restraint.

B. Autonomous Agents

As networks grow beyond the comprehension of any individual, computers will play an increasing part in retrieving information and managing interaction. *Autonomous agents* are programs that assist with some computer-based task, such as arranging a meeting, finding a document across computer networks, or filtering e-mail according to priority. A user might ask an agent to arrange a meeting with selected colleagues around a given date. Once the agent is activated, it carries out the job of arranging a meeting autonomously. It consults the on-line calendars of the colleagues, finds a range of dates and times, suggests a suitable time and venue to the colleagues by mail, and when agreed, confirms the arrangement.

The style of interaction with an autonomous agent is very different from a command language such as DOS or the point and click of direct manipulation. Rather than issuing commands, the user specifies needs and constraints; for example, by partially completing a form or by indicating ranges on a scale. The interaction is one of request and negotiation. An autonomous agent requesting a meeting with the company director may need to ask and respond in a way very different from one that negotiates with a colleague. Computer etiquette and the micropolitics of organizations are new issues for software designers.

C. Ubiquitous Computing

In time, the computer may fade away altogether. An average house already has 10 or more microcomputers. They are embedded in washing machines, video recorders, telephones, remote controllers, thermostats, clocks, microwave ovens, door bells, cameras, toasters, and electric shavers. We do not notice them as computers because they are programmed to perform a restricted task and because their interface or system image is that of a familiar consumer device. However, they use general-purpose computer chips and in the future they will perform a wider range of tasks, such as providing diagnostic information, or communicating with other domestic appliances.

Ubiquitous computing can mean giving everyday objects computing power while retaining their familiar forms. A pad of paper might transmit what is written on it, a telephone might provide a printed transcript of a conversation, or a window might show an image of the scene outside some hours before. Or it can refer to the seamless integration of computer and noncomputer objects. Xerox EuroPARC are developing a DigitalDesk (Newman & Wellner, 1992) to demonstrate the movement of information between paper and computer. They have suspended a video camera and a projector above an ordinary desk, so that electronic documents can be projected onto the desk, and paper ones can automatically be digitized into computer text. Software connected to the camera will be able to recognize hand gestures, so that a person working at the desk can move the projected documents around just as they would push sheets of paper.

Perhaps the consumer device that will change the most as it is invaded by the computer is television. Digital television combines the interactivity of computer games with the image quality of television opening a vista of "edutainment" from interactive soap operas to self-guided tours of the great museums. It demands a new range of skills, combining television production, electronic art, and software design, and it will provide a new dimension to human–computer interaction, as millions of people simultaneously participate in an interactive television production.

D. The Challenge of Human–Computer Interaction

Human–computer interaction is a new discipline, and it has had little opportunity to mature, because computers and their users are changing so rapidly. At its worst, HCI is a mishmash of anecdotes and good intentions. But, at its best, it blends the psychology and technology of computing, begins to turn software design from an art into a science, and offers guidelines for good practice in developing and deploying computer systems. It has responded to new topics such as user-centered design and computer-supported cooperative working; and it has informed the design of exciting and usable computers such as the Apple Macintosh.

HCI must now address the wider social and organizational issues of living in a computer-mediated world. There are no straightforward technical answers to questions such as "what are the consequences of introducing computer networks into organizations?" "should different interfaces be developed for different cultures?" and "what tasks should never be replaced by computers?" The challenge of HCI is to show how computers can be used to empower people, to assist the design of computer systems that we can not only use with ease, but that we can also begin to respect and trust.

References

Apple Computer Inc. (1987). *Apple human interface guidelines: The Apple desktop interface*. Reading, MA: Adison-Wesley.

Baecker, R. M., & Buxton, W. A. S. (1987). An historical and intellectual perspective. In R. M. Baecker & W. A. S. Buxton (Eds.), *Readings in human-computer interaction* (pp. 41–54). San Mateo, CA: Morgan Kaufmann.

Bush, V. (1945). As we may think. *Atlantic Monthly, 76*(1), 101–108.

Card, S. K., Moran, T. P., & Newell, A. (1980). The keystroke-level model for user performance time with interactive systems. *Communications of the ACM, 23*, 396–410.

Card, S. K., Moran, T. P., & Newell, A. (1983). *The psychology of human-computer interaction*. Hillsdale, NJ: Erlbaum.

Diaper, D. (1989). Task Analysis for Knowledge Descriptions (TAKD); the method and an example. In D. Diaper (Ed.), *Task analysis for human-computer interaction* (pp. 108–159). Chichester: Ellis-Horwood.

Dix, A., Finlay, J., Abowd, G., & Beale, R. (1993). *Human-computer interaction*. New York: Prentice-Hall.

Engelbart, D. C., & English, W. K. (1988). A research center for augmenting human intellect. In I. Greif (Ed.), *Computer-supported cooperative work: A book of readings* (pp. 81–105). Palo Alto, CA: Morgan Kaufmann.

Fitts, P. M. (1954). The information capacity of the human motor system in controlling amplitude of movement. *Journal of Experimental Psychology, 47*, 381–391.

Flower, L. S., & Hayes, J. R. (1980). The dynamics of composing: Making plans and juggling constraints. In L. Gregg & E. Steinberg (Eds.), *Cognitive processes in writing: An interdisciplinary approach* (pp. 31–49). Hillsdale, NJ: Erlbaum.

Harel, D. (1988). On visual formalisms. *Communications of the ACM, 31*(5), 514–530.

Hewitt, B., Gilbert, N., Jirotka, M., & Wilbur, S. (1990). *Theories of multi-party interaction* (Technical Report). London: Social and Computer Sciences Research Group, University of Surrey and Queen Mary and Westfield Colleges, University of London.

Hutchins, E. (1990). The technology of team navigation. In J. Galegher, R. E. Kraut, & C. Edigo (Eds.), *Intellectual teamwork* (pp. 191–322). Hillsdale, NJ: Erlbaum.

Jeffries, R., Miller, J. R., Wharton, C., & Uyeda, K. M. (1991). User interface evaluation in the real world: A comparison of four techniques. In *Proceedings of ACM CHI '91* New Orleans, LA (pp. 119–124). New York: ACM Press.

Jeffries, R., Turner, A. A., Polson, P. G., & Atwood, M. E. (1981). The processes involved in designing software. In J. R. Anderson (Eds.), *Cognitive skills and their acquisition* (pp. 255–283). Hillsdale, NJ: Erlbaum.

Kieras, D. E., & Polson, P. G. (1985). An approach to the formal analysis of user complexity. *International Journal of Man-Machine Studies, 22*, 365–394.

Landauer, T. K. (1987). Relations between cognitive psychology and computer system design. In J. M. Carroll (Ed.), *Interfacing thought: Cognitive aspects of human–computer interaction* (pp. 1–25). Cambridge, MA: MIT Press.

Maguire, M. C. (1990). A review of human factors guidelines and techniques for the design of graphical human-computer interfaces. In J. Preece & L. Keller (Eds.), *Human-computer interaction* (pp. 161–184). Hemel Hempstead: Prentice-Hall International.

Malone, T. W. (1981, December). What makes computer games fun? *BYTE*, pp. 258–277.

Michie, D., & Johnston, R. (1984). *The creative computer: Machine intelligence and human knowledge*. Harmondsworth: Penguin.

Miller, G. A. (1956). The magical number seven, plus or minus two: Some limits on our capacity for processing information. *Psychological Review, 63*, 81–97.

Newell, A., & Simon, H. (1972). *Human problem solving*. Englewood Cliffs, NJ: Prentice-Hall.

Newman, W. M., & Wellner, P. (1992). *A desk supporting computer-based interaction with paper documents* (Tech. Rep. EPC-91-131). Cambridge, UK: Rank Xerox EuroPARC.

Norman, D. A. (1986). Cognitive engineering. In D. A. Norman & S. W. Draper (Eds.), *User centered system design* (pp. 31–61). Hillsdale, NJ: Erlbaum.

Papert, S. (1980). *Mindstorms: Children, computers and powerful ideas.* New York: Basic Books.

Reece, J. (1993). *Cognitive processes in the development of written composition skills: The role of planning, dictation and computer tools.* Doctoral thesis, La Trobe University, Melbourne, Australia.

Sharples, M. (1993). A study of breakdowns and repairs in a computer-mediated communication system. *Interacting with Computers, 5*(1), 61–77.

Shneiderman, B. (1992). *Designing the user interface: Strategies for effective human-computer interaction.* Reading, MA: Addison-Wesley.

Spivey, J. M. (1988). *The Z notation: A reference manual.* Hemel Hempstead: Prentice-Hall International.

Sproull, L., & Kiesler, S. (1991, September). Computers, networks and work. *Scientific American, 265*(3), 84–91.

Tesler, L. G. (1991, September). Networked computing in the 1990s. *Scientific American, 265*(3), 54–61.

The Open University (1990). *A guide to usability.* Milton Keynes: The Open University.

Young, R. M. (1983). Surrogates and mappings: Two kinds of conceptual models for interactive devices. In D. Gentner & A. L. Stevens (Eds.), *Mental models* (pp. 35–52). Hillsdale, NJ: Erlbaum.

CHAPTER 11

Artificial Life and the Animat Approach to Artificial Intelligence

Jean-Arcady Meyer

I. WHAT IS ARTIFICIAL LIFE?

"*Artificial Life* (AL) is a novel scientific pursuit which aims at studying man-made systems exhibiting behaviors characteristic of natural living systems. AL complements the traditional biological sciences concerned with the analysis of living organisms by attempting to *synthesize* life-like behaviors within computers or other artificial media. By extending the empirical foundation upon which biology is based *beyond* the carbon chain life that has evolved on Earth, AL can contribute to theoretical biology by locating *life-as-we-know-it* within the larger picture of *life-as-it-could-be*" (Langton, 1989). In other words, AL views life as a property of the organization of matter, rather than a property of the matter so organized. In still other words, whereas biology has largely concerned itself with the *material* basis of life, AL is concerned with the *formal* basis of life.

At the core of the AL research program is the concept of *emergent properties*. These are properties exhibited by a collection of interacting entities whose global behavior cannot be reduced to a simple aggregate of the individual contributions of these entities. In other words, emergent behavior is said to exist when the whole is greater than the sum of its parts. Life, for example, is an emergent property resulting from interactions at a certain level of integration that cannot be explained simply in terms of the sum of the properties of elements interacting at lower levels (organs, tissues, cells, membranes, molecules, and so forth). Because traditional methods in biology are typically reductionist and usually seek to decompose a system into its constituent subsystems and then to study these subsystems in isolation from one another according to a *top-down* approach, it is difficult for these methods to reveal and explain the emergent properties characteristic of living organisms. On the other hand, AL is resolutely *bottom-up* in its approach. Starting with a collection of entities exhibiting behaviors that are simple and well understood, AL aims to synthesize more complex systems in which entities interact in nonadditive ways and give rise to lifelike emergent properties. Such a methodology could help to reveal what sort of elementary entities and what sort of interactions are necessary and sufficient for the appearance of particular emergent properties. As it also permits a very high degree of control and reproducibility, it may prove to be a useful complement to traditional biological approaches (Taylor, 1992).

Research in AL has recently given rise to a number of applications (Langton, 1989; Langton, Taylor, Farmer, & Rasmussen, 1992; Levy, 1992), notably regarding computer viruses, biomorphs and ontogenetically realistic processes, autocatalytic nets, cellular automata, and artificial nucleotides.

One particularly active area of artificial life is concerned with the conception and construction of *animats* (Wilson, 1985)—that is, of animals simulated by computers or by actual robots—whose rules of behavior are inspired by those of animals (Cliff, Husbands, Meyer, & Wilson, 1994; Meyer, Roitblat, & Wilson, 1993; Meyer & Wilson, 1991). This research has a twofold objective. In the short term, it aims to understand and reproduce the mechanisms that enable animals to adapt and survive in changing environments. In the longer term, it aims to contribute to our understanding of human intelligence, an objective similar to that of artificial intelligence (AI).

II. THE ANIMAT APPROACH TO AI

A. Objective and Methods of Standard AI

Research in standard AI, when it is not guided by purely technological objectives, aims at simulating the most elaborate faculties of the human brain—problem solving, natural language understanding, logical reasoning, for example. These simulations rely on computer programs that process "physical symbol tokens"—that is, various objects or physical patterns (like, for example, the set of magnetic moments of the various particles constituting the memory of a computer) that represent something other than themselves (for example, a set of objects in an environment, concepts, desires, emotions, and so forth)—through syntactic rules operating on the physical characteristics of these symbols. The basic claim of standard AI is that such a "physical symbol system" (Newell, 1980) is necessary and sufficient to produce intelligent behavior (Newell & Simon, 1976). According to such a view, the sensory and motor interfaces of an animat in interaction with its environment are collections of symbols processed by a centralized system of rules that reasons from these symbols independent of their meaning.

It is characteristic of simulations in standard AI to use data carefully selected by the programmer and consider restricted application domains whose heterogeneity and predictability are controlled as rigorously as possible. For example, the expert system MYCIN (Shortliffe, 1976), which is devoted to the diagnosis of blood diseases, is quite incapable of detecting that a patient is going to die from a cut artery. Likewise, the plan generator GPS (Newell & Simon, 1963), despite its claim to be a "general problem solver," demonstrates its ability to solve a given problem only if this problem is posed by a human, in a formalism that favors the discovery of the corresponding solution.

B. Objectives and Methods of the Animat Approach

With the aim of explaining how peculiar human faculties might be inherited from the simplest adaptive abilities of animals, the animat approach is based on the conception or construction of simulated animals or robots capable of "surviving" in more or less unpredictable and threatening environments. Like certain animals (Roitblat, 1987), these animats prove themselves capable of actively searching for useful information and choosing behaviors that permit them to benefit from their interactions with the environment. Moreover, they are often able to improve their adaptive faculties thanks to individual learning or to evolutionary processes. From this perspective, the animat approach heavily relies upon recent work on the cognitive behavior of animals (Roitblat & Meyer, 1995) and computational tools inspired by nature, such as *neural networks* and *genetic algorithms*.

The resulting simulations require no symbolic computation to produce adaptive or intelligent behavior. They demonstrate that, if such a manipulation is perhaps sufficient to produce such a behavior, it is not necessary. On the contrary, the animat approach seeks, according to the aims of AL described previously, to cause adaptive and intelligent behavior to appear in the form of emergent functionalities (Steels, 1991) issuing from interactions between simple behavioral mechanisms. Rather than immersing programs that exhibit a narrow competence of a high level in environments simplified to the extreme, the animat approach aims to model organisms that are simple, but complete, interacting in environments as realistic as possible, in which the organisms can feed, reproduce, escape predators, and so forth (Dennett, 1978).

The basic claim here is that it is possible to touch on issues of human intelligence according to a bottom-up approach that, originating in minimal architectures and simple environments, aims to increase progressively the complexity of these architectures and environments. If one takes care to add to these architectures only those features necessary to the primary goals of perception, categorization, and the pursuit of autonomously generated tasks, it will become possible to resolve increasingly complex problems of survival without losing the capacity to resolve the simplest. In the long term, one might hope to understand by what evolutionary mechanisms the adaptive capabilities of bacteria led to human intelligence and why it took so much more time to learn to survive and master the environment than to manipulate symbols. As Brooks put it (1990): "This suggests that problem solving behavior, language, expert knowledge and application, and reason, are all rather simple once the essence of being and reacting are available."

C. How the Two Approaches Complement One Another

It therefore appears, as Wilson (1991) has stressed, that

> Standard AI is basically competence-oriented, modeling specific human abilities, often quite advanced ones. However, while many AI programs exhibit impressive performance, their relevance to the understanding of natural intelligence is, in several respects, limited. In addressing isolated competences, AI systems ignore the fact that real creatures are always situated in sensory environments and experience varying degrees of need satisfaction. Furthermore, the systems attach less importance to such basic natural abilities as perception, categorization, and adaptation than they do to algorithmic processes like search and exact reasoning. This leads to problems connecting the arbitrary symbols used in internal reasoning with external physical stimuli ("symbol grounding"; Harnad, 1990, and to "brittleness" (Holland, 1986), the tendency for AI systems to fail utterly in domains that differ even slightly from the domain for which they were programmed.

The animat approach, on the other hand, places emphasis on the characteristics neglected by standard AI. It is interested explicitly in the interactions between an animat and its environment and particularly stresses the aptitude of the animat to survive in unexpected environmental circumstances. Centered around the study of grounded and robust behaviors, research on the adaptive behavior of animats should avoid the pitfalls of standard AI and improve our knowledge in those domains where this latter has failed notoriously, notably while addressing problems of perception, of categorization, and of sensorimotor control (Brooks, 1991; Maes, 1993; Roitblat, 1995).

III. WHAT IS ADAPTIVE BEHAVIOR?

In a changing, unpredictable, and more or less threatening environment, the behavior of an animal is adaptive so long as the behavior allows the animal to survive. Under the same conditions, the behavior of a robot is considered to be adaptive so long as the robot can continue to perform the functions for which it was built. The survival of an animal is intimately involved with its physiological state, and the successful operation of a robot depends on its mechanical condition. As a consequence, it appears that one can associate with an animat a certain number of state variables on which its survival or successful operation depends and that each of these state variables has a specific range within which the animat's continued survival or operation is preserved. Ashby (1952) referred to such variables long ago as *essential variables*. Their ranges describe a *viability zone* inside the given state space, allowing the animat to be referenced at any instant by a point within this zone (Figure 1). Under the influence of environmental or behavioral varia-

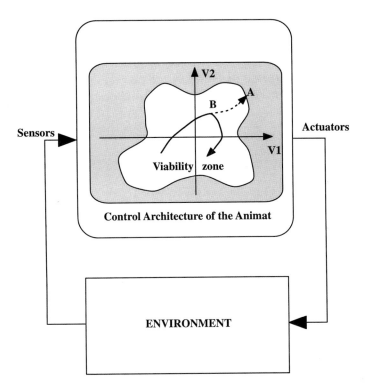

FIGURE 1   Viability zone associated with two essential variables, V1 and V2. The adaptive behavior of the animat is evidenced by the corrective action it takes at point B to avoid a movement outside of the viability zone at point A.

tions affecting the animat, the corresponding reference point moves and may at times approach the limits of the viability zone. In this case, the animat's behavior can be called *adaptive* so long as it avoids transgressing the boundary of viability (Ashby, 1952; Sibly & McFarland, 1976).

Such a behavior can be generated by means of several different or complementary abilities and architectures. For example, the laws governing the animat's operation may rely upon various homeostatic mechanisms thanks to which, if the reference point alluded to earlier moves away from an adapted point of equilibrium (adapted because it is suitably located within the viability zone), this process tends to return it to its original position, thereby decreasing the risk that it will pass outside the limits of the viability zone. Other ways in which to lower this risk involve the use of high-quality sensory organs or motor apparati that allows the animat to detect as early as possible that it is approaching these limits or to move away from them quickly and effectively. In this line of reasoning, it is obvious that the equivalent of a nervous system is mandatory to connect the animat's perceptions with its actions and that reflex circuits activated as quickly as possible increase the adaptive nature of its behavior. It is likewise clear that additional adaptive potential is afforded to an animat capable of responding with more than simple reflexes, particularly when it is able to choose from among several possible reactions the one that proves best adapted to the situation at hand. Such a behavioral control can in particular result from changes in the animat's motivation. Finally, it is understandable that the capacity to memorize the perception–action sequences that have shown themselves to be useful or harmful in the past is of considerable adaptive value to an animat obliged to decide what to do in a given situation and that this adaptive value is enhanced should the animat also be capable of more or less sophisticated forms of planning.

The remainder of this chapter will review significant approaches that make use, separately or in combination, of these various adaptive solutions. This review will be concerned with computer simulations and real robots and will deal with adaptive architectures or organizations that are either fixed (because they are preprogrammed or hardwired) or not (because they result from learning or evolution).

IV. PREPROGRAMMED BEHAVIORS

That adaptive behavior can result from interactions among simple modules can be illustrated by two cases: one in which the modules cooperate or compete to control the behavior of an individual animat and one in which each module is an elementary animat living and interacting in some societal context.

A. Individual Intelligence

Many animats exhibit adaptive behaviors because they were purposely programmed or hardwired this way. For instance, work by Brooks is based on the construction of actual robots whose sizes, morphologies, and missions vary, but all of whom are controlled by the same *subsumption architecture* (Brooks, 1986). Essentially, this architecture consists of superimposed layers of networks of finite-state machines, augmented with various timers and registers. Each layer connects sensors to actuators and implements a control system that achieves a certain level of competence. Higher level layers can subsume the roles of lower levels by suppressing their outputs. However, lower levels continue to function as higher level layers are added and higher levels of competence are achieved. The result is a robust and flexible robot-control system needing much less computation than in more traditional approaches. For example, this architecture allows the robot Genghis to chase infrared sources over rough terrain (Brooks, 1989). Likewise, it permits Squirt—"the world's largest one-cubic-inch robot"—to act as a "bug," hiding in dark corners and venturing out in the direction of noises only after the noises are long gone.

Connell (1990) demonstrates how it is possible to account for the behavior of the coastal snail Littorina by supposing that this behavior is controlled by a subsumption architecture (Figure 2(A)). One can indeed regard this behavior as depending on two basic competence modules: UP, which tells the snail always to crawl against the gravitational gradient, and DARK, which tells it to avoid light by crawling directly away from the source. However, DARK subsumes UP; that is, if a very bright light source is present, the snail will crawl away from it even if it means going downward. In Figure 2(A), this interaction is shown by a circle with an arrow entering it, suggesting that the output of DARK replaces the output of UP. In a similar manner, it can be supposed that a competence BRIGHT subsumes DARK because, if one turns the snail upside down, instead of avoiding light, it will now head toward bright areas. However, because this light-seeking behavior occurs only underwater, another competence module must be added to the control architecture: DARKER, which takes precedence over all the other light-sensitive behaviors when the snail is out of water. Finally, a last module, STOP, halts the snail when it encounters a dry surface and thus keeps it from wandering too far inland.

Fraenkel (1980) explains how this collection of competence modules and their interactions aids the snail in its pursuit of food and how it allows it to arrive at the region of maximum algae concentration, even if it has to negotiate major obstacles along the way (Figure 2(B)).

Other arguments supporting the biological realism of the subsumption architecture—or, more precisely, the logic of decentralized control it

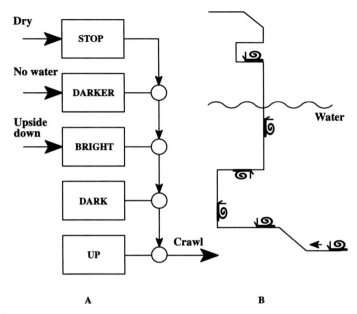

FIGURE 2   (A) The subsumption architecture underlying Littorina's behavior. (B) Littorina's adaptive crawling behavior. (Adapted from Connell, 1990, Figure 1.3, p. 8.)

implies—are to be found in Altman and Kien (1989). Indeed, this logic mobilizes no central control module responsible for analyzing the environmental situation at each instant and then for deciding to activate one specific behavior module or another. On the contrary, each competence module in Brooks's robots reacts in parallel to the environmental characteristics concerning it, and the collective behavior is an emergent property resulting from the interactions between instantaneous behaviors of the modules.

B. Swarm Intelligence

A simple generalization of the previous remark applies to another biological metaphor underlying much work on animats, that of insect society or of *swarm intelligence*. Here, the idea is to use a colony of animats with individual behaviors that may be quite simple, but because they communicate with each other, either directly or by means of the environment, they can exhibit a collective behavior that is relatively complicated and adaptive. In particular, this collective behavior can be maintained even in the event of the dysfunction of one or more individual animats. Maes and Brooks (1990) describe, for example, how a colony of robots exhibiting simple individual behaviors could be sent to the moon for the purpose of collectively building a permanent base. Thus, the interactions and individual behaviors in Table

TABLE 1   Robots Build a Moon Colony

A. Individual behaviors allow a colony of robots to select an open surface:
  1. Each robot maintains a minimum distance from the robots surrounding it.
  2. Each robot matches velocities with the robots in its neighborhood.
  3. Each robot moves toward the perceived center of mass of the robots in its neighborhood.
  4. The velocity of a robot is proportional to the number of big rocks it perceives in its neighborhood (or inversely proportional to the degree of flatness of the local neighborhood).
  5. When a robot has not moved much for a while it goes into a new "mode," adopting a new set of behaviors that is appropriate for the next global task.
B. Individual behaviors allow robots to level the ground and build walls:
  1. A robot tends to adopt the mode of the majority of robots in its neighborhood (the robots emit a certain code that tells what mode they are in).
  2. A robot that senses neighboring robots only on one side, stops its motion, and starts emitting a special signal A.
  3. A robot with an empty scoop tends to move away from robots emitting signal A.
  4. A robot with an empty scoop wanders around randomly; when sensing a slope with its inclinometers, it backs up a little, lowers its scoop and removes a layer of soil until its inclinometers report substantially different data or a specific time period has passed; next it moves its scoop up.
  5. A robot with a full scoop is attracted to the robots emitting signal A.
  6. A robot with a full scoop wanders around until it senses a pile or until some period of time has passed; it then empties its scoop.

1(A) would enable the colony to select an open surface, whereas the interactions and individual behaviors in Table 1(B) would take care of the leveling of the ground and ensure that the soil is deposited in a few piles at the edges of the construction site. Similar individual behaviors can be designed to achieve other global tasks cooperatively, such as pushing a rock or a broken robot out the way, digging out trenches for the habitation units, covering the habitation units with soil from the piles, and so on.

Another application of the swarm intelligence metaphor is described by Colorni, Dorigo, and Maniezzo (1992) and relies on the observation that an ant lays down traces of pheromone on the paths it travels and that these traces incite other ants, which otherwise would wander randomly, to follow this same path. These new ants in turn lay down pheromone traces on the path in question and reinforce its attractive force. These individual behaviors generate an interesting collective property: that of making it possible to identify the shortest path around an obstacle (Figure 3). It indeed appears that, given equal individual speeds of locomotion, a larger number of ants covers path BCE than path BDE per unit time. The attractive force of path BCE is accordingly more strongly reinforced than that of path BDE, with the result that, little by little, the ants will follow only the shortest path. This property is exploited in a program that seeks the optimum solution to the traveling salesman problem. This problem is actually solved collectively

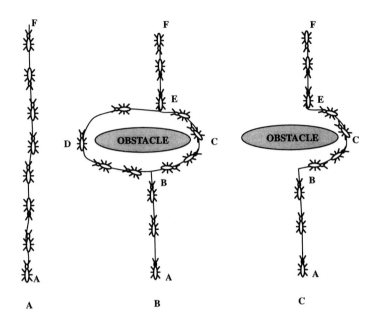

FIGURE 3   Collective problem solving by ants: (A) Some ants are walking on a path between points A and F. (B) An obstacle suddenly appears and the ants must get around it. More pheromones are deposited per unit of time on path BCE than on path BDE. (C) At a steady state, the ants follow the shortest path. (Adapted from Colorni et al., 1992, Figure 1, p. 135.)

by a colony of ants that live in the network of towns and mark the paths they explore.

V. LEARNED BEHAVIORS

Numerous studies address the way in which an animat can improve the adaptive character of its behavior while it experiences new situations in its environment. From this perspective, two types of learning can be claimed to be biologically realistic: unsupervised learning (which permits an animat to learn, to memorize, and to reconstruct a pattern by associating the various parts of this pattern with one another) and learning by reinforcement (which permits an animat to learn to recognize and to favor those behaviors that yield rewards rather than those that yield punishments).

A. Learning in Neural Networks

This type of learning (discussed at greater length in Chapter 5) usually involves artificial neurons, each one of which is characterized by a set of

Input Neurons   Output Neurons

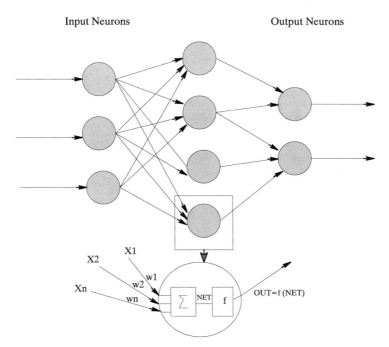

FIGURE 4   An artificial neural network with input and output neurons.

input signals $X1$, $X2$, . . ., Xn and an output signal, OUT (Figure 4). The inputs, collectively referred to as vector X, correspond to the signals into the synapses of the neurons. Each signal is multiplied by an associated weight $W1$, $W2$, . . ., Wn, which corresponds to the synaptic strength of each connection. It is applied to a summation block that simulates the biological cell body and adds all of the weighted inputs algebraically, producing the NET output: NET $= X \cdot W$.

The NET signal is usually further processed by an activation function to produce the neuron's output signal OUT. According to the case considered, the activation function may be

a linear function: OUT $= K \cdot$ NET, $K =$ constant;
a function with a threshold: OUT $= 1$ if NET $> T$; otherwise, OUT $= 0$, $T =$ constant;
any sort of nonlinear function, such as
the logistic function: OUT $= 1 / (1 + e^{-\text{NET}})$
or the hyperbolic tangent function: OUT $=$ tanh (NET).

Naturally, more complex operational laws have been proposed by many authors in the interest of enhancing the biological realism of such artificial neurons.

Since the output of a neuron can become the input to another neuron, artificial neural networks can be designed and their architectures varied with relative ease. These networks contain both input and output neurons (Figure 4). The transformation of input signals into output signals of which they are capable can turn out to be relatively sophisticated, and the power and efficiency of the computations taking place in these networks is strongly dependent on their architecture. This is why a number of different architectures are currently employed: single-layered, multilayered, and fully connected organizations, to name the principal ones. It is clear, however, that the input–output transformations effected by the network are likewise influenced by the way each individual neuron processes the signals as they pass through it.

Insomuch as the processing depends on the current synaptic strengths W, it is evident that a network is capable of learning, provided the synaptic strengths of each neuron can be modified in the course of the network's operation. Several algorithms have been developed for the purpose. Their efficiencies differ, as do the architectures of the network to which they apply.

Other varieties of learning involve the probabilities according to which a given system changes state or the probabilities according to which an action is triggered—as is the case, for example, with DYNA architectures, which will be discussed later.

B. Unsupervised Learning

An example of unsupervised learning is provided by the work of Nehmzow and Smithers (1991) who use a *Kohonen network* (Kohonen, 1988) to allow various robots to distinguish and recognize *landmarks* in their environment.

A Kohonen network is composed of a certain number of artificial neurons, each of which receives the same input vector $\mathbf{i}$. The output $\mathbf{o}_j$ of the neuron j is determined by the scalar product of the input vector $\mathbf{i}$ and the weight vector $\mathbf{w}$ of neuron j and is given by $\mathbf{o}_j = \mathbf{i} \cdot \mathbf{w}_j$.

At initialization, the weight vectors are chosen at random and are all distinct. It follows that, when a given input vector is transmitted to the network, there must be one neuron whose output is stronger than those of the other neurons. The output from the network is then expressed as a simple binary $+1$ response from the winner, and there is no output from any other neuron. In effect, the winning neuron represents the category to which the input pattern belongs.

Unlike most other neural networks, in a Kohonen network only the winning neuron and its physical neighbors (within a distance from the winner determined by the network designer) modify the weights of their connections; the remaining neurons experience no learning. The training law used by the network is $\Delta \mathbf{W} = \eta \cdot (\mathbf{i} - \mathbf{w}_j)$, where η is a learning gain that determines the amount of change experienced by the elements of vector $\mathbf{w}_j$.

Since both the input and the weight vectors are usually normalized to a unit magnitude, each points to a position on a unit hypersphere. Therefore, the winning neuron is the one having the weight vector closest to the input vector on this hypersphere, and the result of a training pass is to nudge its weight vector closer to the input vector, with the size of the nudge depending on the learning gain. The winning neuron's physical neighbors also adjust their weights by applying the same learning equation. Thus, they, too, move their weight vectors closer to the input vector.

After several training passes, not only does the network give typically dissimilar responses to dissimilar input vectors, but also develops regions that respond most strongly to particular types of input vectors. In other words, the network categorizes the input vectors.

The robots of Nehmzow and Smithers possess a control architecture that exhibits emergent functionalities useful for moving and exploring an unknown environment—such as avoiding obstacles, escaping from dead ends, or following walls. These robots are also capable of distinguishing and recognizing various landmarks in their environments, notably those that appear in the form of convex or concave corners. For example, when a robot explores a territory bordered by a wall by following the wall, a convex corner is detected if the time the robot needs to turn toward the wall exceeds a certain threshold time. Likewise, a concave corner is detected if the time it takes the robot to get away from a detected obstacle exceeds the threshold time.

The control architecture used to categorize the environment is a Kohonen network implemented in the form of a 50-neuron ring (Figure 5(A)), and the neighborhood within which the weight vectors are updated is ±2 neurons.

Typically, the input vector given to the network describes whether the actual landmark is a convex or concave corner and whether the previously encountered landmarks were convex or concave corners. Odometry information about the distances between landmarks is also entered into the network. Given such information, it appears that the unsupervised learning procedure just described leads a given cluster of neurons to be more active than other neurons when the robot is in a particular place, where it receives a specific input signal, and leads some other cluster of neurons to be the most active in another place where the input signal is different. Thus, the robot is capable of categorizing its environment; to distinguish, for example, landmarks A to H of Figure 5(B). Moreover, once the corre-

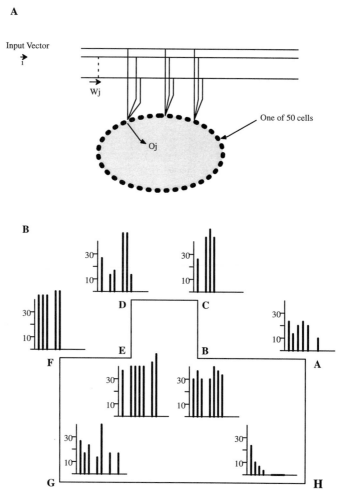

FIGURE 5   (A) The ring of 50 cells used by Nehmzow and Smithers as a self-organizing network. (B) The recognition of corner H when using information about the previous sensor readings. Histograms show the absolute difference between the memorized pattern of cells' activation at every corner and the new pattern obtained at corner H. Such differences are smaller at point H, indicating that the corner is recognized. (Adapted from Nehmzow and Smithers, 1991, Figures 3 and 7, pp. 154 and 156).

sponding learning is accomplished, the robot is capable of moving about the environment and recognizing at any given moment where it is situated. It is possible that such an aptitude has a certain amount in common with the capacity of bees to use landmarks to guide their way and locate food sources (Cartwright & Collett, 1983).

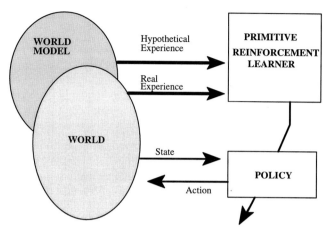

FIGURE 6   The four components of DYNA architectures.

C. Reinforcement Learning

The typical scenario in reinforcement learning is one in which the animat receives a special signal from the environment—usually called a *reward,* although it may be either positive or negative—and must coordinate its actions to maximize its cumulative reward over time. In other words, reinforcement learning is a kind of learning by trial and error from performance feedback. Among the numerous architectures that allow the implementation of learning by reinforcement, the DYNA architecture proposed by Sutton (1991) is original in introducing an internal world model and allowing for planning, a mental activity generally considered to be "cognitive."

A DYNA architecture relies essentially on four interacting components (Figure 6):

- The real world, which changes state in relation with the animat's behavior and distributes rewards;
- The world model, which the animat elaborates for itself and is intended to mimic the one-step input–output behavior of the real world;
- The policy function, relied on by the animat to determine what action to engage in response to each possible state of the world;
- A primitive reinforcement learner, which improves the policy function over time.

In a particular implementation of DYNA architectures, called DYNA-Q, the reinforcement learner makes use of the *Q-learning algorithm* (Watkins, 1989). Such an algorithm uses a utility function $Q(x, a)$ that represents the utility of performing action a in state x. This utility is defined as the sum of the immediate reward r plus the utility $E(y)$ of the state y resulting from the action discounted by a parameter γ between 0 and 1. That is, $Q(x, a) = r + \gamma E(y)$. The utility of a state x, in turn, is defined as the maximum of the utilities of performing each different possible action in that state. That is, $E(x) =$ maximum $Q(x, a)$ over all actions a.

During learning, the stored utility values $Q(x, a)$ have not yet converged to their final values [that is, to $r + \gamma E(y)$]. Hence, the difference between the stored values and their final values gives the error in the current stored values. Therefore, Q-learning uses the following rule to update stored utility values: $\Delta Q (x, a) = \alpha (r + \gamma E(y) - Q(x, a)]$, where the parameter α controls the rate at which the error in the current utility value is corrected.

In general, the action chosen in a given state x by the policy function is the one that has the highest utility $Q (x, a)$. However, to ensure that all states in the state space will eventually be explored and that the utility of every pair (x, a) will be assessed, some randomness is actually introduced in the choices of the policy function.

The novel aspect of DYNA architectures is their inclusion of an internal world model along with mechanisms for learning it. The world model is a function that describes which actions are produced in a real world and which rewards are obtained in response to each possible action of the animat. Consequently, every time an action is performed by the animat and a reward is obtained, the state of the real world changes and the corresponding triple (action : reward : state change) is recorded in the world model. In this context, the Q-learning procedure described previously can be applied to real experiences in the real world as well as to hypothetical experiences in the world model. Such hypothetical experiences, which call on the metaphor of "planning as performing thought experiments," can be interleaved with experiences in the real world.

The results obtained by Sutton with a DYNA architecture demonstrate that it is possible for an animat to learn to reach a goal as directly as possible in an environment encumbered with obstacles. For instance, in the case of Figure 7, the animat's task is to navigate through the maze from the starting state S to the goal state G. In each state there are four possible actions: UP, DOWN, LEFT, and RIGHT, which change the state accordingly, except where the corresponding movement would take the animat into an obstacle—in which case the state is not changed. Reward is 0 for all transitions, except for those leading into the goal state, for which it is +1.

Each time the animat reaches the goal state, thus ending a learning trial, it is placed back at S and starts a new trial. Therefore, the animat's objective is to learn a policy that improves over trials and that ultimately enables it to obtain the maximum rate of reward over time. Incidentally, such a policy will correspond to the discovery of the shortest path leading from S to G.

In this context, although learning from real experiences updates the utili-

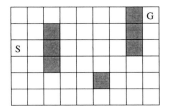

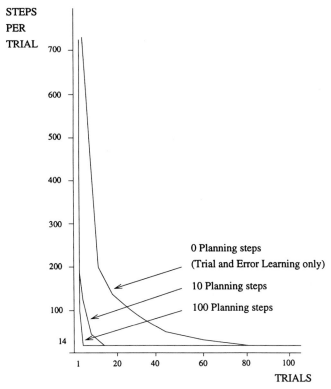

FIGURE 7   An example of the learning curves obtained in a specific navigation task with DYNA architectures. The more hypothetical experiences (k planning steps) using the world model, the faster an optimal path was found. These data were averaged over 100 runs. (Adapted from Sutton, 1991, Figure 4, p. 292.)

ty function according to the actual consequences of each action, planning updates this same utility function for simulated transitions chosen from the world model. Several such updates can be performed between each actual step taken in the real world. However, it should be noted that the world model, on the contrary, is updated only for actual transitions from state to state.

The utility function can be coded in a variety of forms and notably as a neural network. In Sutton's implementation, it is coded as a matrix with elements all set to 0 at initialization. As the probability that the animat will choose action a in state x depends upon the utility $Q(x, a)$, the animat's first trial is a random trajectory through states because all initial utilities are the same. Along such a trajectory, the transitions between old and new states resulting from each real action, together with the rewards obtained in each state, are recorded in the world model. If, at state $G - 1$, immediately preceding G, the animat performs action UP, it gets to state G and receives a reward of 1. It accordingly updates the value of $Q(G - 1, UP)$, changing it from 0 to $\alpha[r + \gamma E(G) - Q(G - 1, UP)] = 0.5 (1 + 0 - 0) = 0.5$, if the value of α is set to 0.5. As a consequence, $E(G - 1)$ now equals 0.5 because, at this learning stage, the best action that can be performed in state $G - 1$ seems to be UP, which has a utility of 0.5.

During the second trial, the animat still wanders at random and still updates its world model. From state $G - 2$, immediately preceding $G - 1$, action UP leads it to state $G - 1$. Therefore, the value of $Q(G - 2, UP)$ is updated from 0 to 0.5 $(0 + 0.9 \times 0.5 - 0) = 0.225$, if the value of γ is set to 0.9. Similarly, $E(G - 2)$ is updated to 0.225. From action UP in $G - 1$, the animat reaches the goal and is rewarded again. The value of $Q(G - 1, UP)$ is accordingly changed to 0.75 because $\Delta Q(G - 1, UP) = 0.5 (1 + 0 - 0.5) = 0.25$.

It is thus seen that, as the process is iterated in the course of successive trials, the world model is progressively filled in according to an order imposed by the order of the various states the animat visits and of the various actions it performs. The utility function, on the contrary, is updated backward from the goal state to the starting state—a process equivalent to that of classical *dynamic programming*—and every $Q(x, a)$ value converges toward its correct value; that is, $r + \gamma E(y)$. Therefore, the trajectories of the animat are less and less random from trial to trial and converge toward the shortest path leading from S to G.

Hypothetical experiences allow for the same adjustments of utility estimates as real experiments. However, although the latter can, for example, adjust $Q(G - 2, UP)$ only when the animat moves from $G - 2$ to $G - 1$, the former can make such an adjustment even when the animat is situated somewhere else. Therefore, planning allows for a quicker back-propagation of utility estimates and accelerates learning, as evidenced by the learning curves on Figure 7.

VI. EVOLVED BEHAVIORS

Following the work of Holland (1975), a number of research efforts have addressed the simulation of processes that improve the behavior of individuals in a population from generation to generation. These efforts involve the implementation of selection processes that eliminate individuals with ill-adapted behaviors and favor the reproduction of individuals displaying behaviors that are well adapted. Most often, they involve a classical genetic algorithm or some variant.

A. Genetic Algorithms

A *genetic algorithm* (Goldberg, 1989; Holland, 1975) manages in parallel a given population of "chromosomes," each of which codes—generally in the form of a chain of binary symbols—a possible solution to a particular optimization problem. Each of these chromosomes can therefore be assigned a "fitness" that assesses the corresponding solution. The application of the genetic algorithm accordingly causes this population to "evolve" from generation to generation. It does this by maintaining, for each chromosome, a probability of reproduction proportional to the chromosome's fitness and using genetic operators such as "mutation" and "crossover" to give rise to new solutions in the population (Figure 8). This type of evolutionary process generally causes chromosomes of ever-increasing fitness to be generated until the optimum value is reached or sufficiently nearly so for all practical purposes.

Genetic programming (Koza, 1992) is a technique derived from the genetic algorithm. This technique allows for the search of solutions to a wide and diverse variety of problems in computer science. Genetic programming can essentially be thought of as the search for a "program" that permits a computer to produce a certain desired set of "outputs" when presented with certain "inputs." In accordance with the terminology of the application, this program can correspond to the action plan of a robot, to a control strategy, to a decision tree, to an economic model, to a system of equations regulating state changes, or more generally, to a *composition of functions.* The inputs associated with these programs can be called *sensory information, independent variables, attributes,* or more commonly, *functional arguments.*

The programs sought in genetic programming are symbolic expressions representing compositions of functions—like those of the LISP programming language. The solutions that are tested and improved by the algorithm consist of trees whose nodes can be functions or terminal symbols. These functions and symbols belong to sets predefined by the programmer according to the problem to be solved. For instance, these functions can be simple arithmetic functions, Boolean operators, functions specific to the domain under consideration, control structures such as IF . . . THEN . . . ELSE, or iterative structures like REPEAT . . . UNTIL. The terminal symbols, similarly, can be variables—such as the state variables of the system—or input data or constants. Figure 9 illustrates how, given the predefined set of logical functions AND, OR, and NOT and a predefined set of Boolean-valued terminals $D0$ and $D1$, genetic programming can

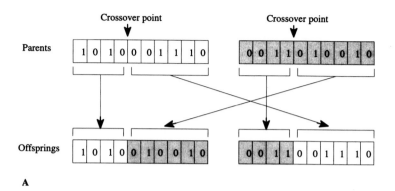

A

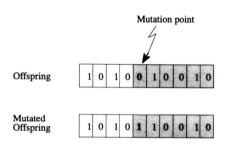

B

FIGURE 8   How new solutions are discovered by the genetic algorithm: (A) Role of the crossover operator. A crossover point is chosen at random within the chromosomes of the parents. Before that point an offspring inherits the genetic material of one parent. After that point it inherits the genetic material of the other parent. (B) Role of the mutation operator. A mutation point is chosen at random within the chromosome of an offspring and the binary value at that point is swapped.

discover a program that calculates the XOR (that is, the *exclusive OR*) of the two logical variables $D0$ and $D1$ thanks to a crossover between two incorrect solutions.

B. Evolution of the Control Parameters of a Neural Network

Beer and Gallagher (1992) considered how to discover, with the aid of a genetic algorithm, a combination of parameters which permit a neural net to control effectively the locomotion of an artificial insect. To control the movements of the six legs of this insect, they used a continuous-time, recurrent network consisting of six input neurons, eighteen motor neurons, and twelve interneurons (Figure 10). The input neurons detect the angular position of each leg. The motor neurons govern the force with which each leg is propelled forward or backward and whether or not the corresponding

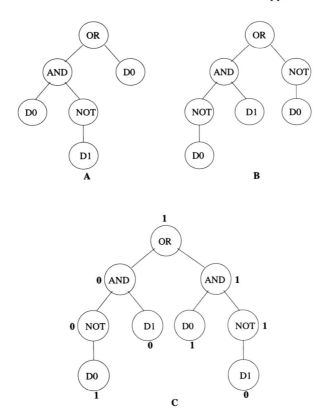

FIGURE 9   How a program able to evaluate the XOR of two logical variables $D0$ and $D1$ can be discovered by genetic programming. The correct solution (C) is obtained from incorrect solutions (A) and (B) by a crossover operation that exchanges two branches of the parents' trees. There are four possible combinations of the two variables $D0$ and $D1$, and the upper node of each tree gives the solution proposed by the corresponding program; that is, the XOR value of each possible combination of $D0$ and $D1$. For instance, tree C suggests that, when $D0 = 1$ and $D1 = 0$, the corresponding XOR is 1, which is true. It is easy to verify that tree C gives four correct answers out of four possible and that its fitness can accordingly be evaluated as 4. Likewise, it can be seen that the fitness of tree A is 2 and that of tree B is 1.

foot is set down. The role of the interneurons is unspecified. To enhance the biological realism of these neurons and model, in particular, some of the dynamic properties of real nerve cells, the instantaneous activity of each neuron is regulated by the equation

$$\tau_i \frac{dy_i}{dt} = -y_i + \sum_{j=1}^{N} w_{ji} \, \sigma_j \, y_j + I_i \, (t)$$

where N is the number of neurons j connected to neuron i.

A

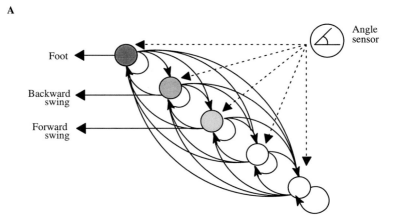

B

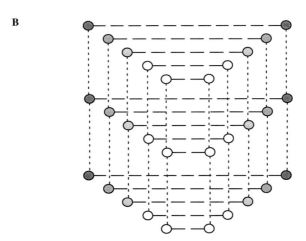

FIGURE 10 Locomotion controller network architecture: (A) Architecture of a simple leg controller. (B) Coupling between leg controllers. Identically shaded neurons have identical time thresholds and time constants. Dashed lines represent cross-body connections, and dotted lines represent intersegmental connections. Connections between identically shaded neurons with the same line style have identical weights. All coupling connections are symmetrical. (Adapted from Beer and Gallagher, 1992, Figure 10, p. 107.)

In this equation, y can be interpreted as the mean membrane potential of the neuron; $\sigma_j\,(\zeta) = (1 + e^{(\theta_j - \zeta)})^{-1}$ is a sigmoidal function giving the short-term average firing frequency of the neuron; θ is a bias term that controls the firing threshold; τ is a time constant associated with the passive proper-ties of the cell membrane; w_{ji} represents the strength of the connection from the jth to the ith neuron; and $I_i\,(t)$ represents an external input to the network such as from a sensor. According to such an equation, each neuron can exhibit, in particular, a rhythmic activity and temporally extended responses to brief stimuli.

Because of the back–front and left–right symmetries of this control architecture, only one set of leg-control parameters needs to be optimized by the genetic algorithm. To accomplish this, a combination of 50 parameters— 5 thresholds, 5 time constants, 25 connection weights, 5 sensor weights, 5 cross-body connection weights, and 5 intersegment connection weights— were coded in each chromosome of the algorithm. The performance measure to be maximized was the distance the insect travels forward in a given amount of time. Because the insect can make forward progress only when it is statically stable, the problem the genetic algorithm had to solve was that of generating 18 motor outputs that interact to maintain the insect in balance while allowing it to advance as rapidly as possible.

The results obtained by Beer and Gallagher show that effective locomotion controllers were evolved in four distinct evolutionary stages. The first stage was marked by the appearance, in a population of insects incapable of motion, of several individuals that succeeded in advancing by placing their feet on the ground and pushing until they fell over. The second stage saw the development of individuals that, although they fell often, succeeded in advancing nonetheless by moving their legs in a rhythmic, but uncoordinated way. In the third stage, insects using statically stable gaits appeared, but their coordination was still suboptimal. In the final stage, the genetic algorithm discovered controllers generating a pattern of leg movement known as a *tripod gait,* which is ubiquitous among fast-walking insects. The discovery of this form of locomotion is owed to the fact that the performance measure puts pressure not just on the development of locomotion controllers per se but on the development of controllers that cause the insect to move as quickly as possible.

The controllers discovered by the genetic algorithm exhibit interesting adaptive capabilities. In particular, when the insect is allowed to evolve alternately in conditions in which it can avail itself of information provided by the angle sensors and in conditions in which it cannot—thus simulating a series of functional breakdowns—the genetic algorithm discovers mixed controllers. Although such mixed controllers exhibit a higher stepping frequency and clearer phasing when the sensors are intact than when they are not, the performances of the controllers are still quite good even in the latter case.

C. Evolution of a Control Program

Koza, Rice, and Roughgarden (1992) studied how an evolutionary process could help the Caribbean anolis lizard to optimize its hunting strategies.

This animal is a "sit-and-wait" predator, typically perching head-down on tree trunks and scanning the ground for desirable insects to chase and eat. It can be supposed that the insects the lizard eats appear infrequently enough that the lizard starts every chase from its perch. It can also be supposed that the evolutionary process thus hypothetized tended to favor those lizards that avoided losing time in attacking insects that were too far away. The problem of developing an optimal hunting strategy can therefore be viewed as a search for a control program permitting the lizard to decide whether or not to attack its prey according to how far away the prey is and to how densely the prey populates the hunting territory under consideration.

The search for such a program can be conducted using genetic programming. To do this, Koza et al. decided that the programs thus generated will use the four variables X, Y, AB, and VEL for terminal symbols or input data, in addition to numerical constants. The variables X and Y represent the coordinates of the prey within the lizard's planar field of vision. The variable AB represents the average density of prey in a certain area (expressed as the probability of appearance per unit of surface area in a single unit of time), and VEL represents the lizard's sprint velocity. The programs were also permitted to use arithmetic functions such as addition, subtraction, multiplication, and division, in addition to mathematical operations like exponentiation or to control structures such as IF . . . THEN . . . ELSE.

Thus, by convention, the program

(IFLTE (SREXPT (% (* 3.0 VEL) (* 3.14159 AB)) (% 1.0 3.0))
    (SREXPT (+ (SREXPT × 2.0) (SREXPT Y 2.0)) (% 1.0 3.0))
    −1.0 +1.0)

corresponds to a control strategy more simply expressed as

$$\text{IF } \left(\frac{3.0 \times VEL}{\pi \times AB} \right)^{1/3} \le (X^2 + Y^2)^{1/2} \text{ THEN ignore OTHERWISE chase.}$$

However, the former formalism presents the advantage over the latter of readily accommodating mutations and crossing over to generate new programs that continue to describe meaningful control strategies.

The fitness of each program was evaluated by simulating the strategy it implemented in various velocity and insect frequency combinations and then counting the total number of insects it allowed the lizard to consume over the course of the simulation. A population of 1000 such programs was allowed to evolve freely.

In a first approach to the optimization problem studied here, it was supposed that the lizard always captures the prey it chases. In such conditions, it turned out that a control program randomly generated when the system was initialized allowed the lizard to capture 1235 insects. The corre-

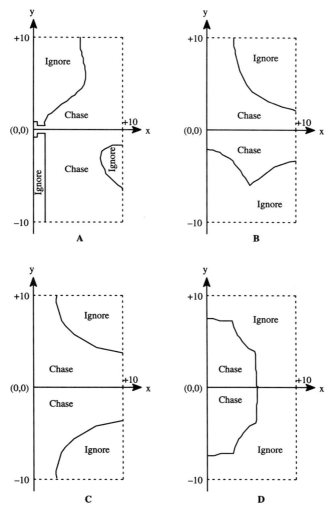

Figure 11   Evolution of food-foraging strategies for the anolis lizard when it necessarily catches every chased insect: (A) Individual at generation 0, scoring 1,235. (B) Best individual from generation 0, scoring 1,460. (C) Best individual from generation 10, scoring 1,514. (D) Best individual from generation 60, scoring 1,625. (Adapted from Koza et al., 1992, Figures 7, 8, 9, and 11, pp. 186, 187, 188, and 190.)

sponding strategy is represented graphically in the *X, Y* space in Figure 11(A). Another individual initialized at random scored 1460 (Figure 11(B)). By generation 10, a control program capturing 1514 insects (Figure 11(C)) was discovered. By generation 60, a control program capturing 1625 insects appeared (Figure 11(D)). This program defines a strategy very similar to the optimal strategy determined by a mathematical model of optimization. This

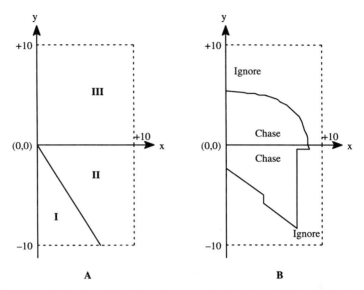

FIGURE 12   Evolution of food-foraging strategies for the anolis lizard when it does not necessarily catch every chased insect: (A) Three regions with different probabilities of capture. (B) Best individual from generation 46. (Adapted from Koza et al., 1992, Figures 13 and 16, pp. 195 and 196.)

optimal strategy dictates the attack of all prey within a semicircle of radius $R = [(3.0 \times VEL)/(\pi \times AB)]^{\frac{1}{3}}$, and it appears to be very similar to that applied by animals in nature.

Koza et al. also studied how the hunting strategy evolved when supposing that the lizard does not necessarily capture all the prey it decides to chase. In one such scenario, the lizard's hunting territory is supposed to be divided into three zones (Figure 12(A)), such that in zone I the lizard never catches its prey, in zone II it always does so, and in zone III the catching probability is 100% along the X axis and decreasing linearly as the angle of vision increases between 0° and 90°. Under such conditions, 46 generations of genetic programming led to the hunting strategy represented in Figure 12(B), which seems well adapted to the problem. As can be seen, not only does the lizard avoid an area that approximately corresponds to region I and chase insects in region II, but also the lizard is willing to travel a distance in region III that is all the greater as the angular location of the prey is closer to 0°.

VII. CONCLUSION

The various efforts discussed here illustrate several of the objectives and methods of the animat approach. Particular instances were stressed where adaptive behavior appears as an emergent property at a level of integration superior to that in which the organisms, neural modules, genome segments, and so on interact to produce that behavior. The animats described here are, notwithstanding, complete organisms, with sensors and actuators linked by the equivalent of a nervous system; and these animats interact with their environment, not their programmer.

The behavior of the animats described in this chapter is, in general, purely reactive. Nonetheless, the robots of Nehmzow and Smithers learn to categorize and memorize their environment, and the animats of Sutton are capable of elementary planning. The literature contains numerous examples of other animats exhibiting more elaborate cognitive faculties (Cliff et al., 1994; Meyer & Guillot, 1991; Meyer et al., 1993; Meyer & Wilson, 1991). Donnart and Meyer (1994), for example, describe the architecture of a *motivationally autonomous animat* that is capable of generating its own goals, assessing the consequences of its decisions, and performing actions that seem to be the most advantageous in attaining the goals in question.

At the same time, it must be recognized that another objective envisaged in the beginning of this chapter remains unattained in the present state of research: that of understanding the adaptive role of cognition. The reason for this deficiency is clearly the lack of comparative approaches that investigate, for example, how well such and such a problem of adaptation can be solved by such and such an architecture and not by some other, or how well such and such an architecture allows such and such a problem to be solved and not some other. From such a perspective, tremendous progress will be made once a typology and a hierarchy of both the environments and the problems of adaptation they pose can be established. Fortunately, the past few years have seen several efforts initiated in this direction (Horswill, 1992; Littman, 1993; Wilson, 1991). Likewise, substantial improvements in our understanding of human cognition could be gained from the five-year research project described by Brooks and Stein (1993) or by Dennett (1994). This project proposes to build an integrated physical humanoid robot—including active vision, sound input and output, dextrous manipulation, and the rudiments of language. Its objectives are to study how a serious exploration of the relationships between intelligence and the subjective experience of a body helps in understanding the modularity of the human mind, how its "representations" are grounded in the sensory modality used to learn them, and how consciousness, symbols, and language are interelated. In other words, this approach might help to bridge the evolutionary gap that, according to Kirsh (1991), separates the sensory–motor connections of the earwig from human concepts and representations.

References

Altman, J. S., & Kien, J. (1989). New models for motor control. *Neural Computation, 1*, 173–183.

Ashby, W. R. (1952). *Design for a brain*. London: Chapman & Hall.

Beer, R. D., & Gallagher, J. C. (1992). Evolving dynamical neural networks for adaptive behavior. *Adaptive Behavior, 1*, 91–122.

Brooks, R. A. (1986). A robust layered control system for a mobile robot. *IEEE Journal of Robotics and Automation, RA-2*(1), 14–23.

Brooks, R. A. (1989). A robot that walks: Emergent behaviors from a carefully evolved network. *Neural Computation, 1*, 253–262.

Brooks, R. A. (1990). Elephants don't play chess. In P. Maes (Ed.), *Designing autonomous agents. Theory and practice from biology to engineering and back* (pp. 3–15). Cambridge, MA: MIT Press.

Brooks, R. A. (1991). Intelligence without representation. *Artificial Intelligence, 47*, 139–159.

Brooks, R. A., & Stein, L. A. (1993). *Building brains for bodies* (AI Memo No. 1439). Cambridge, MA: MIT, Artificial Intelligence Laboratory.

Cartwright, B. A., & Collett, T. S. (1983). Landmark learning in bees. *Journal of Comparative Physiology, 151*, 521–543.

Cliff, D., Husbands, P., Meyer, J. A., & Wilson, S. (Eds.). (1994). *From animals to animats 3. Proceedings of the Third International Conference on Simulation of Adaptive Behavior*. Cambridge, MA: MIT Press.

Colorni, A., Dorigo, M., & Maniezzo, V. (1992). Distributed optimization by ant colonies. In F. J. Varela & P. Bourgine (Eds.), *Toward a practice of autonomous systems. Proceedings of the First European Conference on Artificial Life* (pp. 134–142). Cambridge, MA: MIT press.

Connell, J. H. (1990). *Minimalist mobile robotics. A colony-style architecture for an artificial creature*. San Diego, CA: Academic Press.

Dennett, D. C. (1978). Why not the whole iguana? *Behavioral and Brain Sciences, 1*, 103–104.

Dennett, D. C. (1994). The practical requirements for making a conscious robot. *Philosophical Transactions of the Royal Society of London, Series A*. 349, pp. 133–146.

Donnart, J. Y., & Meyer, J. A. (1994). A hierarchical classifier system implementing a motivationally autonomous animat. In D. Cliff, P. Husbands, J. A. Meyer, & S. Wilson (Eds.), *From animals to animats 3. Proceedings of the Third International Conference on Simulation of Adaptive Behavior* (pp. 144–153). Cambridge, MA: MIT Press.

Fraenkel, G. (1980). On geotaxis and phototaxis in Littorina. In C. R. Gallistel (Ed.), *The organization of action: A new synthesis* (pp. 149–165). Hillsdale, NJ: Erlbaum.

Goldberg, D. E. (1989). *Genetic algorithms in search, optimization, and machine learning*. Reading, MA: Addison-Wesley.

Harnad, S. (1990). The symbol grounding problem. *Physica D (Amsterdam), 42*, 335–346.

Holland, J. H. (1975). *Adaptation in natural and artificial systems*. Ann Arbor: University of Michigan Press.

Holland, J. H. (1986). Escaping brittleness: The possibilities of general purpose machine learning algorithms applied to parallel rule-based systems. In R. Michalski, J Carbonell, & T. Mitchell (Eds.), *Machine learning: An artificial intelligence approach* (Vol. 2, pp. 593–623) San Mateo, CA: Morgan Kaufmann.

Horswill, I. (1992). Characterizing adaptation by constraint. In F. J. Varela & P. Bourgine (Eds.), *Toward a practice of autonomous systems. Proceedings of the First European Conference on Artificial Life* (pp. 58–63). Cambridge, MA: MIT Press.

Kirsh, D. (1991). Today the earwig, tomorrow man? *Artificial Intelligence, 47*, 161–184.

Kohonen, T. (1988). *Self-organization and associative memory*. Berlin: Springer-Verlag.

Koza, J. R. (1992). *Genetic programming: On the programming of computers by means of natural selection*. Cambridge, MA: MIT Press.

Koza, J. R., Rice, J. P., & Roughgarden, J. (1992). Evolution of food-foraging strategies for the Caribbean Anolis lizard using genetic programming. *Adaptive Behavior, 1*, 171–199.

Langton, C. G. (Ed.). (1989). *Artificial life*. Reading, MA: Addison-Wesley.

Langton, C. G., Taylor, C., Farmer, J. D., & Rasmussen, S. (Eds.). (1992). *Artificial Life II.* Reading, MA: Addison-Wesley.

Levy, S. (1992). *Artificial Life. The quest for a new creation.* London: Jonathan Cape.

Littman, M. L. (1993). An optimization-based categorization of reinforcement learning environments. In J. A. Meyer, H. L. Roitblat, & S. W. Wilson (Eds.), *From animals to animats 2: Proceedings of the Second International Conference on Simulation of Adaptive Behavior* (pp. 262–270). Cambridge, MA: MIT Press.

Maes, P. (1993). Behavior-based Artificial Intelligence. In J. A. Meyer, H. L. Roitblat, & S. W. Wilson (Eds.), *From animals to animats 2: Proceedings of the Second International Conference on Simulation of Adaptive Behavior* (pp. 2–10). Cambridge, MA: MIT Press.

Maes, P., & Brooks, R. A. (1990, May). Robot insect societies. *Data Manager Magazine,* pp. 1–6.

Meyer, J. A., & Guillot, A. (1991). Simulation of adaptive behavior in animats: Review and prospect. In J. A. Meyer & S. W. Wilson (Eds.), *From animals to animats: Proceedings of the First International Conference on Simulation of Adaptive Behavior* (pp. 2–14). Cambridge, MA: MIT Press.

Meyer, J. A., Roitblat, H. L., & Wilson, S. W. (Eds.) (1993). *From animals to animats 2: Proceedings of the Second International Conference on Simulation of Adaptive Behavior.* Cambridge, MA: MIT Press.

Meyer, J. A., & Wilson, S. W. (Eds.). (1991). *From animals to animats: Proceedings of the First International Conference on Simulation of Adaptive Behavior.* Cambridge, MA: MIT Press.

Nehmzow, U., & Smithers, T. (1991). Mapbuilding using self-organizing networks in "really useful robots." In J. A. Meyer & S. W. Wilson (Eds.), *From animals to animats: Proceedings of the First International Conference on Simulation of Adaptive Behavior* (pp. 152–159). Cambridge, MA: MIT Press.

Newell, A. (1980). Physical symbol systems. *Cognitive Science, 4,* 135–183.

Newell, A., & Simon, H. A. (1963). GPS, a program that simulates human thought. In E. A. Feigenbaum, & J. Feldman (Eds.), *Computers and thought* (pp. 279–293). New York: McGraw-Hill.

Newell, A., & Simon, H. A. (1976). Computer science as empirical enquiry: Symbols and search. *Communications of the ACM, 19,* 113–126.

Roitblat, H. L. (1987). *Introduction to comparative cognition.* New York: Freeman.

Roitblat, H. (1995). Comparative approaches to cognitive science. In H. Roitblat & J. A. Meyer (Eds.), *Comparative approaches to cognitive science* (pp. 13–25). Cambridge, MA: MIT Press.

Roitblat, H., & Meyer, J. A. (Eds.). (1995). *Comparative approaches to cognitive science.* Cambridge, MA: MIT Press.

Shortliffe, E. H. (1976). *Computer based medical consultations: MYCIN.* Amsterdam: Elsevier.

Sibly, R. M., & McFarland, D. (1976). On the fitness of behavior sequences. *American Naturalist, 110,* 601–617.

Steels, L. (1991). Towards a theory of emergent functionality. In J. A. Meyer & S. W. Wilson (Eds.), *From animals to animats: Proceedings of the First International Conference on Simulation of Adaptive Behavior* (pp. 451–461). Cambridge, MA: MIT Press.

Sutton, R. S. (1991). Reinforcement learning architectures for animats. In J. A. Meyer & S. W. Wilson (Eds.), *From animals to animats: Proceedings of the First International Conference on Simulation of Adaptive Behavior* (pp. 288–296). Cambridge, MA: MIT Press.

Taylor, C. E. (1992). "Fleshing out" Artificial Life II. In C. G. Langton, C. Taylor, J. D. Farmer, & S. Rasmussen (Eds.), *Artificial Life II* (pp. 25–38). Reading, MA: Addison-Wesley.

Watkins, C. J. (1989). *Learning with delayed rewards.* Unpublished doctoral dissertation, University of Cambridge, UK.

Wilson, S. W. (1985). Knowledge growth in an artificial animal. In J. J. Grefenstette (Ed.), *Proceedings of the First International Conference on Genetic Algorithms and Their Applications* (pp. 16–23). Hillsdale, NJ: Erlbaum.

Wilson, S. W. (1991). The animat path to AI. In J. A. Meyer & S. W. Wilson (Eds.), *From animals to animats: Proceedings of the First International Conference on Simulation of Adaptive Behavior* (pp. 15–21). Cambridge, MA: MIT Press.

Index

355